NOAH WEBSTER

Noah Webster at age sixty-five. Engraving by A. B. Durand from an original portrait (1823) by Samuel F. B. Morse and used as the frontispiece for the first edition of *An American Dictionary of the English Language*. (Yale Picture Collection, Manuscript and Archives, Yale University Library.)

NOAH WEBSTER

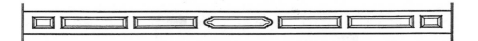

The Life and Times
of an American Patriot

Harlow Giles Unger

John Wiley & Sons, Inc.

New York • Chichester • Weinheim • Brisbane • Singapore • Toronto

Text designed by Sona Lachina in Linotype Didot, based on a typeface family created in 1783 by Firmin Didot and updated for digital technology by Adrian Frutiger in 1992. The sign *Typographie de Firmin Didot* still hangs at 56 rue Jacob in Paris, where on September 3, 1783, John Adams, John Jay, and Benjamin Franklin signed the Treaty of Paris granting the United States independence. This book was composed by Lachina Publishing Services, Inc.

This publication is designed to provide accurate and authoritative information in regard to the subject matter covered. It is sold with the understanding that the publisher is not engaged in rendering professional services. If professional advice or other expert assistance is required, the services of a competent professional person should be sought.

Library of Congress Cataloging-in-Publication Data

Unger, Harlow G.
    Noah Webster : the life and times of an american patriot / Harlow
  Giles Unger.
        p.   cm.
  Includes bibliographical references and index.
  ISBN 0-471-18455-1 (acid-free paper)
  1. Webster, Noah, 1758–1843. 2. Lexicographers—United States—
Biography. 3. Social reformers—United States—Biography.
4. Educators—United States—Biography. I. Title.
PE64.W5U54   1998
423'.092—dc21
[B]   98-15707

Printed in the United States of America

10 9 8 7 6 5 4 3 2 1

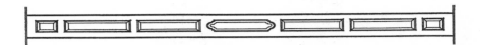

Contents

Illustrations

Acknowledgments

ULTIMATELY, IT IS THE EDITOR of every book who transforms it from manuscript into book, from a stack of pages off the word processor into the magnificent product that finds its way into stores, libraries, and homes. The editor of this book is Hana Umlauf Lane, senior editor at John Wiley & Sons. It was she who decided to publish the book and guided its metamorphosis so skillfully from manuscript to book, and I thank her first and foremost. She would never have seen the manuscript, however, had it not been for Edward Knappman at New England Publishing Associates, who has been my agent, adviser, and friend, and to whom I owe my deepest thanks. One other person has been equally important in the genesis of this book—Randi Ladenheim Gil, my former editor and, as ever, my good friend.

From the beginning of this project, Sally Whipple, the executive director of Noah Webster House, has given generously of her time and knowledge and placed the resources of that wonderful institution at my disposal. Anne Keirstead, the office manager at Noah Webster House, has also been unstinting in her help.

And of those who have had a direct impact on this work, I owe special thanks to Doris Newnham, my friend and mentor of forty years, for her wise counsel and constant encouragement.

Many archivists and librarians have also contributed generously of their time, knowledge, and resources. Particularly helpful were William R. Massa Jr., public services archivist, and Judith Ann Schiff, chief research archivist, in the Manuscripts and Archives Division of the Sterling Memorial Library at Yale University. Nor can I forget the cheerful welcome and enthusiastic help of these other members of the Manuscripts and Archives staff at Yale: Chris Connolly, Anthony P. Massarelli, and Sandy Staton.

Archivists overseas were equally welcoming and helpful—especially Jonathan Smith at the Wren Library, Trinity College, Cambridge University; S. R. Tomlinson, assistant librarian at the Bodleian Library, Oxford University; Mme. Bernard Billaud, conservateur, Bibliothèque Historique de la Ville de Paris, Paris; and Mme. Chassagne and the entire staff at the Bibliothèque de l'Institut de France, Paris.

    Douglas Kneeland, a Latin scholar of the highest rank from the Hotch-kiss School and Swarthmore College, was particularly helpful by providing what turned out to be a truly difficult translation and evaluation of Noah Webster's complex Latin declamation from his student days at Yale.

    I also want to express my sincerest thanks to Diane Aronson at John Wiley & Sons and—most especially—to Chuck Antony, the brilliant copy editor who prepared my manuscript for production.

To my friend
Doris Newnham
and
my son
Richard

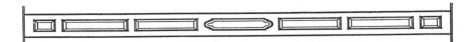

Chronology

1758	October 16. Noah Webster born in West Hartford, Conn.
1770	Boston Massacre.
1773	Boston Tea Party.
1774	NW enrolls at Yale College.
1775	Revolutionary War begins at Lexington and Concord.
1776	Continental Congress signs Declaration of Independence.
1778	NW graduates from Yale.
1779–80	Teaches school in Hartford and West Hartford.
1780–81	Studies law in Litchfield; admitted to the bar; begins work on spelling book.
1783	Practices law in Hartford; publishes *A Grammatical Institute of the English Language.* England signs peace treaty granting U.S. independence.
1785	NW publishes *Sketches of American Policy,* with new form of American constitution and government.
1785–86	NW obtains nation's first state copyright laws. Shays's Rebellion, in Massachusetts.
1786–87	Constitutional Convention, in Philadelphia.
1787–88	NW edits, publishes the *American Magazine* in New York; Constitution ratified.
1789	George Washington inaugurated as first president; NW marries Rebecca Greenleaf; moves to Hartford to practice law.
1790	First child, Emily, born on August 4.
1792	Washington elected to second term as president.

1793   Second child, Julia, is born. NW moves to New York to publish daily newspaper, *American Minerva,* and semiweekly *Herald;* confronts French ambassador-spy Edmond Genet.

1797   Harriet, a third daughter, is born; Vice President John Adams elected to succeed Washington.

1798   NW retires to New Haven to practice law, publish scientific and literary works; publishes monumental *History of Epidemic and Pestilential Diseases*.

1799   Fourth child, Mary, is born.

1800   Federal government moves to Washington, D.C. Jefferson defeats Adams for the presidency.

1801   First son, William, is born.

1803   Eliza, the sixth Webster child, is born.

1806   NW publishes 40,000-word *Compendious Dictionary of the American Language*. Second son, Henry Bradford, is born; dies nine weeks later.

1808   Eighth and last child, Louisa, is born. Madison elected to the presidency.

1812   NW moves to Amherst; begins *American Dictionary of the English Language*. U.S. declares war on Britain; Madison elected to second term.

1814   NW helps organize Hartford Convention; demands changes in Constitution; Federalists threaten secession of Northern states. British burn Washington, D.C.

1819   Webster's favorite child, Mary, dies at 20.

1822–23 NW moves to New Haven; Yale awards him LL.D.

1824–25 Travels to Paris, then Cambridge University, to complete research for dictionary.

1828   Publishes 70,000-word *American Dictionary of the English Language*.

1830   Convinces Congress to enact new, federal copyright law.

1833   Publishes revised edition of the Holy Bible.

1841   Publishes second edition of *An American Dictionary*.

1843   May 28. Dies in New Haven; buried in Grove Street cemetery, next to Yale College.

1847   Rebecca Webster dies and is buried beside her husband.

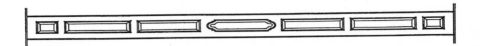

Prologue

O F THE THOUSANDS OF STUDENTS AND TOURISTS who visit Noah Webster's birthplace, in Connecticut,* each year, some, unfortunately, confuse Noah with his distant younger cousin Daniel Webster—often knowing as little about Daniel as they do about Noah. Most, however, realize that "Noah's the one who wrote the dictionary" and assume that's all he did in the course of his eighty-five years. Webster's name, after all, has always been an American household word. Say "dictionary" and Americans almost automatically respond, "Webster's." Indeed, Webster's dictionary has become so much a part of American daily life that it has obscured its author's other achievements—many of which were of far greater import than his dictionary.

Noah Webster was one of the towering intellects of his generation. Long before he even thought about writing a dictionary, Webster had assumed a place among the nation's founding fathers as the father of cultural independence, whose words reached American minds in every home and classroom and transformed the nation from a Babel of conflicting tongues— English, Dutch, French, German, and innumerable others—into the first nation on earth where generations of diverse people would speak and think in one language as one people.

"There has never been a great nation with a universal language without dialects," proclaimed a newspaper editorial in 1857, more than a decade after his death. "The Yorkshireman can not talk with a man from Cornwall.

---

* The Noah Webster House, where Noah Webster was born, in 1758, and lived until his graduation from college, is a national historic landmark that was restored in 1965. Now a public museum, it is furnished with period pieces and maintained by the Noah Webster Foundation, which offers guided tours lasting about one hour, every day except Wednesdays and major holidays, from 1 to 4 P.M.

The peasant of the Ligurian Apennines, drives his goats home at evening, over hills that look down on six provinces, none of whose dialects he can speak. Here [in the United States], five thousand miles change not the sound of a word. Around every fireside, and from every tribune, in every field of labor, and every factory of toil, is heard the same tongue. We owe it to Webster."

Webster really led two different lives in the span of a single lifetime, with the end of the eighteenth century serving as a division between the two. Each was dramatically different from the other and illustrious enough to have provided any ordinary man with a lifetime of brilliance. But Webster was no ordinary man. A descendant of New England's first Puritan settlers, he devoted the first half of his life to a relentless war against political and social disunion and the forces of anarchy. His powerful essays helped ensure ratification of the Constitution that united the thirteen feuding states of the Confederation. Then, by word and deed, he faced down raging street mobs and anarchists and helped expose foreign plotters conspiring to overthrow the American government and dismember the new nation.

He fought for universal public education and created a national "system of instruction" he hoped would eradicate illiteracy and educate "all ranks of society." Lecturing in town after town, North and South, he harangued listeners with the notion that the survival of liberty in a self-governing nation depended on a universally educated, literate electorate and that national unity depended on linguistic unity, with all Americans speaking a single common language.

Webster was the nation's first great social reformer. He was one of the first American leaders to campaign for universal public education, women's education, unemployment and workman's compensation insurance, social welfare for the poor and homeless, child care, city planning, public sanitation, public health, advanced methods of agriculture, free commerce and trade, dredging of rivers and canal construction, copyright protection for authors, and historical preservation. He was one of the early champions of emancipation and fought for everyone whose rights were unprotected.

And all of this before he turned forty.

Webster spent the second half of his life weaving the fabric of American cultural and linguistic unity. Calling language "a band of national union," he invented the concept of "America" in his textbooks for children. Designed to teach Americans to "speak alike," Webster's books did more than teach children to read, write, and speak American. They taught children to live, breathe, and think American. For more than a century, Webster's textbooks gave millions of illiterate native- and foreign-born children a new, common heritage as well as a new, common language. Webster's books not only served his own generation, but every generation of Americans that followed, including our own.

Until Webster, no great nation on earth could boast of the linguistic unity that Webster created in the United States. More than a lexicographer, Webster was a teacher, philosopher, author, essayist, orator, political leader, public official, and crusading editor. Webster's life thrust him into every major event of the early history of our nation, from the Revolutionary War to the War of 1812. He touched the lives of the most renowned Americans—and the most obscure. He earned the love and friendship of many, the hatred of some, but the respect of all. Noah Webster helped create far more than an American dictionary; he helped create an American nation.

Ironically, the shadow of his colossal work all but obscured the dramatic contributions he made to the nation's survival and the unification of its people. Webster never sought high public office or political power—a decision that did not enhance his chances for memorialization in bronze or stone. The absence of national monuments, however, does not diminish his importance to the United States. He was and remains one of the most exciting and fascinating figures in American history—and one of the most overlooked. Celebrated during his lifetime as a towering figure among the nation's founding fathers, Webster disappeared into the pages of his own dictionary. For the last thirty years, Noah Webster House, his birthplace, in West Hartford, Connecticut, has celebrated him in his home state; now this long overdue book will celebrate him across the nation and around the English-speaking world.

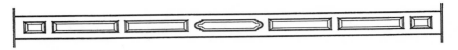

CHAPTER ONE

Patriot

I

THE AMERICAN COLONIAL WILDERNESS was awash with war when Noah
Webster was born, in the fall of 1758. French forces had swept southward
from Canada, past Lake Champlain and Lake George, to the northern edge
of the Berkshire Hills, less than two hundred miles north of the Webster
farm. Although the clamor of cannons and the cries of the wounded were
well beyond earshot, they posed a fearful threat to Webster's little farming
community, in the west division of Hartford, Connecticut. Only a year earlier, his father had barely escaped slaughter at Fort William Henry, at Lake
George, New York. He had been part of a vastly outnumbered column of
thirty-five hundred untrained colonial conscripts—mostly farmers like himself—whom the British had positioned as a human barrier to the French
advance. Faced with massacre, the helpless colonists laid down their comic
fowling muskets to surrender—only to be set upon treacherously by the
French army's savage Indian forerunners. Only fourteen hundred colonists
survived, among them Noah Webster's father, who fled into the Berkshire
wilderness and struggled home to his farm to pick up the pieces of his life.
A year later, on October 16, 1758, his fourth child, a son, was born, and he
passed on his own name, Noah, to the boy. It was an appropriate name for
the times, for the Webster farm seemed, indeed, an ark adrift in a sea of uncer-
tainty, with only the Websters' God privy to their ultimate national destination.

The British hold over the American colonies was deteriorating rapidly—not just in New England but in almost every other area of North
America. The French already controlled parts of western Pennsylvania, and
French-speaking colonists in Vermont and Maine were in open rebellion
against British rule. In eastern Pennsylvania, Benjamin Franklin railed
that German settlers were turning Pennsylvania into "a German colony.

1

Instead of learning our language, we must learn theirs, or live as in a foreign country. Already the English begin to quit particular neighborhoods [of Philadelphia], being uneasy by the disagreeableness of dissonant manners."

The English confronted similar "disagreeableness" in Swedish-speaking areas of Delaware and Dutch-speaking areas of New York, where, as in Pennsylvania, talk of independence from Britain among the non-English threatened to erupt into open rebellion. Even English-speaking settlers—Noah Webster's father included—now spoke openly about disunion from the British motherland. Throughout New England, the British had conscripted colonists to battle the French and the Indians—and taxed their families to pay for the war. Parliament reasoned that inasmuch as British troops were fighting the French and Indians to protect the colonists, the colonists themselves should bear the burden—by paying taxes, by billeting British regulars in their homes, and by shouldering arms and marching alongside the regulars to battle. It was a heavy burden—more than many were willing or able to carry.

The atmosphere of disunion at the time of his birth would permeate Noah Webster's entire life, as it had that of his father and generations of his forebears. For centuries, the Webster ancestors had resisted disunion by tempering their ardor for individual freedom with respect for the sanctity of societal bonds. As deeply as they yearned for the former, they feared that liberty unleashed would devolve into anarchy and leave them as enthralled to the mob as they had been to king and clergy.

Webster's ancestors were drawn into the stream of Puritans that flowed from England to America during the reigns of King James I (1603–25) and his son Charles I (1625–49). Both monarchs equated religious dissent with treason and branded Puritans who sought congregational independence from the Anglican bishop of London as separatists. "I will make them conform themselves," King James shouted to his court, "or harry them out of the land. . . . No Bishop, no King."[1]

James made good on his threat, forcing a group of Puritan farmers from Yorkshire and their pastor, John Robinson, to flee to Leyden (now Leiden), Holland, in 1609. One of them was nineteen-year-old William Bradford, Webster's maternal great-great-great-grandfather. As aliens, with no lands of their own to cultivate, the Puritans found life intolerable in Holland. After ten years, they returned to England to answer a call from the Virginia Company for "adventurers" to exploit the wealth of England's unexplored continent across the Atlantic. In 1620, they sailed to America aboard the *Mayflower*. On December 21, the first one hundred settlers stepped ashore in New England, at "Plimouth," and a year later, they elected Bradford their governor, a post he held for twenty-five of the next thirty years until his death.

The first Webster came to America about ten years later.[2] By then, Charles I had succeeded James to the throne and had grown even more hostile to the Puritans than his father. The stream of religious dissenters to America turned into a torrent. Two thousand arrived in Boston alone in 1630. More than eighteen thousand followed in the next decade. Among them was John Webster, another Yorkshire farmer, Noah Webster's great-great-grandfather. By the time that first Webster arrived in Boston, he found that the earlier, established settlers had established Congregationalism as the official state religion and restricted voting on civic matters to church members. This left Massachusetts government in the hands of a Puritan theocracy that brooked as little dissent in the New World as the bishop of London had in the old.

Finding himself no freer under Puritan rule in Boston than he had been under Anglican rule in Yorkshire, John Webster moved to rural Newtowne (now Cambridge), where the Reverend Thomas Hooker, a strong supporter of universal suffrage, had defied the Puritan theocracy and opened his congregation to all.

Puritan leaders were quick to punish such nonconformists, however. In 1635, they forced Roger Williams to flee his Salem pastorship when he criticized civil authorities for using their power to enforce church doctrine.[3] The following year, Hooker fell out with colony leaders over the issues of limited suffrage and magisterial authority, and he left Newtowne with fifty of his congregants, including John Webster and John Steele, who had married Melatiah Bradford, a daughter of Plymouth's William Bradford.

As a small child, Noah Webster often listened to his mother, the descendant of the Steele-Bradford union, describe their Puritan ancestors' trek through Massachusetts to Connecticut—then still part of the Massachusetts Bay Colony. She recounted how they had to cross "a hideous and trackless wilderness . . . through swamps, thickets and rivers. They had no cover but the heavens and no lodgings but such as nature afforded them. They drove with them one hundred and sixty head of cattle, and subsisted by the way on the milk of their cows. They were nearly a fortnight on their journey, singing psalms in the wilderness."[4]

One hundred miles to the southwest, they reached an expanse of rich, tillable land, sparkling streams, and lush forests abounding with game—already peopled, however, by less-than-hospitable Pequot Indians, who feared farmers would clear the forests and drive away the game on which they depended.

Edward Winslow of Plymouth had established the first white settlement in Connecticut, called Windsor, in 1635, and a year later, just before the Hooker party left Newtowne, the Massachusetts General Court granted Connecticut settlers limited independence and the right to create some self-government.

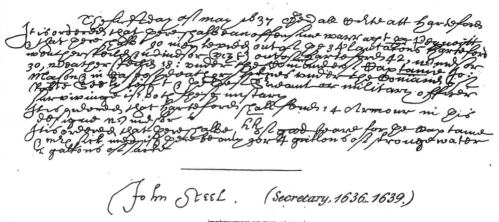

The first day of May, 1637, Genʳall Corte att Harteford.

It is ordered that there shalbe an offensiue warr agt the Pequoitt, and that there shalbe 90 men levied out of the 3 Plantacons, Harteford, Weathersfeild & Windsor (vizt) out of Harteford 42, Windsor 30, Weathersfeild 18 : vnder the Comande of Captaine Jo : Mason & in Case of death or sicknes vnder the Comand of Robᵗe Seeley Leift, & theᵗldest Sᵗreant orᵗmilitary officer survivinge, if both these miscary.

It is ordered that Harteford shall send 14 Armour in thisᵗdesigne, Windsor 6.

It is ordered that there shalbe 1ʰʰ of good beare for the Captaine & Mʳ & sick men, if there be only 3 or 4 gallons of stronge water, 2 gallons of sacke.

Noah Webster's mother, Mercy Steele Webster, traced her ancestry to John Steele and Melatiah Bradford, the daughter of William Bradford, a governor of Plymouth, who arrived on the *Mayflower* in 1620. Steele and John Webster, Noah Webster's great-great-grandfather, were among fifty religious dissidents who carved Hartford from the wilderness. The order signed by John Steele sent ninety settlers from three towns to war against the Pequot Indians, who were all but exterminated before the end of 1737. (Webster Papers, New York Public Library.)

"Arriving late in the season," Webster's mother told her children, "they had to endure all the hardships and trials of a severe winter, with the labors of clearing the forest, constructing their rude dwellings, securing food, and of protecting themselves against cold and wet, the ravages of wild beasts, and the warlike savage."[5] Although Hooker's band survived the winter, their efforts to clear the forest for spring plantings encroached on Pequot hunting grounds, and in May, the inevitable conflict erupted between farmer and hunter, colonist and native, Christian and savage. Within a year, the Christians had all but exterminated the Pequot.

The settlers renamed their community Hartford, after the English birthplace of many Hooker congregants, and together they began to clear the wilderness and create what was then the largest settlement in the new colony of Connecticut (an Indian word for "place of the long river"). They built their church and homes; they planted and harvested the fruit of the vine and of the earth for six days each week; and they scrupulously observed the Sabbath. From the very first, they taught their children "His Word" and sent their children to school to learn to read and recite the scriptures.

They created a new England, with individual liberties restricted only by scriptural law and the "commonweal" of the community—a new England where people's common struggle against the wilderness erased social distinctions, where everyone worked and helped his or her neighbor, and where each person's skill was an essential thread in the fabric of the community. Love of labor and of God determined individual worth, both in productivity and communal respect. Hooker, the spiritual leader, encouraged independent thought and the search for a personal relationship with God. His concept of individual liberties, limited only by the broader public interest and the laws of God, would become the basis of Connecticut's Fundamental Orders, the colony's first written constitution.[6]

As one of the largest landholders, John Webster was elected a magistrate in Connecticut's first General Court, a combined legislature-judiciary, and in 1642, he helped write the colony's first criminal code. Cited for his "prudence, piety, skill and private worth," he was elected deputy governor in 1655 and, two years later, governor. He died in 1671, but his progeny, like that of the Steeles and Bradfords, grew into a sizable and important clan that held high posts in church and state, including several governorships. Indeed, the only blight ever to touch a leaf on the Webster family tree was an accusation of witchcraft against Mary Reeve Webster, who had married one of John Webster's sons and settled in Hadley, Massachusetts. Angry townsfolk dragged the poor woman from her house, stripped her, and searched for witch marks "on her teats," then sent her to jail and a trial in Boston, in April 1683.

Although the Boston court acquitted her, for the rest of her life Hadley invariably blamed "the power of this enchantress" for every unexplained misfortune—including the illness of a Lt. Philip Smith in 1685. "While he lay dying," according to an account from that era, "a number of brisk lads . . . dragged her out of the house . . . hung her up until she was near dead, let her down, rolled her some time in the snow, and at last buried her in it, and there left her; but it happened that she survived and the melancholy man died. It is not known that Mary Webster annoyed the people of Hadley by her witch pranks after 1685."[7]

The tragedy of Mary Reeve Webster notwithstanding, most Websters retained their good names, prominence, and wealth during the rest of the seventeenth century. John Webster divided his property among his sons, and they, in turn, did the same, leaving each generation of sons with smaller and smaller estates. By the mid–eighteenth century, the various Webster holdings, like those of most New Englanders, were too small to subdivide into farms large enough to support one family each. Most farmers had little choice but to keep their lands intact and restrict inheritance to their oldest

sons. Younger boys either learned crafts, went into business, or moved west-
ward to carve new farms out of the New York or Pennsylvania wilderness.

For boys with enough intellectual promise, the eighteenth century offered another option with the addition of four new colleges, in Princeton,
Philadelphia, New York, and Providence. Together with Harvard, Yale, and
the College of William and Mary, the new schools expanded the opportunities for young men to prepare for the ministry, medicine, or law. Noah
Webster would be one of these young men.

2

WHEN NOAH WEBSTER WAS BORN, his father's farm amounted to only
ninety acres, scattered across four or five parcels of orchards and fields of
corn, wheat, oats, flax, and tobacco, in the west division of Hartford. The
house was a standard Connecticut farm dwelling—a square wooden box,
two stories tall, clad in simple white clapboards with a peaked roof. Inside,
plain pine planks covered the floors, and burly hand-hewn beams stretched
across the ceilings.

A massive brick chimney sliced the house in half and delivered heat
through fireplaces on either side. A mammoth fireplace in the kitchen let
the Webster women lean in easily to swing the iron dogs and kettles on and
off the fire. The kitchen was the social center of the house—a living and
dining room, as well as a cooking room and bakery. A second fireplace
opened from the other side of the chimney into the formal parlor (where
Noah was born). Near the window, staring sternly at all who entered, a plain
black Bible lay on the unvarnished Puritan table surrounded by a stand of
straight-backed chairs. A small settee stood against the opposite wall. Up-
stairs, a small fireplace was the only luxury in each of the two plain bed-
rooms.

The Websters were a middling family financially, albeit well nourished
by a cottage garden, grapevines, fruit trees, and a variety of barnyard animals. A cow provided milk, and a horse took them to church and into town.
The small size of his estate did not diminish the elder Noah Webster's influence in the community. Indeed, he was a pious man, and his conduct
only enhanced the value of the historic name he bore. As his forebears had
done, the elder Webster tempered Calvinist orthodoxy with a tolerance that
assumed equality of condition among freemen. Webster measured individual worth on the basis of work, personal behavior, church attendance, and
readiness to help one's neighbor and community. Webster himself ranked
high in each of these respects.

Born in 1722, the elder Webster was a leader of his church and his community in peace and in war. He was a lieutenant in the town militia and held a succession of important church posts, including the deaconship—the highest office his church could bestow. For fifteen years he was also justice of the peace, thus holding the town's highest secular as well as clerical posts. His neighbors addressed him with respect—either as Deacon Webster or Squire Webster.

On January 12, 1749, the great-grandson of John Webster married Mercy Steele, the great-great-granddaughter of William Bradford. The following November, their first offspring, also named Mercy, was born. Abram followed in September 1751, and a second daughter, Jerusha, in January 1756.

The mid-eighteenth century was not the most auspicious time to marry, raise children, and begin life as an independent farmer. The summer before Jerusha Webster was born, her father had marched off to the disaster at Fort William Henry. In his absence, Mercy Webster tended the fields herself. Like her Bradford ancestors, she was intelligent, well educated, capable, and energetic. The younger Noah's wife, Rebecca, would later describe her mother-in-law as "a gentle loving mother and care-taker, looking well to the ways of her household. She carried on the farm quite successfully"[8] when her husband marched off to war.

Mercy Webster displayed her emotions more openly than most women of her generation, easily bursting into tears of joy or sorrow. But she was better schooled than other women in both the domestic and the ornamental arts. The domestic arts—needlework, sewing, making clothes, cooking, housekeeping, and gardening—left little time in most farmhouses for the ornamental arts, such as music and reading, yet Mercy Webster found time to read to her children and play the flute, and to teach each of the children to do the same. Each evening she led the family in singing the popular psalms of Isaac Watts[9] after her husband's Bible reading. The children all became skilled readers, strong writers, and gifted flutists—and all knew the Bible intimately.

The Websters' fourth child, Noah, was born in October 1758. Their fifth and last child, Charles, was born four years later. Noah's early childhood was unremarkable. Like other colonial children, he busied his days with farmyard chores, helped his mother tend the cottage garden, and joined his sisters in attending to his younger brother.

Noah's bony frame carried a serious though pleasing little face, topped by a mop of red hair and punctuated by brownish grey eyes that stared in wonder at his father's huge, godlike presence in the fields. By the time he was four, daily recitations of the Our Father left him certain that his father was God and that heaven lay somewhere in the fields where his father toiled.

He thus grew up in the tranquil, certain omnipresence of his stern, loving, all-embracing God, adoring both God and the fields about him and unaware of the turmoil beyond the horizon of the Webster farm, which for young Noah was nothing less than Eden. He felt God everywhere, in his coming in and going out, and each day he did his chores unquestioningly because, as his mother told him, God and his father expected him to. And unlike Cain and Abel, Noah Webster and his brothers and sisters loved one another deeply.

Peace and harmony ruled also in the immediate community surrounding the Webster farm—largely because of the familial continuity on which the town had been built. The Websters and Steeles continued to till the same lands their forebears had tilled since they had driven the last Pequot from the forest, and at their little church, the Reverend Nathaniel Hooker, descended directly from the Reverend Thomas Hooker, led his flock in prayer from the pulpit his ancestor had occupied. Mutual affection thus joined with devotion to the commonweal to repel those who threatened peace, tranquillity, or doctrinal unity.

If there was an imperfection in young Noah's personal paradise, it lay only in education. Indeed, his school apparently stood as close as any Hartford child could ever get to the gates of hell. By the time he entered school, his mother had already taught him his alphabet from a primer, along with the Lord's Prayer, the Apostles' Creed, and the Decalogue. As in almost every colonial Connecticut home, the King James Bible was the most important cultural influence, and the Websters read from the Bible each day, individually and communally. Young Noah knew his Bible by the time he was six and was fully prepared for school. His mother had even taught him his numbers.

Like Massachusetts, Connecticut had enacted compulsory education laws in the mid–seventeenth century, requiring every town with fifty or more householders to establish a common school and teach children and servants to read, write, and calculate. Both states retained their official ties to the Puritan Congregational Church, whose teachings remained the heart of common-school education. As in most common schools, Webster's teachers were untrained transients whose names went unrecorded in town annals. Sometimes they were college students in need of funds to continue their own education, but more often they were unskilled, out-of-work passersby with little intellect or love for children. Webster recalled the teachers of his youth as the "dregs" of humanity. "The principal part of instructors," he said, "are illiterate people"[10] who teach with ferules and whips.

Children did not attend school for long periods of time or for many years—only for eight to twelve weeks a year, between the autumn harvest and spring planting, when their parents had little work for them in the fields or pastures. The purpose of schooling was as much to incarcerate the potentially unruly as it was to educate, although some education did inevitably result.

"When I was a schoolboy," Webster recalled later, "the greatest part of the scholars did not employ more than an hour in a day, either in writing or in reading; while five hours of the school time was spent in idleness, in cutting tables and benches to pieces, in carrying on pin lotteries, or perhaps in some roguish tricks."[11]

As in other common schools, the books at Webster's school were limited to a King James Bible, a psalter, a catechism, and Thomas Dilworth's *New Guide to the English Tongue.* First published in London in 1740, Dilworth's was a beginners' spelling book, syllabarium, and reader that indoctrinated children in religious dogma. It sought to save "poor creatures from the Slavery of Sin and Satan" by placing "the word of God for a Lantern to our Feet and a Light to our Paths." The word *God* appeared in every sentence of even the earliest lessons, with words of only three letters:

> No Man may put off the Law of God.
> The Way of God is no Ill Way.
> My Joy is in God all the Day.
> A bad Man is a Foe to God.

"The instruction in schools was very imperfect," Webster explained. "No geography was studied . . . no history was read . . . no book for reading was used. . . . Before the revolution & for some years after, no slates were used in common schools; all writing & the operations in Arithmetic were on paper. The teacher wrote the copies & gave the sums in Arithmetic; few or none of the pupils having any books as a guide."[12]

According to Webster's daughter Emily, "The 'nurture and admonition of the Lord' were almost the only education he received until his fourteenth year, for secular studies were then confined within very narrow bounds."[13]

3

FROM HIS EARLIEST YEARS, Noah Webster lived in a political storm of biblical proportions, which eventually pulled him into its vortex as an eager, active participant for much of his life.

The clouds began gathering after the end of the French and Indian War, in 1763. Although British troops had turned the tide of battle against the French the year after Noah's birth and eventually won the war, they faced colossal debts from the conflict. The British government's inveterate penchant for governing without the consent of the governed smothered the colonial economy with taxes to pay for the war—first on sugar, then, one by one, on coffee, wines, silks, and calicoes.

The taxes, due in silver, increased living costs and destroyed the value of colonial paper currency. Suddenly, paper money that the Websters and other families had saved was worthless, and farmers and merchants turned to barter to survive.

By 1765, when Noah was seven, depression had gripped New England, and many communities lay bankrupt. Tax collectors added to the woes by invading homes without warrants to collect their due. In 1764, Connecticut's first newspaper, the weekly *Connecticut Courant,* had been founded in Hartford, and it carried news of British outrages into colonial homes across the state. Angry colonists near Webster's home responded by dragging at least three tax collectors to tar-and-feather parties.

Farm life now demanded twice the labor for half the profits. Infuriated, Noah's father read the *Courant* aloud to his family, while his wife patiently explained phrases such as *confiscatory taxes* and *taxation without representation* to the children. Like their neighbors, the Websters talked of justice and, if necessary, independence as a last resort for obtaining it.

Britain's insatiable appetite for revenues reached a new peak with the infamous Stamp Act, which taxed newspapers, pamphlets, and legal papers. Colonists responded violently, and repeal of the Stamp Act the following year did little to restore calm. More taxes followed—on paper, glass, lead, paints, and, finally, tea. By 1770, colonists' hostility evolved into rebellion, and on March 5, British regulars fired at an angry mob in Boston, killing five people—and rupturing the last Puritan ties to the motherland.

The *Courant*'s Journal of Occurrences reported the Boston massacre and roused Connecticut to arms. Hartford and other towns held extraordinary weekly meetings to develop appropriate responses. The elder Noah Webster, by then an overage militia captain of forty-eight, organized and trained an "alarm list" of volunteers who were over forty-five years old—with three exceptions: twelve-year-old Noah Webster and his brothers, nineteen-year-old Abram and eight-year-old Charles, each shouldered muskets and marched proudly at the rear of the column.

Young Noah had grown lanky, bony. His strong jutting chin, high cheekbones, and still-unruly red hair belied his quiet personality and thoughtful mind; his straight, thin lips made it difficult to know whether he was about to smile or to explode in anger. Like other common-school boys, he had worked long hours alongside his father and older brother in the fields during the spring plantings and autumn harvests and had attended school only during slack periods in winter and midsummer.

Unlike other boys, however, he was a Webster, a member of a family that had settled and helped lead Hartford from its beginnings and had continuing responsibilities to the community. Endless hours of Congregational upbringing at home and an eternity of Sundays in the forward Webster pew had taught young Noah to listen and learn, and to prepare for eventual accession to community leadership. His father's militia drills reinforced his love of country and pride of family—and his sense of obligation to lead.

In the west part of Hartford, as in other Connecticut towns, the Puritan Congregational Church was the foundation of government as well as religion, with Sunday services blending into late-afternoon town meetings. Church elders were almost always town officials, and town officials, elders. While the women and young children left for home, the men and older boys remained in church with the minister to debate church discipline, school curriculum, and local taxes, and to settle disputes between neighbors. All who loved God could join the church, and all who joined the church could vote. Noah had been raised on his father's reports of these proceedings, and at twelve, he, too, remained in church and stood beside his father, learning to be what he later described as a "good republican."

"New England," he wrote later, "is certainly a phenomenon in civil and political establishments, and in my opinion not only young gentlemen from our sister states, but from every quarter of the globe would do well to pass a few years of their life among us, and acquire our habits of thinking and living."

Those habits, he said, "are formed by a singular machinery in the body politic, which takes the child as soon as he can speak, checks his natural independence and passions, makes him subordinate to superior age, to the laws of the state, to town and parochial institutions—initiates him in the business of government by making him an active party in local regulations, and in short molding him into a peaceable citizen, an intelligent man, and an independent, but rational freeman."[14]

In 1772, the elder Noah Webster decided that of his three sons, his middle one should go to college. The reason was straightforward, as his granddaughter Emily Ellsworth Fowler Ford explained years later:

> When my father was a boy of fourteen, he showed a decided love for study and books. He would take his Latin Grammar into the field, and his rests under the apple trees were quite too long for a farmer's son. He was led to reflect on the advantages of a collegiate education, and the native ardor of his mind awakened and directed to this end, was able to obtain it. My Grandfather was a wise man, and, finding Noah stretched on the grass forgetful of his tasks, he decided to permit him to follow his inclinations, and he was placed under the tuition of the Rev. Nathan Perkins, the pastor of the Congregational church in West Hartford. With him my Father fitted for College.[15]

That same year, Perkins, a graduate of Yale College, in New Haven, replaced Hooker as West Hartford's minister after the latter's death. Webster became the first of 150 boys that Perkins would prepare for college during his sixty-six years there. Although young Webster spent half his time helping his father in the fields, he completed his studies in two years, learning basic Latin and Greek, studying the ancient classics and histories, and committing the scriptures to memory. Perkins awarded Webster a certificate attesting to his character and scholastic achievements, and Yale admitted the boy at the age of sixteen, in September 1774.

Although college costs would combine with the collapsing economy to leave his father deeply in debt, the father was committed to ensuring his son's success, often displaying his commitment with uncharacteristic displays of tenderness as well as financial sacrifice. As the elder Noah Webster's granddaughter put it, "The father was deeply interested in his son's career, for he mortgaged the farm to pay his college expenses, and more than once rode [the fifty miles] on horseback to New Haven to bring his boy home, once walking back and letting his son ride, saying that he was best able of the two."[16]

4

ONCE THE FONT OF THE PURITAN MINISTRY, Yale had changed dramatically by the time the two Websters, father and son, arrived in New Haven with their horse, in September 1774. The Great Awakening had weakened the foundations of Puritanism, and Yale College was collapsing with the church, physically as well as spiritually.[17]

Orthodox Calvinists had founded Yale in 1701 as a bastion of Puritanism in Connecticut, where Congregationalism was the official state religion and property taxes supported church and state—and Yale. Preservation of all three institutions depended on a ministry formally educated to interpret the Bible and prevent error from eroding religion and government. Yale began as "a religious society" to train that ministry.[18]

Four decades after its founding, however, only half its students were preparing for the ministry. (Thirty-five years later, when young Webster enrolled, the number of divinity students in his class of forty had dwindled to four, the smallest percentage in Yale history.) The Puritans themselves were responsible for the decline. By limiting voting membership in their Congregational churches to an elite of propertied first families, they had shattered Puritan unity and driven the unpropertied into a nonpracticing Christian netherworld, yearning for salvation but barred by the church itself. Led by the inspiring call of Yale's Jonathan Edwards, who graduated in 1720, dissenting ministers took to the fields to call their disenfranchised brethren back to Christ. Their fiery evangelism ignited a conflagration of religious fervor across New England. They cast a "new light" on biblical teachings, with a few even implying that God had created all men in his image without predestining any—first families or field hands or even the king—for heaven or hell. They promised to open the gates of heaven to all and sowed the first seeds of political as well as spiritual revolution in America.

In New Haven, a New Light Congregational Church sprang up beside the Old Light church on the green, just down the slope from the college. Students routinely violated college rules by darting away from campus to attend services and revival meetings.

Yale's president, the orthodox Calvinist minister Thomas Clap, called the Great Awakening Satan's effort to undermine authority and discipline. In a statement reminiscent of James I, Clap declared that "the Laws of God and the College are one," and he set out to crush student dissent. He expelled New Light students, banned all New Light preaching on campus, and imposed a cruel and complex system of regulations, with stiff fines for violators.

Bridling under Clap's harsh rules and byzantine system of fines and punishments, students went on "a rampage of firing guns" in April 1758, "ringing bells, and breaking windows to the great Amazement and Terror of all that were near."[19] According to faculty reports, tutors called in the sheriff to quell the rioters, but he was able only to restore temporary calm. The boys assaulted Clap's home during a fellows' meeting, "damaged the window sashes and clapboards and broke off and removed the gates." They smashed "about 30 squares of glass," injuring the sixty-three-year-old president with flying shards. The students then went on strike and harassed tutors until they resigned. The trustees had no choice but to send students home and close the college. Eight years of turmoil followed. Broken and exhausted, Clap resigned in September 1766 and died four months later, leaving Yale in shambles.

By the time Webster enrolled, the years of rioting had reduced the number of students from 170 to 100, and those who remained were bristling with rebellion. The state, still officially Congregational, withdrew its financial support, and Yale's trustees installed the gentle divinity professor Naphthali Daggett as acting president to try to restore peace on campus. Daggett would become one of the most tragic figures in Yale history.

An orthodox minister who had been pastor at a Presbyterian church, Daggett was the first Yale graduate to head the school—a member of the class of 1748, which had suffered much of Clap's "natural Despotism and high notions of Dominion." Daggett dismantled the hated system of "gradation," which seated boys by social rank, and replaced it with a democratic system of alphabetical seating.[20]

He also adapted the curriculum to changing times by condensing divinity studies from two days a week to a half day on Saturday and allowing students to use English instead of Latin as the language of recitation in secular classes. The indivisibility of church and state required Yale to prepare students for "important stations in civil life" as well as the ministry. The school, therefore, offered algebra, astronomy, botany, advanced mathematics and calculus, physics, anatomy, surveying, and navigation, as well as traditional studies for the ministry, such as theology, philosophy, ethics, and scriptural studies in Latin, Greek, and Hebrew.[21] With only four members

Timothy Dwight (1752–1817), a lifelong friend and confidant of Noah Webster, was a tutor at Yale when Webster attended. A grandson of Jonathan Edwards, Dwight graduated from Yale and was an accomplished poet and author, as well as a Calvinist minister. He founded several academies before becoming president of Yale, in 1795. (Library of Congress.)

of Webster's class bound for the ministry, Daggett added English composition and literature to the curriculum, at the suggestion of two of his tutors, John Trumbull and Timothy Dwight. Trumbull and Dwight were among the most brilliant men ever to graduate from Yale, the former a future poet and lawyer, the latter a grandson of Jonathan Edwards and a future president of Yale.

The curricular reforms combined with the abolition of social rankings to foster democratic social interaction between students. They formed discussion groups and literary societies that enriched college scholarship and stimulated political and social debate. Once-forbidden topics—the morality of slavery, the rights of man, the role of the state, the church, and the crown—all became fodder for heated discussions. Indeed, an inflammatory dialogue on "The Rights of America and the Unconstitutional Measures of the British Parliament" was the centerpiece of the commencement exercises—along with fireworks and celebratory dancing—that greeted Webster and his classmates when they enrolled, in September 1774. (Unlike today's graduation ceremonies in late spring and early summer, commencement exercises, as the term implies, began the academic year.)

5

YOUNG WEBSTER LEARNED ALMOST IMMEDIATELY that the "rights of America" had little to do with the rights of Yale freshmen. The curriculum was daunting, and the difficulties of being "new boys" subdued much of the exuberance he and his classmates felt after the heady commencement exercises. First-year studies remained unaffected by curricular reforms—or the Age of Enlightenment. They included arithmetic and intense study of "tongues," or the original languages of the Old and New Testaments: Latin, Greek, Hebrew, Chaldee, and Syriac. Students had to learn to read, write, and speak Latin fluently—and recite from Virgil and Cicero's orations, as well as the Bible. Each student also declaimed in Latin and English every week; Yale men were expected to graduate as finished public speakers, prepared for either the pulpit or the public platform.[22]

Although the college president and one or two professors lectured the students regularly each week, their primary instructor was the class tutor—a college graduate usually only a few years older than the students, but nonetheless learned enough to conduct day-to-day classes, hear student recitations, and grade them. The tutor remained with his class for the full four years. Webster's class tutor was Joseph Buckminster, a pious, gentle twenty-three-year-old minister who would remain Webster's close friend for the remainder of his life.[23]

In addition to daily classes, the published rules of the school required Webster and the others "to attend the publick worship of God in the Chapel every Lord's Day . . . to excite them to some particular Duty, and to Caution them against some particular Sin" as well as "all Excesses and Extravagance [and] vain Affectation of Show." The services were "to instil in their Minds true Notions of Honor, Politeness, and a Love of Virtue."[24]

Freshmen rose at five-thirty, went to prayer services at six and then two hours of recitation beginning at seven—all before breakfast. They attended school the year round, with the academic year divided into quarters. A "vacancy" of several weeks at the end of each quarter permitted Webster and other farm boys to return home to help with spring plantings, autumn harvests, and other farm chores. They lived two to a room in Connecticut Hall, one of three Yale structures huddled on a barren plateau above the New Haven green. A gem of colonial architecture, Connecticut Hall stands today as the sole vestige of Webster's Yale.[25] To Webster and his classmates, however, it was their "Brick Prison." A beehive of small, square, cell-like rooms, its brick veneer made it an oven in summer, while wood-burning fireplaces funneled out the heat during the bitter New Haven winters. Outside the hall, winter ice and spring mud turned excursions to the pump or privy into unpredictable adventures.

Looming over Connecticut Hall and adjacent to it was the 125-foot-tall steeple of the college chapel, which served as an auditorium as well as a house of worship. The first college church in America when it opened, it was built by Clap in 1763 to dissuade students from attending New Light churches in town. It also housed a four-thousand-volume library and a museum of deteriorating stuffed birds and animals for science classes. Classes met in a third, tumbledown wooden structure called Old College, which students burned to the ground in 1782.

Noontime dinners usually consisted of "Injun pudding" (a kind of cornmeal) and a broth with dandelion greens, a cabbage leaf, turnip, two potatoes, and a bone that was sometimes overlaid with shreds of chicken or beef. Supper, at five, offered only brown bread and milk—but it was, Webster said, by far the tastier of the two meals served. Students could supplement their meals at the buttery, a small store then common in British colleges, where the porter sold sweets, baked goods, fruit, beer, cider, and metheglin (mead).

Although some younger students blamed the British for the bad food and food shortages, upperclassmen knew it also reflected financial mismanagement—and they protested regularly by hurling a barrage of bones at the faculty, who sat in formal wigs and black academic robes at an elevated table at the end of the dining hall.[26]

Rules for freshmen were strict. Yale summarily expelled students for "blasphemy, cursing, robbery, fornication, forgery . . . [and] utterance of heretical opinions." An "indecent rout, tumult, noise, or hallooing . . . in the presence of the president or a tutor" meant a two-shilling fine, and according to Yale records, one freshman who rang the chapel bell at 9 P.M. had "his ears boxed by the president."[27]

An eighteenth-century engraving of Connecticut Hall and the chapel at Yale College, where Noah Webster was a student from 1774 to 1778. The chapel was the first college church in America when it opened. Students lived in Connecticut Hall, which is the only building that remains of Webster's Yale. (Yale Picture Collection, Manuscripts and Archives, Yale University Library.)

Making life more dismal for freshmen was their lowly status as lackeys to upperclassmen—they had to split or fetch wood for the older boys, tend their fireplaces, and perform other menial chores. The freshmen were humiliatingly conspicuous in ordinary street clothes, ordered about by their given names, while upperclassmen and graduate students wore gowns and were addressed as "sir"—Sir Trumbull, Sir Dwight, and so on.

The average age of Webster's freshman class was sixteen, although it ranged from fourteen to twenty, and one student, the son of the New Haven mayor, was only twelve. They were a distinguished group, from some of Connecticut's most notable families—families (such as the Websters) who had carved New England's most productive fields from the wilderness in the previous century and built the state's thriving towns, cities, and ports. Their heirs—young Webster and the rest—would help build a new nation. Indeed, historians later described the class of 1778 as "Yale's most distinguished class up to the Civil War."[28]

Webster made friends easily, and he and they would remain lifelong friends. As leaders of their state and nation, their lives would intertwine. Webster's closest friend in Connecticut Hall was a high-spirited Connecticut farm boy, Joel Barlow, whose ancestors had cleared 170 acres of prosperous farmlands in Fairfield County, at Redding, not far from New Haven. At twenty, Barlow was the oldest of Webster's circle. A glib opportunist and adventurer, Barlow would become a prominent, though forgettable, poet (*The Hasty Pudding, The Vision of Columbus, The Columbiad*) and a diplomat. He would suffer a cruel death in the snows of eastern Europe.

Oliver Wolcott Jr. would fare better. Only fourteen and the youngest of Webster's friends in the freshman class, he would later succeed Alexander Hamilton as secretary of the Treasury and eventually become governor of Connecticut, a post held by his father and grandfather before him.

Webster's other close friends included Uriah Tracy, nineteen, a future U.S. senator from Connecticut; Josiah Meigs, seventeen, who became a Yale professor of mathematics and science and, later, president of the University of Georgia; and Zephaniah Swift, who, at fifteen, was a year younger than Webster and would become chief justice of Connecticut's Supreme Court.

From the moment of their arrival on campus, the growing national rebellion captured their attention. The First Continental Congress was meeting in Philadelphia, and its deliberations converted Yale's Brick Prison into a hotbed of scholastic and nonscholastic intrigue—an exciting center of intellectual ferment for a boy like Webster, just emerging from small-town isolation in the Connecticut wilderness.

Webster joined Brothers in Unity, whose library of several hundred books included works by Locke, Bacon, and Webster's personal favorite, the "great genius . . . the immortal Newton." Newton swept superstition from Webster's mind and impassioned him with an insatiable, lifelong love of science. Three works by Locke—*Essay Concerning Human Understanding* (1690), *Treatises on Government* (1690), and *Some Thoughts Concerning Education* (1693)—helped him resolve the conflict he perceived between orthodox Calvinism and the normal libertarian yearnings of adolescence. Without abandoning his love of God, Webster rejected the Puritan concept of "a speaking aristocracy in the face of a silent democracy"[29] and adopted one more in keeping with the spirit of the American Revolution—that "all power is vested in the people."[30]

Webster combined what he learned from Locke and from his experiences watching self-government in his father's West Hartford church in an undated essay, found among his papers; it concluded that universal public education was essential to the preservation of liberty in a self-governing electorate. "It is scarcely possible," he wrote, "to reduce an enlightened people to civil or ecclesiastical tyranny. Deprive them of knowledge, and they sink almost insensibly in vassalage. Ignorance cramps the powers of the mind, at the same time that it blinds men to all their natural rights. Knowledge enlarges the understanding, and at the same time, it gives a spring to all intellectual faculties, which direct the deliberations of the cabinet and the enterprises of the field." Webster would use the material from the essay in his later political writings.[31]

Webster rejected the Puritan concept of original sin, which had long guided orthodox parents and teachers to "beat the devil" out of children to make them learn. Convinced that kindness was a more effective teaching tool than the ferule or whip, Webster embraced the Lockean concept of tabula rasa—an infant is born innocent, free of sin, and with a "clean slate" on which to inscribe knowledge. He extended the concept of universal public education to include women: "The importance of female education," he wrote, "is evident from the influence that women have over the manners of civilized society." Webster prized his essay and later published it in his own magazine in 1788,[32] and then in a more extensive work, "On the Education of Youth in America," in 1790.[33]

In ordinary times, Webster's ideas might have earned him rebuke, as contrary to Puritan orthodoxy. But 1774 was not an ordinary year in America or at Yale. By midwinter of their first year, Webster and other patriot students had given up tea to protest British duties. They organized a militia of their own and engaged two regular soldiers to drill them each day after classes. "The military Art just begins to dawn in the generous breasts of the Sons of Yale," a friend on campus wrote to the schoolteacher Nathan Hale, who had graduated two years earlier and was about to join the town militia. "College Yard constantly sounds with, *poise your firelock, cock your firelock & c.* These warlike noises are continually in College."[34]

In March 1775, Webster and the others built breastworks and ramparts that converted their hilltop campus into a fortress to repel advances by

British regulars, who were rumored to be on their way. Yale became a center of rebellion—or as one royalist alumnus put it, "a nursery of sedition, of faction, and republicanism."[35]

In April, Yale and the rest of the world heard the fateful shots fired at Lexington and Concord. As chapel bells tolled, chaos spread through the city. "Today," one student wrote in his diary, "tidings of the Battle of Lexington, which is the first engagement with the British troops, arrived at New Haven. This filled the country with alarm and rendered it impossible for us to pursue our studies to any profit."[36]

The local apothecary, Capt. Benedict Arnold, left his shop to muster the governor's guards on the New Haven green, below the Yale campus. Joined by older Yale students, they stormed the powder house and seized British stores of arms and ammunition. To the cheers of students and assembled townsfolk, they marched off to Boston to confront the British.

6

TOO YOUNG TO GO TO WAR, Webster stayed behind with the other sixteen- and seventeen-year-olds to defend fortress Yale. Tutor Buckminster, whose scholastic skills lay in "tongues and logick," tried to coax his charges to concentrate on class work, but news of the war continually interrupted lectures and recitations and inevitably provoked debates on military and political strategy and the rights of man. Life behind the Yale breastworks grew more and more chaotic, but as Webster's granddaughter later wrote, "Those lads who were called out to drill daily, and to build breastworks when New Haven was threatened by the British, had a realizing sense of what country and duty meant."[37]

At the end of May, Ethan Allen and Benedict Arnold captured Fort Ticonderoga, and in June, the Second Continental Congress, in Philadelphia, unanimously elected George Washington commander in chief of the Continental Army in Massachusetts. Within a few days, he and Maj. Gen. Charles Lee arrived in New Haven on their way to assume command of the Revolutionary forces in Boston. Webster and the Yale students invited them "to see a military company of students of Yale College perform their manual exercises," Webster later recalled in his memoirs. "They expressed their surprise and gratification at the precision with which the students performed the customary exercises then in use."[38]

Indeed, according to Webster, the two generals were so impressed they invited the boys to march with regulars the next morning and escort them out of town in parade. On the morning of April 29, they assembled on the New Haven green.

"It fell to my humble lot to lead the company with music," wrote Webster, who strutted proudly at the head of the Yale militia, piping "The Yankee Song" ("Yankee Doodle") on his flute as they led America's commander in chief off to war. As it turned out, Washington and his force left two weeks too late to prevent defeat by British troops at Breed's Hill and Bunker Hill, in Boston.

In June, the mood at Yale grew uglier. Student militiamen posted TORY signs on the doors of students who even hinted at loyalty to the crown. On June 13, a student committee demanded that each student declare himself. Several students fled. Abiathar Camp Jr., a sophomore, called committee members "damn rebels" and vowed he would kill them when he joined British troops. College records state euphemistically that he was treated with "utmost neglect," and he withdrew from Yale.[39]

On July 6, 1775, the Continental Congress issued a "Declaration of the Causes and Necessities of Taking Up Arms." The resolution continued to reject independence but asserted that Americans were ready to die rather than be enslaved. Although the students made a pretense of studying occasionally, the war dominated their lives and crushed scholarly debate of the issues underlying the war.

Webster's friend Joel Barlow wrote home:

Honored Mother:

. . . The students are sensibly affected with the unhappy situation of publick affairs, which is a great hindrance to their studies; and for that reason there has been talk of dismissing college; but whether they will tis uncertain. . . . If your circumstances are such as to want me at home, send a horse at any time & I shall be ready to come.[40]

After a brief respite at the end of August, Webster and the other sophomores returned to college in a somber mood to begin what would be their last complete year on the Yale campus. By then the war had touched almost all the boys personally. Both Webster's and Barlow's older brothers had marched to war in Canada under Richard Montgomery. In November, Montgomery's force took Montreal and was preparing to assault Quebec with Benedict Arnold's force. Over Christmas, however, colonist fortunes changed. The assault on Quebec failed when French settlers refused to join the rebellion. Montgomery was dead, Sam Barlow had been killed, and three hundred colonist soldiers were taken prisoner. Webster's family had no idea of Abram's whereabouts. In April, Noah received and read this letter to his tearful parents:

Montreal, April 14th, 1776.

Loving Brother:

by the time this gets to Hartford I expect you will be there for Spring vacancy, and since Providence has ordered that I must not be there to see you, I must content myself with informing you by these lines, that

> I am through goodness of God in good health and Tolerably Contented
> with a Soldier's life, though it is attended with Care and fatigue as well
> as many and great temptations. I cant write now the 1/4 part of what
> I want.

After describing his astonishment at Roman Catholic rituals, which he had
never witnessed in Calvinist Hartford, Abram reported,

> They have a College and a number of students but the greater part of
> the people Can neither read nor write. I hope you and others of my
> friends will write to me, for I have not heard a word from home since
> I left the place, for which I am very anxious. You may direct your letters
> to Quebeck as I expect to be there soon. My love to you and all my
> friends.
>
>   Your loving brother.[41]

British troops captured Abram shortly after he sent his letter, but he
contracted smallpox and was released for fear he would spread the disease
among them. He tried to find his way southward. Noah described his older
brother's ordeal: "He could not travel—he was obliged to resort to a cabin
inhabited by a French woman, where he lay with the disease so bad that it
seemed to him his flesh would leave his bones and without friend or nurse
or physicians. He had nothing to sustain him but milk."[42]

7

WHEN WEBSTER AND THE OTHER SOPHOMORES returned to Yale in the
spring of 1776, the constant flow of reports and rumors from the war made
study all but impossible. In addition to the Greek Testament and Horace,
their curriculum had expanded to include such secular subjects as logic,
rhetoric, algebra, geometry, geography, and English grammar, but they
talked largely of war and battle strategy, of Tom Paine's fiery essays—and
Joel Barlow's forays into town, usually with Webster along, to court every
girl who would listen to his absurdly adolescent poetry.

At twenty-two, Barlow was already the consummate opportunist, using
the younger, somewhat shyer Webster's illustrious name to inveigle invitations to dances and social gatherings at the homes of the city's most prominent citizens. For the now handsome, eighteen-year-old Webster, full grown,
with a soldierly bearing, the invitations provided a welcome chance to hone
his own social skills and to meet and attract young ladies to his side. He so
mastered the art that younger classmates such as Zephaniah Swift, Connecticut's future chief justice, wrote for advice:

> . . . to be solely a man of Letters or a man of the world is not sufficient,
> for one pleases the learned and the other the unlearned, and by these

means neither of them cannot please but half the World. The way to avoid this will be to mix both these characters. . . . Your opportunities and the time you spend with the Ladies will enable you to reach both, but as for myself I fear I shall reach neither but be a medium fit for no company. I am averse to frequent changes or trivial conversation which will not allow me to be a man of the world. I fear I shall never be able to obtain learning sufficient to be called a man of letters and if so I shall be a nobody. . . . Fail not to send me a letter by the next post.[43]

Webster later admitted that he fell into "vicious company at college . . . [and], despite being educated in a religious family, under pious parents, I . . . contracted a habit of using profane language." At the time, however, he seemed quite proud of his social skills with the ladies. In a rambling Latin declamation entitled "Youth and Old Age," Webster wrote, with evident personal pride, "*Juventutem bene actam, Senututem parere felicem*"—a well-spent youth is the proper preparation for a felicitous old age.

"Young men," he added, "turn their backs on weighty matters during their immature years and are carried headlong to the delights of pleasure." Webster's tutor, the Reverend Joseph Buckminster, described the work as "second-rank."[44]

Although the war undoubtedly eroded the quality of work at Yale, Webster's scholastic efforts were, after all, those of a farm boy with little more than an elementary-school education, and Yale, like America's other colleges, was little more than an academy—the equivalent of today's college preparatory schools and well below the standards of Britain and Scotland's great universities of that era. Although Webster and his classmates gained some fluency in Latin and Greek, they used it almost exclusively for biblical studies. In the end, Yale's greatest contributions to its students were to stimulate their love of learning and transform them into obsessive autodidacts for the remainder of their lives.

8

BY THE SPRING OF 1776, campus life reflected the temper of the nation: despair, after the British pushed American forces out of Canada; exultation, after the colonists repulsed British troops at Charleston, South Carolina. After Congress issued the Declaration of Independence, news reached New Haven that New York City faced imminent invasion by General Howe's troops on Staten Island. General Washington called for volunteers to supplement his force of seventeen thousand near Coney Island. Connecticut governor Jonathan Trumbull issued a proclamation to colonists on August 12: "Be roused, therefore & alarmed to stand forth in our just and glorious cause" and form companies to join Washington.[45]

Yale's trustees granted seniors their diplomas and sent them off to battle for whichever country they embraced as their own. According to Yale records, Timothy Dwight, tutor of the sophomore class, stood "wholly dressed in the manufactures of our own country"[46] and delivered the emotional farewell address to Yale's first war class on July 25, 1776: "You should by no means consider yourselves as members of a small neighborhood, town or colony only, but as being concerned in laying the foundations of American greatness. Your wishes, your designs, your labors, are not to be confined by the narrow bounds of the present age, but are to comprehend succeeding generations. . . . Remember that you are to act for the empire of America, and for a long succession of ages."[47]

In September, Yale gave the nation its first Revolutionary War hero, when the British executed Lt. Nathan Hale, of the class of 1773, as a spy. His last defiant words inspired every student on the Yale campus: "I only regret that I have but one life to lose for my country."

The older Yale students immediately enlisted. Under the command of Oliver Wolcott's father, a member of the Continental Congress and signatory of the Declaration of Independence, the Connecticut militia of several thousand men marched to New York City and the battle of Long Island. Included in their number was Webster's friend Joel Barlow.

Too young to join up, Webster returned home to West Hartford, where, to his relief and delight, he found his brother Abram home from war and in the final stages of recuperation. Several weeks later, after he had fully recovered, Abram prepared to return to his company in Whitehall (New York) and asked Noah to accompany him to bring home his horse. For Noah, the ride proved a disillusioning first glimpse of a soldier's life:

> We took horses and traveled through Bennington to Skeenborough (Skenesboro), now Whitehall, passing the last twelve miles through a forest of marked trees.
>
> At that place, the head of South Bay, I found Ashbel Wells, the companion of my youth, a soldier in the troops at that place. The musketoes were so numerous that the soldiers could not sleep at night except by filling their tents with smoke. I spent one night in the Wells tent in that condition.
>
> The next night I slept in a batteau on South Bay. When we arrived at Mount Independence [now Mount Defiance, across Lake Champlain from Fort Ticonderoga] we found about half the soldiers sick with dysentery, and fever, so that the very air was infected.
>
> I returned through the woods, sleeping one night on the floor of a hospitable farmer.[48]

When Webster returned to Yale, he found the college overcrowded. The dormitory wing of the crumbling Old College had collapsed, forcing four boys to squeeze into rooms built for two, in Connecticut Hall. In October, Barlow returned from the disastrous campaign on Long Island and rejoined Webster. Having experienced life on or near the battlefield, he and other veterans chafed under the schoolboy rules, the intolerable living conditions, and what they considered a dull curriculum that bore little relationship to the explosive events in the world about them. In December, food shortages forced the college to close.

"So impoverished was the country at one time," according to Webster, "that the steward of the college could not supply the necessary provisions of the table, and the students were compelled to return ... home." Although college reopened on January 7, 1777, food supplies were exhausted by mid-March. Sugar had all but disappeared. "At one time," Webster recalled, "goods were so scarce that the farmers cut corn-stalks and crushed them in cider-mills, and then boiled the juice down to a syrup, as a substitute for sugar."[49] Wood supplies ran so low that students burned straw in their fireplaces and almost set Connecticut Hall aflame.

Although respected for the patriotic fervor of his sermons, Pres. Naphthali Daggett could no longer maintain control over the students. Barlow and another student demanded that Daggett resign, with Barlow issuing a scathing attack on the embattled divinity professor and on life at Yale, in a parody he wrote of the Book of Chronicles:

> And it came to pass on the third day of the tenth month, that there went forth a decree from Naphthali, the son of Zebulon, that all the captives throughout his dominion should depart for a little season, into the land of their nativity, to buy themselves some bread. . . . Now Naphthali was a great man and ate much bread . . . and lifted his voice in the midst of them and said, "Forasmuch as the famine is sore in the land, insomuch there is hardly bread enough for me and my household; Wherefore ye sons of the captivity of Naphthali, behold you may return to your houses in the land of your nativity, where ye can get some bread, lest ye die.
>
> "Nevertheless, when you shall hear the voice of my decree in the land of your fathers, saying unto you, return into the land of Naphthali. Then it shall come to pass, that ye shall return and sojourn again in the land of captivity." Thus was it done according to all the words of Naphthali.[50]

Although students could hardly contain their laughter as Daggett began his sermon the following Sunday, their mood turned sour as Daggett condemned Barlow for blasphemy and announced his imminent dismissal. Webster and twenty-five other students walked out of chapel in protest.

Threatened with dismissal, they agreed to sign a "Confession of Causing a Disturbance in Chapel," acknowledging their "audacious Contempt of all the Authority of the College, and a practical Countenancing and Approving of the Crimes of others.

"We publicly condemn ourselves," the confession went on, "and confess we justly deserve a very severe punishment on account of it; we humbly ask forgiveness of the Rev'd. President and all the other Authority of the

College whom we have hereby offended. We cast ourselves on their clemency . . . sincerely promising that we will for the future carefully avoid all such like disorderly behavior." It was signed by twenty-six students of the Yale College class of 1778, including Noah Webster.[51]

Before the devastated Reverend Dr. Daggett could punish Barlow, British military and naval encroachments in mid-March punished New Haven so severely that the college once again closed and sent students home. In April, the British seemed determined to capture New Haven, because of its strategic coastal position. While their ships squeezed closer to the harbor from the south, British troops closed in by land from the west, overrunning nearby Danbury and burning valuable food supplies. Webster's young classmate Oliver Wolcott, just seventeen, was "routed out of bed to join the militia" under Gen. Benedict Arnold and helped to repel the British.[52]

After the colonists pushed the British back to the Hudson River, Yale's trustees decided to resume instruction on April 30, but to disperse students and much of the library to the safety of inland towns, where food supplies were more plentiful. Dwight gathered the seniors in Wethersfield, while freshmen went to study with a tutor in Farmington for the summer. Two classes settled at a school in Glastonbury, not far from Webster's West Hartford home: the juniors, including Webster, under Buckminster, and the sophomores, under Prof. Nehemiah Strong.

Throughout the summer, however, the war moved relentlessly closer. Gen. John Burgoyne's seventy-seven hundred British and German troops swept down from Canada to link up with forces in New York and isolate New England. By July 1, Burgoyne had recaptured Fort Ticonderoga, at the foot of Lake Champlain. A week later, his forces had driven through Skenesboro, taken Fort Ann, and reached Saratoga, and were preparing to move on Albany.

Word reached Hartford's newspaper that Burgoyne's advance had left a swath of "terror and devastation . . . throughout the northern counties of New York, and the adjacent settlements of Vermont." Especially terrifying was the tale of Burgoyne's Indian forerunners' having shot and scalped young Jane (Jenny) McCrea and left her nude body at Fort Edward, midway between Fort Ann and Saratoga—despite Burgoyne's order that "aged men, women and children and prisoners must be held sacred from the knife or hatchet." Jenny was the daughter of a Presbyterian minister; she had been awaiting her Tory fiancé, who was, ironically, a soldier with Burgoyne's own troops.[53]

News of the murder of Jane McCrea became a call to arms across New England against the hated Tory. Rather than await the Redcoats in their fields, farmer-militiamen surged out of their villages to attack the British. Patriot general Horatio Gates fired their anger with a widely publicized letter to Burgoyne:

. . . that the savages of America should . . . mangle the unhappy prisoners who fall into their hands is neither new nor extraordinary; but that the famous Lieutenant General Burgoyne, in whom the fine gentleman is united with the soldier and scholar, should hire the savages of America to scalp Europeans and the descendants of Europeans . . . is more than will be believed in England. . . . Miss McCrea, a young lady lovely to the sight, of virtuous character and amiable disposition, engaged to be married to an officer of your army . . . was scalped and mangled in the most shocking manner.[54]

In West Hartford, Noah's father, by then captain of the alarm list, mustered his old men—all of them over forty-five—and prepared for battle. The courage of their fathers brought the sons flocking to their sides. Fifteen-year-old Charles Webster joined his father's band, as did the oldest Webster boy, Abram, whose company Burgoyne had decimated at Skenesboro. Although college students were exempt from military duty, Noah, who was home from college between quarters, also joined, and in late September, he and his brothers marched away with their neighbors to war, under his father's command.

A forced march of two days brought them to the east bank of the Hudson River, where other militia companies were preparing to prevent Burgoyne from linking forces with Gen. Sir Henry Clinton, who was advancing northward on ship and shore from New York City. Across the river, still more militia had gathered to defend the state capital, at Kingston. On October 6, Clinton's forces captured Forts Clinton and Montgomery, to the south, and three days later, his fleet sailed into view.

The next day, however, as despair gripped Webster's camp, a few sudden cheers gradually swelled into an exultant roar. News had arrived that militiamen to the north had repelled two British onslaughts and sent Burgoyne in full retreat toward Saratoga. On October 13, the Americans, under Gens. Philip J. Schuyler, Horatio Gates, and Benedict Arnold, surrounded Burgoyne's forces at Saratoga and made English defeat inevitable. Too late to save Burgoyne, Clinton began a retreat toward New York. To cover the withdrawal, he ordered his ships to fire on Kingston and set the town ablaze. Across the river, Webster and his father and brothers watched in horror as flames consumed the state capital throughout the night "and the whole country around was fleeing in consternation."

The next morning, with Clinton's fleet out of view and Kingston a blackened mass of debris, "a courier waving his sword in triumph" galloped into Webster's encampment, "crying out as he passed, 'Burgoyne is taken; Burgoyne is taken.'" According to his granddaughter, Webster, even in old age, "could never speak of it or of his feelings, as the shout of the courier rang through the ranks of the regiment, with a strength of emotion, which was often expressed by tears."[55]

With no further need of their support, the little band from West Hartford packed their gear and began the long march home to their farms,
across sixty miles of wilderness, without ever firing a shot at the enemy.
Their mood, however, was ebullient, according to Webster. "Well might
every American who had shared in the conflict, or who was hastening to
meet the foe, exult in such a victory."

Webster's pride in the service he rendered as a volunteer militiaman
never diminished, and sixty years later, he sent a letter of outrage to the editor of the *Palladium,* a Boston newspaper that had dared label Webster an
"aristocrat" because of his Federalist political philosophy.

"In the most critical period of the revolutionary war," Webster coun-
tered, "when the British were attempting to cut off the communication between the Eastern & Southern states, when the companions of my youth
were sinking into the grave by the sword of a deadly pestilence, I offered
to hazard my life to protect the liberties which *you,* Sir, now enjoy in common with others; I marched, a volunteer, to the bank of the Hudson, ill able
to bear the fatigues of a soldier, & glad at times to find a bed of straw in a
barn or a shed."[56]

9

NOW A HARDENED VETERAN, Webster prepared to return to Yale—but Yale
was nowhere to be found. After the disorderly summer quarter had ended,
Yale's trustees appointed a new president: the Reverend Dr. Ezra Stiles, acknowledged as the most learned educator in New England—and an outspoken patriot. Fifty years old, Stiles was a biblical scholar, with a mastery
of Arabic, Hebrew, Syriac, and Armenian. He was also a noted philosopher,
scientist, and historian, and a close friend and confidant of notable American leaders, such as Benjamin Franklin. A graduate of Yale and a former
tutor, Stiles had served as pastor of the Second Congregational Church in
Newport, Rhode Island, and had helped found Rhode Island College (now
Brown University). The approach of British forces had forced him to flee
Providence to Portsmouth, New Hampshire, to escape capture at the beginning of the Revolution.

Although appointed Yale president in 1777, Stiles was not able to reach
New Haven until late spring of 1778 because of the risk of capture by the
British. Yale remained closed throughout the winter until his arrival. He
proved to be a gifted, charismatic orator and a brilliant teacher. His erudition electrified Webster and his classmates. Stiles, in turn, was impressed
with their thirst for and innate ability to absorb knowledge. He personally
took charge of the seniors' education. Webster and the others had barely
completed three months of instruction that year, and they asked him to give

them two recitations a day instead of the usual one during the month that remained before graduation.

On the morning of July 23, Webster, Barlow, and the other seniors, according to Stiles's diary, took their public examinations, "touching their knowledge and proficiency in the learned languages, the liberal arts and sciences, and other qualifications requisite for receiving a bachelor's degree." That afternoon Stiles, the fellows, tutors, students, and "other gentlemen of liberal education" met to hear seniors deliver their orations, recitations, and disputations.

The central disputation was the heady "twofold question 'Whether the Destruction of the Alexandrine Library, and Ignorance of the Middle Ages caused by the ... Goths & Vandals, were Events unfortunate to Literature?'" Stiles commented in his diary that the participants "disputed inimitably well; particularly Barlow, Swift, Webster, Gilbert, Meigs, Sage & c."[57]

The graduation oratory followed:

> a Cliosophic oration in Latin by Sir Meigs
> a poetical composition in English by Sir Barlow
> a dialogue in English by Sir Chaplin, Sir Ely, and Sir Miller
> a Cliosophic oration by Sir Webster.
> a disputation in English by Sir Swift, Sir Wolcott, and Sir Smith
> a valedictory oration by Sir Tracy

Named for Clio, the Greek muse of history, Webster's Cliosophic oration was "A Short View of the Origin and Progress of the Science of Natural Philosophy, with Some Observations on the Advantages of Science in General."

Barlow's poetic composition, "The Prospect of Peace," typified the visionary poems of the day, portraying a future America where

> love shall rule and Innocence adore,
> Discord shall cease, and Tyrants be no more.

Stiles noted gratefully that Barlow began speaking at 3:59 and ended thirteen minutes later.

In September 1778, Stiles awarded the degree of bachelor of arts to Webster and his classmates in the college chapel, although "the customary public celebration [was] omitted on account of the state of the country." Students continued the custom of giving the president a parting gift. Webster's was $10, according to Stiles's diary—a sum worth only about one-quarter of its value when Webster had enrolled four years earlier. Stiles also noted that he absorbed a personal financial loss of about £25 teaching the class of 1778.

Before leaving Yale, Stiles's first class prayed fervently for independence from England. Webster and each of his classmates envisioned America as a new nation destined for greatness, and each intended to help assure and preserve that greatness. The nation would need new laws and a constitution guaranteeing universal suffrage and individual liberties—and universal public education to ensure wise self-governance. Webster envisioned a literate, civil, pious, and united society not unlike the harmonious community in which he had been raised, West Hartford, where the inevitable conflicts of individual self-interest were resolved in the best interests of the whole community.

Webster's formal education and that of his class "was so disrupted by war," wrote one historian, "that it may be wondered if they got much more from college than their diplomas, but nonetheless this class of forty men must be singled out for special mention . . . [as] one of the greatest classes to graduate from Yale."[58]

Tutor Joseph Buckminster said Webster had obtained "at least [a] tolerable" knowledge of Latin and Greek, along with a familiarity with all the political and social ideas the collection of library and literary society books could offer.

Webster's college education "was in many respects extraordinarily limited compared with that now given by the colleges of New England," according to his granddaughter. "Yet the study of the classics, 'dead languages' though they were, nourished the living patriotism of the students. The welfare of the country, the good of the State, the sacrifice of the individual to public good, are the very warp and woof of the older Latin and Greek writings, and when the call came to military service some of the college lads were ready. Thus the whole college course had its value."[59]

Buckminster urged Webster to continue his education by obtaining "an acquaintance with Men and manners . . . by travailing, by the conversation of Gentlemen of improvement who have gone before us in this perverse world, and by a critical tho just observation of those around us."[60] Webster would do just that, and like Benjamin Franklin and other American scholars of his day, Webster would eventually obtain the bulk of his enormous education by independent study.

Whatever Webster did learn from the faculty and books at Yale, he learned at least as much from his classmates—and they from him. His granddaughter put it this way:

> Webster's college life . . . was known to be full of friendships, some of which were prolonged through life. . . . Much is also to be ascribed to the action of those young and gifted minds upon each other, an influence which is always powerful in college classes. . . . But in their case there was a yet greater influence, which was potent to excite and develop all their faculties, and to put them at that test of *self* training without which there is no education worth the name. The age in which, and for which, they were born, the agitations among which they first became cognizant of things around them, the great events that were transpiring

during the progress of their college life, and the prospects that were opening before their country and before them as American citizens in such an age—these things talked about in their classroom, in their walks, in their sports—these things perpetually revolving in their minds, mingling with their studies, shaping and coloring all their hopes, were of far more effect in their education than all the advantages the best furnished university could have provided without such incitements and impulses. Their souls were nourished with noble food.[61]

Noble food notwithstanding, Webster and his classmates left Yale as little more than naive schoolboys, believing literally in the ideals stated by the Declaration of Independence. Isolated in rural Connecticut, far from the nation's cosmopolitan centers, they had no way knowing how differently other Americans interpreted the words of that document.

IO

YALE PRESIDENT STILES AND TUTOR BUCKMINSTER remained Webster's staunch friends and champions for the rest of their lives. Immediately after Webster's graduation, Buckminster moved to Portsmouth, New Hampshire, to assume the pulpit that Stiles had held during his exile from Rhode Island. Despite periodic student uprisings, Stiles remained president of Yale until his death, in 1795, and he helped restore the college to national prominence.

In July 1779, the year after Webster left, President Stiles and divinity professor Daggett led a valiant but unsuccessful effort by the Yale student militia to defend New Haven against an assault by two to three thousand British troops. According to Stiles's diary, he took his boys to the east while old Daggett, armed with only "a fowling piece," rode off on his black mare in the opposite direction. Stiles's force was overrun, and after a campaign of "Plunder, Rape, Murder, Bayoneting, Indelicacies toward the Sex, Insolence and Abuse and Insult toward the Inhabitants in general," the British prepared to burn the town and college. "A Loyalist officer [who] had been educated within their walls," however, used his influence with his father-in-law, the British commanding general, to spare the town and college from destruction. Yale later awarded the young man, Edward Fanning, an honorary LL.D.[62]

To the west of town, in Milford Mill, British soldiers captured the fifty-one-year-old Daggett. They beat and robbed the poor man and forced him to quick-march at bayonet point, barefoot, more than five miles, after which he collapsed and was left to die. He gathered enough strength to return home but died from his injuries the following year. As his only obituary, he left a letter to his son with the message he had often repeated in the sermons that had so influenced Webster and the boys in the chapel at Yale:

> When I considered the controversy to be truly and simply this: whether this large and fertile country, settled with infinite toil and dangers by our fathers, should be our own free possession or at the disposal of a bankrupt prodigal State in Europe, I could not hesitate a moment, and I cannot but view it in its probable, or rather certain, consequences the most important contest that hath taken place on the globe for many centuries past. . . . Under this view of the justice and high importance of the controversy, I feel willing to risque my temporal all in support of it.[63]

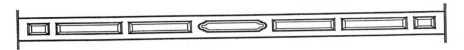

CHAPTER TWO

Schoolmaster

I

WHEN NOAH WEBSTER JR. CAME HOME FROM YALE, his family was penniless. The proud man who was his father proffered his son an $8 bill, which was all he had left of the family's savings. "Take this," he said. "You must now seek your own living. I can do no more for you."[1]

Shocked by his father's announcement, the devastated young graduate climbed the stairs to his room and stayed there "in a state of anxiety" for three days, groping with the future. He later described his state of mind: "Having neither property nor powerful friends to aid me and being utterly unacquainted with the world, I knew not what business to attempt nor by what way to obtain subsistence. Being set afloat in the world at the inexperienced age of twenty, without a father's aid which had before supported me, my mind was embarrassed with solicitude and overwhelmed with gloomy apprehension."[2]

For both Noah Websters, son and father, Yale was to have been the first big step toward the study of law and assumption of leadership in Hartford. Although not as costly as college, the study of law also entailed expense.

America had no law schools—nothing comparable to the formal legal training at England's Inns of Court. Throughout the seventeenth and most of the eighteenth century, local ministers or sheriffs settled most disputes—especially in small towns, where disputants were usually neighbors who sat together in church. Lawyers were little more than notaries who drew up one-page contracts or wills.

By the time Webster went to Yale, however, the legal climate was changing. A vast expansion of commerce required more complex contracts. Independence was coming, and the states needed jurists with skills to write new laws, constitutions, and other weighty documents. The law was clearly the path to state and national leadership. Two of Webster's closest friends at Yale, Oliver Wolcott Jr. and Uriah Tracy, were already on their way to Litchfield, Connecticut, to read law with Tapping Reeve, the renowned attorney who had founded the nation's first law school.[3] Noah Webster had planned to join them.

But four years of war had depreciated paper money by three-quarters of its value, and when young Webster got home from college in September 1778, his father was repaying $8 for every $2 he owed on the mortgage he had obtained on his home to pay for his son's education. In the meantime, no new cash was coming in. Farmers had lost faith in paper money and relied exclusively on barter, and the elder Noah Webster was getting only logs for the fireplace or butter for the grain he grew — no cash. All that remained of his savings was the $8 bill he gave his son — and it was really worth only $2 in silver.

"The period at which [I] entered upon life," Webster later wrote in his *Memoir*, "was an unpropitious one for a young man to be cast upon the world without property. The country was impoverished by the war to a degree of which it is difficult . . . to form any just conception; there was no prospect of peace; the issue of the contest was felt, by the most sanguine, to be extremely doubtful; and the practice of law . . . was in good measure set aside by the general calamity."[4]

Nor was there any indication the situation would improve. The war was going badly. Although Washington's forces had recovered somewhat from the disastrous winter in Valley Forge, Butler's Indian Rangers, led by the Tory John Butler, had swept through northeastern Pennsylvania, massacring patriot families, and were threatening to move northward into New York.[5] Meanwhile, forces loyal to the crown were preparing a sweep through the South, while the French fleet backed away from a planned assault on the British in New York.

With the economy continuing to deteriorate, Webster had few career choices open to him. The study of law would require money that he didn't have. Remaining on the farm would only increase the number of people absorbing his family's precious food resources, without raising productivity. His father and younger brother were already extracting maximum yields from their ninety acres without his help. Nor was there any work elsewhere. Every farmer and merchant was bartering to survive and had no cash to pay extra hands.

There was only one type of work open: teaching common school. Most communities had difficulties finding teachers. The low pay — usually between £1 and £2 a month — the difficult work of cleaning and maintaining the building, and the necessity of "boarding round" from home to home made a schoolmaster's life disagreeable at best. Moreover, most country schools were sievelike shacks that leaked torrents when it rained and offered slim protection against the snow and icy blasts of winter. The stove did little but turn the school into a firetrap. Students were often unpleasant packs of snarling little savages.

Webster, however, needed money, and Glastonbury, where he and his Yale classmates had spent the summer quarter of his junior year, needed a schoolmaster for the winter term. He took the post and, to his surprise, discovered a deep joy and satisfaction in teaching—but an equally deep frustration with the low pay, the poor facilities, and the lack of schoolbooks.

His friend Barlow, also penniless at graduation, was teaching in New Haven. "You and I," he wrote to Webster, "are not the first in the world to have broken loose from college without friends and without fortune to push us into public notice. Let us show the world a few more examples of men standing upon their own merit and rising in spite of obstacles. . . . I have too much confidence in your merits, both as to greatness of genius and goodness of heart, to suppose that your actions will not be conspicuous; and I hope you have too much confidence in my friendship to suppose that I don't speak from the heart." After four months, Barlow quit teaching and used his college degree and Yale's history as a divinity school to talk his way into an army chaplaincy.[6]

In the spring of 1779, Webster became a schoolmaster at the elite Brick School House in Hartford. He boarded with Oliver Ellsworth, a prominent lawyer who would later become one of Connecticut's first two senators and then chief justice of the U.S. Supreme Court. A graduate of Yale himself, Ellsworth was state's attorney for Hartford and a representative in the Continental Congress; he would represent the state at the Constitutional Convention. The two became close, lifelong friends, and Webster's eldest daughter would marry one of Ellsworth's sons.

Ellsworth opened his huge law library to the young man, who was thus able to read law, as he had originally intended, while earning his keep as a teacher. Passionate about both occupations, he worked himself cruelly: at school for six mornings and five afternoons a week, then back to Ellsworth's to read law by candlelight until early each morning. He fell ill—to a combination of exhaustion and an undefined illness (common then, probably influenza) that left him so weakened he had to suspend his studies, resign his teaching post, and return to his parents' home to recuperate.

After Christmas, he took the only job he could find—teaching at the little West Hartford school that he himself had attended as a boy. The winter was the coldest in more than a century, and for three months that winter, he walked to and from his school—nearly four miles in all—through "drifts of snow which completely covered the adjoining fences."[7]

At school, his shivering students fought to draw closer to the stove, with the smallest inevitably pushed to the rear by older, stronger boys. Webster converted his winter experience into a series of essays on elementary education and school reform that decried "the most usual defects of our country schools."[8]

"The general institution of schools in this country," he wrote in his essay,

> is full proof that . . . people never misapply their economy so much, as
> when they make mean provision for the education of children. The only
> practicable method to reform mankind is to begin with children. . . .
> Education, in a great measure, forms the moral characters of men, and
> morals are the basis of government. Education should therefore be the
> first . . . article in the code of political regulations, for it is much easier
> to introduce and establish an effectual system for preserving morals than
> to correct, by penal statutes, the ill effects of a bad system.

In addition to broad principles of reform, Webster described the horrors he had encountered as a teacher—"the absolute impossibility of obtaining books," the run-down condition of schools, inadequate heating, and school benches and tables too large and too high off the floor for the youngest children and too small and squat for the oldest. Lack of teacher training and overcrowding—with as many as seventy to eighty boys and girls of all ages in a classroom—made effective education impossible, he said.

"Children will be educated cheaper," he wrote, "if there are never more than twenty or twenty-five pupils under the charge of one instructor. The pupil should have nothing to discourage him." Webster suggested creating new types of children's books, with entertaining stories to make reading pleasurable. He also emphasized pupil health and comfort and was the first American educator to suggest comfortable, properly proportioned desks and chairs to assure correct posture for growing children of every age. He criticized teachers who frightened or beat children into paying attention and warned that children would never enjoy learning or delight in books "under the lash of a master's rod."

In a radical break with Puritan tradition, he called for extensive teacher training and the use of rewards instead of flogging as a method of enticing children to study. As a schoolmaster, he rejected the popular dictum "Spare the rod and spoil the child"[9] and condemned the practice of "beating the devil" out of students to make them learn.

"Some trifling gratuity on quarter-day," he said, would do more "to engage children to be diligent and make them fond of books than all the reasoning in the world or ten thousand rods of correction."[10]

Although eager to reform American education, Webster recognized that such reforms would require political power not available to a schoolmaster in an isolated country schoolhouse. He realized he would need a law degree and close ties to the powerful network of political leaders, jurists, and lawyers from Yale who were helping to shape the new nation.

Although he could not afford to apprentice with Tapping Reeve at Litchfield, he developed a strategy to achieve the same end. In the summer of 1780, a family friend—a judge in West Hartford—arranged for him to live with Jedediah Strong, a judge and register of deeds in Litchfield, who was suffering from "nervous disorders" and needed an assistant.

The job gave Webster the opportunity to learn about deeds and records—then an important part of day-to-day law—and left him enough free time to study general law on his own, with the amiable Judge Strong giving him a good deal of instruction. In addition, he was in the heart of one of Connecticut's most important communities, a center for the study of law, in a rich social, cultural, and economic environment, and only a few miles from his sister Jerusha's home, in Salisbury, which he visited regularly. He was in day-to-day contact with his friends Tracy and Wolcott and other young lawyers in training, and in the end, his winning ways gained him access to many of Reeve's lectures and discussions. He was thus able to earn enough to live and to learn the law amid the joys of family and friends.

2

BY AUTUMN OF 1780, even the most optimistic young patriots had begun to despair for the future of the new nation. Early in January, speculators had hoarded silver and destroyed the value of the paper continentals that the Continental Congress was printing in reams for Washington's army to buy supplies and shelter.

That army stretched along the Hudson from New Jersey to Newburgh, New York, devouring every ounce of food the region's farmers could produce. Soldiers went without meat for days on end. When farmers refused payment in continentals and loan certificates, the soldiers simply took what they needed and burned the property of farmers who protested too much.

At the end of September, even Benedict Arnold, a hero when Webster watched him leave New Haven, decided the colonist cause was lost. He handed over plans of the Continental Army's fortifications at West Point to British major John André and deserted to the Tories. André was caught in civilian clothes and hanged as a spy—with the ever-opportunistic Joel Barlow attending as chaplain.

As winter approached, the fate of the Revolution did not improve. In January, troops in Pennsylvania and New Jersey mutinied. The value of paper money—eight-to-two when Webster graduated from Yale in September 1778—had plunged to forty-to-one by January 1781, and was virtually worthless. Then, on March 1, the Continental Congress lifted the nation's spirits by giving the nation a name—the United States—and it ratified the Articles of Confederation that united the thirteen former colonies into a league of friendship. United against common enemies in war, each of the states would retain "its sovereignty, freedom and independence" in peace. With renewed optimism, Webster went to Hartford to take his examinations for the bar. He was admitted on April 3.

3

THE WARTIME ECONOMY OF THE 1780s offered little work for lawyers— especially inexperienced ones. The states were already overrun by lawyers, and every young man who wanted to make a name for himself was trying to join them—only to find Poverty and Anonymity as the only certain clients.

Demand for teachers, however, remained constant and insatiable because of the low pay and poor school conditions that drove even the most dedicated teachers out of the profession. Applying his ingenuity to take advantage of these conditions, Webster decided to open a private academy, where he could earn more than a salaried teacher in common school and test his burgeoning educational theories. The decision proved of historic importance. As his granddaughter put it, "had the condition of the country been peaceful and prosperous at the time he was admitted to the bar, he would probably have opened a law office and the world might have lost him in his distinctive character as a lexicographer."[11]

The Reverend Cotton Mather Smith, a Yale graduate and friend of Yale president Stiles, gave Webster the use of the spacious attic of Sharon House, his home in Sharon, near the New York State border. At the time, Sharon harbored many prominent patriot families who had fled British forces in New York City, where their children had attended the finest private academies. They were loath to send them to rural common schools and eagerly responded to Webster's announcement in the *Connecticut Courant:*

> The subscriber, desirous of promoting Education, so essential to the
> interest of a free people, proposes immediately to open a school at
> Sharon, in which young Gentlemen and Ladies may be instructed in
> Reading, Writing, Mathematics, the English Language, and if desired,
> the Latin and Greek Languages—in Geography, Vocal Music, &c. at the
> moderate price of Six Dollars and two thirds per quarter per Scholar.
> The strictest attention will be paid to the studies, the manners and the
> morals of youth, by the public's very humble servant,
>
> NOAH WEBSTER, Jun.[12]

To the grateful relief of Sharon's wealthy Whig families, Webster opened his school on June 1, 1781, and they sent their children there in droves. The huge and powerful Livingstons of New York and New Jersey sent their five children to him. Mrs. Theodore Provost, a widow who later married Vice President Aaron Burr, sent her two sons, as did Garret Augustus Hobart, a future vice president.

The school was an immediate and overwhelming success, with Webster developing a depth of mutual affection with his students—and their influential parents—that was almost unheard of in that era. In addition to honing his teaching skills, Webster added French to his scholastic repertoire. Pursuing his love of music, he also taught an evening singing school once a week that "drew together the best of the local society" and gave him a chance to enjoy "ladies' society," of which, according to his daughter, he "always remained fond . . . and was a favorite with them."[13] In the midst of his success and popularity, he found time to develop and write the first elements of his new theories of education. He rebelled at the idea that girls should receive a different education than boys and criticized the common notion that "a *good* education is that which renders the ladies correct in their manners, respectable in their families, and agreeable in society [and] that education is always wrong, which raises a woman above the duties of her station." He urged subordinating the "ornamental arts" (music, drawing, dancing, and so on) to arithmetic, history, geography, and teaching women "to speak and write their own language."[14] He concluded that schools should teach girls their legal rights, so that they could protect their interests and property if they were left without a father, husband, or other protector.[15]

To add to the joys of Webster's personal success, the summer of 1781 saw a turnaround in the fortunes of the nation, with the arrival of a huge French fleet off the coast of Virginia. On August 30, fleet commander Comte François de Grasse set up a naval blockade of the Cornwallis garrison at Yorktown, Virginia. The fleet landed fresh troops to join the forces of the marquis de Lafayette, who had hemmed Cornwallis in by land. On September 5, a British fleet engaged the French, but it fled to New York after four days, abandoning Cornwallis and leaving the French in control of the seas.

By then, Webster had converted his summer's notes on teaching into a dissertation, which he presented for his master of arts degree at the Yale commencement exercises in September 1781, at the end of the school quarter.[16] A master's degree required no campus study or attendance and was granted routinely to any alumnus who paid the appropriate fee and presented a dissertation at commencement three or more years after receiving his bachelor's degree.

Yale's commencement exercises of September 1781 were especially joyous—the first public exercises there in seven years and the first in the new United States of America. Although the last battle of the Revolution had yet to be fought, French naval victories off the Virginia coast had made British defeat inevitable. With American victory near, Yale's commencement became a scene of unrestrained jubilation. Adding to Webster's joy was the presence of two of his dearest friends from college days, Joel Barlow and Oliver Wolcott. Wolcott had just been admitted to the Connecticut bar at Litchfield, while Barlow had completed a year as an army chaplain. All had shared the dream of national independence as boys and had cut short their college days to fight, however briefly, for their nation. They now shared the elation of receiving their master's degrees together at Yale's first public commencement in the new nation they had helped create.

To add to their exhilaration, the man who presented their degrees was their friend, mentor, and former professor, Yale's patriot president Ezra Stiles. Barlow read extracts from his epic poem in progress, *The Vision of Columbus,* a suitably patriotic lyric, for which, Stiles noted cryptically in his diary, "Mr. Barlow was clapped."[17]

4

AFTER COMMENCEMENT, Barlow resumed his army chaplaincy and Wolcott went to Hartford to practice law with Oliver Ellsworth. Webster returned to Sharon, cloaked in the "worthy and imposing dignity" of his new academic honors. The fortunes of the colonist forces continued improving. An army of about nine thousand Americans and seventy-eight hundred French troops laid siege to the British positions in Yorktown. On September 30, Cornwallis abandoned his outer line of fortifications, permitting allied guns to move forward and fire on his inner defenses. On October 19, he ordered his troops to lay down their arms.

The good fortune of the young nation, however, did not translate into good fortune for Webster. The patriot victories made it safe for most of the refugee families to return to their homes in New York, and Webster was left with too few students to make the academy worthwhile. For the moment, the frugal young schoolmaster was not penniless. He had saved enough to spend the winter studying. He pressed ahead with his French studies. Fascinated by comparative grammar, he added Italian, Spanish, and German, while expanding his study of history, law, and literature with works such as Rousseau's *Social Contract* and *Emile* and Thomas Paine's essays in *The American Crisis.* Rousseau and Paine, he said, shaped his amorphous ideas on the injustice of slavery, popular sovereignty, the relationship of governors to the governed, and the dangers of an established church. Rousseau solidified his belief in formal education as central to liberty in a self-governing society. Together with Locke's concept of tabula rasa, his winter studies in Sharon gave Webster a clear direction to follow: to create a complete system of universal public education that would give "all classes" of

Americans the intellectual skills to govern themselves and the practical skills to sustain themselves and their families.[18]

5

ALTHOUGH YORKTOWN DID NOT END THE WAR, the surrender of Cornwallis all but assured American victory and independence, and Webster began to work out his new system of education to ensure Americans the literacy skills and education to govern themselves. He realized that unless he acted swiftly, a literate aristocracy—pro-British Tories in the North and slave owners in the South—stood poised, as they had in the old Puritan churches, to seize the reins of government and reenslave the illiterate majority.

In addition to literacy, he reasoned, Americans would need a knowledge of history, geography, and political science. He deemed arithmetic essential to virtually every type of useful employment. He rejected Latin and Greek as impractical for all but those destined for college and the "learned professions"—that is, divinity, law, and medicine.

In what seemed nothing short of heresy, he rejected the Bible as a school textbook, maintaining that overuse would diminish its value as a spiritual guide without teaching the self-reliance and independent thought needed for self-government. In place of the Bible, Webster envisioned new types of reading materials and literature prepared especially for American children. No such literature existed. He would have to prepare it himself.

Just as he was completing the design for his new curriculum, Webster was distracted by a series of newspaper articles in the *New-York Packet* in early 1782. The Tory newspaper called it folly to continue the war and urged return to British rule. The colonists had proved their point at Yorktown, said the paper, and the time had come for peaceful reunion with the parent country. Citing the earlier "Declaration to the Inhabitants" by Sir Henry Clinton,[19] whose forces had burned Kingston while Webster and his father and brothers watched, the *Packet* argued that Parliament had shown its "affectionate and conciliatory intentions" by exempting the colonies from future taxation. The exemption eliminated the "grounds of discontent" that provoked the Revolution, and "the door is thus again thrown open . . . for commencing negociations which may instantly terminate the miseries" of the war. Like Clinton, the *Packet* warned that America's alliance with France placed the colonists in risk of "being delivered over to Popish and arbitrary nations."

The articles infuriated Webster, and he responded with four essays he called "Observations on the Revolution of America." Calling the *Packet* articles propagandistic trickery, he said King George had forfeited all right to the allegiance of the American people by imposing "unconstitutional and oppressive laws" and confiscating property. "Great Britain, having experienced the inefficacy of fleets and armies to support her illegal claims . . . is making use of sophistry, fraud, and bribery to disunite the Americans and overturn our independence."[20]

Webster called the American Revolution a historic event that would have "considerable influence in unfettering the shackles which are so generally rivetted on the human race." A return to British rule would be nothing less than "a return to vassalage."

His article had more impact than he had anticipated. The widely read *Salem Gazette* in Massachusetts reprinted Webster's first article, giving him notoriety in Boston as well as New York and Connecticut. He wrote a second article two weeks later,[21] refuting the logic that American colonists were "children and brethren of England" and that "a separation of such relations is unnatural." He said that Britain's violent assault on Americans and its appropriation of American properties was not responsible parental behavior and that Britain had, therefore, defaulted all parental privileges.

"America," he said, "is now an independent empire. She acknowledges no sovereign on earth, and will avow no connexions but those of friends and allies, in which characters all nations are invited to her commerce."

Intoxicated by his writing success, Webster wrote a third article,[22] declaring that "dependence on foreign government is incompatible with the tranquility of America." He predicted correctly that, within the ensuing twenty years, America would have "more tons of shipping in traffic than any power in Europe." In his fourth and most explosive article, Webster attacked established religion and called for religious tolerance and freedom, and complete separation of church and state.

"They tell us that a separation from Great Britain will . . . [mean] that the protestant religion will lose ground, if not be totally extirpated, through the influence of a popish ally. To liberal minds, these dangers are phantoms, mere illusions of a distempered imagination," he wrote. Acknowledging himself "a sturdy son of Congregational Connecticut," Webster called separation of church and state essential to individual liberty and possible only with independence from Britain.

"The very idea of a system of religious principles and a mode of worship, prescribed and established, by human authority," he wrote, "is totally repugnant to the spirit of christianity. Every establishment is only a milder term for tyranny. . . . It is an insult, a solemn mockery of all justice and common sense." Established churches, he charged, had retarded progress and been responsible for "tumults and massacres which have deluged kingdoms in blood and filled the Christian world with rancor and animosity. All the dangers to which any government can be exposed by sectaries, must arise wholly from intolerance; and the Roman Catholics, when indulged the free exercise of their religion, make as good subjects, as peaceable citizens as any sect of protestants."

America, he proclaimed,

> founds her empire upon the idea of universal toleration: She admits all
> religions into her bosom—She secures the sacred rights of every individ-
> ual; and (astonishing absurdity to Europeans!) she sees a thousand dis-
> cordant opinions live in the strictest harmony of friendship; the privilege
> of unprecedented toleration . . . will finally raise her to a pitch of great-
> ness and lustre, before which the glory of ancient Greece and Rome
> shall dwindle to a point, and the splendor of modern Empires shall fade
> into obscurity.

Webster's articles not only earned him his first public recognition, they taught him the use of his pen as a new and powerful instrument.

6

IN THE SPRING OF 1782, Lord North's government fell, and his successor, Lord Rockingham, the minister who had repealed the Stamp Act in 1766, abandoned the war in America and opened peace negotiations. By then, Webster had exhausted his funds and needed a job. Young farmers and merchants were streaming from the congested fields and towns of New England to the fertile wilderness of New York State. Reasoning that new settlements would need teachers and, perhaps, lawyers, Webster set his sights in the same direction.

Across the Hudson, the village of Goshen, New York, had become a major agricultural center. Many of its largest landowners were among the nation's most prominent leaders, including some of the Livingstons, who had known Webster in Sharon. The town had opened its first common elementary school, and the wealthier, better-educated citizens who had migrated from Connecticut had established the exclusive Farmers' Hall Academy to prepare their sons for college. The war had forced its closure, and no schoolmaster had come along to reopen it. Webster packed his things and left Sharon with a letter of introduction from Minister Smith to the Reverend Dr. Nathaniel Kerr, Goshen's Congregational minister, a Connecticut native and Yale graduate who knew and respected the Webster name.

The first leg of his journey took him forty miles southwest, and he crossed by ferry to Newburgh, New York, on the west bank of the Hudson, where the American army had massed to await disbandment. He spent a day there in the encampments of troops and westward-bound migrants. What he saw so stunned him that he changed the entire direction of his approach to education.

Instead of the joyous celebrations he expected among a newly independent people, he heard a dizzying cacophony of languages and accents — Dutch, French, German, Swedish, Gaelic, and varieties of English that the Connecticut Calvinist from Yale had never heard before: the muddy drawls of the rural South, the gargled grunts of Philadelphia Negroes; and the clipped utterances of militiamen from the northern reaches of New Hampshire. He could not understand them, and the sporadic fights he saw told him that many of them could not understand one another, either. Far from producing unity, the independence for which they had fought so long and hard had turned them into a nasty, squalling mob. Webster had come expecting warmth and mutual affection between his countrymen but found only strangers thrashing about in a raging sea of anarchy.

He left with what he described as an "extreme depression & gloomy forebodings" about the future of the nation, but pressed on to Goshen, twenty miles to the west. He arrived exhausted, with only seventy-five cents left in his pocket, and "in a desponding state of mind," but determined to undertake "an employment which gave a complexion to [my] whole future life. This was the compilation of books for the instruction of youth in schools."[23]

Like the fertile Israelite lands of biblical antiquity, Goshen became a source of light amid a plague of darkness. He reopened the Farmers' Hall Academy and "received pupils from the most respectable families of that village & its vicinity."[24] Webster's reputation had preceded him, and parents filled his school to capacity with children, some coming forty miles or more to study and board with him. The demand for his services gave him "the advantage of receiving the pay for tuition in silver, an advantage rarely enjoyed in any business at that time."[25]

With his personal confidence renewed, he resumed his work of developing a new system of instruction. Although he had been distraught at the disunion at Newburgh, his experience there had yielded an astonishing revelation—that speech was as essential to education as spelling, reading, and writing. Even more important, he realized that only a uniform method of speaking—a common language—would ever ensure the fraternity Americans needed to remain united in nationhood and govern themselves peacefully.

Only four years out of college and a mere twenty-four years of age, Noah Webster believed he could unite the American people by creating a new, common language, or as he called it, a "federal language."

He began developing the new language on his first day in his Goshen classroom. He listened carefully to the voices of the children—almost all of them from families who had migrated from other parts. He listened to the differences in speech: some children said *dew* and *tew* instead of *do* and *too;* others, *datter* for *daughter,* *sass* instead of *sauce,* *bust* when they meant *burst,* *sparrowgrass* for *asparagus,* *chimbley* instead of *chimney,* and *ax* instead of *ask.*

"Pronunciation of words, as taught in our schools," he concluded, "is wretched." He decided to "demolish those odious distinctions of provincial dialects which are objects of reciprocal ridicule in the United States."[26] He decided to combine instruction in spelling and grammar with readings from the most inspired works of American patriots, which would teach all elementary school children to read, write, and speak uniformly. It was one of the most audacious and fateful decisions in American cultural history—one that changed not only Webster's own life but the lives of tens of millions of American children for the next century.

7

WEBSTER RECOGNIZED that the spread of literacy would depend on developing a new "system of instruction" that would make it easier for young children to learn to read, write, and speak. He began by studying existing grammar books and spellers, along with spellings commonly used in letters, manuscripts, and literature. What he recognized was that spellers did not teach spelling, let alone writing or speaking. Nor were they meant to. They were meant to teach *reading*—especially reading of the scriptures. They used spelling merely as an incidental tool for learning to read. This was the alphabet method of teaching, as opposed to the whole-word and phonics methods that would be developed in the nineteenth and twentieth centuries.

Originated in England in the sixteenth century, the alphabet method taught children to use the alphabet and letter combinations as sounding devices with which to build words and phrases. Spellers were divided into three parts: The first table presented the alphabet. The second part was a syllabarium, which listed syllables in alphabetical order (for example, *ba, be, bi, bo, bu, by*). The third part consisted of word lists of successively increasing difficulty, progressing from monosyllabic words of two, three, four, and more letters to words of two, three, and more syllables. Each word list ended with one or more short reading lesson incorporating words from that list.

Thus, the first lesson in Thomas Dilworth's *New Guide to the English Tongue*,[27] then the most widely used speller, listed monosyllabic words of two and three letters, followed by a reading lesson for the children to practice using the words they learned:

> No man may put off the Law of God.
> The Way of God is no ill Way.
> My joy is in God all the Day.
> A bad man is a Foe to God.

Using the alphabet method, the children recited the first line by pronouncing each letter and word as they read: "En, o, No; emm, ai, en, man;

emm, ai, wy, may; pee, you, tee, put; o, double eff, off; tee, aitch, ee, the; ell, ai, double you, Law; o, eff, of; gee, o, dee, God."

They recited longer words by syllables in this fashion: "*example:* ee, ex, ex; ai, emm, am; ex, am, exam; pee, ell, ee, ple; ex, am, ple, example."[28]

Although Webster himself had learned to read from Dilworth's as a boy, as a teacher he recognized it as an incomprehensible morass of contradictory rules and spellings—as in the last syllable of the word *example,* which, logically, should either have been pronounced "pee, ell, ee, plee" or have been spelled *pul,* as in *exampul.* Webster also concluded that the rules for capitalization, punctuation, and pronunciation—when there were any—were incongruous with everyday spoken language. Many words were spelled in different ways—*choose* and *chuse, seize* and *seise, cheer* and *chear, might* and *mite,* and so on. All were acceptable—and confusing.

"The want of some standard in schools has occasioned a great variety of dialects in Great-Britain and of course, in America," Webster pointed out. "Every county in England, every State in America and almost every town in each State, has some peculiarities in pronunciation which are equally erroneous. . . . And how can these distinctions be avoided?" Webster called the sounds of English letters "more capricious and irregular" than those of any other Western alphabet. He complained that some vowels and consonants have four or five different sounds, while the same sounds are often expressed by as many as seven different characters, none of which have any marks of distinction to show beginning readers how to pronounce them correctly.

"How," he asked,

> would a child or a foreigner learn the different sounds of *o* in these words, *rove, move, dove* or of *oo* in *poor, door?* Or that *a, ai, ei,* and *e,* have precisely the same sound in these words, *bare, laid, vein, there?* Yet these and fifty other irregularities have passed unnoticed by authors of Spelling Books and Dictionaries. They study the language enough to find the difficulties of it—they tell us that it is impossible to reduce it to order—that it is to be learnt only by the ear—they lament the disorder and dismiss it without a remedy.
>
> Thus the pronunciation of our language . . . is left to parents and nurses—to ignorance and caprice—to custom, accident, or nothing.

"And while this is the case," he warned, "every person will claim a right to pronounce most agreeably to his own fancy, and the language will be exposed to perpetual fluctuation."[29]

Webster's remedy, and the first practical product of his research, was to design and draft a new spelling book that would change forever the approach to teaching American children to read, write, and speak. Saying that "the spelling book does more to form the language of a nation than all other books,"[30] he called the early drafts of his book *The American Instructor,* but never actually published it under that name. At the urging of Yale President Ezra Stiles, Webster would change the title the following year,

Tne ALPHABET.

Roman Letters.		Italic.		Names of the Letters.
a	A	*a*	*A*	a
b	B	*b*	*B*	be
c	C	*c*	*C*	ce
d	D	*d*	*D*	de
e	E	*e*	*E*	e
f	F	*f*	*F*	ef
g	G	*g*	*G*	ge
h	H	*h*	*H*	aytch or he, more
i	I	*i*	*I*	i (properly,
j	J	*j*	*J*	ja
k	K	*k*	*K*	ka
l	L	*l*	*L*	el
m	M	*m*	*M*	em
n	N	*n*	*N*	en
o	O	*o*	*O*	o
p	P	*p*	*P*	pe
q	Q	*q*	*Q*	cu
r	R	*r*	*R*	ar
s	S	ſ	*S*	ef
t	T	*t*	*T*	te
u	U	*u*	*U*	u
v	V	*v*	*V*	ve
w	W	*w*	*W*	double u or we
x	X	*x*	*X*	eks
y	Y	*y*	*Y*	wi or yi
z	Z	*z*	*Z*	zee
&		*&*	*	and

V O W E L S.

a, e, i, o, u, y, w, oo, au, oi, ou.
aw, oy, ow.

D O U B L E   L E T T E R S,

ſt, ff, ffi, ffl, fi, fl, fk, fh, fi, fk, fl, ff, ffi, ft

D I R E C T I O N

* This is not a letter, but a character standing for *and*. Cl
ildren should therefore be taught to call it *and* ; not *and per se.*

The alphabet, from a facsimile of Noah Webster's original speller, published in 1783. (Noah Webster Foundation.)

1783, to the cumbersome *A Grammatical Institute of the English Language,* and the first published edition bore that name. In 1787, however, he would rename it *The American Spelling Book*—a title it would bear for the next forty years.

In designing his own new spelling book, Webster experimented with different classroom teaching methods at Goshen and gradually produced a simple approach that unified the language and speech of the children he

[28.]

DIRECTIONS.

Let a child be taught, firſt the Roman letters, both ſmall and great---then the Italics---then the ſounds of the vowels; not pronouncing the double letters *a* and *u*, &c. ſeparately, but only the ſound that thoſe letters united expreſs---then the double letters. All this a child ſhould know before he leaves the Alphabet and begins to ſpell. A child ſhould never be put to a ſecond leſſon, before he has perfectly learnt the firſt.

TABLE I.

LESSON I.							LESSON III.				
ba	be	bi	bo	bu	by		ab	eb	ib	ob	ub
ca	ce*	ci*	co	cu	cy*		ac	ec	ic	oc	uc
da	de	di	do	du	dy		ad	ed	id	od	ud
fa	fe	fi	fo	fu	fy		af	ef	if	of	uf
ka	ke	ki	ko	ku	ky		al	el	il	ol	ul

LESSON II.							LESSON IV.				
ga	ge	gi	go	gu	gy		ag	eg	ig	og	ug
ha	he	hi	ho	hu	hy		am	em	im	om	um
ma	me	mi	mo	mu	my		an	en	in	on	un
na	ne	ni	no	nu	ny		ap	ep	ip	op	up
ra	re	ri	ro	ru	ry		as	es	is	os	us
ta	te	ti	to	tu	ty		ax	ex	ix	ox	ux
wa	we	wi	wo	wu	wy		av	ev	iv	ov	uv

LESSON V.							LESSON VI.				
bla	ble	bli	blo	blu			bra	bre	bri	bro	bru
cla	cle	cli	clo	clu			cra	cre	cri	cro	cru
pla	ple	pli	plo	plu			pra	pre	pri	pro	pru
fla	fle	fli	flo	flu			gra	gre	gri	gro	gru
ſha	ſhe	ſhi	ſho	ſhu†			pha	phe	phi	pho	phu

TABLE

---

* A child ſhould be taught to pronounce *ce*, *ci*, *cy*, like ſe, ſi, ſy.
† It would be a great improvement in education, if *ch*, *sh*, *th*, and *ph*, were called by a ſingle name, viz. *che*, *ſhe*, *the*, and *phe*. Some of the letters may be too hard for young children to pronounce diſtinctly; when they firſt begin to ſpeak, they will found

The syllabarium *(above)* and a table of single-syllable words *(facing page)*, arranged by Webster to make learning to read English easier than it had ever been before, from a facsimile edition. (Noah Webster Foundation.)

taught and made it remarkably easier for them to learn reading, writing, and speaking than ever before. Within a few years, it would do the same for the entire American people and their children, both foreign- and native-born.

Superficially, his book would resemble other spellers of the day. It was a tiny book for tiny hands—120 pages, six and a quarter inches long and only about three and a half inches wide. Indeed, after it was published, it

[29]

TABLE II.

Words of three and four letters.

N. B. The following columns are to be read down-wards . All the words in the same column being founded alike, when a child has the found of the firft, the others will very naturally follow.

A figure placed over the firft word, marks the found of the vowel in all that follow in that column.

LESSON I.

Bag	big	bog	bug	den	cap	bit	dot
cag	dig	dog	dug	hen	gap	cit	got
fag	fig	fog	hug	men	lap	hit	hot
gag	jig	hog	lug	pen	map	pit	jot
hag	pig	jog	mug	ten	rap	fit	lot
rag	wig	log	tug	wen	tap	wit	no

LESSON II.

Man	fob	bad	bed	bid	fop	bet	but
can	job	had	fed	did	hop	get	cut
pan	mob	lad	led	lid	lop	let	hut
ran	rob	mad	red	hid	mop	met	nut
van	fob	fad	wed	rid	top	yet	put

LESSON III.

Belt	gilt	band	bled	brag	clod	brad
melt	hilt	hand	bred	drag	plod	clad
felt	milt	land	fled	flag	fhod	glad
pelt	jilt	fand	fhed	ftag	trod	fhad

LESSON

---

the vowels and fome of the eafieft confonants ; but cannot poffibly pronounce *l*, *r*, or *th*. Parents and inftructors ought to be very cautious not to let them attempt fuch difficult founds at firft ; for a habit of lifping or ftuttering is often contracted by fuch attempts.

But when the tender organs are brought to utter the eafy founds, let them be brought gradually to pronounce thofe that are more difficult. In this children may be much affifted by being told how to place the tongue and lips to make any found ; this is a point in which inftructors are very deficient.

C 2

---

looked suspiciously like the two most widely used English spellers: Dilworth's *New Guide* and Daniel Fenning's *The Universal Spelling Book; or, a New and Easy Guide to the English Language* (1756), which was beginning to replace Dilworth's in England.

Like these and every other speller after the Reformation, Webster's little book began with the alphabet, followed by a syllabarium and lists of words of increasing syllabic length, and finally by a sequence of reading materials. Webster's presentation of the alphabet was the same as Dilworth's, except for the name of the letter z, which Webster listed as "zee" instead of the British "zed." Webster's syllabarium—*ba, be, bi, bo, bu, by,* and so on—remained unchanged.

Where Webster's speller diverged sharply from its predecessors was in the way he grouped words in lists—according to pronunciation rather than similarities in spelling. The change seemed inconsequential, but it was one that proved revolutionary in the history of elementary education. Dilworth listed words with the same number of letters, dictionary style: *age, all, ape, are,* for example, or *babe, beef, best, bold.* Webster, on the other hand, intuited the laws of association from his work as a schoolmaster. A truly gifted instructor who was genuinely fond of young children and interested in the way they learned, he found that young children delighted in rhymes and that they learned and remembered groups of words that sounded alike more easily than words with unrelated sounds.

Thus, in Lesson I, he grouped words that sounded and were largely spelled alike: *bug, dug, hug, lug, mug,* and *tug.* Lesson XII continued the practice but added more letter variations: *be, pea, sea, tea, flea,* and *key.* Webster turned learning and practicing the spelling variations of the same sounds into an amusing classroom game that held student attention while also making them literate. The lessons proceeded logically and easily from monosyllabic words of two, three, and four letters to "easy words" of two syllables—first those accented on the first syllable, then those accented on the second. Similarly, he went through words of three, four, five, and six syllables, each list providing words pronounced with the accent on the same syllable.

In contrast, Dilworth's lists often addled the minds of instructors as much as small children with explanations such as this: "Words of five, six, etc. letters, viz: two vowels and the rest consonants; the latter vowel serving only to lengthen the sound of the former except where it is otherwise marked." One historian called the passage "nearly as luminous as a direction in knitting."[31]

Dilworth's speller forced children to learn to spell polysyllabic biblical names such as *Abelbethmaachah*[32] and *Merodachbaladan,*[33] along with what he called "abbreviations likely to be of use," such as *Ldp., Bp., Rt. Wpful, Rt. Honble, Ast. P.G.C.,* and *P.M.G.C.* As too many children in the American wilderness learned after a blow from the ferule, *Ast. P.G.C.* was the abbreviation for *Astronomy Professor of Gresham College,* and a *P.M.G.C.* was a professor of music at Gresham College, Dilworth's alma mater in England.

Dedicated to "the Reverend and Worthy Promoters of the several Charity Schools in Great Britain and Ireland," Dilworth's speller had little meaning to American children. It was an English book that espoused loyalty to the king and to Great Britain. It listed only English towns and shires, some so obscure and unpronounceable that they represented nothing less than torture for innocent six-year-old American farm boys.

"One half of the work is totally useless," said Webster, recalling his own childhood instruction in Dilworth's, "and the other half defective and erroneous."

Webster wrote his book for American children, limiting his list of the longest, six-syllable words to a dozen commonly used terms such as *divisibility, impossibility,* and *superiority.* All the words in his speller were in common use and of practical value—"the names of domestic articles, animals, fruits, &C . . . collected for the use and pleasure of children."[34] He mercifully omitted Dilworth's "monstrous absurdities"—to wit, *Abelbethmaachah* and *Merodachbaladan.* Rather than torture his students, he made it as easy as possible—and even entertaining—to learn. He became the first teacher-author to dissect and classify the sounds of the English language and present them in a form that simplified teaching literacy. His speller represented a giant step in the history of education and the spread of literacy.

Along with the names of foreign countries and their capital cities, Webster listed in his geography section the American states and their capitals, towns, and counties, and the last two pages of his book contained "A Chronological Account of Remarkable Events in America," from the discovery of America by Columbus, in 1492, to the end of the Revolutionary War, in 1783.

Webster's speller was also the first to show the teacher how to teach. Usually untrained and not overly literate themselves, teachers had used repetition and a rod or whip to force children to pronounce correctly—often punishing children cruelly for repeated errors. Webster gave the teacher a simple and effective method for describing sounds for students to repeat easily and without error: "The consonant *c* is hard like *k* before *a, o, u, l, r,* and at the end of words, such as *cat, cord, cup, cloth, crop, public;* but is always soft like *s* before *e, i, y;* as *cellar, civil, cypress.*

"*G* is also always hard before *a, o, u,* as *gat, got, gum.*"[35]

He also classified sounds of individual vowels and vowel combinations—for example, *sky, lie, eye,* and *buy*—and he introduced a new, "natural division" of words to coincide with the way people spoke. For the first time, children were able to see words on paper that looked the way they sounded: *clus-ter, hab-it,* and *bish-op,* with the accents squarely on the first syllable. In contrast, Dilworth demanded that children pronounce the words as *clu-ster, ha-bit,* and *bis-hop.*

That first season in Goshen saw only the beginnings of the language improvements Webster would make in the course of his life. They evolved over several decades, in innumerable editions of his speller. He never stopped improving his speller or encouraging suggestions from other scholars.

He made one of the most important and most controversial improvements at the suggestion of Prof. (later president) Samuel Stanhope Smith of the College of New Jersey, at Princeton. Dilworth's and other traditional spellers had insisted that the suffixes -cion, -sion, and -tion be pronounced as two syllables, that is, -ci-on, -si-on, and -ti-on. Children learned to pronounce the words *nation* and *salvation* as, respectively, three and four syllables: *na-ti-on* and *sal-va-ti-on*. Although these words were still pronounced that way in some psalm singing, those pronunciations had long earlier dropped out of conversational speech, and Webster's speller changed the syllabic divisions to read *na-tion* and *sal-va-tion*.

Indeed, he went a step further, pointing out that the letters *t, s,* and *c* in *-tion, -sion,* and *-cion* were pronounced *sh,* as in *na-shun*. Religious traditionalists were quick to spew venom at Webster's speller for teaching sacrilege. "A book by a Yankee lad called Wobster is teaching the children agenst the Christian religion!" went one anecdote in the orthodox Calvinist press. "Why, he's changing the psalms of David and making children say *salvashun* instead of *sal-va-ci-on,* the way we sing it in church."[36]

Even more absurd than pronunciations such as *-ti-on* was Dilworth's treatment of silent letters, as in *often* and *subtle,* and nonphonetic pronunciations in words such as *ocean* and *righteous*. Dilworth's insisted that children pronounce every letter of *sub-tle* and *o-ce-an*. Webster combined all such words into a single list of more than one hundred "irregular" terms, for which "the spelling and pronunciation . . . are very different." He then listed each word alphabetically alongside its pronunciation:

Written	Pronounced
accoutre	ac coo ter
acre	a ker
antique	an teek
ocean	o shun
sceptre	sep-ter
subtle	sut l

He grouped homophones to simplify learning their spellings:

Bare	naked
Bear	to suffer
Bear	a beast

Webster singled out for special attention all commonly mispronounced words—*chimney, asparagus, ask,* and so on—and provided their correct pronunciations. It was an entirely new approach to spelling instruction.

Webster recognized the schoolmaster's role in teaching children moral behavior and patriotism, and he supplemented spelling instruction with reading instruction. He selected aphorisms, fables, dialogues, and stories "to inspire the minds of youth with an abhorrence of vice, indolence and meanness; and with a love of virtue, industry and good manners."[37] He taught morality by equating it with practical success and patriotism. In addition to relating George Washington's virtues, Webster gave children straightforward advice:

> Be a good child; mind your book; love your school; and strive to learn.
>
> Tell no tales, call no ill names; you must not lie, swear, nor cheat nor steal.
>
> A good child will not lie, swear nor steal. He will be good at home, and ask to read his book; when he gets up, he will wash his hands and face clean; he will comb his hair, and make haste to school; he will not play by the way as bad boys do.
>
> Happy is the man that findeth wisdom. She is of more value than rubies.[38]

Always the caring teacher, Webster composed his own advice for children on managing their time at home and at school:

> Sloth keeps such a hold of some clowns, that they lie in bed when they should go to school; but a boy that wants to be wise will drive sleep far from him.
>
> If you want to be good, wise and strong, read with care such books as have been made by wise and good men; think of what you read in your spare hours; be brisk at play, but do not swear; and waste not too much of your time in bed.[39]

The speller ended by teaching practical conversational skills. Entitled "Familiar Phrases, and Easy Dialogues, for Young Beginners," the lessons ranged from the elementary:

> I hope you are very well.
> I am very well, Sir, I thank you.
> How do they do at your house?

to the practical:

> What o'clock is it?
> It is half an hour after five.
> Indeed! I did not think it was so late.
> Is dinner ready?
> If you are thirsty, call for a drink.

to the teaching of good manners:

> Come let us go home; it is time for tea.
> I believe it is; and the ladies expect us.
> Sir, I have the pleasure to drink to your health.
> Sir, I am much obliged to you.

to the teaching of morality:

> A tatler is a very mean character, indeed.

I despise the boy who meddles with what is not his business; runs from one to another and whispers foolish stories—and makes mischief in the school.

A tatler is only a softer name for a liar, and a liar is the meanest and worst being that lives.

Unlike most Puritan schoolmasters, Webster appreciated the value of laughter as a teaching tool:

How came you so late to school?
I stopped to pull off my hat to a Gentleman.
How long did that hinder you?
A considerable time.
Pray, Sir, how do you make your manners?
I parade myself with my face to the person, take off my hat with both hands, make several bows and scrape with my right foot.
I do not wonder you are late at school, for surely if you meet several persons, it must employ most of your school hours.[40]

Eventually, Webster's system of instruction evolved into three texts—a speller, a grammar, and a reader. His speller alone not only changed the course of education in the United States, it eventually changed the English language as no other book had or ever would. It made every previous speller obsolete and gained a virtual monopoly in American classrooms for more than a century. No book other than the Bible would ever reach as many Americans. It created a new language for a new nation and ensured that all Americans would speak alike.

"But for the all-prevailing presence of this book throughout our wide extended country, nothing could have saved us from as great a diversity of dialects as there is in England," the *New Haven Daily Herald* would say the year before Webster died.[41]

Until Webster, Americans had lived in what one nineteenth-century Webster biographer called cultural and "literary vassalage" to their countries of origin.[42] Webster's speller was a declaration of American cultural independence, conceived to unite Americans in peace, much as the declaration of political independence had united them in war.

"Americans," he declared a few years later, in 1787,

unshackle your minds and act like independent beings. You have been children long enough, subject to the control and subservient interest of a haughty parent. You have now an interest of your own to augment and defend: you have an empire to raise and . . . a national character to establish.

Now is the time and *this* the country in which we may expect success in attempting changes to language, science, and government. Let us then seize the present moment and establish a *national* language as well as a national government.[43]

8

WHEN WEBSTER REOPENED THE SCHOOL in Goshen for the summer quarter of 1782, he had incorporated his classroom teaching methods into a first draft of his speller, along with some grammar and many short reading selections. Reading, he knew, was the subject children enjoyed most at school. Rhymes turned spelling into entertainment, but reading opened the world of imagination and dreams. Unlike other teachers, whose reading selections were limited to scriptural texts and English literature, Webster gave older children inspiring works by American authors to read—orations by Hancock and Washington, essays by Thomas Paine, poetry by his friends Joel Barlow and Timothy Dwight—to imbue them with a spirit of patriotism that made their parents proud.

His system was a huge success. The children were astonished by the ease and rapidity with which they learned to read—and how much they enjoyed school for the first time. By the end of the quarter, the regional accents and speech patterns of the children had all but disappeared, and all spoke virtually alike. Parents were equally astonished by the rapid progress their children made. Recognizing the value of his work, Webster prepared to publish it, but first he needed to protect it with a copyright.

By then, however, the United States were as independent of British laws as they were of British government. England's copyright law of 1710, the Statute of Anne, had no validity in America, and Americans had not yet replaced it with a law of their own. Armed with letters of introduction from the most prominent parents of his former students, Webster set out boldly from Goshen at the end of August 1782 to ask the Continental Congress of the United States in Philadelphia for copyright protection for his little spelling book.

Outside Independence Hall, he collared such powerful men as New York's James and Robert Livingston and Virginia's James Madison and Thomas Jefferson. All approved Webster's scheme for a national system of instruction and agreed to support copyright protection, but, they pointed out, the Articles of Confederation gave Congress no power to enact, let alone enforce, such a law. The Congress could only resolve to recommend that each of the states pass its own copyright legislation. That being the situation, Webster determined to go to each state legislature himself.

The Pennsylvania state legislature, however, was out of session while Congress used its chamber in Independence Hall, and Webster left for Trenton, New Jersey, with a sense of dissatisfaction with the Articles of Confederation and the impotence of the federal Congress. He stopped overnight at the College of New Jersey, in Princeton, where Madison had graduated, in 1771, and recommended him to its professor of classics and moral philosophy, Samuel Stanhope Smith. The clever young schoolmaster enlisted Smith's aid in improving the speller, and Smith suggested the valuable changes in the pronunciation of the suffixes -cion, -sion, and -tion, which Webster immediately incorporated into his little book. Pleased by the young instructor's deference, Smith, who now had a personal investment in the speller, wrote a testimonial to the state legislature supporting Webster's plea for copyright legislation. Smith was not without influence. In addition to James Madison, his students included Aaron Burr Jr. (the future vice president), ten future cabinet officers, sixty future members of Congress, and three future Supreme Court justices.

Because the state legislature, in Trenton, was out of session, however, Webster approached Gov. William Livingston, whose cousin's children he had taught in Sharon. A graduate of the Yale class of 1741, Livingston pledged to take up Webster's cause at a future session. Somewhat discouraged, Webster moved on to New Haven to show his book to Yale president Ezra Stiles. Instead of the blessing he expected from his old teacher, Webster faced more frustration. This time it was the annoying dilemma of all who seek counsel from the powerful: whether to accept it or risk insult to, and possible loss of, a vital ally.

To Webster's astonishment and disappointment, Stiles found the title, *The American Instructor,* too commonplace for so important a project as the creation of a new system of American education. Comparing Webster's new laws of language and education with John Calvin's laws of religion in the *Institutes of the Christian Religion,* he urged Webster to call his work *A Grammatical Institute of the English Language.* Webster felt he had no choice but to comply if he expected to win the endorsement of Stiles and Yale College.

He regretted the decision immediately. He felt the new title lacked the essential adjective *American* and the equally essential word *Instructor,* which explained the book's purpose. He also found the word *Institute* to be pompous, and he feared—justifiably—that its obvious derivation from Calvin's monumental work would expose him to criticism for vanity, a disadvantage he did not need or seek so early in his career.

Now even more discouraged because he had no copyright protection, Webster nevertheless pressed onward on his unproductive journey—this time to Hartford, where he asked the General Assembly to appoint a committee to examine the manuscript of his new work and, if it approved, to pass a law that would "vest in your memorialist & his assigns the exclusive right of printing, publishing & vending the said *American Instructor* in the State of Connecticut for & during the term of thirteen years from the passing of said act, or for such other term of time as this honorable assembly shall in their wisdom see proper."

His petition was the first effort in the United States to obtain passage of a copyright law for authors, and it earned Webster the title "Father of Copyright" in the United States.[44]

His petition came too late to obtain a hearing at that session of the Assembly, however, and the young schoolmaster prepared to return to Goshen to reopen his school for the autumn quarter without having obtained copyright protection for his little spelling book.

Frustrated by his inability to obtain such simple, obvious justice from government, he began to think the unthinkable—that the new nation might not survive in its present form. The Articles of Confederation did not give the central government the power even to protect the nation's authors against piracy of their literary works, much less the nation's citizens against piracy of their property and possessions.

Before returning, he stopped for a few days to visit his parents in West Hartford, where the high spirits and adolescent optimism of his younger brother, Charles, renewed his own spirits. Webster asked his parents to let the boy return with him to Goshen and enroll in Farmers' Hall Academy. Though young Noah did not yet earn enough to repay the £120 his father had spent for his Yale education, he could at least provide his younger brother with the benefits of an academy education.

By the time Webster arrived in Goshen with his brother for the autumn quarter, word had spread of Webster's remarkable teaching success. Students packed the school to learn from the brilliant young schoolmaster. Charles Webster made excellent progress, and after Thanksgiving,[45] Webster wrote to his parents to tell them of his brother's good work and the success of his school. He received this reply:

Hartford 16th December 1782

Dutiful Son

I rec/d yours of the 5th instant, this day in which you inform me your school is large and also that Charles may make out pretty well. I rejoyce to hear that there is a prospect of doing good and benefiting yourselves. I wish to have you serve your generation and do good in the world and be useful and may so behave as to gain the esteem of all virtuous people that are acquainted with you and gain a comfortable subsistence, but especially that you may so live as to obtain the favor of Almighty God and his grace in this world and a saving interest in the merits of Jesus Christ, without which no man can be happy. . . .

Your Affectionate Parents

N. Webster
M. Webster[46]

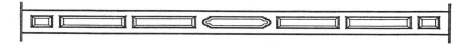

CHAPTER THREE

Author

THE JOY OF HIS YOUNGER BROTHER'S PRESENCE and Goshen's enthusiasm for his teaching skills so renewed Webster's spirits that he doubled his efforts to revise and perfect his speller and system of instruction. As he had done earlier in Hartford, however, he pushed himself too hard, and by the end of the year, the multiple tasks he had undertaken proved overwhelming. Recognizing that he had the strength to pursue but one full-time career successfully, he decided to close the academy for the winter quarter and devote all his energies to developing and improving his spelling book, which he still called *The American Instructor*. (He was still reluctant to adopt the Stiles title of *Institute*.)

He first expanded it into a two-part spelling book and grammar. He also decided to concentrate on obtaining copyright protection in Connecticut and New York, where his former classmates, their powerful families, and other important Yale graduates could influence the highest levels of government. If with so much influence he failed to gain copyright protection in these two states, he resolved, he would abandon his project and try to return to law.

He gathered his various letters of endorsement from "distinguished gentlemen," and on January 6, 1783, he sent his saddened and disappointed younger brother home to West Hartford by way of Sharon, to deliver the letters of endorsement to the influential attorney and Connecticut assemblyman John Canfield, whose daughter Noah had taught and whose help he now sought in obtaining copyright protection in the Connecticut Assembly.

"I have been indefatigable this winter," he wrote Canfield.

I have sacrificed ease, pleasure, and health to the execution of it, and have nearly completed it. . . . The more I look into our language and the methods of instruction practiced in this country, the more I am convinced of the necessity of improving one and correcting the other. And however some may think a book of this kind too trifling for public notice, I am fully of the opinion that the reformation of the language we speak will some time or other be thought an object of legislative importance. I must think that next to the sacred writings, those books which teach us the principles of science and lay the basis on which all our future improvements must be built, best deserve the patronage of the public. An attention to literature must be the principal bulwark against the encroachments of civil and ecclesiastical tyrants. . . . America must be as independent in *literature* as she is in *politics,* as famous for *arts* as for *arms;* and it is not impossible but a person of my youth may have some influence in exciting a spirit of literary industry. . . . A folio on some abstruse philosophical subject might, at first thought, appear to be a work of some consequence and attract public attention; but this would be read only by a few, and its utility seldom reach further than the philosopher's head, while a little fifteen-penny volume, which may convey more useful knowledge to the remote obscure recesses of honest poverty, is overlooked as a matter of trivial notice. The former like a taper gives light only in the chamber of study. The latter like a star casts its beams equally upon the peasant and the monarch.[1]

Deeply moved, Canfield left immediately for Hartford, where he presented Webster's petition for copyright protection—and convinced the legislature to pass a general copyright law granting authors the exclusive right to earnings from publication of their works for fourteen years. On January 18, an elated Webster rode to Kingston to petition the New York State legislature, repeating almost verbatim the plea he had presented to the Connecticut legislature, "to secure to your petitioner the benefits of his own labors to which he conceives himself solely entitled but which are not protected by the laws that protect every other species of property."[2] Again, his friends worked on his behalf. The Livingston family, whose children Webster had taught in Sharon, had written to Gen. Philip J. Schuyler, a member of the state Senate, who pushed through a copyright law in his state.

Optimistic about his prospects for eventual success, Webster returned to Goshen and redoubled his efforts to complete his spelling book. At the same time, he wrote to virtually every friend and contact to explain his project and enlist support for copyright legislation in other states. To each he sent the same message: his books would simplify instruction, spread literacy throughout the land, and unify the American people by teaching them to speak alike, using a new American language, free of the "improprieties and vulgarisms . . . from various parts of Europe." He pledged publicly that his books would "inspire youth with a contempt of the unmanly vices of mankind, and a love of virtue, patriotism and religion"[3] by exposing them to the best of American literature.

His letters elicited phenomenal results. Timothy Dwight, the tutor and poet he and his classmates had revered at Yale, was now a prominent minister in Northampton, Massachusetts. He had founded a coeducational school there, preached in several churches, and been elected to the state House of Representatives. In March 1783, Dwight pushed Webster's copyright legislation through the Massachusetts legislature. In May, James Madison won a resolution from the Continental Congress, in Philadelphia, recommending that states grant a fourteen-year copyright to authors and publishers of new, previously unprinted books. It was fortunate for Webster that Congress acted when it did. A month later, on June 24, several hundred angry militiamen marched on Independence Hall demanding overdue wages from the war, and Congress fled to Princeton.

Although pleased by the congressional resolution, Webster remained frustrated by the central government's impotence under the Confederation. To protect his property, he would need to get copyright laws passed in ten more states. In any other great nation, a more powerful central government would have been able to pass a single law to give him blanket protection in the entire nation.

By the time Congress passed its resolution, Webster had finished a second revision of his system of instruction. It would now consist of three separate and distinct parts: a speller, a grammar, and a reader. The speller was already complete and ready for publication. Webster returned to Hartford, where many of his closest friends had settled and where, if he could find a printer, his work would be fully protected by the state's new copyright law. Although he was, according to his memoirs, "destitute of the means of defraying the expenses of publication,"[4] his old friends rallied behind him— poet Joel Barlow; John Trumbull, the poet-turned-lawyer; and Oliver Wolcott Jr., also a lawyer. Trumbull had built a profitable law practice and invited Webster to stay at his home. Trumbull was still versifying and had written the widely acclaimed *M'Fingal*,[5] a three-thousand-line mock epic satirizing British bungling during the Revolution.

Joel Barlow and his wife, the former Ruth Baldwin of New Haven, were also in Hartford. Discharged from his army chaplaincy, Barlow seemed interminably busy, dabbling at various occupations—publishing, business, and law—but still writing poetry and psalms. He spent all the money he earned furnishing his and his wife's lavish home, where Webster and his friends were frequent guests for soirees of poetry readings and witty repartee.

Oliver Wolcott Jr. was still single and delighted in the resumption of his companionship with Webster, whom he introduced to Hartford's leading families. Together they attended all the fashionable dances, according to Webster's diary, and "sang and rode with the Ladies."

With Trumbull, Barlow, and Wolcott as Webster's sponsors, Hartford society gave the schoolmaster a warm welcome. His name and ancestry were well known, and he quickly blended into literary groups and meetings of young lawyers. Although there was a lot of legal work in Hartford, there were too many lawyers and fees were small. Lawyers such as Trumbull and Wolcott garnered the most lucrative cases because of their family connections, and they gave Webster their surplus cases to help him supplement his income.

Webster's illustrious family name did little to help him get his speller published, however. "Most persons, who were apprised of its design," he explained, "considered it as visionary . . . and no printer or bookseller was found to undertake the publication at his own risk."[6] In fact, few printers or booksellers ever published a book at their own risk. It was up to the author to be both editor and publisher and assume all financial risks. He not only provided the finished manuscript, he also purchased paper and other printing supplies, engaged the printer and binder, paid for their services in advance, and then sold and distributed the finished books to booksellers and other buyers. The author either financed the project himself or found subscribers willing to do so.

Aside from his lack of cash, Webster ran into another problem trying to get printers to handle his speller. Most were already handling Dilworth's, whose vast sales assured them a steady cash flow with each new school quarter. Benjamin Franklin had made a substantial fortune as the first printer to publish Dilworth's speller in America, in 1747, eleven years before Webster's birth, and many other printers were still profiting from it.

With Trumbull's help, Webster finally convinced Barzillai Hudson and George Goodwin, the publishers of Hartford's *Connecticut Courant,* of the merits of his little book. They agreed to accept Webster's personal note for the printing bill in exchange for exclusive rights to produce the speller and all succeeding editions for an "indeterminate" term of years.

Barlow contributed $500; Webster acknowledged that Barlow's "generosity far exceeded his means."[7] The far wealthier Trumbull gave an undisclosed sum to cover paper, typesetting, and other costs. Although Webster claimed initially that his book would "make its own way in the world"[8] on the basis of merit, he recognized the importance of a subscribers' list, and he never ceased adding to the roster of endorsers. In addition to Barlow, Trumbull, and Wolcott, the list for the first edition of the speller included the two former Yale tutors Joseph Buckminster and Timothy Dwight. Recognizing how essential an endorsement from Yale College would be to future sales, he finally decided to change the name of his work to the one suggested by college president Ezra Stiles, adding a subtitle of his own to emphasize its American roots. Instead of *The American Spelling Book,* Webster's speller took on the cumbersome title *A Grammatical Institute, of the English Language, Comprising, an Easy, Concise, and Systematic Method of*

A

Grammatical Inftitute,

OF THE

ENGLISH LANGUAGE,

COMPRISING,

An eafy, concife, and fyftematic Method of

EDUCATION,

Defigned for the Ufe of *Englijh* Schools

IN *A M E R I C A.*

IN THREE PARTS.

PART I.

CONTAINING,

A new and accurate Standard of Pronunciation.

By N O A H W E B S T E R, A. M.

Ufus eft Norma Loquendi.   CICERO.

H A R T F O R D:

PRINTED BY H U D S O N & G O O D W I N,

FOR THE AUTHOR.

A facsimile of the title page from the first edition, October 1783. (Noah Webster Foundation.)

Education, Designed for the Use of English Schools in America. In Three Parts. Part I. Containing, a New and Accurate Standard of Pronunciation, "by Noah Webster, A.M."

Webster emphasized the words *Education* and *America* on the title page to give them prominence in the otherwise pompous title. But the title was the one devised by Ezra Stiles, and it earned the enthusiastic endorsement of the college, its faculty and trustees, and, naturally, President Stiles. On

August 14, 1783, Webster obtained a Connecticut copyright at Hartford, and Hudson & Goodwin began production of the first American speller.

2

WHILE WEBSTER WAITED for the first copies of his speller to come off the press, the first threads of the fragile American Confederation were beginning to unravel in Connecticut. Disgruntled over congressional efforts to establish an impost, or tax, to compensate Revolutionary War veterans, a group of citizens organized one of New England's periodic citizen conventions in Middletown, about fifteen miles south of Hartford, to unseat the war leadership of the state government and possibly force state withdrawal from the Confederation.

As English colonies, each commonwealth had been independent of the others. Each had its own unique commercial, judicial, and social system, with military allegiance to the king the only common tie—and a tenuous one at that. The colonies severed that tie when they declared independence and replaced it with a fragile military alliance. With the war over, however, none was eager to relinquish independence, and powerful social and economic forces within each state sought to prevent the Confederation from assuming any powers that might infringe on state sovereignty.

Under the Articles of Confederation,[9] Congress was little more than a loose-knit council in which each state retained so much "sovereignty, freedom . . . Power, Jurisdiction and right" that the central government was impotent. It had no president, and each state had one vote in the unicameral Continental Congress, which required a two-thirds majority to approve any measure. The result was that Congress approved few measures, and most of them were only recommendations that did not have the force of law—as Webster had discovered when he tried to obtain copyright protection.

Indeed, Webster had been fortunate to obtain any action from Congress. Most of the states were feuding over boundaries and territorial claims and seldom agreed on anything. Eight states had armies. Pennsylvania's militia had actually fired at settlers from Connecticut in northeastern Pennsylvania. Connecticut sent Ethan Allen's Green Mountain Boys to defend the settlers, and Webster's friend Oliver Wolcott drew up a constitution that declared the area independent and created a new state called Westmorland.

The result was near anarchy. Each state printed its own currency, imposed duties or embargoes on goods from other states, and tried to control immigration from neighboring states. Even powers expressly granted to Congress—to conduct war, sign treaties and alliances, issue coins, run the postal system, and borrow money—were too limited to be effective. Congress could not tax the people; it could only ask the states to do so with an impost—an unusual tax that any state could, and usually did, refuse to pay.

During the Revolution, Congress had printed more than $200 million in paper certificates to buy supplies and pay soldiers, but by 1779 they were worthless—valued at about one cent on the dollar.[10] Without money to feed themselves, officers threatened to desert. Congress promised them a bonus of five years' pay, to be raised by a national tax.

When Congress asked state legislatures to approve the tax, Americans rose in protest. Ordinary soldiers and noncommissioned officers demanded similar bonuses. Civilians complained that their own economic losses equaled or surpassed those of the officers. The war had destroyed their homes and shops; they had been forced to billet soldiers and surrender their crops to feed the army. Their paper money was as worthless as the certificates with which the soldiers had been paid. After a band of angry soldiers marched on Independence Hall in Philadelphia and forced Congress to flee, James Madison predicted the dispute over the impost would lead to general anarchy.

"The opposition was more general & violent in Connecticut," Webster reported. "Inflammatory publications roused the people of many towns to call meetings, & discussion. . . . It was alleged that . . . [the impost] was unjust: that the officers of the army had not suffered more by the war than other citizens."

Knowing that any state could thwart the will of Congress, opponents of the tax organized a convention in Middletown to prevent the resolve of Congress from being carried into execution. The Middletown Convention was a milestone in the life of Noah Webster, marking the beginning of his career as a political writer.

Still naive enough to believe in the possibility of national unity and, indeed, unanimity, Webster was convinced that dissent would provoke national disunion and was, therefore, tantamount to treason. He devoted the weeks and months before and during the convention "to support[ing] the resolves of Congress" and attacking opponents of the Confederation.[11] He suspected that Tories, who favored return to British rule, were behind the thrust for disunion, which would leave the states vulnerable to piecemeal reconquest by British forces in Canada. Continued independence, he argued, depended on national unity, which in turn required a new, stronger central government with power to enact laws and force each state to obey and enforce them. Echoing the views of a small but growing camp of so-called Federalists, Webster picked up his pen to engage disunionists. In "An Address to the Discontented People of America,"[12] Webster accused the organizers of the Middletown Convention of "high treason against the United States" and called any resolution the convention might approve "illegal and unconstitutional." He said the state constitution and Articles of Confederation gave only the state Assembly the right to approve and disapprove congressional measures. The people had no direct say, although they could elect or remove from office state legislators with a voice in Congress.

If the state legislature had abused its power and oppressed popular dissent, he conceded, "conventions and town-meetings, for the purpose of petitioning the legislature, would have been legal and honorable. But when the people conceive themselves injured by an act of Congress, it belongs to the legislature to make the proper representations to Congress, and solicit a redress of grievances. . . . No people have clamoured more about the breaches of public faith than those, who are now endeavouring to commit the same crime: A crime which would dissolve the confederation."[13]

Webster called the Middletown Convention an invitation to anarchy and civil war. He said its organizers were "men of intrigue, who are artfully working upon the passions of the multitude to answer their own selfish purposes. . . . Of all situations in the world," he warned, "anarchy is the most to be dreaded."[14]

The ferocity of his attack would typify Websterian criticism for the rest of his life and earn him almost as many foes as it did friends and supporters. That his criticisms were usually valid and justified did little to assuage his targets when he thwarted their personal ambitions. His sense of honor (his critics called it arrogance and self-righteousness) seldom permitted him to be gracious to those he criticized—or to coax them to change their position before he publicly criticized them. He gave them so little room to acknowledge the merits of his criticism that they had little choice but to defend themselves in kind.

Never before in American journalism had readers seen such explosive, personally directed polemics as Webster demonstrated in his political commentaries. Indeed, his articles inaugurated a new era, in which opinions would be printed in vitriol—much to his regret later in life, when he urged Congress to pass libel laws.

On September 2, the day before the Middletown Convention was to assemble, Webster fired another short but powerful salvo. Writing in the *Courant* under the Latin pseudonym "Amicus Patriae" (a friend of the nation), he asked readers whether the representatives to the convention, "irregularly chosen, and acting without an oath," should be "entitled to greater confidence from the people than those who are regularly chosen . . . and who act under the Solemnity of an oath?" He warned that if rump conventions such as that of Middletown prevailed, they would "very soon overthrow the Constitution of our free government and expose the people to the deprivation of all their rights and liberties."[15]

Webster's thunderous articles had their desired effect: they discouraged so many delegates from going to Middletown that, when the convention began, on September 8, only a minority of towns were represented. Without a quorum, it had to adjourn until September 30. When it reconvened, more than fifty towns—five-sevenths of the state—sent representatives, but according to Webster's granddaughter, "many noted characters came to the support of Congress. . . . One of the most earnest," she wrote, "was a young man then all but unknown to fame, but who, by sheer force of his natural abilities, raised himself in after years to great eminence and made his name a household word wherever the English language is spoken. Noah Webster was then in his twenty-fifth year."[16]

The stalwarts against disunion included Webster and a core group of his brilliant young friends, such as Barlow, Wolcott, and Trumbull. Together they defeated all the measures at Middletown, except a call to reconvene at the beginning of the new year, in January 1784.

Webster earned the praise and attention of Connecticut governor Jonathan Trumbull, whom George Washington addressed amiably as "Brother Trumbull." Webster left Middletown an acknowledged leader in the state, a fierce guardian against rump conventions that try to usurp the right to govern from duly elected legislatures. Although pleased by his newfound public stature, he was more elated by the power of his pen to influence minds and events. It was a power he would use compulsively, unceasingly, and somewhat redundantly the rest of his life.

3

A WEEK AFTER WEBSTER'S TRIUMPH AT MIDDLETOWN, the young man cupped his hands lovingly about the first bound copy of his little 120-page spelling book.[17] On the same day, October 7, 1783, the *Connecticut Courant* printed this advertisement: "Just published 'The First Part of a Grammatical Institute of the English Language, Containing a new and accurate Standard of Pronunciation,' by Noah Webster, A.M. 10s [shillings] per dozen or 14d [pence] per single book."

The timing could not have been better. Most of the schools that had closed during the war were just reopening and in need of new books. The spirit of patriotism was high, and teachers and parents naturally turned to an American book rather than an English text that taught loyalty to the hated monarch they had just overthrown.

"The success," Webster wrote in his memoirs, "was better than . . . expected, the edition of five thousand copies being exhausted during the following winter."[18] With sales of five hundred to a thousand books a day, Hudson & Goodwin would publish two new editions of the speller the following year and one new edition a year for decades to follow.

The published version of Webster's spelling book differed somewhat from the draft he had shown Jefferson and Madison a year earlier. The published speller contained an expanded introduction that not only emphasized the patriotic nature of the book but brutally assailed Dilworth's as a

British book for British children—a book that was not only improper for teaching freeborn American youth but also "defective" as a speller. The clear implication was that its use by any American teacher not only bordered on sedition but would result in poor and unacceptable instruction:

> As Mr. Dilworth's New Guide (which by the way, is the *oldest* and most imperfect guide we use in schools) is commonly used and his authority become as sacred as the traditions of the Jews, or the Mahometan bible, I shall take the liberty to make some remarks upon it with that plainness that is due to truth. . . .[19]
>
> His Grammar, being founded entirely upon the principles of the *Latin* language, is in fact worse than none, as it is calculated to lead into error. The only circumstance that renders it tolerably harmless is that it is very little used and still less understood.[20]

Almost every part of Dilworth's speller, Webster went on, "was originally defective; and is rendered still more so by the improvements made in our language since it was first published. But the late revolution has rendered it still more improper in America; and yet tens of thousands of these books, are annually reprinted and find rapid sale, when one half of the work is totally useless and the other half defective and erroneous."

Webster's criticism of Dilworth was only partially justified. It was indeed old and out of date, and its British orientation was certainly inappropriate for American boys. Beyond this, Webster's criticism was somewhat unfair. When first published, in 1740, Dilworth's represented an important advance over previous spellers by subdividing monosyllabic words into separate lists of two-, three-, and four-letter words instead of mixing them haphazardly. Moreover, Dilworth was actually a daring progressive for his day, urging that girls be taught to read, write, and calculate as well as boys.[21]

Nevertheless, Dilworth's remained an English speller. In contrast, Webster's was an American speller, indeed the first *American* speller ever available to American children.[22] His preface made it clear that the aim of his book differed from that of previous spellers:

> "The author wishes to promote the honour and prosperity of the confederated republics of America; and chearfully throws his mite into the common treasure of patriotic exertions.

"This country," he declared,

> must in some future time, be as distinguished by the superiority of her literary improvements, as she is already by the liberality of her civil and ecclesiastical constitutions. . . . American glory begins to dawn at a favourable period, and under flattering circumstances. We have the experience of the whole world before our eyes; but to receive indiscriminately . . . the manners and literary taste of Europe and make them the ground on which to build our systems in America, must soon convince us that a durable and stately edifice can never be erected upon the mouldering pillars of antiquity. It is the business of *Americans* to select the wisdom

of all nations—to prevent the introduction of foreign vices and corruptions and check the career of her own,—to promote virtue and patriotism,—to embellish and improve the sciences,—to diffuse an uniformity and purity of language,—to add superior dignity to this infant empire and to human nature.[23]

As soon as he received the first copies from the Hartford bindery, Webster took personal command of marketing and promoting his new book. He sent copies to friends and classmates throughout the Northeast. He traveled everywhere—on horseback or by stagecoach—to present copies personally to "distinguished gentlemen" such as Yale president Ezra Stiles and former Yale tutor Timothy Dwight. Dwight had just moved to Greenfield Hill, about twenty-five miles west of New Haven, where he had taken over the Congregational church and was founding an academy.

It was essential to the success of the *Institute* to win the endorsements of such educators. They were the men who trained future ministers and teachers and dictated educational standards. Webster made it his top priority to meet eventually with every college president in the nation. Next to college presidents, ministers were most important to the success of the *Institute*. In each New England town, where the minister did not conduct the elementary school himself, he appointed the instructor and determined which speller the instructor should use.

Webster's old tutor from Yale, the Reverend Joseph Buckminster, who had succeeded Ezra Stiles in the pulpit at Portsmouth, New Hampshire, was overjoyed with the *Institute*. He wrote that Webster reminded him of "the old Psalmist . . . [who] grew wiser than his teachers."[24]

Buckminster's letter was almost modest compared to the huzzahs of Webster's other friends, classmates, and teachers. Letters flowed from other sources as well, one of the most notable coming from the camp at Newburgh, New York—the same site the discouraged young Webster had visited a year earlier, where the American army was still awaiting orders to disband.

Concerned that his son was not receiving a proper education, the U.S. quartermaster general, Col. Timothy Pickering, had ordered a copy of Webster's speller, and "instead of sleeping I read it through last night," he wrote to his wife in Salem, Massachusetts.

"I am much pleased with it," he continued.

> The author is ingenious, and writes from his own experience as a schoolmaster, as well as the best authorities; and the time will come when no authority, as an English grammarian, will be superior to his own. It is the very thing I have so long wished for, being much dissatisfied with any spelling book I had seen before. I now send you the book, and request you to let John[25] take it to his master, with the enclosed letter; for I am determined to have him instructed upon this new, ingenious and at the same time easy plan. I am a stranger to Mr. Webster,

> but I intend, when I can find leisure, to write him on the subject, using the liberty (which he requests) to suggest some little matters which may be altered and improved in his next edition; for I think the work will do honor to his country, and I wish it may be perfect. Many men of literature might think it too trifling a subject; but I am of a different opinion, and am happy that a gentleman of Mr. Webster's genius and learning has taken it up. All men are pleased with an elegant pronunciation, and this new Spelling-Book shows children how to acquire it with ease and certainty.[26]

A Harvard graduate and lawyer, Pickering would eventually hold two cabinet posts in the Washington administration and win election as U.S. senator from Massachusetts. He later sent Webster some suggestions to improve the speller, and the two began a deep, lifelong friendship that tied them politically as well as intellectually. Like all of Webster's other admirers, Pickering happily added his name to the list of prominent subscribers to the *Institute*.

Pickering's enthusiastic endorsement was typical of those who had fought for national independence in the Revolutionary War. To them, Webster's deep-felt nationalism was irresistible. They had risked their lives for independence, and here, in Webster's little speller, was a tangible symbol of their triumph—one they could use to teach their children a new, American way of reading, writing, speaking, and, indeed, thinking, as free and independent Americans. The speller promised a new and independent American literature and history that freed their children from the English past and promised to ensure a cultural unity never before achieved in any major nation. All who believed in preservation of the new nation recognized how essential Webster's speller would be in unifying people from so many different nationalities and language groups.[27]

Another characteristic of Webster's speller that stood out was its relative secularity. It was the first children's book to teach morality as an end in itself, unrelated to any particular religion, and it omitted almost all references to the Deity. "Nothing has greater tendency to lessen the reverence which mankind ought to have for the Supreme Being," Webster explained, "than a careless repetition of his name upon every trifling occasion."[28] Gone, too, were the threats of death and eternal damnation that previous spellers had used to frighten children into learning their lessons.

Webster's attack on Dilworth, of course, drew considerable criticism—even from friends such as Buckminster, who thought that "you are a little too severe upon our friend Mr. Dilworth."[29] Webster, however, seemed to have innate marketing skills and knew that any publicity—good or bad—is better than no publicity. From the beginning, he intended inciting Dilworth's defenders, knowing that their cries—and his well-reasoned, logical, and patriotic replies—would provide his new speller with widespread attention and would spur the curious to buy and examine the new book—if only to see what the fuss was about. Once in the hands of enough curious parents and schoolmasters, he was certain, its simplified approach to reading instruction would make its introduction into schools inevitable.

He was correct. His broadside provoked angry outcries from schoolmasters who had grown used to the old book and were uninterested in learning new teaching methods. It also produced angry responses from orthodox Calvinists who saw Dilworth's lessons from the Bible as essential to the education of the young. They charged Webster with "sanctimony" for refusing to use the name of the Deity. Tories were the most outraged because of Webster's assault on all things English—especially their beloved English language and pronunciations.

Behind the scenes, some of the outrage was the work of printers and booksellers whose livelihood depended on regular production and sale of Dilworth's with each reopening of school. Because so many schools had closed during the war, booksellers were caught holding stocks of Dilworth's speller that they might never sell if schools adopted Webster's book.

Webster spent the rest of 1783 working on his grammar book and touring the state—a consummate Yankee peddler, he visited friends, relatives, churchmen, and schoolmasters, stopping at every school to expose his new book to as many people of influence as possible and to win their endorsements. One effective promotion he invented was the presentation of his work as a gift to each schoolmaster. The technique invariably led to its adoption in the teacher's school and sales of hundreds of books to area students.

Webster's essays and speeches at the first two Middletown Conventions had made him a renowned public figure in New England, and as he had hoped, almost every Connecticut personage of any consequence eagerly endorsed his work—if not for its new approach to instruction, at least for its fervent patriotism and its focus on American geography and history. His tour—the first book tour ever by an American author—produced sales of thousands of spellers and a sense that national success awaited him beyond the state's borders. He returned to Hartford bent on opening a school of rhetoric to exploit his new fame and expand on his teaching successes in Sharon and Goshen. A letter awaited him from Governor Livingston of New Jersey saying that the legislature had passed the copyright law, thus expanding the area of protection for his new book.

Elated by the news and perhaps swelled with overconfidence, he placed a pompous advertisement in the *Connecticut Courant* of December 30, 1783:

A RHETORICAL SCHOOL

The subscriber, having devoted himself for a considerable time to the cultivation of the English Language, and having lately obtained the best standard of pronunciation hitherto published, in order to diffuse propriety and uniformity of speaking as well as to gratify the wishes of particular Gentlemen, proposes to open an Evening School in this town for instructing young Gentlemen and Ladies in the most elegant modern pronunciation, from the simple sounds that compose words to a just and graceful elocution.

The School will begin as soon as thirty scholars shall enter their names. . . .

There was no interest, and the school never opened.

4

ONLY SLIGHTLY DISMAYED by the failure of his rhetorical school, Webster pressed on with the preparation of his grammar—and some new oratory for the next Middletown Convention, which was to convene on January 17. The grammar was to be different from all previous grammars in that Webster no longer based the rules of English on the rules of Latin. In so doing—and this was his greatest innovation—he eliminated a huge body of unnecessary grammatical terminology that did not reflect actual usage or changes in word forms. By eliminating the declension of nouns, for example, he spared children the painful, meaningless exercise of labeling each noun as being in the nominative, objective, dative, or ablative case. If a noun appeared before the verb, it was, simply, the subject; after the verb or preposition, it was the object. No more cases. Webster also did away with the subjunctive mode and the traditional Latin grouping of verbs into three groups: transitive, intransitive, and neuter. Instead, he labeled a small handful of verbs, such as *to be,* as "auxiliary" and grouped all the rest as either transitive or intransitive.

Webster's grammar also represented a practical, economic advance that pleased parents and teachers: it was published as a separate book from the speller. Previous spellers and grammars had been published in a single volume, with the grammar filling the rear pages, to be studied after the child mastered the spelling materials in the first half of the book. As a caring schoolmaster, Webster had noticed that, by the time the child advanced to the grammar section, constant handling by tiny hands had usually torn the book to shreds, leaving the grammar section indecipherable. Parents invariably had to buy a second, identical book to allow their children to proceed with their studies of grammar. Webster cleverly offered the two books for the price of one.

In addition to his work on the grammar, Webster continued firing broadsides at organizers of the Middletown Convention. The December 30, 1783, *Courant*—the same issue that ran his ill-fated advertisement for the rhetorical school—renewed his charge of "treason against the State." The assault had its desired effect: the convention again had to adjourn for lack of a quorum.

The organizers said they would reconvene in the spring, but Webster anticipated their every move. He warned *Courant* readers that "the dignity, safety, and happiness of America are inseparably connected with a union of all the states." In early April, he ridiculed convention leaders as nothing less than "rogues."

"What a vile mixture of misrepresentation and falsehood is this!" he wrote of the convention's agenda. "What an insidious attempt to play upon the ignorance, the passions and the interests of the multitude." After the final Middletown Convention, Webster urged citizens to vote against any convention members who might run in the May elections for the state legislature.

Just after the convention, part II of the *Grammatical Institute*—the grammar—came off the presses, and Webster returned to his studies of law, which he now recognized as essential to participation in political affairs. For the first time in a year, the young author found himself with ample time to attend court trials and pore over the latest law books in Trumbull's and Wolcott's libraries. He expanded his studies into related areas, such as economics, devouring Adam Smith's *Inquiry into the Nature and Causes of the Wealth of Nations,* which he used as a basic reference for the rest of his life whenever writing on economic affairs.

Despite his attention to scholarship, Webster never neglected his social life, and his diary frequently reports his visits with "the Ladies in the evening as usual."

"If there were but one pretty girl in town," he lamented facetiously on April 8, 1784, "a man could make a choice—but among so many! One's heart is pulled twenty ways at once. The greatest difficulty, however, is that after a man has made *his* choice, it remains for the Lady to make *hers.* "[30]

On May 8, the voters handed organizers of the Middletown Convention a crushing defeat. As Webster put it, the months he had devoted "to the object of enlightening & tranquilizing the minds of [my] fellow citizens . . . [had] a degree of success which more than answered expectations. The discontent was greatly allayed; & at the election of the spring of 1784, three fourths of the members of the house of representatives were chosen from the supporters of government. The Middletown Convention ended in smoke."[31] A week later, Connecticut approved a federal tax of 5 percent to fund military pensions. The legislature honored Webster, asserting that he had "done more to allay popular discontent and support the authority of Congress at this crisis than any other man."[32]

Governor Trumbull, who was almost seventy-four and exhausted by the turmoil of Middletown, retired from public service after the convention, and a new governor was elected. Trumbull thanked Webster publicly for putting down the threat to disunion and invited the young man to join him at the official retirement ceremonies.

"For those labors," Webster wrote in his *Memoir,* "[I] received the thanks of Governor Trumbull; and Mr. Mitchell, then a member of the council, & afterwards Chief Justice of the State, coming from the state house one day during the session of the legislature in May . . . said to [me], 'You have done more to appease public discontent, & produce a favorable change than any other person.' "[33]

Webster later received a letter from the Revolutionary hero Samuel Adams of Boston, supporting his stand against the Middletown Convention:

> County conventions and popular committees served an excellent purpose when they were first in practice [under colonial rule]. No one needs regret the share he may have had in them. . . . But there is decency and respect due to constitutional authority; and those men who, under any pretence or by any means whatever, would lessen the weight of government, lawfully exercised, must be enemies to our happy Revolution and the common liberty. . . . I candidly own that is my opinion . . . that as we now have constitutional and regular governments, and all our men in authority depend upon the annual elections of the people, we are safe without [rump conventions].[34]

5

Webster's attacks against the Middletown Convention brought him widespread notoriety—plaudits from budding Federalists and hate-filled replies from Tories who sought reunion with Britain. Sensing the political strength of his position and aware of his brilliant gifts as a writer and teacher, Webster followed up his Middletown victory with two essays for the *Courant* outlining a "Policy of Connecticut" to reinvigorate the state's economy. In the first article, only ten days after the convention, he proposed a plan for improving the state's foreign balance of trade. He urged merchants to form purchasing and marketing cooperatives to buy imports in quantities large enough to command discounts, and to price their exports together and prevent buyers from playing one merchant off against the other.

In his second article, a week later, he urged merchants to build their own, cooperatively owned wagons to take goods to market in large lots rather than each merchant hiring an individual transport contractor. He suggested development of aggressive new marketing techniques to export products native to Connecticut, such as lumber, flax, potash, meat, and fish.[35]

His articles thrust Webster further to the center of the Connecticut political stage, and he immediately took advantage of that position by setting off on his horse for a monthlong tour of New England to promote his *Institute.* The tour proved an overwhelming success, with Webster personally selling his books to schoolmasters, churchmen, and community leaders across Connecticut, Massachusetts, and southern New Hampshire.

A born promoter, his approach was simple and effective—and one he would use for the rest of his life. As he had done before, he first obtained letters of endorsement for his speller from prominent figures—governors, college presidents, leading clergymen, and thinkers—whose recommendations carried all but the force of law in education. He then flooded the local press with advertisements and essays praising the speller. He signed some of the ads with his own name, others pseudonymously.

Applying this formula before approaching local schoolmasters in eastern Massachusetts, he stopped in Boston to see the new governor, Samuel Adams, the Revolutionary War hero who had praised Webster's stand at Middletown. Adams, in turn, sent Webster to have tea with and present copies of the *Institute* to James Bowdoin, a close Adams friend who had founded and was president of the American Academy of Arts and Sciences. A future governor himself, Bowdoin joined Adams in endorsing Webster's book and recommending it to area schoolmasters. Few dared refuse. Webster assured press coverage of his meetings and travels by placing advertisements of the book with details for purchasing it singly or in quantities. Thus, the same day's paper would report the governor's meeting Webster and praising his work, while providing an advertisement that told readers how to buy it.

After meeting with the printer Elisha Babcock of Springfield, Webster rode across the Charles River to Cambridge, for tea with Harvard College president Joseph Willard. He gave Willard a special leather-bound edition of the *Institute* for the college library—a presentation that was duly reported in the Massachusetts newspapers. In return, Willard proudly endorsed the *Institute*—a gesture that Webster knew would ensure sales of thousands more copies. Then, riding from town to town, Webster met with every schoolmaster and minister in every community, presented each with a sample copy of his speller, displayed his letters of endorsement, and pointed out the patriotic duty of every teacher to use the *Institute* to teach American children to read, write, and speak "American" and to love their country. It was an infallible sales presentation—especially for a Calvinist New Englander in Calvinist New England.

After touring Massachusetts, Webster reached Portsmouth, New Hampshire, by stagecoach and on horseback, for a weekend with his old Yale tutor the Reverend Joseph Buckminster, whom he enlisted as an informal agent for the *Institute*. Though tired, Webster nevertheless attended Buckminster's church services and, the following evening, "attended a ball" where he was "agreeably entertained; had a fine Partner, but she is engaged."

Webster returned home to Hartford by way of Worcester, where he met with Isaiah Thomas, a printer whose proindependence newspaper, the *Massachusetts Spy*, had forced him to flee the British but had made him both a hero to American patriots and the official patriot printer. He had expanded into magazine, almanac, and book publishing when Webster arrived, and like many printers, he was a bookseller as well. Webster agreed to send him seven dozen copies of the speller for his shop.

Webster arrived home in Hartford on July 3. After a day's rest visiting his parents in "Westdivision," as West Hartford was called, he resumed his law studies with his friend John Trumbull, while directing his infant publishing enterprise. Besides promoting his books, he had to protect his property against piracy by obtaining copyright legislation wherever possible, and to beat back critics who might hurt sales.

During his absence, the organizers of the Middletown Convention had been nursing the deep political wounds Webster had inflicted on them and contemplating ways to topple the arrogant young man from his newfound political perch. They thought they had found an effective weapon in a series of letters pseudonymously signed "Dilworth's Ghost." The Ghost had sent a stream of letters to newspapers criticizing Webster's *Institute* for attempting to standardize pronunciation. He accused Webster of plagiarism and arrogance for taking Calvin's title *Institute* as his own. The first letter appeared in the *Connecticut Courant* in June, just after Webster had returned from his New England tour.

Webster shrugged it off with a cursory reply to the *Freeman's Chronicle:* "Mr. Printer, if the Ghost you have introduced to this city be really Mr. Dilworth's, I suspect that some petty schoolmaster or bungling printer, who has a large number of Dilworth's books on hand and finds them less saleable than formerly, has called up his Ghost to defend the books and help the sale."[36]

Thinking he had laid the Ghost to rest, Webster turned his attention to expanding copyright protection by writing to James Madison, a leader in the Virginia House of Delegates. "From the small acquaintance I had with you at Philadelphia and the recommendation of Mr. Jefferson," Webster wrote, "I take the liberty to address you on the subject of literary property and securing to authors the copyright of their productions in the State of Virginia. It is my request, Sir, that you would move for a law of this kind in your next session of Assembly."[37]

By midmonth, a stream of orders for his *Institute* was flowing from Boston—most of it the result of press publicity regarding his visits with Harvard president Willard, Gov. Samuel Adams, James Bowdoin, and other "distinguished men," and their endorsements of his work. The chore of packing and shipping books began to eat into his time. By midmonth, his diary reflected the monotony of his daily activities:

> [July 16] Put some boxes of books aboard Capt Moses Williams to carry to Boston.
>
> [July 21] Very steady, over books and paper.

[July 23] At Books.

[July 26] Engaged with books.

[July 28] At books.[38]

In the meantime, letters arrived at the *Connecticut Courant* defending Webster's *Institute* against the Ghost's assault. One writer, who signed his letter "Thomas Dilworth," said, "I am happy to see later writers improve on mine."[39]

Webster himself remained silent and so out of character that some friends and critics began chiding him and asking whether he himself "or some friend of mine wrote [the Ghost's letters] to excite public attention and increase the sale of my books."[40]

Webster finally fired back, answering the charge of plagiarism by saying that "the most eminent scholars in America, particularly some of the instructors at Nassau Hall [Princeton] and the University of Pennsylvania," had attested to its originality. As for arrogance, Webster pointed out that he had not selected the title—indeed, that "it had been christened by the gentleman who presides over literature in Connecticut," Yale president Ezra Stiles.[41]

"Proud and arrogant as you represent me," Webster continued,

> I have not a single wish to impose any thing on my countrymen. I offer them what I esteem a better system of education than that which has been generally used; and they have a sovereign right of receiving or rejecting it at their pleasure. . . . If the system I have proposed is on the whole good, neither printing errors nor your own petulant errors can overturn it. But if upon the whole it shall be found not preferable to those which have gone before it, you may be assured, Sir, that it will fall into neglect and oblivion without your assistance.[42]

Dilworth's Ghost's letters of criticism continued without letup for a year, appearing in newspapers in every major city. At first, Webster seemed annoyed at the requests of editors for responses. In his letter of July 5 "To the Printer" of the *Freeman's Chronicle,* Hartford, Webster voiced suspicions that Dilworth's Ghost was actually "the Ghost of the late [Middletown] Convention, for the styles and spirit of the remarks exactly resemble those of their writers, and they seem to be produced in a fit of peevishness." Dilworth himself, Webster added, "was a scholar and a respectable character when living, and unless he is much degenerated since his death, his Ghost could not have been the author of . . . such indecent remarks."[43]

Webster eliminated the rancor from his replies, however, when he realized how effective a platform the Ghost had created for explaining the logic and benefits of the new speller to potential buyers in virtually every American city. He even began enjoying the correspondence as a pastime that overcame the weariness of endless travel by horseback to sell books to schoolmasters, churchmen, and parents.

As the correspondence continued, Webster was able to use the pages of every newspaper to detail every theory that underlay his new method of instruction. Readers followed the feud like a modern-day soap opera, and sales of Webster's book soared, from five hundred books a week to one thousand.

"I am under ten thousand obligations to that restless spirit," Webster wrote, "for his spiteful attempt to depreciate my publications. Had not his scurrilous remarks appeared, people would have taken less pains to examine the design, the plan, and the merit of the *Institute*. The result of a critical examination has generally been in its favour, not only in Connecticut, but in other States."

Obviously enjoying himself, Webster signed his letter in the courteous fashion of the day: "I am, Mr. Printer, Your's and his Ghostship's most humble Servant, N. Webster, Jun."

With some disappointment, Webster eventually learned the identity of the Ghost—he was no one more interesting than an obscure schoolmaster named Hughes, who was variously described as "an old Litchfield schoolmaster" and "a retired New York City schoolmaster" and who may have intended publishing his own speller. In his final response to the Ghost, Webster pointed out that by obtaining copyright laws to protect authors, "future writers (perhaps you, Mr. Ghost, if you should publish a grammar) will be indebted for the security of their literary property."[44]

After signing his letter, Webster could not resist a last word: "P.S. I was always at some loss, Mr. Ghost, to discover your real motives in decrying the *Institute*. Since I finished the foregoing address, I am informed you are preparing or have prepared a grammar for publication. This develops your plans; it unfolds the whole mystery. But if my *Institute* is such a wretched performance, it will do yours no injury. Publish a better, Mr. Ghost, and it will soon supersede the use of mine."[45]

6

HAVING ESTABLISHED his *Institute* as the universal text in New England schools, Noah Webster, Jun., Esq., had little to occupy his time when he returned home, and with ample funds in his pocket, he decided to fulfill his original ambition. He opened his first law office in Hartford in the summer of 1784, three years later than he had anticipated, but he now did so knowing that clients who turned to him would do so because of his own name, not those of his forebears. He was both a successful author of textbooks and a crushingly effective political essayist. His stand against disunion had earned him a position of prominence in Connecticut.

Although his law office attracted a reasonable number of cases, he faced competition from other young attorneys with equally prominent names in Connecticut—his friends John Trumbull and Oliver Wolcott Jr. Theirs was not a bitter rivalry by any means, and indeed, the summer proved one of the most pleasant Webster would ever spend. Royalties from his books were flowing nicely, allowing him to repay his debts. He and his father experienced the joy of sharing a courtroom together, as the son pleaded—and won—a case before the father, who sat as justice of the peace.

Webster also had enough leisure time in the summer of 1784 to read poetry, reread the works of Locke and Rousseau, and sing in the church choir. Apart from Sundays at church and weekly visits to his parents in Westdivision, Webster divided his time between "the Ladies and books" and frequent dinners with his friends Trumbull, Wolcott, and Barlow. "If I cannot devote my time to books," he wrote in his diary, "I can to the Ladies."[46] In September, his law practice and social life grew substantially, with Webster organizing a major ball, which he described as "a brilliant Assembly and an agreeable evening" that left him "much fatigued."[47]

Webster's Hartford was a friendly, close-knit community of about five thousand, with about three hundred of the most handsome homes spread atop the banks above the Connecticut River. Tall, stately elms shaded the green at the town center, where townspeople of all ages gathered to exchange news and invite one another to tea, evening dances, or bees of one type or another. Young people were as comfortable with their elders as they were with their peers. Webster knew the entire community, and the entries in his diary provide a census of Hartford society—especially the young ladies—and paint a warm and inviting portrait of the young lawyer's everyday life:

[July] 23. At Books
24. do. a dull day
25. Sunday. At Church . . .
27. Rode to West division [parents' home] with Mr. Barlow, & c.
29th. Drank tea at Dr. Hopkins.
30. Sober as a Judge.
Sunday. August 1. At Church. Singing performed AM wretchedly; PM We did better.
2. First ate Watermelons. Received the Coat of Arms of our Family engraved on Copper Plate, & c.
3. Very warm. At evening attended the Serenade.
4. Too warm to stir.
9. Returned Mr Bliss his hat which he left in place of mine at Norwich 30th January.
10. Amusing myself with books and with a flute. What an infinite variety of methods have mankind invented to render life agreeable! And what a wise and happy design in the organization of the human

frame that the sound of a little hollow tube of wood should dispel in a few moments, or at least alleviate, the heaviest cares of life!

12. Read a little Law and some poetry, if a man lays up a few ideas every day and arranges them, it is enough.

14. Capt. Israel Seymour of the City killed by Lightning, as he was standing near the front door of his own house. . . . The house was considerably damaged.

16. Mortified to find my eyes too weak to study. But if I cannot devote my time to books, I can to the Ladies. A Remarkable hurricane at Southington.

28. Get Grapes in the North Meadow.

September 6. Divide my time between the Ladies and books.[48]

On October 11, the Marquis de Lafayette, the French hero of the American Revolutionary War, arrived in Hartford on his triumphal tour of the United States, and Webster was among the city's leaders who dined with him the following evening. Five days later, Webster's diary records, "My birthday. 26 years of my life are past. I have lived long enough to be good and of some importance. Introduced to Miss S Dwight of Springfield, a fine Lady."[49]

The continuing economic crisis, however, left him short of money, despite a steady flow of income from his law practice. He complained to his diary that "money is so scarce that I cannot borrow 30 £ for a few weeks, giving 12 pr cent interest and good security."[50] In November, he received a major legal assignment from the Susquehanna Company, whose investors included his father. The company asked Webster to prepare a statement of claims against Pennsylvania for land in the Wyoming Valley, where the state militia had driven off Connecticut settlers. He wrote seven articles describing the history of the controversy, asking, in conclusion, "If all the states rush to claim the unseated lands within the limits of their overlapping, carelessly defined colonial grants, will not a civil war arise on a greater, more terrible scale than at Wyoming? If a large state begins a campaign to extend its borders, what power can stop the aggressor from conquering and absorbing its neighbors?

"The safety and harmony of the whole depend on a proper equality in the several individuals," said Webster, who went on to call for revision of the Articles of Confederation. He urged forming a new, stronger central government, with "a federal head, vested with powers to compel any particular State to comply with the measures that are adopted by the majority of the States."[51]

His was not the only voice calling for strong central government, but it was certainly one of the first and most audible. The earliest may have been that of the young New York attorney Alexander Hamilton, who in 1780 had written the first of a series of critical letters and essays advocating greater powers for Congress.[52] Another of the early advocates of federal government was Pelatiah Webster, a cousin of Noah Webster, though a generation older, and one of Philadelphia's prominent merchants.[53]

An outspoken critic of the excessive use of unsecured paper money, Pelatiah Webster published his first pamphlet on Federalism in 1781. In it, he called for a continental convention to draw up a new, stronger federal constitution. Pelatiah cried out for Federalism again in 1783, but thereafter it was his cousin Noah's voice that echoed throughout the land.

7

IN NOVEMBER 1784, Noah Webster obtained permission from his old friend Timothy Dwight to include extracts of Dwight's epic poem *Conquest of Canaan*[54] in the third volume of the *Institute,* a reader that would include the finest American literature. Webster finished his manuscript before Christmas, and on February 5, 1785, the first copies of his 186-page reader came off the press bearing the forgettable title *A Grammatical Institute, of the English Language, in Three Parts: Part III, Containing, the Necessary Rules of Reading and Speaking, and a Variety of Essays, Dialogues, and Declamatory Pieces, Moral, Political and Entertaining; Divided into Lessons, for the Use of Children.*

Despite its title, the reader was a significant—indeed, pioneering—work in the history of American education and school texts, for it was the first literary anthology for children ever published and in addition, the first anthology of any kind containing a significant amount and variety of literature by American authors. Webster also included dialogues, on the theory that by having students read the dialogues aloud, teachers could use the speller as a teaching tool to improve student speech.

As he had in his two previous books, Webster began his reader with a provocative preface that he knew would stir public controversy and create publicity for his book. The absence of literary anthologies, he pointed out, had previously restricted American children to using the Bible as their reader—a practice he called "reprehensible" because its archaic and uniform style of writing hindered acquisition of "a complete knowledge of words and of the modern manner of writing." Moreover, just as he had eliminated the name of the Deity from his speller, he said that "common use of the Bible [as a reader] is a kind of prostitution of divine truth to secular purposes."[55]

His choice of words proved unfortunate in Calvinist America. Unlike the prefaces in his previous books, Webster had to change this one in subsequent editions of his reader. It was one thing to target Dilworth's book as inimical to the education of the young, but quite another to assail the Bible. Reflecting widespread public opinion, Dr. Benjamin Rush, the great patriot-physician who had been surgeon general and a signatory of the Declaration of Independence, wrote Webster that children could not study the Bible too much. Far from turning Rush and Webster into adversaries, however, the controversial preface was instrumental in making them lifelong friends because of their mutual support for universal public education.

Moreover, most of the preface displayed the same patriotic zeal as his previous books. "In the choice of pieces," Webster explained, "I have been attentive to the political interests of America. Several . . . masterly addresses of Congress written at the commencement of the late Revolution, contain such noble sentiments of liberty and patriotism that I cannot help wishing to transfuse them into the breasts of the rising generation."[56]

The title page bore the counsel of the French orator and revolutionary Mirabeau, whose brother had fought with the Americans: "Begin with the infant in his cradle: let the first word he lisps be Washington."[57]

The first chapters of the anthology contained easy-to-read proverbs, passages, and aphorisms that exuded piety, virtue, and love of country, and exposed children to easy-to-read "select sentences" from great literature. Included, among others, were Swift, Shakespeare, Johnson, Pope, Bacon, Dryden, Addison, and Benjamin Franklin. There were two addresses from Congress—one by Hancock, the other by Livingston—an address by Washington, an extract from Thomas Paine's *Crisis,* no. V, and at the end of the little book, a letter by Thomas Day warning Americans that they faced "the dilemma of either acknowledging the rights of your Negroes, or of surrendering your own."[58] Its inclusion marked Webster's first act as a champion of abolition.

In addition to literature by celebrated American writers, Webster published several short stories of his own that he had created for the book. Nor did he forget his friends: he included extracts from the epic poetry of Joel Barlow and Timothy Dwight and a portion of John Trumbull's popular poem *M'Fingal.*[59]

Webster finished correcting the last printer's proofs of his reader on February 5, 1785, and was able to turn his attention to a greater goal—achieving universal use of his books to ensure a nationwide standard of language that would unify the American people. The speller was already an overwhelming success in New England, with more than twelve thousand copies sold in about eighteen months. Webster received a royalty of one cent per copy—hardly a fortune, but enough to make it a self-sustaining enterprise that, together with his law practice, left its author solvent for the moment. The books sold for ten cents a copy in uncut sheets and sixteen cents when cut, bound, and "covered with blue paper"—which eventually gave the speller its nicknames "The Blue-Back Speller" and "Old Blue Back."

With his books still unprotected by copyright in the middle and Southern states, he began planning to tour those regions as he had New England,

New York, and New Jersey. He would visit the legislatures, petition for copy-right protection, then travel from town to town, introducing his *Institute* to instructors, churchmen, and men of influence. Although his voyage would mean abandoning his growing law practice, he sensed disunion growing about him, and he believed his scheme for a common language and national culture was the key to national unity.

His ardor for his cause totally eclipsed his other interests, including the practice of law. Indeed, he found certain aspects of daily practice distressing. Just before correcting the last proofs of part III of the *Institute,* he had the unpleasant task of representing his father's cousin Ebenezer Webster in a suit to collect an overdue loan from Medad Webster, another of his father's cousins. Debt collection paled in comparison to the creation of a national language.

Although the number of his court cases continued increasing, his diary entries evince little enthusiasm. On November 22 and 23 he "heard the Case of the State against John Benton for lascivious carriage . . . found not Guilty."[60] On the twenty-fourth, he pled "the cause of a Mr. Brown . . . Caleb Bull versus Brown—Book debt."[61] In another case, the court ruled on a parent's right to rescue his daughters from a religious sect. "The Plaintiff brought an action against the Defendant, a *Shaking Quaker,* vulgarly so called,—on[e] Mechum of Enfield—for harbouring his 2 daughters, who had been persuaded to embrace that curious religion. On evidence it appeared that they were convinced that this new fanaticism was the *way of God,* (to use their own expression) and had left their father's house, merely to enjoy their worship unmolested. Judgement for the Defendant."[62] The routine of court cases was broken only by an opportunity to read a draft of his friend's Barlow's epic *Vision of Columbus,*[63] just before Thanksgiving.

The birth of a son and heir to his brother Charles, however, brought much joy, as did the "jovial mirth" of holiday celebrations—"at my Fathers as usual, with my brother Charles and Sisters."[64] True to form, he took great pleasure going to balls—especially when the ladies outnumbered the men. At the New Year's Eve ball, he wrote in his diary, there were "60 Ladies and 40 Gentlemen. . . . Feel exceedingly well after dancing; close the year."[65]

In preparing to travel southward, Webster knew that the Webster name and what it stood for in Connecticut would have little meaning or influence in the South. He set to work writing a document outlining the political philosophy that underlay his *Institute*—a document he would give to men of influence throughout the South to convince them of the logic of his argument for using his speller to teach a single, standardized language and promote cultural unity. After three weeks, his argument for cultural unity grew into four powerful essays that detailed a plan for a new form of federal government. Published in a four-part pamphlet, *Sketches of American Policy* contained some of Webster's most important and influential essays. Webster believed they contained "the first distinct proposal, made through the medium of the press, for a new constitution of the United States."[66]

Virtually every educated man in America who participated in the affairs of government read Webster's *Sketches,* and the framers of the Constitution incorporated almost all its principles in the framework they created for the new American government.[67] Although ignored by most historians, Webster's *Sketches* preceded by two and a half years the publication of the *Federalist* essays, which appeared in 1787–88,[68] and both Alexander Hamilton and James Madison borrowed almost all of Webster's concepts for their essays.

Webster never claimed that his ideas were original or that his work represented more than an amalgamation of the best political and social concepts of the Age of Enlightenment. The essays included concepts from the Declaration of Independence, from America's state constitutions — especially Connecticut's — from humanism, from Locke, Rousseau, Paine, and others, and from discussions in churches, courthouses, statehouses, and law and literary societies. Indeed, every intelligent, well-educated man in America was discussing the question of congressional impotence and methods of strengthening central governmental powers when Webster wrote his *Sketches.*

George Washington himself had penned the principles he considered essential to successful government in 1782, when still encamped in Newburgh, New York:

> 1st An indissoluble union of the States under one Federal Head,
>
> 2ndly A Sacred regard to Public Justice,
>
> 3dly The Adoption of a Proper Peace Establishment and
>
> 4thly The prevalence of that pacific and friendly Disposition among the People of the United States, which will induce them to forget their local prejudices and policies to make these mutual concessions which are requisite to the general prosperity, and in some instances, to sacrifice their individual advantages to the interest of the community.[69]

But Washington's suggestions were not a framework for government. Nor were those of Alexander Hamilton, who may have been the first to propose replacing the Confederation with a new, more powerful federal government. Hamilton's letter to Congressman James Duane in 1780 lamented the lack of congressional powers as the "root of all evil" in the Confederation. In contrast to Webster's common language and culture as binding mediums, Hamilton called the army the "essential cement of the union." Hamilton suggested nothing short of a coup d'etat, with Congress using the army to seize "complete sovereignty" over civic, military, and economic life and transforming the nation into a "solid, coercive union."[70]

Even Washington was appalled, saying he had read Hamilton's letter "with astonishment and horror." The army, he said, "is a dangerous instrument to play with. . . . the idea of redress by force, is too chimerical to have had a place in the imagination of any serious mind in this army; but there is no telling what unhappy disturbances might result from distress and distrust of justice."[71]

In February 1783, Pelatiah Webster, Noah's older cousin, whom James Madison described condescendingly as "an obscure but able citizen," had published one of the first vague outlines for a new government. In an essay in the *Pennsylvania Packet*, "The Political Union and Constitution," he proposed a bicameral legislature with expanded power over the states and over law enforcement. He suggested giving broad controls over economic affairs and commercial policies to a chamber of commerce. He outlined three broad principles for a new constitution: establishment of a "supreme power," or a chief executive with independent power to enforce the laws; legislative checks on executive power to prevent abuse of authority; surrender of enough state sovereignty to create an effective, unified confederation.

Without any surrender of state sovereignty, he warned, the confederation will be "a union without bands of union, like a cask without hoops."[72]

Except for its last few words, Pelatiah Webster's article had little impact. The phrase "hoop to the union," however, became the watch cry of every political speech, every newspaper article, and every dinner toast by those who sought a new constitution.

Although few dinner toasts cited phrases from Noah Webster's *Sketches,* the latter had far more impact on the writing of the actual Constitution and made Webster "the first man who proposed the present government" of the United States, according to New York State chancellor (chief justice) James Kent.[73] *Sketches* had a far wider circulation than any other published Federalist document prior to the Constitutional Convention and covered a broader range of issues, including that of executive power. Some critics called it "too democratic," and in a facetious, self-deprecating appraisal a few years later, Webster admitted that his *Sketches of American Policy* "contain many chimerical notions . . . [but] the last sketch was well timed and among the causes of framing a new government."[74]

In a more serious analysis, he wrote, "The remarks in the first three sketches are general, and some of them I now believe to be too visionary for practice; but the fourth sketch was intended expressly to urge, by all possible arguments, the necessity of a radical alteration in our system of general government, and an outline is there suggested. As a private man, young and unknown, I could do but little; but that little I did."[75]

James Madison, himself the author of twenty-nine *Federalist*[76] essays, admitted as much in the notes he took during the debates at the Constitutional Convention, in 1787, in which details of the Constitution were worked out: "In the winter of 1784–5, Noah Webster, whose political and other valuable writings had made him known to the public, proposed in one of his publications, 'a new system of government which should act, not on the States, but directly on individuals, and vest in Congress full power to carry its laws into effect.'"[77] Madison first studied George Washington's copy of the *Sketches* at Mount Vernon, in 1785. "Mr. Madison spoke to me with great approbation of the publication," Webster said.[78] Twenty years later, Madison wrote this personal letter to Webster acknowledging the importance of the *Sketches:*

> The change in our government, like most other important improvements, ought to be ascribed rather to a series of causes than to any particular and sudden one, and to the participation of many, rather than to the efforts of a single agent. It is certain that the general idea of revising and enlarging the scope of the federal authority so as to answer the necessary purposes of the Union, grew up in many minds, and by natural degrees, during the experienced inefficacy of the old Confederation. The discernment of General [Alexander] Hamilton must have rendered him an early patron of the idea. That the public attention was called to it by yourself at an early time is well known.[79]

George Washington, the president of the Constitutional Convention, would also pay homage to the young man's contributions by a personal visit to Webster's lodging in Philadelphia, two days after the convention opened.

8

NOAH WEBSTER PUBLISHED his monumental *Sketches of American Policy* on March 9, 1785. They consisted of four essays:

    I. Theory of Government
   II. Governments on the Eastern [European] Continent
 III. American States; or the Principles of the American [state] Constitutions Contrasted with Those of European States
 IV. Plan of Policy for Improving the Advantages and Perpetuating the Union of the American States

He wrote the first sketch "soon after reading Rousseau's *Social Contract,*" from which he admitted he "imbibed many visionary ideas"[80] that he later rejected. "Men, in every stage of society, have found it necessary to establish some form of government to protect their persons and property from invasion," Webster began his first essay—virtually plagiarizing Rousseau. He said that

> a social compact, either expressed or implied, is the basis of all civil government. This compact is nothing more than an association of all the members of a community, by which each individual, for his own security, consents to obey the general voice.

In this act of association, there is a reciprocal engagement between
the public body and its particular members. The public body engages to
protect the person and property of each member, and each member engages to be obedient to the public body. In other words, each individual
engages to assist his fellow citizens in protecting the rights of the whole,
merely from a regard to his own safety; and each engages to yield obedience to the public voice from the same motive.

A state thus formed by compact is a sovereign power and has a right
to command the services and obedience of each member.[81]

Webster went on to define individual rights and develop the concept
of "equal protection under the law," which would later be incorporated in
the Bill of Rights. "Every individual . . . when he becomes a part of the *body
politic,*" Webster wrote,

voluntarily relinquishes so much of his property as is necessary to defray
the expence of securing the remainder. The public therefore has a right
to call upon every individual for this proportion. But the public has no
right to the property of a partial number of individuals . . . the supreme
power cannot order a single person to . . . militia duty, yet it can call
forth every effective man in the state. . . .

The essence of sovereignty consists in the general voice of the people.
But each individual pursues his own interest; and consults the good of
others no farther than his own interest requires. Hence the necessity of
laws which respect the whole body collectively, and restrain the pursuits
of individuals when they infringe the public rights.[82]

Webster said there were three basic relationships in every well-organized
society: that of the citizens to one another; that of each citizen to the sovereign power, or collective body; and that of each citizen to executive authority: "Every individual has a share of sovereign power—every individual
is a subject of that power—and a few only, who are public servants, are
vested with the right of administering the laws."[83]

9

THE MORE ORIGINAL PART II of Webster's *Sketches* outlined what he perceived as the advantages and disadvantages—and evils—of virtually every
type of European government dating back to ancient Rome and Greece,
and "their effects upon the happiness of society."

"In despotic governments, under which nine tenths of the human race
are included," Webster wrote,

a standing army, at the command of a sovereign, has been generally
established, for the purpose of enforcing obedience to his arbitrary
edicts. . . . In order to secure the obedience of subjects, the terrors of

religion have always been called in to aid the civil power, and in most countries, have been incorporated with the political institutions. It has been the policy of the sovereign to keep his subjects in ignorance, to teach them a blind obedience to the oracles of some deity, commonly fabricated or feigned by human contrivance, to impress their minds with the belief that their rulers and priests were beings of a superior order who had some intercourse with their gods and had power to punish disobedience with the severest judgments. All the events of the natural world, earthquakes, thunder and lightning, eclipse, storms and famine, with the whole catalogue of imaginary prodigies, miracles, dreams, tricks of magic, and fabulous stories of demons, have been converted, by power and artifice, into instruments of tyranny. . . .

These two instruments of despotism, superstition and a military force, command peace and subordination in all the kingdoms and empires on the eastern continents.

In a prescient aside, Webster declared that slavery had survived only in the South, "where education is not so general."[84]

"It is scarcely possible to reduce an enlightened people to civil or ecclesiastical tyranny," he declared.

Deprive them of knowledge, and they sink almost insensibly in vassalage. Ignorance cramps the powers of the mind, at the same time that it blinds men to all their natural rights. Knowledge enlarges understanding, and at the same time, it gives a spring to all the intellectual faculties. . . . The general education of youth forms the firmest security of our liberties. A general diffusion of science is our best guard against the approaches of corruption, the prevalence of religious error, the intrigues of ambition and against the open assaults of external foes.[85]

10

IN THE FOURTH AND LAST PART of his *Sketches,* Webster provided a "Plan of Policy for Improving the Advantages and Perpetuating the Union of the American States," which outlined "new principles in modelling our political system." In effect, it was a sketch of a new American constitution. All but two of its key elements—universal compulsory public education and abolition of slavery—would be incorporated into the Constitution two years later in Philadelphia, and both were nonetheless the subject of intense debate.

Central to his "Plan of Policy" was the separation of church and state. "Religion, by which I mean superstition, or human systems of absurdity, is an engine used in almost all governments, and has a powerful effect where people are kept in ignorance."[86]

Webster's equivalent of a preamble to a constitution declared: "All power is vested in the people. That this is their natural and unalienable right, is a position that will not be disputed. . . . The right of making laws for the United States should be vested in all their inhabitants by legal and equal representation."[87]

Webster cited the Connecticut constitution as "the most perfect on earth" and an ideal model for a new federal constitution. He said the Connecticut constitution did not in any way diminish the power of towns and cities to govern themselves in matters that affected only their own citizens. "As bodies politic, they are sovereign and independent—as members of a large community, they are mere subjects. In the same manner, the head of a family, is sovereign in his domestic economy, but as a part of the state, he is subject."[88]

Webster urged adoption of the same system at the national level, with the states remaining "sovereign and independent" for local matters, but "subjects of the federal head" for "common concerns. . . . Let every state reserve its sovereign right of directing its own internal affairs; but give to Congress the sole right of conducting the general affairs of the continent."[89]

Webster warned that the Articles of Confederation had left the American states in disunion, on the verge of anarchy, with each at liberty to fight its neighbor and "no sovereign to call forth the power of the continent to quell the dispute or punish the aggressor. . . . Either the several states must continue separate, totally independent of each other, and liable to all the evils of jealous dispute and civil dissention—nay, liable to a civil war upon any clashing of interest; or they must constitute a general head, composed of representatives from all the states, and vested with the power of the whole continent to enforce their decisions. There is no other alternative."[90]

Webster then sketched what was the first published outline for a new American constitution. Its provisions are often strikingly similar to those the Constitutional Convention would adopt:

"A supreme power at the head of the union."[91]

(The Constitution of the United States, Article II, Section 1: *The executive power shall be vested in a president of the United States of America.*)

A legislature "in which all the power of all the states is united . . . vested with authority to make laws that respect the states in general and to compel obedience to those laws."[92]

(Article I, Section 1: *All legislative powers herein granted shall be vested in a Congress of the United States. Section 8: The Congress shall have the power . . . to make all laws which shall be necessary and proper for carrying into execution, and all other powers vested by this constitution in the government of the United States.*)

A superintendent of finance shall have "the power of receiving public monies and issuing warrants for collection."[93]

(Not debated at the Constitutional Convention.)

In addition to the core articles describing the form of government, Webster's sketch for a constitution included four other basic provisions:

"A general diffusion of knowledge among all classes of men."[94]

(Defeated at the Constitutional Convention.)

Abrogation of state rights to interfere with interstate commerce or impose duties on goods from other states and from foreign countries.[95]

(Article I, Section 8: *The Congress shall have the power . . . to regulate commerce with foreign nations, and among the several states. . . . No tax or duty shall be laid on articles exported from any state . . . nor shall vessels bound to, or from, one state, be obliged to enter, clear, or pay duties to another.*)

Equal influence among states in public deliberations.[96]

(Article I, Section 3: *The Senate of the United States shall be composed of two senators from each state . . . and each senator shall have one vote.*)

Abolition of slavery.[97]

(Defeated at the Constitutional Convention.)

Webster ended his *Sketches* with a plea for national unity: "We ought not to consider ourselves as inhabitants of a particular state only; but as *Americans;* as the common subjects of a great empire . . . the citizens of this new world, should enquire, not what will aggrandize this town or this state; but what will augment the power, secure the tranquility, multiply the subjects, and advance the opulence, the dignity and the virtues of the united States."[98]

CHAPTER FOUR

Yankee Peddler

I

In EARLY MAY OF 1785, Noah Webster, not yet twenty-seven years old, left for the middle and Southern states to promote passage of copyright laws that would protect his *Grammatical Institute*. At the same time, he intended to knock on the doors of every educator, churchman, and political leader and put his book into as many hands as possible to ensure its use in every school in the land. The diary of his trip reads like a *Who's Who* of eighteenth-century America. His journey brought him to national prominence and into contact with the nation's great figures and founding fathers.

He laid the groundwork for his trip by ensuring a flow of letters from his influential friends and acquaintances in the North. Although he had saved some money for the journey, he knew he would have to earn some more along the way, either by selling books or teaching—or both. He shipped several crates of his books to Baltimore and to Charleston, South Carolina, in anticipation of his visits to each. On April 26, he rode to West Hartford for a farewell with his parents and younger brother, and a week later, he set off for New Haven to catch the schooner to New York. On that same day, his classmate Josiah Meigs, a science tutor at Yale, had organized a balloon ascension—an astonishing new scientific advance that was only a little more than two years old. Nothing since Franklin's electric kite had so excited the world of science and the public generally. "The ingenuity of Mr. Meigs," Webster commented after watching the flight. "It rises several Hundred feet."[1]

Webster set sail for New York on May 4, arriving the following day for the first of many calls on America's most powerful and influential men. His approach was an ingenious refinement of the one he had used in selling his *Institute* in New England. At every stop, he asked every new acquaintance to write letters of introduction to prominent people at the next stop. The result was that, in the course of the year, he built a network of friends that included virtually every man of influence in the nation. He seldom spent a day during his travels without having breakfast, lunch, tea, and dinner with people of note.

In New York, he called on Col. Aaron Burr Jr., the future vice president, and through Burr met members of New York's powerful Schuyler, Van Rensselaer, and Clinton families, and more members of the huge Livingston family he had known in Sharon. Their letters of introduction took him to the doors of influential men in Elizabeth Town, Brunswick, and Trenton on his ride southward through New Jersey. In Philadelphia, then the nation's premiere city, he obtained certificates of copyright to protect his *Institute* in Pennsylvania. Then he dined and spent the night at the home of Pelatiah Webster, his older cousin, who "constantly proved himself a valuable and sympathetic friend."[2]

The next morning, he left on horseback for Baltimore, traveling along "terrible roads" often severed by ruts six or eight feet deep.[3] Webster found Baltimore an unattractive boomtown of about ten thousand. Its port disgorged hundreds of unruly Scottish and Irish immigrants every day. On Sundays, "hundreds of blacks collected for pastime," according to Webster, "cracking their whips, elevating kites into the air, breaking each others' heads with clubs, and alarming whole streets with their quarrels."[4]

Baltimore was America's fastest-growing city and, like most of the South, a mine of opportunity for enterprising Yankees. Most of the South was a rural backwater, where a huge slave population produced profitable tobacco and cotton crops for a handful of wealthy white plantation owners. Cities such as Baltimore served as transit points for those crops on the way to Northern U.S. and foreign markets, and they grew into huge, bustling trading centers, stocked to capacity with profits for clever buyers and sellers. Several of Webster's friends from Hartford had already settled in Baltimore, and they urged him to make it his base for his Southern venture. They introduced him to merchants who agreed to stock the *Institute* and to the publisher of the *Maryland Journal,* which ran an advertisement for his books.

Webster's friends also took him to hear Dr. Henry Moyes, a Scottish scientist who was touring America, lecturing on light, sound, and other scientific subjects. Webster found the talk on light particularly remarkable because, as it turned out, Moyes was blind. The performance convinced Webster that he, too, might use the speaker's platform to advantage.

After three days, he sent a letter home to his parents—he always wrote to them at least once a week when he traveled—and rode off to Alexandria, Virginia, to meet legislators and win support for a copyright law in their state. Then, with a letter of introduction in hand from Connecticut governor Trumbull, the intrepid young schoolmaster rode a few miles more to

Mount Vernon, where he dismounted and strode confidently to the door of the world's most revered American.

"I proceed," Webster recorded, "to Genl Washington's seat, 9 miles from Alexandria, down the River Potowmack, an elegant situation on the bank of the river; treated with great attention . . . agreeably entertained by him and family . . . continue with him the night. Play whist with the Genl and his Lady, who is very social."[5]

Webster was seldom as verbose in his diary as he was in his public writings. In fact, the visit that he describes so casually produced one of the most important political friendships of his life. For Webster, Washington was a larger than life American hero, a father figure whom he elevated to godlike status in his books for American children. Indeed, when a printer used a portrait of Washington as a frontispiece in the Webster speller, an embarrassed Webster ordered its removal, saying, "It is using the General disrespectfully to make him a passport for spelling books."[6]

Webster and Washington got along famously. Webster gave the general a copy of the *Sketches*, and the two spent the afternoon discussing the most controversial topics of the day—national unity, the need for a strong federal government, abolition of slavery, agriculture, and education. Earlier in the year, Washington had convened politicians from Virginia and Maryland to resolve interstate navigation conflicts on the Potomac River and Chesapeake Bay. When new problems arose with Delaware and Pennsylvania, James Madison had suggested convening all the states in Annapolis the following year to discuss granting Congress the power to regulate and tax interstate and foreign commerce. Webster's *Sketches* outlined just such a scheme, and Washington said he would show it to Madison.

The young man impressed the general and charmed both Washington and his wife with his wit and skills as a raconteur—even evoking a rare burst of laughter from the general with banter about a bowl of molasses.

"At dinner," Webster later recalled,

> the last course of dishes was a species of pancakes which were handed around to each guest, accompanied with a bowl of sugar and another of molasses for seasoning them, that each guest might suit himself. When the dish came to me, I pushed by me the bowl of molasses, observing that I had enough of that in my own country. The general burst out with a loud laugh, a thing unusual with him.
>
> "Ah," said he, "there is nothing in that story about . . . Yankees eating pork and molasses together . . . in New England."[7]

After breakfast the next morning, Webster returned to Baltimore and prepared to sail for Charleston, South Carolina. Before leaving, he placed an advertisement in the *Maryland Journal,* "To the Inhabitants of Baltimore," announcing plans to open a school. He would teach "young Gentlemen and Ladies in Reading, Speaking and Writing the English language with propriety and correctness. He will also teach Vocal Music in as great Perfection as it is taught in America. He expects as an indispensable condition that the School should be patronized by Families of Reputation; and he himself will be responsible for the success of the undertaking."[8]

2

INSTEAD OF THE NORMAL SEVEN TO TEN DAYS, Webster's ship spent twenty-seven days at sea. It encountered squalls that "beat [me] to pieces" and endless days in the doldrums, rocking sickeningly beneath a stifling summer sun. The only stop had come too soon to ease the distress of the long voyage—at Norfolk, Virginia, less than a day out of Baltimore. Webster took advantage of his day ashore to meet the city's largest merchants.

Norfolk, he wrote in his diary, "consisted of about 300 houses before the war, but was burnt [by the British], & is not wholly rebuilt. . . . Considerable business is done here: but little attention is paid to religion, education or morals. Gentlemen are obliged to send their children to the Northward for education. A shame to Virginia! I leave 3 dozens of the Institute . . . to be sold. Green peas are plentiful."[9]

After two weeks at sea, food supplies were exhausted aboard Webster's ship and the remaining fresh water was rationed. The crew managed to harpoon three dolphins and a shark to assuage passenger hunger. To add to his woes, the ship ran aground and lay stranded offshore for ten hours. When it finally landed in Charleston on a Sunday morning, the young Calvinist was so grateful that he attended three different church services—Saint Michael's Church in the morning, the "White meeting" in the afternoon, and the Methodist church at night.

Webster was "pleased with the appearance" of Charleston. "The people . . . are very civil & polite. They behave with great decency at church, & the slaves attend in greater numbers & behave with more decorum than I have seen in America."[10]

He could not have arrived at a more propitious time. Unlike the North, the South had no tradition of educating its young. A century earlier, when every Connecticut village of fifty or more families had a common school, the fiercely royalist Virginia governor Sir William Berkeley had proclaimed proudly, "I thank God, there are no free schools nor printing [in Virginia], and I hope we shall not have these [for one] hundred years; for learning has brought disobedience and heresy and sects into the world, and printing has divulged them, and libels against the best government. God keep us from both."[11]

God apparently did, for when Noah Webster arrived in 1785, the South still had no common schools. Most white children were as illiterate as their black counterparts, who by law were not permitted to learn to read or write. A few of the cities such as Charleston had an academy, but there was only one college in the entire region at the beginning of the Revolutionary War: Virginia's William and Mary, in Williamsburg.[12]

"An eminent merchant in Alexandria," said Webster, "informed me that of 50 planters in Virginia who sold him Tobacco, 4 or 5 only could write their names but made a mark on the receipts. O New England! how Superior are thy inhabitants in morals literature, civility & industry."[13]

With independence, however, the South began to recognize the need for lawyers, doctors, teachers, and other professionals, and Yankee intellectuals were flocking southward to take advantage of the demand. South Carolina had just founded three colleges when Webster landed in Charleston, and before the year was out, Abraham Baldwin, one of Joel Barlow's brothers-in-law from Yale, would found the University of Georgia. (Two years later, Georgia voters would send him as their representative to the Constitutional Convention.)

Webster spent about ten days in Charleston, using letters of introduction to meet the city's most prominent citizens, presenting each with copies of his *Sketches* and his *Institute* and obtaining pledges of their support for a state copyright law. After a leading merchant agreed to stock and advertise the *Institute,* Webster again demonstrated his marketing genius by presenting two hundred spellers and one hundred grammars to the powerful Mount Sion Society, which had just opened a new local college. The newspaper turned the presentation into a major civic event, with the secretary of the society declaring that "the production of a native of America at so early a period after her arduous and successful struggle for freedom and independence, must reflect the highest honour on the ability and liberality of the author."[14] Within months, South Carolina passed a copyright law, and Webster's *Institute* was adopted by every churchman and educator in South Carolina. To the astonishment of its printers, the *Institute* remained the standard in every new school that opened in South Carolina until the middle of the twentieth century.

An elated Webster celebrated July 4 in Charleston. He described the event in his diary: "Independence Celebrated with Cannon, musquetry, fire works &c. a balloon set off, takes fire, falls on the market, but the fire extinguished. I ascend the steeple to take view of the town from the steeple; Charleston is very regular; the most regular of any in America, except Philadel & New Haven. They have a good chime of bells."[15]

Four days later he sent his usual letters to family and friends in Connecticut and set sail for Baltimore. He arrived a week later and learned that his advertisement had attracted too few applicants to found a school. The resourceful Webster lost no time contacting the minister of the Congregational church, who needed a choir and let Webster organize a singing school at the church. After six weeks of practice, he and his ten-member choir made their singing debut at church on the first Sunday of September. They "astonished all Baltimore" with their skills, Webster noted in his diary,[16] and set off a deluge of applications to study singing with him. He auditioned and admitted twenty-one students, each of whom paid twelve shillings for books, and a dollar (or seven shillings, six pence) per lesson for instruction. With cash in scarce supply, he occasionally accepted payment in kind. A pair of gloves from Miss Jenny Boyd earned a credit of three shillings, nine pence toward her tuition. Haberdasher Samuel Owings paid his entire tuition with a pair of shoes worth thirteen shillings, nine pence, a pair of slippers worth twelve and six, and a pair of silk stockings worth one pound, one shilling.

Enrollment in Webster's choirs more than doubled, and they soon "fill[ed] the churches of Baltimore with music"[17] on Sunday, with Webster himself singing so many solo parts that his voice was in as much demand as his choral groups. His choir proved valuable in many ways. The members expanded his social life and his insatiable need for the company of young ladies his age. They also yielded enough money to buy a comfortable standard of living, even allowing him to pay for advanced French lessons. Fluency in French was essential in the world of international affairs, which he believed he would soon frequent through his acquaintance with men such as Washington, Jefferson, and Madison.

The choir also raised Webster to a position of prominence in a major Southern city, and he took full advantage. In addition to writing a few essays for the *Maryland Journal,* he decided to follow Dr. Moyes's example and lecture. He wrote five "dissertations"—"History of the English Language," "Pronunciation," "Errors in Pronouncing," "Errors in the Use of Words," and "General Remarks on Education"—and ran this advertisement in the *Maryland Journal:*

> The objects of these lectures are to point out and reconcile, on established principles, the most material differences and pronunciations and use of words in the American States; to check the errors and abuses which the fashion of another country is palming upon us for propriety; to prove that some of the received rules for the construction of our language are founded on erroneous principles; to show the defects of our present mode of education; to draw the outlines of a system better adapted to our forms of government; and to detach Americans from that dependence on foreign opinions and manners, which is fatal to efforts of genius in this country.

The price of admission was two shillings for each lecture or seven and six for the series.[18]

Public lectures were one of the few forms of entertainment in eighteenth-century America, and with Webster a popular figure in Baltimore because of his singing, he filled the church where they were delivered to capacity. His lectures were vintage Websteriana, with powerful calls for national unity to be achieved through universal public education and adoption of a common American language as presented in his *Institute*.

"Nothing but the establishment of schools and some uniformity in the use of books can annihilate differences in speaking, and preserve the purity of the American tongue," he declared. "As an independent nation our honor requires us to have a system of our own, in language as well as government."[19]

Americans, Webster declared, should determine how Americans speak—not the British aristocracy:

> Let Englishmen notice that when I speak of the American yeomanry, the latter are not to be compared to the illiterate peasantry of their own country. The yeomanry of this country consists of substantial independent freeholders, masters of their own persons and lords of their own soil. . . . In the [New England] states there are public schools sufficient to instruct every man's children, and most of the children are actually benefitted by these institutions. The people of distant counties in England can hardly understand one another, so various are their dialects; but in the extent of twelve hundred miles in America, there are very few, I question whether a hundred words, except such as are used in employments wholly local, which are not universally intelligible.[20]

Webster was, of course, talking only about the native American yeomanry—not the foreign born who continued speaking foreign languages. Indeed, he warned that the flood of immigrants from all parts of Europe bore dialects that would erode the perfection of American speech:

> Nothing but the establishment of schools and some uniformity in the use of books can annihilate differences of speaking and preserve the purity of the American tongue.
>
> Now is the time, and this the country, in which we may expect success, in attempting changes favorable to language, science and government. . . . Let us then seize the present moment, and establish a *national* language, as well as a national government. Let us remember that there is a certain respect due to the opinions of other nations. As an independent people, our reputation abroad demands that, in all things, we should be *federal*; be *national*; for if we do not respect *ourselves*, we may be assured that *other nations* will not respect us. In short, let it be impressed upon the mind of every American, that to neglect the means of commanding respect abroad, is treason against the character and dignity of a brave, independent people.[21]

The audience rose as one and roared its approval. His talk earned widespread coverage by the press—both in Baltimore and elsewhere. At twenty-eight, Webster was certain that he had at last arrived on the national scene as a political philosopher whose views the nation's leaders would respect.

"The Lectures have recd so much applause," Webster wrote excitedly in his diary, "that I am induced to revise and continue reading them in other towns."[22]

He celebrated his triumph in mundane fashion the following day at the decidedly un-Calvinistic racetrack. To his delight, he had discovered that "Horse-Races in these [Southern] States, every spring & autumn, are holidays; like the Election & Thanksgiving in Connecticut. 7 horses enter the lists, 5 run 3 four mile heats. The Brilliant wins the purse £75."[23]

3

WITH STATE LEGISLATURES RECONVENING throughout the South, Webster prepared to return to the road in November to pursue his quest for copyright legislation. Virginia had failed to act despite earlier assurances from the legislators in Alexandria. A few days before his departure he received a warm, complimentary message from the quartermaster general of the United States, Timothy Pickering, in Philadelphia—the same Pickering who had been so taken with the speller two years earlier that he had urged his wife to use the book to instruct their son. The letter initiated a close, lifelong friendship.

Philadelphia Oct. 19. 1785

Sir,

Some time since I met with the two first parts of your grammatical institute of the English language; and was so well pleased with the plan & execution, that I wished to have them introduced universally into the schools of America. Being a subscriber to the funds for supporting the Episcopal Academy lately established here, I took the liberty to recommend your institute. . . . I was pleased to see the spelling book and grammar in separate volumes.

After noting that his own children had learned to read using the speller, Pickering suggested, "If business should lead you to Philadelphia, I shall be happy to see you."[24]

Webster was delighted, answering by return that he was "honoured by your attention to my publications." Never one to refuse an invitation, he solicited Pickering's aid in preparing the way for a visit to Philadelphia as the first itinerant American lecturer:

I hope to be there by the first of December, and probably shall read my Lectures in that city. As I am the first American, who has entered on such important plans and a youth, as well as a Yankee, I shall need the countenance of Gentlemen of your established Character. In order to prepare the minds of the people for such an event, I could wish that a paragraph may be inserted in a Philadelphia paper, informing that I may be expected to read a course of Lectures on the English language some-time this winter.[25]

4

ON NOVEMBER 4, 1785, Webster left Baltimore for Richmond to press the copyright issue a second time. Knowing that a message from George Washington would force legislators to act, Webster went by way of "Gen. Washington's hospitable mansion" at Mount Vernon to obtain letters of introduction, such as the following, that Washington had promised in cor-respondence over the summer:

> To his Excy. the Governor; the Speaker of the Senate, & the Speaker of the House of delegates [of Virginia].
> Sir,
>
>   This letter will be handed to you by Mr. Webster whom I beg leave to introduce to your acquaintance. — He is author of a Grammatical Insti-tute of the English language — to which there are very honorable testi-monials of its excellence & usefulness. — The work must speak for itself; & he, better than I can explain his wishes.
>
>   I am & c.
>
>   G. Washington.[26]

Although less than overwhelmed by its tone, Webster hid his disap-pointment and spent the rest of the day and evening in conversation with Washington and his family. At dinner, the general said he planned writing to Scotland to find a secretary who could do double duty as tutor to Mrs. Washington's three grandchildren.[27] Webster bristled at the idea, asking how European nations would react if, after "the exhibitions of great talents and achievements in the War for Independence, the Washingtons, of all people, turned to Europe for a tutor to teach the rudiments of learning to their grandchildren."

"What shall I do?" asked Washington, obviously taken aback. "There is no person to be obtained here for my purposes."

Webster insisted that excellent candidates could be found at any of the Northern colleges, and after dinner, as the two were walking in the hall, Washington said, "Sir, I have been thinking of what you said in regard to a Secretary. I have indeed a letter partly prepared to send to Scotland on this subject, but if you can recommend to me a person who will answer my views, I will lay aside my letter." Webster said he had no name in mind, but promised to write to friends in the North to find suitable candidates.[28]

Webster left the next morning for Richmond, stopping at Alexandria to meet with the principal of the academy there. In Richmond, his letter from Washington opened the door to the governor's mansion, where he dined with the governor and speaker of the house, who in turn invited Webster to deliver his lectures in the Capitol. Webster appeared in the elegant chamber of the House of Delegates, where "about 30 respectable Gentlemen" listened "politely," though less enthusiastically, apparently, than the Baltimore audience.

Webster met with James Madison, who greeted the New Englander warmly and recalled their previous meeting and subsequent correspondence with enthusiasm. He "spoke with praise of [the] contents" of the *Sketches,* which Washington had shown him and which he had studied carefully. Madison's newfound enthusiasm combined with Washington's letter to win passage of copyright legislation.

Webster left Richmond and visited the state's other principal cities. He found Petersburg "unhealthy"—perhaps because his lecture drew so few listeners. He thought Williamsburg "a pleasant city" but in a state of decay. After meeting the faculty and lecturing at the College of William and Mary, he concluded, "The Virginians have much pride, little money on hand, great contempt for Northern people, & amazing fondness for Dissipation. They do not understand grammar. . . . There is not any free school in Virginia at present, Novr 1785. The College at Williamsburg is well endowed & pretty respectable; one Academy at Prince Edward & one at Alexandria are most of the schools in the State. The education is very indifferent. Plays, horse-races & games are almost the sole objects of pursuit."[29]

Webster returned to Alexandria and read his lectures "to a larger audience." Filled with a growing sense that success was nearly at hand, he returned to his lodgings and wrote a letter of heartfelt gratitude to General Washington, remembering, at the same time, Washington's need for a tutor for his stepgrandchildren:

Alexandria, December 16, 1785.

Sir,

I have just returned from Richmond where I was happy enough to succeed in my application to the legislature. For this success I acknowledge myself indebted . . . to your politeness.

Should the same success attend me in the states of Delaware and New York, my whole plan will be accomplished; and if on my return to the northern states I find myself in tolerably easy circumstances, I propose to sit down and devote my attention to literary pursuits. This has long been my plan, and to this I direct all my views. Within a few days past a new idea has struck me and made so great an impression on my mind that I have determined to write you on the subject.

I have thought, Sir, that it might be possible for me to answer your views in the superintendence of your children's education and at the same time to pursue my own designs. Could these two points be reconciled, Mount Vernon might furnish an agreeable philosophical retreat. The particular motive which has influenced me to mention this is that a part of my plan would probably be a work in the execution of which I should have the occasion for letters and other papers in your possession. At any rate I should want many articles of intelligence which I could not obtain in any way so well as by the assistance of your letters.

If your wishes could be gratified in a person of my character and abilities, I should expect no compensation for any services but your table and other domestic conveniences. . . .

If any material objection should at once oppose itself to this idea, a line from you, Sir, will satisfy me. If, on the other hand, the plan should strike your mind favourably, I should wish for a more particular explanation before I proceed on my journey, as I must, within five or six days.

At any rate, no person can be more ready to render you any services in his power, than, Sir, Your most obliged, most obedient, and very humble Servant,

Noah Webster, Jun.

P.S. I have been repeatedly solicited to permit the *Sketches of American Policy* to be retailed in the public papers. I have hitherto declined, partly on account of some exceptionable passages. If, Sir, some extracts from the pamphlet can have any influence in harmonizing the views of the citizens of the different states, I am willing to see them made and published. But I have no copy, and there is none in the State but that in your possession. If you will mark such passages as you deem most useful and send the pamphlet . . . to me . . . it shall be returned as soon as convenient.

N.W.[30]

Washington marked passages of the *Sketches* he believed should be published in the national press and sent his copy back to Webster, along with a letter saying that, in addition to educating the grandchildren, a tutor at Mount Vernon would also have to serve as a full-time secretary to the general. Webster answered immediately, with a frank admission that "I have no idea of continuing single for any long period . . . my feelings forbid it." Moreover, he added, "I wish to enjoy life, but books & business will ever be my principal pleasure. I must write—it is a happiness I cannot sacrifice. . . . The education of three children would not interfere with my pursuits . . . [but] if your business requires a man's whole attention & will require it for years, I am not the person."[31]

Webster returned to Baltimore and sailed to the state capital at Annapolis, where the legislature was about to reconvene. He arrived "precisely at 12 oclock PM," according to his diary. "Enter Annapolis & the New Year, at the same time."

By January 4, Webster had met the governor, attended a dance, met "a brilliant circle of ladies," and concluded that Annapolis was "a pleasant city . . . more elegant houses in proportion than in any town in America."[32]

On January 3, an article in the *Maryland Journal* praised him, his lectures, and the *Institute,* and urged favorable action by the legislature. Two days later, the House of Delegates approved Webster's copyright legislation and invited Webster to read his lectures in the State House—which he began to do that afternoon "to about 30 respectable people." He finished his lectures on the fifth and dined with the governor and a group of state senators on the following day before returning to Baltimore on the tenth. The *Maryland Gazette* featured a flood of letters from senators who had attended his lectures. One wrote: "The elegance of his style, the energy of his reasoning, his profound knowledge of the subject, and especially the candour and independent spirit with which he delivers his sentiments, are well calculated for a reform [of the English language]. Great Britain will yet be indebted to America for the last improvement in the language."[33] The tidal wave of praise swept beyond Baltimore to Philadelphia, New York, and Boston, which not only publicized Webster's *Institute,* but reprinted his *Sketches* and lifted him onto the dais of national leadership.

In ten days, the clever Yankee peddler had obtained copyright legislation to protect his books in Maryland, earned about three hundred shillings ($40–50) from his lectures, arranged for Baltimore's major bookseller to stock his books and for the academy to use them, became an intimate of the governor of Maryland and ten state senators and assemblymen, and achieved national prominence. Webster had turned twenty-seven only three months earlier.

On the return to Baltimore, he stopped at Frederick, Maryland, to deliver another lecture and place his books with the local minister. His horse took "a fright" on the road back to Baltimore and fell, injuring Webster's leg and rendering him "quite lame," according to his diary. He eased the pain in his own, peculiar way—an "evening with the Ladies," telling them "pretty stories."[34]

5

ON JANUARY 30, 1786, Webster left for Dover, Delaware, to repeat his brilliant Annapolis performance. He arrived on February 1 and presented his petition to the Assembly.

"Among all modes of acquiring property, or exclusive ownership," said Webster, "the act or operation of *creating* or *making* seems to have the first claim. If anything can justly give a man an exclusive right to the occupancy and enjoyment of a thing it must be that he *made* it. The right of a farmer and mechanic to the exclusive enjoyment and right of disposal of what they *make* or *produce* is never questioned. What, then, can make a difference between the produce of *muscular strength* and the produce of the *intellect?*"[35] Delaware summarily granted his petition on the first reading, and Webster rode off for Wilmington, the state's largest city. The trustees of the academy there agreed to adopt the *Institute* and invited Webster to use the school for his lectures. He spoke "to a crouded audience, whose applause is flattering. More taste for science in these States than below."[36]

From Dover, Webster set off for Philadelphia, the altar of national prominence, where endorsement of his books and his new, American language would be essential to their long-term success. His first priority was to meet Col. Timothy Pickering, the Harvard graduate, whom Webster called "one of the best of men."[37] In an instant, they were old friends. A man of his word, Pickering had arranged for Webster to meet the most prestigious citizens of the community: the legendary physician Benjamin Rush; the United States attorney general, Andrew Bradford; the president of the College of Philadelphia, John Ewing; and the revered national hero Benjamin Franklin. It was Franklin who had obtained French recognition of American independence, along with the military and financial aid that doomed British hopes for victory in the Revolutionary War.

The ostensible reason for Webster's meeting Franklin was the latter's position as president of the board of trustees of the College of Philadelphia. Webster would need his permission—indeed, blessing—to present his lectures at the college. He received both, and despite the huge difference in their ages, the two began a warm, affecting friendship that added enormous joy to Franklin's few remaining years. Webster had been profoundly interested in science since he had first studied Newton's *Principia* at Yale. He admired all scientists, but none more than the great Dr. Franklin, an American scientist of Olympian stature who had earned the Royal Society's Copley Medal and honorary degrees from Yale, Harvard, Edinburgh, and Oxford for his pioneering work in electricity and other scientific areas.

Webster returned again and again to Franklin's home to be in the great man's presence. Already eighty, Franklin had only four more years to live, but he would use them in his typically productive style. He found his meeting with young Webster particularly fortuitous because of his lifelong interest in universal public education and his search for simplified methods to teach literacy.

Ironically Franklin, like Webster, had earned some fame and fortune with a spelling book. For it was Franklin who had obtained the first, exclusive rights to print Dilworth's *New Guide to the English Tongue*[38] in the United States—the very book that Webster was now displacing in American classrooms with his *Institute*. Dilworth's was first published in England in 1740, and Franklin, then publisher of the *Philadelphia Gazette,* obtained rights to it in America for seven years. Franklin, who accumulated handsome profits by the time his rights expired, had been responsible for establishing the monopoly in classrooms for Dilworth's speller that Webster now sought for his own.

Benjamin Franklin, a close friend and mentor of Noah Webster, developed the first spelling reforms in the United States and enthusiastically encouraged Webster to perfect his Americanization of the English language. (Library of Congress.)

Unlike Webster, Franklin had almost no formal education. He was the consummate autodidact—the symbol of the quintessential self-made American in a nation top-heavy with formally educated leaders. He had loathed school as a child, and except for a year at Boston Latin when he was eight and a year of private tutoring in writing and arithmetic, he had educated himself. Having suffered the deficiencies of public education, he developed an obsessive interest in its improvement and directed much of his printing and publishing to that end. He published a newspaper, the *Philadelphia Gazette,* and an array of classical literature. He wrote and published *Poor Richard's Almanac,* which he "considered a proper vehicle for conveying instruction among the common people."[39] In 1731, he founded the Library Company of Philadelphia, America's first subscription library, designed "to render the benefit from books more common."[40]

In 1749, Franklin raised the hackles of the education community with his *Proposals Relating to the Education of Youth in Pennsylvania,* which advocated universal public education at a time when formal academic and college education was reserved for the sons of the elite.[41] Two years later, he founded the Public Academy in the city of Philadelphia. By the time Webster met him, "Franklin's academy" had expanded and changed its name to the College of Philadelphia, although it was called "the university" in anticipation of a new charter that would name it the University of Pennsylvania in 1791.

As a publisher of primers and spelling books and then as an educator, Franklin, like Webster, had searched for ways to make it easier to learn to read and write. To that end, he developed a phonetic alphabet, with a character for every sound, which he published in 1768 as a *Scheme for a New Alphabet and a Reformed Mode of Spelling.* Fascinated by Webster's work in the same area, Franklin suggested collaborating to improve English spelling. He explained his own scheme to the young teacher during their frequent conversations, which continued late into the night.

"This indefatigable gentleman," said Webster, "amidst all his other employments, public and private, has compiled a Dictionary on his scheme of a reform, and procured types to be cast for printing it. He thinks himself too old to pursue the plan; but has honored me with the offer of the manuscript and types, and expressed a strong desire that I should take these types & prosecute the plan."[42]

Franklin's system of spelling added six new characters to twenty-two familiar ones, in the standard alphabet, along with a host of digraphs, or compound letters. He eliminated *c, w, y,* and *j.* He added a modified *a,* representing the drawl in *ball;* a modified *u,* with an extended descender (the letter was virtually an upside-down *h*) for the clipped sound of the *u* in *unto;* an overlapping *s* and *i* (essentially an *s* with a vertical slash) for the *sh* sound; a *y* with a curled tail for the *ng* sound; a modified *h,* with an extended right descender, for the short *th* sound, as in *thin;* and another modified *h,* with a wavy appendage at the top, for the long *th* sound in words such as *thy.*[43]

Although flattered by the chance to collaborate with the great Franklin, Webster believed "that any scheme for introducing a new alphabet or new characters is & will be impracticable."[44] Webster favored spelling rather than alphabet reforms, and in his spare moments during his journey to the

South, he had changed many spellings for the next edition of his speller. His speller had already respelled words like *musick* and *publick* — as *music* and *public*. For the next edition, he decided to simplify the spelling of *colour, honour, humour,* and similar words ending in *-our* by eliminating the *u*. He was also considering reversing the *r* and *e* at the end of such words as *centre, sceptre,* and *theatre,* as well as dropping double consonants that had no effect on pronunciations, as in *traveller* and *waggon*.

Nevertheless, Webster realized that Franklin's collaboration would mean the endorsement of America's greatest thinker, a certified genius whose name would ensure universal embrace of the speller and its spelling reforms. Webster decided to incorporate some of Franklin's reforms in the next edition of his speller. Franklin was elated. He began mentoring Webster, urging him to enlarge the scope of the *Institute* to include more history, geography, and literature. He also suggested that Webster broaden the scope of his publishing enterprise to include works that would encourage adult education — perhaps with an almanac and works on history and geography geared to adult interests. In addition to his notes for a phonetic alphabet, Franklin gave Webster "free access to his library" and immediately plucked a two-volume set from its shelves to lend Webster — James Elphinston's *Principles of English Grammar,* a bizarre approach to grammar then in use in England, containing the first hints of an equally bizarre phonetic system of spelling that Elphinston was developing.[45]

Webster sent Franklin a note of thanks marked by a reverence shown not even to General Washington, who was no less a hero of his, but in a far different way. Washington stood in Webster's pantheon of political and military leaders; Franklin stood with Newton among the great minds of the ages. His note to Franklin was the first in a warm and frequent correspondence between the two:

> Mr. Webster presents his respects to his Excellency President Franklin and begs him to peruse the enclosed papers and correct any mistake in the principles. It is designed to collect some American pieces upon the discovery, history, war, geography, economy, commerce, government &c. of this country and add them to the third part of the *Institute,* in order to call the minds of our youth from ancient fables and modern foreign events, and fix them upon objects immediately interesting in this country. A selection for this purpose should be judicious, and the compiler feels his need of assistance in the undertaking. He will do himself the honor to call in a few days and take the advice of his Excellency, whose library may also be of service. The bearer will return the first volume of Elphinstone's [*sic*] *Principles.*[46]

Webster could not have composed a more charming message to the old man. It cemented Franklin's affection for him.

Webster, however, harbored many doubts about alphabet and spelling reforms and they grew in the years that followed. Five years later, he wrote:

The question now occurs: ought the Americans to retain these faults which produce innumerable inconveniences in the acquisition and use of the language, or ought they at once to reform these abuses, and introduce order and regularity into the orthography of the AMERICAN TONGUE? . . . Several attempts were formerly made in England to rectify the orthography of the language. But I apprehend their schemes failed of success rather on account of their intrinsic difficulties than on account of any necessary impracticality of a reform. It was proposed, in most of these schemes, not merely to throw out superfluous and silent letters, but to introduce a number of new characters.

Webster cited as a prime example James Elphinston's *Inglish Orthography Eppittomized and Propriety's Pocket Diccionaary*—a work that drew nothing but ridicule, with spellings such as *dhe* for *the, hwich* for *which, singuel* for *single, poartion* for *portion,* and *occazzion* for *occasion.* "Any attempt on such a plan," Webster said, "must undoubtedly prove unsuccessful."[47]

6

THE PICKERINGS INVITED WEBSTER to tea and dinner several times a week during his month in Philadelphia, to meet Philadelphia's first families—the Biddles, the Boudinots, the Austins, and others who either governed or controlled the governance of America. Webster formed close friendships with Dr. Benjamin Rush, who was professor of chemistry at the university, and his friend David Rittenhouse, the university's great astronomer and expert on optics, who had invented the collimating telescope and the use of crosshairs (he used spiderwebs) for accurate sighting.[48] In addition to his ideas on education, Webster's interest in Newtonian physics and optics immediately won over the two scientists, with whom he took tea and dined several times during his stay in Philadelphia.

After signing the Declaration of Independence, Rush had embarked on "a one-man crusade to remake America,"[49] and he eagerly embraced Webster's ideas on education. "The business of education," said Rush, "has acquired a new complexion by the independence of our country. The form of government we have assumed, has created a new class of duties to every American. It becomes us, therefore, to examine our former habits upon this subject, and in laying foundations for nurseries of wise and good men to adapt our modes of teaching to the peculiar form of our government."[50]

Rush would later collaborate with Webster in a number of crusades to "remake America," including abolition of slavery and—just as ambitious for the times—the abolition of epidemic diseases.

Webster's insatiable appetite for scientific knowledge lured him continually to the sightless Dr. Moyes's popular lectures on scientific phenomena. To his delight, Webster also met and made a point of befriending Jean-Pierre-François Blanchard, the French aeronaut who had made the first balloon ascent two years earlier and then made the first balloon crossing of the English Channel. Blanchard had also invented and used a parachute and was in Philadelphia to make the first manned balloon ascents in America. As with the other personages he met, Webster dined with Blanchard several times during his month in Philadelphia.

As always, Webster also sought out the company of young women, but found that "the Ladies [in Philadelphia] will not dance with strangers, if they can avoid it—polite indeed. People in high life suppose they have a right to dispense with the rules of civility."[51]

On February 27, only two weeks after Webster's arrival in Philadelphia, Pickering introduced him to one of the young man's literary heroes—"Mr. T. Paine, Common Sense." At the time, Paine was living quietly in Philadelphia, working on a design for an iron bridge without piers that he would later try to market in England. Webster noted in his diary: "examined his plan of a bridge, supported by angles solely, executed in miniature, with success."[52]

Webster began his lectures in University Hall the following day, "to an audience of about 100 reputable characters." They included Philadelphia's most notable personages, whose number and enthusiasm grew each night, attendance reaching 150 on the evening of his last lecture, which they greeted "with great applause."[53]

On March 15, Webster read a lecture to three hundred listeners and raised "a handsome sum" for the benefit of Benjamin Franklin's favorite project, his own Pennsylvania Hospital. For his effort, Webster won the praises and warm approval of Philadelphia's leading families as well as Franklin himself.[54] By now the scope of his lectures had expanded to include American history and manners, as well as language. Though he still punctuated his talks with nationalistic fervor, he also laced them with humor and anecdotes gleaned from American heroes such as Washington, with whom he could now claim intimate acquaintance.

At a dinner at Colonel Pickering's, Webster met the great American portraitist Charles Willson Peale, who had just opened America's first museum, at the exhibit hall of Franklin's American Philosophical Society. Peale took Webster and Pickering to the new exhibit, which included not only the collection of his portraits but also some startling mastodon bones and an impressive collection of preserved birds, snakes, fish, fossils, insects, minerals, and plants from around the world. Peale intrigued Webster with a new technique of "moving pictures" that combined projections of glass transparencies with sound and lighting effects.

Webster's ties to Philadelphia's most prominent men assured quick passage of copyright legislation in Pennsylvania, which was the last of the thirteen states of the Confederation to enact such legislation. Passage there assured protection of his and other authors' works everywhere in the nation. Authors hailed Webster as the father of America's copyright laws. The laws were not uniform by any means, but they were on the books, with specific penalties for pirating an author's works, ranging from £1 to £2,000 or equal to as much as twice the value of all pirated copies printed. The length of time an author retained exclusive rights to his works varied, with four states—New Hampshire, Massachusetts, Rhode Island, and Virginia—limiting it to either twenty or twenty-one years, with no renewal. The other states granted the author exclusive rights for fourteen years, with the right to renew for another fourteen years if he survived the first term. Later in life, Webster would win enormous improvements in copyright legislation, but in the meantime, the *Institute* was safe from piracy.

"In my journeys to effect this object," he wrote, "I expended nearly a year of time. Of my expenses in money I have no account, but it is a satisfaction that a liberal statute for securing to authors the fruit of their labor has been obtained."[55]

Webster's battle for copyright protection achieved a twofold victory, for at the same time, he had made acquaintances and often won the lasting friendships of the nation's most influential figures. In so doing, he moved to the center of national influence and closer to his goal of unifying the American people by teaching them to read, write, and speak a uniform American language, with his textbooks as the universal medium of instruction.

On Sunday, March 19, Webster entertained Philadelphia society at his quarters by way of reciprocation and "to bid my friends adieux." Before leaving, however, he agreed to adopt Pickering's suggestions for improving the *Institute* by developing abridged, elementary versions of the speller, grammar, and reader for five-year-olds. Pickering assumed the responsibility of publishing Webster's abridged speller, which he called *The New-England Primer*—the name borne by the speller that had preceded Dilworth's as the most widely used American speller in the seventeenth and early-eighteenth centuries.

7

HAVING SECURED COPYRIGHTS and ensured the use of his books in schools in South Carolina, Virginia, Maryland, Delaware, and Pennsylvania, Webster left Philadelphia for Princeton, New Jersey. There, he dined with his old friend Samuel Stanhope Smith, the College of New Jersey professor who had contributed to the improvement of the speller and whose letter of endorsement helped obtain copyright legislation in New Jersey. To his chagrin, Webster found the college library and beautiful Nassau Hall "almost ruined by the [British] soldiers." Only sixteen students showed up for his first lecture, and he abandoned the series and moved on to New York, where Congress was meeting.

Webster again met with the powerful Col. Aaron Burr Jr. and the equally powerful New York congressman James Duane, who arranged a meeting with the mayor and secured City Hall for Webster's lectures. As he had in Philadelphia, Webster worked day and night, enriching his social life and building a network of powerful friends and allies to support his scheme of a uniform system of national education with the *Institute* at its core. He attended theater, went to teas, and appeared at important exhibits, including one at Columbia College, where he heard "8 dull speakers" but secured the friendship of Dr. William Samuel Johnson, the founding president.

He made certain to meet his share of "the Ladies" and visited his mother's cousin Josiah Steele, whom he invited to his lectures at City Hall. The lectures drew "a very polite audience of 100," including Columbia's Dr. Johnson and many members of the Continental Congress. One of the latter was Dr. David Ramsay, the scholarly Revolutionary War field surgeon from South Carolina, who was acting president of Congress during John Hancock's illness.[56] An author himself, Ramsay immediately became an enthusiastic supporter of Webster's spelling reforms and new, American language. Ramsay urged Congress to pass a resolution recommending that all books printed in America conform to Webster's American spellings. He urged Congress to declare English a foreign tongue. But before the Continental Congress would ever consider the proposal, it voted its own permanent dissolution, in favor of a new, bicameral congress under a new constitution.

Webster's lectures, however, drew ever larger audiences—often two hundred or more of New York's most celebrated personalities. The prospect of his visit to schools in New York was enough to assure awe—and the immediate adoption of his *Institute*.

Webster did not lack for critics, but his defenders far outnumbered them. "It is strange," the editor of New York's powerful *Daily Advertiser* chastised them in one editorial,

> that curiosity should be so dormant and partial to an American in his own country. The lectures of Mr. Webster, although of much public and private utility, do not seem to meet the encouragement in this city they so evidently deserve. What a pity it is he has all his faculties about him! if he had glass eyes or wooden arms, he would not fail of meeting the most unbounded encouragement—men, women and children all would go to see the man with glass eyes and wooden arms—if he were to advertise that he would go into a quart bottle or dance a hornpipe upon the slackwire, his company would be numberless. Alas! what a misfortune it is to be endowed with genius! A man may trudge on through the common beaten track of humanity without an idea above the most vulgar . . . but if he should chance to be cursed with genius,

and competent to instruct his fellow citizens he may pine in want and die in obscurity. The ignorant brute in human shape, whose narrow soul is circumscribed by a purse, contemptuously shakes his dross at the man of science and laughs at his refinement. When we recollect what a crowd attended the lectures of Dr. Moyes [the sightless Scotsman whose lectures Webster so enjoyed in Baltimore and Philadelphia], altho' unimportant to the far greater part of the audience, and a foreigner besides, we cannot but think it a great reproach upon the taste of our ladies and gentlemen, to neglect the truly valuable LECTURES OF MR. WEBSTER.[57]

8

ALWAYS EAGER TO WITNESS THE EXTRAORDINARY, Webster went to the waxworks during his visit to New York, attended a duel—one dueler died of his wounds—and breakfasted at Dr. Ramsay's with a Seneca Indian chief, who had come with five other Indians "on business to Congress."

"They behave with great civility," Webster reported, "& took tea and coffee with decency & some appearance of breeding. When they left the house they shook hands with men & women, without any bow, wearing strong marks of native independence & dignity."[58]

With his property protected by copyright, Webster left for a whirlwind tour of upstate New York, visiting schools in Peeks Kill, Hudson, Albany, and Schenectady and giving lectures wherever he could attract a large enough paying audience. In Hudson, a wealthy family whose children Webster had taught in Sharon gave him, as a token of gratitude, an option in the Susquehanna Company, which had developed the Wyoming Valley of Pennsylvania and in which his father had already invested.

His Albany lecture the next day drew little applause because, as he put it, "The Dutch have no taste for the English language." The promise of meeting several ladies lured him to dinner at the huge Van Rensselaer estate, where he found "four attractive young ladies"—along with the astounding "Miss Ten Broeck . . . a ten thousand pounder."[59]

Webster quickly returned to his lectures, and by the end of May left Albany for another week in New York, where he checked on sales of his *Institute*. To his shock, he found that one bookseller priced his speller too high and kept supplies "in the box in a back room" instead of displaying them in the store. Infuriated, he threatened to cut off supplies to the bookseller and sent an angry letter to Hudson & Goodwin, his printers in Hartford. "It is not at all strange that the Institute sells so slowly when we find what price is set by the booksellers," he wrote. "Mr. Hodge sells both parts at 18 [shillings New] York money per dozen."[60] (Each state printed its own currency.)

Webster had by then grown fairly sophisticated in the ways of publishing. He knew that proper pricing was the key to marketing: a book priced too high made it unattractive to the public, while a book priced too low was unprofitable for both the bookseller and printer. He told Hodge to lower his prices and urged Hudson & Goodwin to give Hodge a contract guaranteeing him a purchase price of fourteen shillings and setting the maximum retail price at fifteen or sixteen shillings. "They will sell very well at 15 or 16 [shillings New] York currency—At any rate please to see them exposed to sale & for a lower price—They are much in estimation here & will soon be in general use if properly managed."[61]

The incident proved to him how little control his printers had over marketing and how involved he would have to remain in the sale and promotion of his works. He also began questioning whether Hudson & Goodwin's monopoly had not become counterproductive to book sales. With orders for the *Institute* pouring in from the entire country, any failure of the printer to meet demand for the *Institute* would force potential buyers of Webster's books to stock other spellers—and the success of the *Institute* was luring a growing number of imitators into the market.

Before he left for Hartford, friends in New York introduced him to Dartmouth College president John Wheelock,[62] who agreed to promote Webster's *Institute* in the middle townships of New Hampshire. By then, Webster had completed his work on spelling reform and sent it to Benjamin Franklin. Webster had judiciously incorporated some of Franklin's alphabet reforms in the work.

New York, May 24th, 1786

Dear Sir,

When I was in Philadelphia, I had the honor of hearing your Excellency's opinion upon the idea of reforming the English alphabet. I had repeatedly revolved in my mind the utility of such a plan and had arranged some ideas upon the subject, but had not ventured to hope for success in an undertaking of this kind. Your Excellency's sentiments upon the subject, backed by concurring opinion of many respectable gentlemen . . . have taught me to believe the reformation of our alphabet still practicable. I know that several attempts to effect it in England have proved fruitless; but I conceive they failed through some defect in the plans proposed or for reasons which do not exist in this country.

Enclosed is a plan for the purpose of reducing the orthography of the language to perfect regularity . . . and it is submitted to your Excellency for adoption, amendment, or rejection.

I am requested to lay the plan before your Excellency, and by a gentleman [Dr. David Ramsay] whose character in public life and particularly in the chair of Congress will give his opinion great weight in this country. Should this or any other plan be adopted, it is desired that your Excellency would lay it before Congress for their critical consideration. . . .

I have the honor to be, with the highest respect, your Excellency's most obedient, most humble servant.

Noah Webster, Jun.

P.S. It would be esteemed a singular favor if your Excellency would publicly recommend the *Institute;* it would facilitate its introduction and confer a particular obligation on me.

I must also beg permission to inscribe my lectures to your Excellency when I publish them, as it is probable I may do within a few months.[63]

Thinking it would show greater respect, Webster sent the letter to his friend Colonel Pickering, to hand-deliver it personally to Franklin. In addition, he asked Pickering to examine the spelling reforms himself and add any improvements he thought appropriate. Webster also hoped that the well-connected Pickering would serve as spokesman in Philadelphia for the new, uniform American language and system of universal public education.

New York, May 25, 1786

Sir,

Enclosed is a letter to Dr. Franklin covering the plan of a reformed alphabet. I am in some haste, preparing for a journey eastward, and consequently have not time to be very explicit. You will be so kind as to wait on his Excellency and will then have an opportunity of examining the plan. I wish, Sir, you would continue your freedom in making remarks and suggesting new ideas.

The advantages expected from a reformation of the alphabet are:

1st. It will render acquisition of the language easy both for natives and foreigners. All the trouble of learning to *spell* will be saved.

2. When no character has more sounds than one, every man, woman, and child who knows his alphabet can spell words, even by the sound, without ever seeing them.

3. Pronunciation must necessarily be uniform.

4. The orthography of the language will be fixed.

5. The necessity of encouraging printing in this country and of manufacturing all our own books is a political advantage, obvious and immense.

6. A national language is a national tie, and what country wants it more than America?[64]

The next morning, Noah Webster set off on the journey home to Hartford, after an absence of thirteen months. He dined with his friend Joel Barlow the evening of his arrival and rode to Westdivision the following morning for a joyful, tear-filled reunion with his parents, family, and childhood friends and neighbors.

Webster spent the next six months—almost the rest of 1786—basking in the love, admiration, and praise of his family and friends. "There is no doubt," he said, "that I shall be able to effect a uniformity of language &

education throughout the continent," he confidently assured them all.[65] Webster looked forward eagerly to displaying his new, self-assured persona as an eminent lecturer at home in Hartford for the first time.

To his consternation, however, vengeful former delegates to the Middletown Convention incited a mob of farmers with no money to pay the admission fee to hurl a barrage of stones through the windows of the North Meeting House during the lecture.

"In the year 1786, there are people in Hartford so illiberal," Webster retorted angrily, "that they will not permit public lectures to be read in a church because they cannot be admitted without paying two shillings! [Webster actually charged three.] The General Assembly to whom I presented tickets, attended. They ought at least to have been secured from the insults of wealthy farmers."[66]

Aside from what he interpreted as a personal affront, Webster was clearly beginning to lose patience with farmers who complained about the declining value of their money but refused to grant Congress powers to tax and to borrow funds to improve the national economy. After little more than two weeks, Webster traveled to Yale College, in New Haven—and once again, a chance to present his lectures to a group of old friends and acquaintances. They received his talks *"avec éclat,"* as he put it. Webster delivered six lectures to an audience "of the best families in town,"[67] including Judge Roger Sherman, the Revolutionary War patriot, signatory of the Declaration of Independence, and treasurer and benefactor of Yale College.

Webster's classmate Josiah Meigs was also there—by then he had founded and was editor of the *New Haven Gazette,* which said that Webster's lectures "command the attention and excite the speculations of our politicians as well as of the literati."[68] Yale president Stiles was no less impressed by his former pupil. He attended the entire lecture series and, on July 1, noted in his diary, "I attended Mr. Websters 6th & last Lecture. He took his leave of me this Morning. He was of the first Class of Pupils whom I instructed at my Accession the Presidency 1778. From him I learn."[69]

After a brief visit with his parents over July 4, Webster set off on a four-month tour that took him to virtually every city of any size in Massachusetts, New Hampshire, Rhode Island, and Connecticut. He met once again with Isaiah Thomas, the Worcester publisher, dined with Massachusetts governor James Bowdoin, attended commencement exercises at Harvard, and had a joyful reunion in Portsmouth, New Hampshire, with the Reverend Joseph Buckminster, his old Yale tutor.

Unlike his tour through the middle and Southern states, the New England trip was a return to old acquaintances and friends. As usual, he dined with every notable at every stop, traveling by carriage wherever possible. Carriage rides gave him an opportunity to sell books and his new "American language." He read his lectures in Newport, Rhode Island; New London and Norwich, Connecticut; in Salem, Marblehead, Newburyport, Newtown,

and Boston, Massachusetts; and in Portsmouth, New Hampshire. He delivered the series twice in Boston, the first time at a schoolhouse,[70] the second time at Faneuil Hall before an audience that included the Revolutionary War hero Samuel Adams.

By selling tickets to his lectures through bookstores, Webster ensured
the sale of his *Institute* as well, and everywhere he traveled in New England,
he reserved time to "do business," as he put it, selling his books to every
bookstore and every schoolmaster and educator he could find. By the end
of his trip, his *Institute* was in use in every school in New England, and
thanks to his lectures and the publicity they engendered, his name had become a household word.

He also began to work on a new edition of his speller, incorporating
many of the spelling reforms he had described earlier to Franklin. In mid-
June he received a warm and enthusiastic letter from Franklin:

> I think the Reformation not only necessary but practicable. But have so
> much to say to you on the Subject, that I wish to see and confer with
> you upon it, as that would save much Time and Writing. . . . Our Ideas
> are so nearly similar, that I make no doubt of our easily agreeing on the
> Plan, and you may depend on the best Support I may be able to give it
> as Part of your Institute, of which I wish you would bring with you a
> compleat copy. . . . Hoping to have soon the Pleasure of seeing you, I do
> not enlarge, but am, with sincere Esteem
>
>   Sir,
>   Your most obedient
>   & most humble servant.
>   B. Franklin[71]

Webster replied immediately:

>   New Haven June 23rd, 1786
> Sir,
>   The letter which your Excellency has done me the honor to address
> me at New York was yesterday received at this place.
>   I am happy that a plan of reforming our Alphabet is so well received
> by a gentleman who thoroughly understands the subject; and am more
> and more convinced from the present sentiments of the Americans that
> a judicious attempt to introduce it needs but the support of a few emi-
> nent characters to be carried into effect.

Webster said he was about to leave for a series of lectures in Boston and
Portsmouth and would come to Philadelphia in early fall unless Franklin
wanted him to cancel the lectures and come sooner.[72]

Franklin answered, encouraging Webster to continue his lectures:

> I think with you that your Lecturing on the Language will be of great
> Use in preparing the Minds of People for the Improvements proposed,

and therefore would not advise your omitting any of the Engagements you have made, for the sake of being here sooner than your Business requires, that is in September or October next. I shall then be glad to see and confer with you on the subject; being with great Esteem,

Sir,

Your most obed.

& most humble Servant

B. Franklin[73]

In addition to his correspondence with Franklin, the peripatetic Webster sent out a stream of letters while traveling, to cement relationships with all the new friends he had made in earlier stops. He also kept in touch with his printers, Hudson & Goodwin, in Hartford. Sales of the *Institute* were lagging in Boston because booksellers often refused to sell books they did not print or bind themselves. Webster decided he could no longer afford to rely exclusively on Hudson & Goodwin.

"By giving you the whole right of printing all parts," he explained, "I make all the printers & Booksellers here enemies to its progress. Much depends on Printers & Booksellers in introducing a School Book—afterwards it may rest on itself or on customs or prejudice."[74]

Hudson & Goodwin were as aware as Webster of market conditions, and finding themselves unable to meet surging national demand for his books, they agreed to relinquish to Webster all printing rights outside New England and to share their monopoly with other printers in the states where they retained the copyright. By the end of August, Hudson & Goodwin agreed to permit Boston printer Benjamin Edes to print an edition of the speller for the Boston area on a commission basis, with Webster to receive his usual royalties, equivalent to 1 percent of sales.

The possibility of multiple printers, however, caused Webster new concerns about publishing uniformity. If the *Institute* was to become the standard elementary textbook in the United States, he would have be certain that each printer published books that were identical to those published by every other printer. "In order to render . . . Edes' and your future editions alike," he wrote to Hudson & Goodwin, "it is necessary that a copy should be corrected by the one I have left with you."[75]

9

BY MID-AUGUST, discontented Massachusetts farmers were blocking country roads and staging demonstrations that slowed Webster's travels. New England's farms had grown ever smaller and poorer as their owners used up the land. Elsewhere, forward-looking farmers had produced record crops for two successive years by joining "scientific societies" and introducing such advances as crop rotation and selective livestock breeding. But the small, low-quality root crops of backcountry dirt farmers in Massachusetts left them constantly fending off bankruptcy.

In 1785, seven states printed paper money to pay for government expenses, but six other states, including Massachusetts, imposed taxes—a method that stabilized money supplies but infuriated taxpayers. By August, Massachusetts farmers had taken up arms.

"There is political ferment in this state," Webster wrote from Salem in August to his friend Colonel Pickering in Philadelphia. "Some towns are disposed for a convention to redress grievances, the principal of which are *taxes*. . . . Sutton has burned its tax bill, and another town has voted not to pay taxes."[76]

Losing patience with the protesters, Webster began to rethink the basic principle of his *Sketches*—namely, that all power be vested in the people as an indisputable right. "It is a fact, demonstrated by correct calculation," he told Pickering,

> that the people of this country drink rum and tea sufficient every year to pay the interest of the public debts—articles of living which, so far from doing them any good, injure their morals, impair health, and shorten their lives. A man has a right in a political view to make himself sick or drunk when he pleases, provided he does not injure himself or his neighbors; but when by these means he renders himself unable to fulfil the duties of society or comply with the laws of the state, very little indulgence should be granted to his vices. The best way to redress grievances is for every man when he gets sixpence, instead of purchasing a pint of rum or two ounces of tea, to deposit his pence in a desk till he has accumulated enough to answer the calls of the [tax] collector. Every man who does this sacredly redresses his own grievances.[77]

On August 15, while Webster was in Marblehead, north of Boston, angry protesters gathered at Worcester, in the middle of the state. A week later, delegates from fifty towns gathered in Hadfield, in western Massachusetts, to condemn lawyers, the high costs of justice, the tax system, and the Massachusetts Senate. They called for the state to print paper money to pay the public debt. Three days of angry speeches provoked mob violence. On August 31, armed men prevented the court from sitting at Northampton, and on September 5, another mob forced the court at Worcester to flee. The rioting spread across the state. Gen. Henry Knox, the former commander of the Revolutionary Army's artillery and a trusted aide to George Washington, warned that armed mobs numbering twelve to fifteen thousand were in Concord preparing to march on Boston. Webster, who was lecturing in Haverhill, near the New Hampshire border, was infuriated by the spreading anarchy and the failure of the state's central government to crush the mobs. He sent a letter, "On Redress of Grievances," to the *Essex Journal,* in nearby Newburyport:

Mr Printer . . . in my humble opinion, there are but two effectual methods of redressing grievances; one depends on the people as individuals, and the other on the Supreme Executiv [*sic:* Webster was already using his own phonetic spelling system] authority.

As to the first, let every person, whether farmer, mechanic, lawyer, or doctor, provide a small box, (*a small box* will be big enough) with a hole in the lid. When he receives a shilling, let him put six pence into the box, and use the other six pence in providing for his family; not rum . . . but good bread and meat. Let this box remain untouched, until the collector shall call. Then let it be opened, the tax paid, and the overplus of cash be expended on gauze, ribbands, tea and New England rum. Let the box then be put into its place again, to receive pence for the next collector. This method, Mr. Printer, will redress all grievances, without the trouble, noise and expense of town meetings, conventions and mobs.

Webster said the other method for redressing grievances was for the "Executiv" authority to crush insurrection so that "our lives and our properties should be secure under the law and constitution of the State."[78]

Webster returned to Boston to offer his services to his friend James Bowdoin, who had been elected governor the previous year. "I would fight the insurgents," he advised the governor. "The mob is headed by some desperate fellows, without property or principle. . . . The same principle which leads a man to put a bayonet to the breast of a judge, will lead him to take property where he can find it, and when the judges dare not act, where is the loser's remedy. Alas, my friends, too much liberty is no liberty at all. Giv me anything but mobs. . . . I would shoot the leader of a mob, sooner than a midnight ruffian."[79]

About five hundred insurgents wielding muskets and pitchforks marched into Springfield, led by Daniel Shays, a destitute farmer who had risen to captain during the Revolutionary War. As Webster had suggested, Bowdoin sent six hundred militiamen to protect the state Supreme Court, which was then sitting in Springfield, only twenty-five miles north of the Webster family home, in West Hartford. The militia arrived too late to thwart Shays at the court, but it was able to prevent a rebel raid on the federal arsenal that could have led to outright civil war.

With mobs roaming the Massachusetts countryside, Webster abandoned his overland itinerary and set sail along the coast to Newport, Rhode Island. He was thoroughly disillusioned by the spreading rebellion and anarchy unloosed by the weak Confederation. Webster had expected victory over British tyranny to bring contentment and peace to Americans. Instead it seemed to be producing nothing but bitter internecine disputes and threats of fratricide.

After lecturing in Newport, Webster went to the state capital, Providence, where his fury mounted as the governor told him that a convention of unelected citizens had forced the state legislature to print £100,000 in paper money. The mob had also forced the legislature to legalize barter and make it illegal for creditors to refuse payment in goods as well as paper money to settle debts.

Webster could no longer contain his anger. He feared the disorder would lead to civil war and open the nation to invasion by British troops from the north. Everywhere he looked, mobs were attempting to seize control of duly elected state governments, while the governments themselves were threatening war with one another over territorial claims in wilderness far from their population centers. Pennsylvania and Connecticut were still feuding over conflicting claims in the Wyoming Valley; New Hampshire, New York, and Massachusetts were feuding over Vermont; New York and Massachusetts each claimed territory along Lakes Ontario and Erie; and Connecticut and Massachusetts were claiming lands in faraway Ohio that Virginia claimed as its own.

Webster sent the *United States Chronicle* of Providence a letter filled with rage. "The Devil Is in You" (as it was called) earned Webster the bitter, lasting enmity not just of Tories who sought reunion with England but of all New Englanders—and indeed, Americans—who favored local rule unfettered by state or federal regulations and controls.

"Too much liberty is the worst of tyranny," Webster railed.

> . . . when all men seek to be masters, most of them will inevitably become the slaves of those who succeed. While you attempt to trade to advantage, without a *head* to combine all the States into systematic uniform measures, the world will laugh at you for fools. While merchants take and giv credit, the world will call them idiots, and laugh at their ruin. While farmers get credit, borrow money, and mortgage their farms, the world will call them fools, and laugh at their embarrassments. While all men liv beyond their income, and are harassed with duns and sheriffs, no man will pity them, or giv them relief. But when mobs and conventions oppose the courts of justice and Legislatures make paper or old horses a legal tender in all cases, the world will exclaim with one voice— *Ye are rogues, and the devil is in you!*[80]

To accuse New England's devout Christians of being in the grasp of the devil was a serious charge. Signed "Tom Thoughtful," the article appeared in newspapers throughout New England and effectively polarized voters and legislators alike, both Federalists and antifederalists—those who favored strong central government and those who favored local popular rule. The polarization, which ultimately proved essential for organizing the Constitutional Convention, gained impetus as Webster continued his relentless attacks on the disunionists. He fired another barrage when he reached New London, where Connecticut populists were also demanding that the state print money to ease cash shortages.

"Americans!" he wrote.

You talk of a scarcity of cash. Well, the only remedy is, to enable Congress to place our commerce on a footing with the trade of other nations. Foreign States have nothing to do with Massachusetts or New York. They must make treaties with *United America*, or not make them at all. And while we boast of the independence of particular states, we lose all the benefits of independence. For fear that Congress alone would abuse their powers and enrich themselves, we, like the dog in the manger, will not even enrich ourselfes. We complain of poverty, and yet *giv* the profits of our trade to foreign nations [by buying imports]. Infatuated men! We have one truth to learn—*That nothing but the absolute power of regulating our commerce, vested in some federal head,* can restore us cash, or turn the balance of trade in our favor.[81]

Webster sailed up the Thames River from New London to Norwich before returning home to Hartford on October 27. He arrived, however, deeply shaken by the spreading anarchy in Massachusetts and convinced that the democratic political views he had developed during the Revolutionary War were utterly wrong. In Hartford, antifederalists attacked him in the press as one of a group of "ambitious, tyrannical men, who are aiming at power and office at the expense of the people at large."[82]

IO

WEBSTER EARNED ENOUGH MONEY on his New England tour to pay off his debts, including his printing bill. He renegotiated his arrangement with Hudson & Goodwin. His friend Joel Barlow, who had become an attorney, drew up a new contract that freed Webster to sell the copyrights to anyone in the middle and Southern states. It left Hudson & Goodwin with the "exclusive right of printing & vending all parts of the Institute in New England and Vermont . . . for the whole term granted me by the [copyright] laws of the several states."[83] Hudson & Goodwin also had the right to sell printing rights within New England, but the firm would have to pay Webster £5 in copies of his books (ten) for every thousand copies sold of any of the three parts of the *Institute*. He was free to sell them independently, receiving, in effect, a 1 percent cash royalty on the sale of his books. It was not an uncommon arrangement for printers to pay authors in copies. Authors like Webster bore much of the responsibility for marketing their books. In so doing, they sold their own copies to every bookseller they encountered for the first time, receiving cash, and only then referring the bookseller to the printer for additional supplies.

To Webster's relief, sales of the *Institute* were now great enough to cover the costs of paper and supplies for subsequent printings, thus eliminating the need to raise cash. Webster even repaid some of his debt to his father for college tuition by giving him the Susquehanna Company option that he had received as a gift while touring upstate New York.

His debts settled, Webster turned his thoughts to earning a living. Although selling well, his books would provide him with royalties of only about £100 a year at current sales levels, and he had read his lectures to virtually every literate person in every city in America. He knew that few would come to listen to the same lectures a second time, although he believed they might have value in published form as a pamphlet for congressmen debating his plan of education. He wrote to Colonel Pickering to set the venture in motion: "I propose to print 1500 copies, large octavo, and it will make, probably, 400 pages. . . . I shall want about 80 reams of the finest *demi* (I believe they call it) which can be made. It should be equal to the best writing paper. . . . I must request you, Sir, to contract for the paper and have it made before cold weather. I expect to pay cash and at least half in hand."[84]

Although not a certainty, it seemed likely that the states would assemble in convention the following spring in Philadelphia to consider drafting a new constitution to strengthen the federal government. Representatives of only four states had attended Madison's Annapolis Convention to draft an interstate commerce agreement, but Alexander Hamilton averted failure at that meeting with a call to all states to reconvene in Philadelphia in May 1787 to discuss *all* matters necessary "to render the constitution of the Federal Government adequate to the exigencies of the Union."[85]

Recognizing the import of the convention, Webster decided to move to the center of power, Philadelphia, to have a hand in shaping the new constitution and ensure adoption of his plan for a national language and system of universal public education. Unfortunately, he was not earning enough money to support himself in a strange city. He knew he would have "to seek a living" there, and hoped the wealthy Benjamin Franklin, as chairman of the board of trustees at the College of Philadelphia, might help.

"I labor under some embarrassments which I take the liberty to mention to your excellency," he admitted in a letter to Franklin in October.

> The profits on the sale of my books, which amount now to about £100 per annum, was all appropriated to reimburse the expense I have incurred in prosecuting my designs, so that I cannot with propriety expect any assistance from them for the coming year. My lectures, which have supported me hitherto, are closed; and I have nothing to depend on for subsistence this year but my further expectations in some business. I can hardly bear my expenses to Philadelphia, much less can I support myself there without some business which is not ascertained.

Webster hoped Franklin might help him either to obtain subscriptions for a repetition of his lectures in Philadelphia or to obtain a professorship at the university.

"I shall wait here a few days for your Excellency's answer," Webster wrote,

> if an answer will not be too great a trouble; for in my present situation
> I know not how to act.
>
> I wish for business: it is my life, my pleasure, as well as my support.
> But I began a vast design without a shilling, and I know the world too
> well to ask pecuniary assistance from any person. I want none; I will
> take none but what I can earn. . . . If your Excellency can furnish me
> with any prospects in either of the ways mentioned or in any other, it
> would be a satisfaction to me and enable me to make such arrangements
> as will be necessary, if I leave this state.
>
> I have the honor to be with perfect respect, Your Excellency's most
> obliged and very humble servant,
>
> Noah Webster, Jun.[86]

Webster set his departure for Thanksgiving Day, November 23, when travel to New York would be relatively light. He spent his last week in Hartford visiting with his closest friends—Barlow, Wolcott, Tracy, and Trumbull. He then spent a long last day at his boyhood home, in West Hartford, with his aging parents, who grieved openly about the prospects of losing their son and dying without ever seeing him again.

But Webster was intent on going to Philadelphia to help write a new constitution. Instead of seeking to vest political power in the people, as he had suggested in his *Sketches,* he now sought to limit the power of his once-beloved American yeoman. Against the advice of all his friends, he proclaimed his new position in an essay to the *Connecticut Courant,* which published it on November 20, 1786, three days before his departure.

"People in general," he wrote, "are too ignorant to manage affairs which require great reading and an extensive knowledge of foreign nations. This is the misfortune of republican governments. For my own part, I confess, I was once as strong a republican as any man in America. *Now,* a republican is among the last kinds I should choose. I would definitely prefer a limited monarchy, for I would sooner be the subject of the caprice of one man, than to the ignorance and passions of the multitude."[87]

For Webster, who had joined his father, brothers, and other countrymen in marching against the perceived injustices of the British monarch, this essay represented a complete reversal of the position he had espoused in *Sketches.* The yeomen he praised so lavishly in *Sketches* were now the targets of his attack for expressing their grievances against their own government. His article did not sit well with Connecticut farmers, and it seriously endangered Webster's chances for election by the state legislature as a delegate from Connecticut to the Constitutional Convention. Undaunted, Webster, barely twenty-eight years old, left Hartford, "perhaps for life,"[88] to begin the next phase of his career—shaping a new American government.

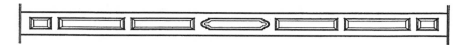

CHAPTER FIVE

Essayist

I

NOAH WEBSTER RETURNED to his intellectual home, New Haven, before going to Philadelphia. Angry and disillusioned about the ability of Americans to govern themselves, he placed himself once more under the tutelage of Yale president and fiery revolutionary Ezra Stiles.

Good instructor that he was, Stiles agreed that Shays's armed rebellion was an improper way to seek redress, but he exposed the economic grievances of insurgent farmers as real. Massachusetts had imposed taxes four times higher than other states and sent to debtors' prison farmers who could not pay them or seized their lands and sold them to pay the back taxes. A "rage for emigration"[1] to escape high taxes sent land prices plunging to near giveaway prices. Making matters worse, the majority of legislators were themselves wealthy men who snapped up lands at bargain prices from poor farmers who could not afford the taxes that the legislators had imposed. It was this combination of profiteering and disregard of legitimate grievances, Stiles explained to Webster, that provoked violence—not farmers' pitchforks. Only by granting Congress more powers, he said, would the violence end, and he encouraged Webster to participate in any way he could in Philadelphia.

Fueled with new understanding, Webster left for Philadelphia. Franklin had arranged for him to deliver a series of Saturday lectures in January, but competition from theaters and from Mr. Peale's exhibition of motion pictures at the museum kept audiences and revenues meager. Webster's advertisements probably did not help; they warned that his lectures were "not designed for amusement. They are designed for people who have leisure and inclination to devote an hour to *serious* reflection, as their object is to unfold some of the less visible causes of our political embarrassments."[2]

Webster tried developing a new system of spelling with Franklin's complex phonetic alphabet. He knew Franklin's name would ensure acceptance of his plan for spelling reform, but after a month he found the task impossible. He found Franklin's alphabet "neither practicable, necessary nor expedient,"[3] but he did not know how to say so without hurting the old man's feelings. He genuinely liked Franklin and enjoyed the many evenings the two spent together that winter. They become close friends, even sharing several evenings "with the Ladies."[4]

Webster said that instead of integrating the two orthographies, he would take Franklin's types and publish a new dictionary, based on Franklin's orthography, if he could obtain public subscriptions to underwrite the project. There is no evidence that he ever pressed ahead with the work, however.

By February, Webster found a Philadelphia printer to publish the *Institute* in Pennsylvania, and in March, for whatever reason, he decided to venture back into the political arena. It was a costly—and puzzling—decision, for he took up a cause that was not at all central to his life's work.

The nation was engaged in a furious debate over repayment of the public debt—especially back pay and pensions to Revolutionary War soldiers. Congress and the state governments had issued millions of dollars' worth of paper certificates—the equivalent of today's bonds—whose worth had eroded anywhere from 50 percent to 100 percent of face value. Holders had often sold their certificates at huge discounts to speculators, who gambled that the government would eventually redeem them at face value. Many speculators were themselves legislators and government officials who stood to profit by enacting redemption legislation.

The central question in the debate was which certificates to redeem and at what value. Every citizen had an opinion; to agree with one citizen's opinion automatically invited the rage of another. The debate was an emotional hornets' nest that neither rational arguments nor reasonable solutions could calm. But Webster could not resist the opportunity to express an opinion. It was simply ingrained in his character—especially when he suspected corruption and conflict of interest in high places. Webster charged into the fray, firing off a letter to his friend Massachusetts governor James Bowdoin. Interpreted as an assault on speculators and investors, it found its way, in whole or in part, into newspapers around the nation, including his home state of Connecticut.

In it he told Bowdoin that "to pay the debt to the men [speculators] who now hold evidences of it [that is, certificates], appears to me the most iniquitous measure that a legislature can adopt." Instead of redeeming certificates held by speculators, said Webster, the government should pay the original certificate holders the full face value in silver and let them buy back the certificates they had sold to speculators, at the prices the speculators had paid, plus interest. Speculator purchases would thus be treated

Noah Webster, the young man. Engraving from a portrait by the great artist-inventor Samuel F. B. Morse. This is the youngest likeness of Webster that remains. (Yale Picture Collection, Manuscripts and Archives, Yale University Library.)

as simple loans, entitled to legitimate interest but not to the huge profits speculators had counted on. In effect, the Webster proposal would send the market for certificates crashing.

A storm of invectives immediately befell the poor man. Almost every influential American, including newspaper owners, had been buying certificates at huge discounts from former soldiers in the expectation of redeeming them at full value.[5] Newspapers everywhere printed brutal attacks that not only damned Webster's scheme for handling the public debt but denounced his *Institute* and imputed his character. No less an eminence than Pres. John Ewing of the College of Philadelphia denounced Webster as a "fomenter of rebellion" and demeaned him as nothing but a "retailer of nouns and pronouns" with "hell-born opinions."[6] The essays not only cost Webster his lectureship at the university, they cost him all chances of appointment by the Connecticut legislature as a representative from Connecticut to the Constitutional Convention. As in all states, the legislature counted among its members many who had speculated in certificates and stood to lose fortunes if Webster's scheme were adopted. Moreover, many of the men whom Webster's ink had smeared at the Middletown Convention now sat in the legislature, and they gleefully avenged that humiliation by refusing to consider him for the convention.

2

THE END OF HIS APPOINTMENT at the university left Webster in need of income, and in April, Colonel Pickering arranged a six-month appointment to teach at the Episcopal Academy, for a stipend of £200. The targets of his essays, however, continued assailing the defenseless schoolteacher—probably to discourage any legislators who might have been considering Webster's scheme for redeeming certificates. Five days after Webster started at the academy, and only two days after the bishop of Pennsylvania laid the cornerstone for the academy's new building, the *Freeman's Journal* published an editorial signed "Seth," which was the pseudonym of the paper's fanatically antifederalist editor, Thomas Freeman.

> The uncertainty of all human affairs never appeared more manifestly than in the case of NOAH WEBSTER, jun. esq, whose extraordinary abilities and unparalleled knowledge of the English language, have enabled him to write that masterpiece of instruction, his *Grammatical Institute*. His consciousness of his own great learning and genius, had justly led him to imagine, that, by his becoming an itinerant lecturer through the United States, he would, by this means, be one of the most valuable citizens of our new empire, and have his name ranked among the great men of this western world.—But, alas! all his well-digested plans and schemes have vanished into smoke, his *learned* and *useful lectures* have been neglected, and he himself suffered to starve, or to join one of the most Herculean pieces of labor that ever any poor man engaged in, *to wit*, that of a schoolmaster.
>
> This learned man, whose extraordinary knowledge and abilities gave him good reason to expect at least *one thousand guineas* a year clear profit from his lecturing, is now obliged to accept of *two hundred pounds* a year of paper money, which at present, allowing for discount, is scarcely one hundred pounds sterling. . . . This is surely a strange reverse of fortune on the part of Noah Webster, Esq. Would to God that he may have magnanimity of mind sufficient to bear all this.[7]

Aroused by Seth's letter, Webster fired back an essay signed "Adam"—
Seth's biblical father. Calling Seth "stupid," "vile," and a "scribbling fool,"
Webster wrote that as a teacher he was walking in the footsteps of "antient
kings and sages [who] taught children and schools." He said his motives for
teaching were "the noblest that can actuate the human mind" and that he
would have willingly taught without compensation.[8]

On May 8, he slipped deeper into the quicksand of the debate over the
public debt. In a long, rambling reply to those who attacked him, he declared, "I have only to inform the public that threatening is thrown away
upon me. I live in a free country and claim the privilege of thinking and
speaking as I please, a privilege I shall resign only with my breath."

He reiterated that his

> political creed on this . . . consists of two short articles:
> 1st. That every farthing of the debt ought to be repaid.
> 2d. That the rulers of America cannot be justified in the view of the
> world or of God Almighty if they suffer public delinquency to injure a
> numerous and respectable class of original creditors. They ought either
> to make some compensation to them for their losses, or exempt them
> from taxation imposed for the payment of the money which they have
> lost.[9]

Webster's letter added nothing to the national debate except to make
his name a continuing target of invective in many newspapers, including
the *Connecticut Courant,* in Hartford. His parents were upset.

"I have had a hint from some Gentlemen and some Newspapers," his
father wrote,

> as though you had made some Unfriendly to you by some of your writings
> and done yourself damage. I would caution you to be wise as a Serpent
> as well as harmless as a dove[.] have Courage but temper the Same with
> prudence. . . . Publick matters at this time of year seem to rest much as
> they have been of late[.] Coppers now pass two for a penny[.] as to our
> Crops, the Rye Comes in pretty well the wheat is much damaged by the
> insect[.] ours is a good Berrie what grew and stood upright at Harvest.
> we have got in all our Harvest in good order and Hay, except Second
> mowings, which may be Considerable by reason of the wet season[.] flax
> good . . . we heard from Mr Steele of Egremont that about a month ago
> Some Insurgents, alias Roberts Entered his House in the night and took
> away from him in Cash, household furniture and provisions to the value
> of 30 or forty pounds. . . . Hoping to hear from you soon I write no more
> at present only that I hope you will Come to Hartford as soon as you
> well can Consistent with your interest
>
> I Remain Your Effectionate Father.

Noah's younger brother, Charles, sent Noah his support, saying he believed the criticism had been "written by . . . Scoundrels to Injure your In-

stitute but I believe you have nothing to fear from them. . . . I should flee from among them as Lot did from Sodom. Mamma says I must tell you she wants to [see] you more than ever. Your affectionate Brother."[10]

Fortunately, Webster's personal charms belied the rectitude of so much of his writing, and in the end, his public assault on investors cost him few, if any, of his private friendships. Throughout the winter, Webster dined with Philadelphia's most influential families, and by early spring, he could count more than two-thirds of the fifty-five delegates at the Constitutional Convention among his acquaintances. Many were close friends. More than half were college graduates and lawyers. Some were scholars whom Webster enjoyed enormously—as they apparently enjoyed him. He had met many of them before, of course—Washington at Mount Vernon, and Madison in Philadelphia and Richmond. Abraham Baldwin of Georgia was Joel Barlow's brother-in-law, and Webster had known him when Baldwin was a tutor at Yale. Yale president Stiles had introduced Webster to Roger Sherman, and Webster had boarded with Judge Oliver Ellsworth and studied law with him while teaching school in Hartford.

As usual, Webster met his share of "Ladies," but on March 1, one stood out from the rest: Miss Rebecca Greenleaf. By March 7, Webster's diary elevated her to "Sweet Miss Greenleaf"; by the eighth she was "the agreeable Miss Greenleaf"; and by the twenty-second she was "the lovely Becca." For the first time in his life, Noah Webster was deeply, irretrievably in love.

Rebecca Greenleaf had just turned twenty-one and had come from Boston with her older brother James to visit their newly married sister. "Witty, sensible, sociable" Rebecca had bright dark eyes and dark hair, "was little of stature, and of light weight, but," according to her daughter Emily, "was very erect and graceful." Although her family was not as significant historically as the Websters, the Greenleafs were not inconsequential and more than made up in financial stature what they lacked in historical distinction. Rebecca was the thirteenth of fifteen children of Mary and William Greenleaf, the latter a prosperous merchant-trader who was sheriff of Suffolk County, which included Boston. Descended from French Huguenots who had fled Catholic persecution in France, they anglicized the name "Feuillevert" when they settled in Devonshire in the mid-1500s. The first Greenleaf in America arrived in the Massachusetts Bay Colony in 1635. His son bought Nantucket Island with his father-in-law for £30 and two beaver hats, and a grandson married a doctor's daughter, Elizabeth Gookin, who became the first woman to practice medicine in America.

Subsequent generations of Greenleafs attended Harvard. Rebecca's uncle founded Boston's first insurance company, and her father risked his life to proclaim the Declaration of Independence from the balcony of the old State House on King Street (later State Street) in July 1776. Although the Revolutionary War eroded the family fortune, Rebecca's brother James was a brilliant speculator who had turned unwanted land into gold and rebuilt the Greenleaf treasury by the time Webster met Rebecca. A warm, extremely loving friend and relative who generously shared his wealth with his entire family, James Greenleaf formed an immediate and deep friendship with Rebecca's new suitor.

Rebecca's mother, Mary, was descended from John Browne, a magistrate in Plymouth with Gov. William Bradford, Noah Webster's maternal ancestor.[11] In contrast to the warmth of the Greenleaf men, Rebecca's mother "was said by some," according to Emily Ellsworth Fowler Ford, "to have been a cold, haughty woman, handsome and highbred . . . a queen of society, but neither domestic nor affectionate to her brood." Rebecca sensed her mother would reject the suit of a young schoolmaster with only £300 a year to support her daughter.[12]

Undiscouraged, Webster saw Rebecca no less than eight times in the month of March and twice as often in April. Poor though he may have been in comparison with the Greenleafs, he was not threadbare. He was handsome, always charming, with a gift of conversation and enough accumulated knowledge and travel experience to give substance to his words and hold his listener's attention. He kept his few suits immaculate and was impeccably groomed. Noah took Rebecca to concerts, dinners, and other festivities—although he was never averse to spending quiet evenings with her at her sister's home. He recorded these in simple, touching phrases: "At my favorite place," "With the most lovely," "With the best of women," "With my heart," and finally, "Visit my best friend."

He proposed to her in early June, shortly before she was to return to Boston.[13] Although she returned his love, she told him she was certain that her parents would never approve of their marriage until Webster could support her in a style at least equal to that of her family. Her answer can be construed from this reply Webster sent before her departure:

> Philadelphia, June 20th [1787].
>
> The hour approaches, my dear Becca, when I must lose the pleasure of your company and conversation. The prospect throws a gloom round my heart and makes me regret the revolutions of day and night. Call it not weakness that a tear steals down my cheeks; I would forbid it but cannot. Sensibility is given us to be the source of pleasure; and however it may sometimes occasion pain, yet I must hope that the same susceptibility which has received lively impressions of your loveliness and worth will yet make us both permanently happy. This hope, my sweet girl, when you are gone, will be my only dependence.
>
> I have been happy with you; I could have been happier had it not been for some restraints which you judged prudent and which for that reason I believe to be so.
>
> My attachment gives me anxiety as well as pleasure, and you know the reason why. But a few months may remove it and open brighter prospects.

I am happy in your confidence and esteem of your good brother. Permit me to assure you that your *esteem—your* friendship—is now *my* only happiness, and *your* happiness the great object of my pursuit. And if I am permitted to indulge a hope of mutual attachment, your inclinations will always be consulted in my future determinations. *Without you* the world is all alike to me; and *with* you any part will be agreeable. As a pledge of my sincerity, accept a lock of hair, and keep it no longer than I deserve to be remembered. You must go, and I must be separated from all that is dear to me; but you will be attended by guardian angels and the best wishes of your sincere and respectful admirer.

N. Webster[14]

Becca went home to Boston four days later.

3

NOAH WEBSTER BEGAN TEACHING at the Protestant Episcopal Academy in Philadelphia on Friday, April 13, 1787. The following month, on May 25, a quorum of delegates from seven states assembled at Independence Hall and unanimously elected George Washington their presiding officer. On the evening of the second day, Washington went to visit Webster at the latter's quarters and reviewed Webster's *Sketches*.[15] Washington returned to the convention and suggested replacing the Articles of Confederation with a new constitution. There is no concrete evidence that Washington's visit with Webster—or the subsequent visits of other delegates with Webster—directly affected deliberations over, or the final form of, the Constitution. It may, however, be more than coincidental that after each such visit to Webster, Washington and the delegates returned to the convention and reached compromises suggested by Webster, or inserted language in the Constitution that was similar to or exactly that found in Webster's *Sketches* or other writings.

On May 29, Washington's colleague from Virginia Edmund Randolph proposed a Virginia Plan of Union, including a bicameral legislature not unlike the one suggested by Webster—with a lower house elected directly by the people and representing the population of each state. Once installed, the lower house would choose members of the upper house from nominees selected by state legislatures. The plan called for a chief executive and a judiciary—a supreme court and lower courts—to be chosen by the legislature.

States with small populations rose in opposition to Randolph's plan, which gave the South undue power by including slaves (who did not vote) in their population counts. The day after his meeting with Washington, Webster spent the afternoon "in the Gardens" with, among others, former Rhode Island governor Stephen Hopkins, a longtime member of the

Continental Congress. Hopkins expressed bitter opposition to the Virginia Plan. He agreed with delegates from other small states that each state should retain its sovereignty and that any change in the Articles of Confederation should be limited to the area of interstate commerce. On June 15, New Jersey's William Patterson introduced resolutions that would retain the Confederation but give Congress new powers to tax and regulate foreign and interstate commerce and to name an executive governing body and a supreme court.

On June 19, the convention finally voted to scrap the Articles of Confederation (thus defeating the New Jersey Plan) and to work toward a new national government, as Washington had suggested after meeting with Webster. The convention began reconsidering Randolph's Virginia Plan. Although Webster had no direct access to the convention—by agreement, its proceedings were secret—he had extensive evening discussions with the garrulous Franklin. His diary records frequent visits and late dinners with William Samuel Johnson, Roger Sherman, and Oliver Ellsworth of Connecticut; Abraham Baldwin of Georgia; Rufus King of Massachusetts; William Livingston of New Jersey; James Duane of New York; Thomas Fitzsimmons of Pennsylvania; and Edmund Randolph and James Madison of Virginia. His diary also refers cryptically to meetings with untold numbers of other "Convention Gentlemen"—almost always in the days preceding key decisions.

The debate over the Virginia Plan centered over whether the new government should be *national*, with representation in the new congress based on population, or *federal*, with each state having an equal number of votes. The North, with a smaller population, favored a federal system.

On June 9, Webster dined with Columbia College president William Samuel Johnson, who was a Connecticut native and represented that state, rather than New York, in both the Continental Congress and the Constitutional Convention. Dining with them was Abraham Bishop of New Haven, who, at twelve, had been Webster's youngest classmate at Yale. The next day, July 10, Webster met with Abraham Baldwin, the transplanted New Havenite who had founded the University of Georgia and represented that state at the convention.

On July 12, Connecticut and Georgia—two unlikely allies, brought together at the Webster dinner table—joined in winning convention agreement to a compromise: each state's representation in the lower house of the new government would be based on its total white population and three-fifths of its black population. Four days later, the convention agreed on Roger Sherman's Connecticut Compromise, which made representation in the lower house proportional to population and gave each state an equal vote in the upper house, or senate. The Connecticut Compromise also reserved to the states all powers not "expressly delegated" to the central government.

An elated Webster spent a joyful Independence Day with Connecticut's Johnson and Georgia's Baldwin, whose views he had helped reconcile. His influence, however, galled the antifederalist editor at the *Freeman's Journal,* who constantly attacked Webster during the convention. Not knowing any details of the secret proceedings, the newspaper could not attack its participants. But Webster was an easy target as he darted in and out of the lodgings of convention participants. In an open letter to the convention in June, Freeman accused Webster of spreading "disorder, confusion and error."[16]

Webster ignored the attack, preferring to concentrate on maintaining ties to the men who were writing the new constitution. For the rest of the summer, he dined with them frequently, along with Pelatiah Webster, Colonel Pickering, and Benjamin Franklin. On August 22, as convention delegates watched from the shore, he sailed on the Delaware River with Franklin and James Greenleaf, Rebecca's brother, on the maiden demonstration of John Fitch's first American steam-powered boat—a forty-five-foot craft with steam-powered oars. It was a heady summer for young Webster—still not even thirty years old, he was walking (and sailing) among the nation's founding fathers and thoroughly accepted by them as one of their number.

In the midst of all this activity, the enterprising schoolmaster managed to teach English at the academy each day and to study Spanish and German grammar. He also wrote a seventh edition of his spelling book, which he had renamed *The American Spelling Book*—a title he had always preferred over Yale president Stiles's Calvinistic *Institute.* Philadelphia printer William Young paid Webster £42 for exclusive printing rights in Pennsylvania, Delaware, Maryland, and Virginia for three years, with Webster to receive royalties of one-twentieth (5 percent) on the speller and one-fifteenth (6⅔ percent) on the grammar and reader. Young's edition was the first to include engraved illustrations.

In addition to revising the speller, Webster doubled the size of the reader to 372 pages and changed its title to *An American Selection of Lessons in Reading and Speaking.*[17] Brim full of patriotism and enthusiasm for the new federal government being created, *An American Selection* included John Hancock's speech on the Boston Massacre, the Declaration of Independence, four congressional orations, Washington's Farewell Orders to the Army, speeches by three governors, a speech by Joel Barlow, and two poems by Philip Freneau: "Columbus to Ferdinand" and "On General Washington." It included also one of Webster's own lectures on the importance of good manners and speaking the same national language.

Webster wrote fifty pages of new material for the book, including a history of the discovery and settlement of North America and a history of the Revolutionary War, with "Authentic Accounts of the Principal Battles," from Bunker Hill to the capture of Cornwallis. *An American Selection* became the

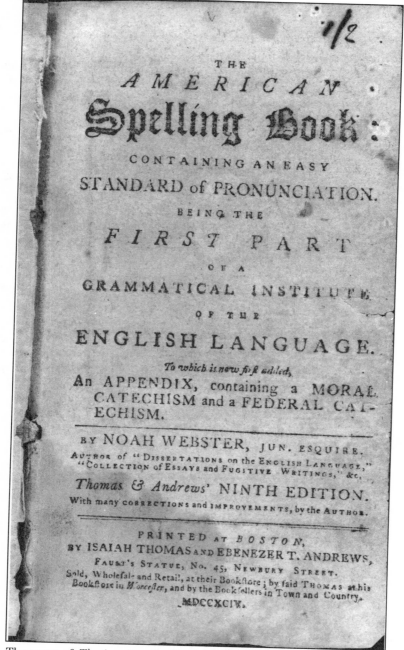

The cover of *The American Spelling Book,* Noah Webster's innovative text for teaching children to read and write. (Beinecke Rare Book and Manuscript Library, Yale University.)

first schoolbook ever to detail the history of the events leading up to the creation of the United States.

Another innovation was a brief geography of the United States and the thirteen states, along with a glossary of geographic terms, such as *island, cape, bay, strait,* and *gulf stream.* The geography, however, did not represent much of an innovation. In fact, Jedidiah Morse, the religious leader who had graduated from Yale five years after Webster, had published a widely used and much acclaimed geography in 1784, called *Geography Made Easy,*[18] which exuded the same patriotic spirit as Webster's book. Webster had no intention of competing with Morse, and the two met in Philadelphia during the summer of the convention to work out a long-term collaboration for a new, expanded textbook called *The American Geography.* Published two years later, in 1789, it combined a thirty-six-page history of the United States by Webster with Morse's geography text; within five years, it made its way into virtually every school.[19] It made the geography portion of Webster's *American Selection* redundant, and he eventually eliminated it.

Despite the summer's frenetic activities, Webster did not forget his family in West Hartford—or his beloved Rebecca in Boston, to whom he lamented, "Such a distance between us! But I must not complain: time will shorten that distance and bring me where my happiness centers."[20] References to visits with the ladies were notably absent from Webster's diary that summer.

In addition to delegates and congressmen, there were many other men of influence in Philadelphia who affected the outcome of the convention, and Webster met with them with varying degrees of frequency. They included Francis Hopkinson, the poet and essayist, a signatory of the Declaration of Independence; David Rittenhouse, the wealthy and influential scientist; the Reverend Jedidiah Morse; and John Marshall, the influential Virginia legislator and friend of Washington, who invited Webster to spend an evening with "Convention Gentlemen" in mid-August, a month before the convention ended.[21]

By that time, virtually every member of the convention had a copy of Webster's *Sketches* in hand, and the similarity between *Sketches* and several basic principles of the Constitution is too great to be mere coincidence—especially given the lack of any competing document with similar carefully outlined ideas. Webster had traveled the nation calling for national unity and was first to call for federal copyright protection for authors. As he had done in Virginia a year earlier, Webster turned to James Madison, who once again sponsored and succeeded in winning such protection.[22] Article I, Section 8, Paragraph 8 of the U.S. Constitution granted Congress the power, *inter alia,* "to promote the progress of science and useful arts, by securing for limited times to authors and inventors the exclusive rights to their respective writings and discoveries."[23]

It is pure Webster, as are key segments sketching the powers of the president and the legislature and their relationship to the individual states. His ties to the convention became evident on September 15, two days before ratification of the final draft, when Pennsylvania delegate and eventual signatory Thomas Fitzsimmons asked Webster to use his pen "in support of the New Federal System, which is almost finished."[24]

"I shall make you no apology for addressing myself to you upon the present occasion," Fitzsimmons wrote to Webster,

> because you must be equally interested with me in the event, and having contributed my mite to the service of our common country, I have some right to call upon others for their assistance. I consider the present moment, as the crisis that will determine whether we are to benefit by the revolution we have obtained or whether we shall become a prey to foreign influence & domestic violence. The business of the convention is nearly at an end, & a few days will bring before the people of America the constitution prepared for their future government. That it is the best which human wisdom could devise, I mean not to assert; but I trust it will be found consistent with the principles of liberty, and calculated to unite & bind together the members of a great country. It is already too evident that there are people prepared to oppose it, even before they are acquainted with its outline, and it is as easy to foresee that if unreasonable jealousies are disseminated, its adoption may be at least protracted. In my mind, to delay is to destroy. There are so many interests, foreign & domestic, opposed to order & good government in America, as to warrant an apprehension of their interfering, if time is given for cabal & intrigue.
>
> It too often happens that men whose views are upright, trust to the goodness of their cause; while men of opposite views are indefatigable in misrepresenting theirs.
>
> Under these opinions & from a conviction that your abilities may be eminently useful on the present occasion, I am induced to call your attention to this subject. If as a friend to your country, you can support the act of the convention, I hope you will exert yourself to that purpose. I ask it only upon that condition.
>
> > I am Sir, your most obedient Servnt
> >
> > Thomas Fitzsimmons
>
> Walnut Street
>
> > 15 Sept. 1787.[25]

Webster was elated by the call to national service. He knew the convention had not permitted Fitzsimmons to select him as publicist for the Constitution without careful deliberation—and despite strong opposition from those he had insulted in his essay on speculators. In the end, Webster had triumphed, and he wrote to his dear Becca:

Philadelphia, September 15, 1787

Well, my dear Friend, another week is gone, and I am retired to pass a few minutes with Becca. These few minutes are to me the most precious. They revive your image in my mind and call into view your smiles, your friendship, and virtues. Every recollection of this kind awakens some agreeable sensations; it, in some measure, repeats the pleasures I have received in your conversations. I imagine my self hearing some sprightly remarks from your lips, some censure upon vice, or some encomiums upon the amiable and the good. This imaginary scene revives my attention to my own character and has a tendency to make me better. My attachment to you would tempt me to love every thing that is good. This, you will say, I ought to do without that attachment, but we are apt to stray without some friend to call us back. Be that friend to me, Becca, and you will make me very happy.

I shall leave Philadelphia in October, but must attend the Assembly in Delaware and probably make a journey to Albany before I see New England. But in all places and at all times I am really what I profess to be: Your friend and devoted admirer.

N. Webster[26]

The convention gave its final approval to the Constitution on September 17, and on the following day, Webster accompanied Benjamin Franklin to the official farewell to George Washington before going on to Independence Hall. Webster's diary described the day's events succinctly: "Genl Washington leaves town. Dr. Franklin presents the Speaker of the House of Assembly in Pennva with the Federal System, which is read. Bells ring. All America awaits anxiously for the Plan of Government."[27]

4

WITH THE COMMISSION from Fitzsimmons in hand, Webster spent the next three weeks studying the Constitution, discussing it with Franklin, and reviewing the essays he had written on the Middletown Convention and Shays's Rebellion. Webster disagreed with certain aspects of the document, as did Franklin, who had favored a unicameral legislative body. Webster saw two major failings in the new document: its failure to abolish slavery and its failure to create a system of universal public education. The convention had scrapped both concepts as part of a compromise to win the support of Southern states for ratification.

Franklin nevertheless urged Webster to give the Constitution his full support, saying, "I have been all my life changing my opinions on many subjects, & in this case, I have yielded my own opinion to those of other men."[28] Webster agreed and began writing an essay whose impact on the ratification of the Constitution would rank with that of Thomas Paine's essays in support of the Declaration of Independence.

Dedicated to Benjamin Franklin, Webster's *Examination into the Leading Principles of the Federal Constitution*[29] was distributed throughout the nation. Webster signed the document "A Citizen of America," knowing that his name would unnecessarily provoke the fury of his enemies and blunt the potential benefits of his essay.

Unlike *Sketches of American Policy,* the *Examination* was not addressed to political leaders but to the people of the United States, in language they could understand. For they would elect the state legislators who, in turn, would vote for or against the Constitution. It was important that these voters understand what the Constitution was all about.

Divided into three parts, his essay explained the importance of the Constitution in historic terms, its meaning in practical terms (how the new government would work), and its benefits to ordinary citizens.

Comparing the Constitution to "promulgation of the Jewish laws at Mount Sinai," Webster wrote that "the origin of the AMERICAN REPUBLIC is distinguished by peculiar circumstances. Other nations have been driven together by fear and necessity. . . . In the formation of our constitution the wisdom of all ages is collected—the legislators of antiquity are consulted, as well as the opinions and interests of the millions who are concerned. In short, it is an *empire of reason.*"

Webster called the Constitution

> an *improvement* on the best *constitutions* that the world ever saw. In the house of representatives the people of America have an equal voice and suffrage. The senate will be composed of older men, and while their regular dismission from office once in six years will preserve their dependence on their constituents, the duration of their existence will give firmness to their decisions and temper the factions which must necessarily prevail in the other branch. The president of the United States is elective, and what is a capital improvement on the best governments, the mode of chusing him excludes the danger of faction and corruption.

Like the schoolmaster he once was, Webster argued for ratification with an explicit lesson on the differences between liberty and license:

> I cannot quit this subject without attempting to correct erroneous opinions respecting *freedom* and *tyranny* and the principles by which they are supported. Many people seem to entertain an idea that liberty consists in a *power to act without any control.* This is more liberty than even the savages enjoy. But in civil society political liberty consists in *acting conformably to the sense of a majority of the society.* In a free government every man binds himself to the *public voice,* or the opinions of a majority, and the *whole society* engages to *protect each individual.* In such a government man is *free* and safe. But reverse the case; suppose every man to act without control or fear of punishment—every man would be free, but no man

would be sure of his freedom one moment. Each would have the power of taking his neighbor's life, liberty, or property, and no man would command more than his own strength to repel the invasion. The case is the same with states. If the states should not unite into one compact society, every state may trespass upon its neighbor, and the injured state has no means of redress but its own military force.

Webster admitted that the Constitution had faults, but added that it was absurd to oppose it for that reason alone:

> Let every man be at liberty to expunge what *he* judges exceptionable, and not a syllable of the constitution will survive the scrutiny. A painter, after executing a masterly piece, requested every spectator to draw a pencil over the part that did not please him; but, to his surprise, he soon found the *whole piece* defaced. Let every man examine the most perfect building by his *own* taste and, like some microscopic critics, condemn the *whole* for small deviations from the rules of architecture, and not a part of the *best* constructed fabric would escape. But let *any* man take a *comprehensive view* of the whole, and he will be pleased with the general beauty and proportions and admire the structure. The same remarks apply to the new constitution. I have no doubt that *every* member of the late convention has exceptions to *some part* of the system proposed. Their constituents have the same, and if *every* objection must be removed before we have a national government, the Lord have mercy on us!
> Perfection is not the lot of humanity.[30]

Ten days after publication of Webster's *Examination*, the *Independent Journal* in New York published the first of seventy-seven essays by "A Citizen of New York" (Alexander Hamilton's favorite pseudonym). The essays appeared regularly from October 17, 1787, to April 12, 1788, with most of the later articles signed "Publius." Together with eight additional essays, they were republished the following spring in a two-volume work, *The Federalist*. Alexander Hamilton wrote fifty-one of the essays, James Madison, twenty-nine, and John Jay, five, and historians have traditionally credited their essays, rather than Webster's *Examination*, with swinging national opinion in favor of ratification.

Although the *Federalist* papers unquestionably won votes for ratification in cosmopolitan Northern cities, they had far less circulation elsewhere and almost none among ordinary Americans. In the end, Webster's short, easy-to-read pamphlet was at least as influential as the *Federalist* papers, if not more so, in less populated states, where isolated farmers eschewed all contact with governmental authority. It was to these men that Webster's arguments for ratification were directed, and he obviously knew how to address their concerns—far more than the citified Hamilton. Although most readers would not vote directly for ratification, they would elect the state legislature that would do the voting. Webster's article urged them to vote for legislators who would support ratification.

Antifederalists made up the majority of the voting population in New Hampshire, Massachusetts, Rhode Island, New York, Virginia, and the Carolinas when the Constitutional Convention adjourned, and historians have been careless in failing to credit Webster's pamphlet for its influence in winning ratification in these rural states. Some of the oversight can be traced to Webster's failure to write a self-aggrandizing autobiography during the cloudy twilight years when great and not-so-great men embellish the past to elevate the significance of their own contributions and diminish those of their contemporaries. By the time historians began studying the history of the Constitution a few decades later, only a handful of octogenarians such as Madison survived to describe the secret proceedings at Philadelphia, and after years of vilification by Webster and other Northerners for the War of 1812, he was less than generous in praising any political enemies. Fortunately, other documents from the time of the Constitutional Convention remain. Dr. David Ramsay, the South Carolina surgeon, scholar, and political leader who had served as acting president of the Continental Congress and had strongly supported ratification, wrote to Webster from Charleston about the impact of the latter's *Examination* in that state: "I have read it with pleasure, and it is now in brisk circulation among my friends. I have heard every person who has read it express high approbation of its contents. It will doubtless be of singular service in recommending the adoption of the new Constitution."[31]

A week before completing his essay, Webster resigned from the Episcopal Academy. Although he would continue to be "schoolmaster to America" through his textbooks for children, he would never again teach in a classroom.

The day after he finished writing his essay on the Constitution, he wrote to Rebecca Greenleaf, who had replied unfailingly to his letters but had apparently grown prudish about his wasting of paper:

> I thank you, my kind girl, for your caution to take care of my health. There is some need of it. I accept it as a proof of your goodness and the interest you take in my happiness. But what shall I do with your commands to fill the paper that I send? I find you have an aversion to the blank side of a letter. And yet if a letter is not filled with good sense or something entertaining, two sides at least should be blank. . . .
>
> Among other instances of my readiness to obey your wishes, you may rank the mode of dressing my hair. I have turned it back. . . .
>
> I am just leaving Philadelphia, having finished the business that has detained me. Notwithstanding the noise made about me last spring, everything is calm, the party that opposed me is almost sunk into obscurity by their opposition to the new government, and it would be as easy for me to establish myself in this city as anywhere else. But I shall return to the eastward and endeavor to enter upon some permanent business. Where I shall sit down is uncertain, or where you will hear from me next. It is equally uncertain whether I shall see you this fall or not.

. . . You know I am unsettled and therefore unhappy. But no circumstances shall prevent my exertions or interrupt my attachment to the best of women. Your happiness, Becca, is one principal object of my pursuit, and I cannot hope I may yet have it in my power to unite your felicity with my own.[32]

The day after publication of his *Examination,* Webster turned twenty-nine. "I have been industrious," he wrote in his diary, "[and] endeavored to do some good, & hope I shall be able to correct my faults & yet do more good."[33] He was nevertheless still without work and would have to supplement the £300 a year he was earning from the *Institute* if he was ever to support a wife. His work in Philadelphia was now complete, and he packed his trunk and put it on a coach bound for New York. He spent his last two evenings in Philadelphia discussing his future with Benjamin Franklin, who was now approaching eighty-two and had but two and a half years to live. Franklin lavished Webster with counsel that would deeply influence the young man for many years. A publisher himself, Franklin encouraged his young proselyte to continue to write and make his views known to the American public—just as Franklin himself and as Thomas Paine had done. It was the last time Webster would see the old man.

5

CONVINCED HE HAD AFFECTED the course of the new nation, Webster believed he could ensure national unity by continuing to write essays. Franklin suggested that Webster found his own magazine of commentary and literature. Printer Isaiah Thomas had founded such a magazine in Boston, and Matthew Carey and Francis Hopkinson had founded the wildly successful *Columbian Magazine* in Philadelphia. Webster's Yale classmate Josiah Meigs had launched the *New-Haven Gazette, and the Connecticut Magazine* three years earlier, and it had gained widespread attention, publishing the poetry of Timothy Dwight, Joel Barlow, John Trumbull, and other "Connecticut Wits," as they were called. Most of their work satirized antifederalists in verse. They humiliated advocates of confederation, the mob rule of conventions, and the proponents of paper money. Surprisingly, New York, the seat of the Congress and best suited as a national distribution center, had no similar publication.

Webster left Philadelphia for New York on Thursday, and by the following Wednesday, he had raised $200 to found his new magazine. Unfortunately, the money came from the impetuous sale to the unscrupulous printer Samuel Campbell of exclusive rights to publish *The American Spelling Book* in New York for five years. The transaction would come back to haunt him.

Webster spent the next month traveling through Connecticut to raise more money and provide a cushion of capital to keep the publication going for several months. He sold five hundred subscriptions for his new publication to all the familiar figures of the Yale network—Baldwin, Dwight, Stiles, Tracy, Trumbull, Wolcott, and the rest—all the while writing to friends elsewhere throughout the country, such as Rush, Pickering, and Buckminster. From each, he obtained promises of literary contributions as well as subscriptions.

Always committed to his familial obligations, Webster spent several days during his travels visiting relatives—his parents, in West Hartford, his sister in Salisbury, and assorted relatives elsewhere in the state.

By November 29, he was back in New York with more than enough money to publish his magazine for at least six months. In quick succession, he signed a year's lease for his lodgings, a contract with a printer, and a contract to buy paper. On December 5, 1787, he opened the offices of the *American Magazine* and began to write.

There was much to write about. On December 6, Delaware became the first state to ratify the Constitution—by unanimous vote of the legislature. Convinced his powerful essay on ratification had produced Delaware's unanimity, Webster unsheathed his pen and wrote with renewed vigor. Pennsylvania ratified six days later, despite the bitter opposition of the German settlements. New Jersey ratified a week after that. On New Year's Eve, as Webster prepared to ship the first issue of his magazine, he bet an unmarried lady friend in New York, Miss Kate Marsh, that he would marry first. The stakes: "a pair of Wedding Gloves."[34]

6

THE FIRST ISSUE of the *American Magazine* appeared on January 1, 1788, bearing a cover date of December 1787 and the motto "Science the guide, and truth the eternal goal."[35] The advantages of New York City as a shipping hub gave the magazine wide circulation throughout the nation—and Webster's editorial skills placed it among the best in the United States.

In many respects, it was the first modern magazine in America: the first to organize materials by category rather than at random; the first to appeal to a broad, general audience; and, in the most radical innovation, the first to invite women as both readers *and* contributors. His goal for the magazine was the same as it had been for the *Institute*—to educate and unite Americans in every corner of the United States and to promote his agenda for a common, federal language and system of education.

With the ordered mind of a schoolmaster, Webster presented materials subject by subject. His topics included news ("Foreign Intelligence" and

"American Intelligence"), "Curiosities," government, agriculture, fashion, and theology—along with poetry, reviews, notices of marriages and deaths, and miscellaneous essays. He kept items brief, giving them the quality of the modern digest. He often serialized essays to prevent them from monopolizing space in any edition. The table of contents appeared on the cover. Unfortunately, many of the contributions that other writers had promised never arrived, and Webster was forced to write nearly one-third of the sixty-four-page publication himself.

His first issue began with the lively, confident introduction of all good teachers on the first day of school:

> The Editor of the *American Magazine* presents his compliments of the season to all his readers, and wishes them all the blessings they wish for themselves. He begs leave, on the auspicious opening of 1788, to usher into the world a *New Publication* which he designs to continue, as long as it shall be profitable to himself or entertaining to his countrymen.
>
> It is the Editor's wish to gratify every class of readers—the divine, the historian, the philosopher, the statesman, the moralist, the poet, the merchant and the laborer—and his *fair readers* may be assured, that no inconsiderable pains will be taken to furnish them with entertainment; at the same time he flatters himself, that many of the ladies who are the favorites of Minerva and the Muses, will be found in the number of his correspondents.
>
> The *American Magazine* will be open for every species of decent and valuable Essay; for fair discussion, general satire and wit and humor and for the production of imagination. At the same time the Editor will find it necessary to reserve to himself the right of deciding on the merit of the Essays communicated, and the propriety of admitting them into the work; as personal invective, ribaldry and immoral writings will form no part of the proposed selection.
>
> The Editor is sensible of the arduous task, he has imposed upon himself, in attempting to please the various tastes of his readers, and render the publication worthy of encouragement . . . and if *great faults* should be found in the *American Magazine;* the Editor will freely consent to discontinue publication.[36]

As he promised, he filled the pages with learned ideas, information, good discussion and argument, and old-fashioned joy, laughter, and entertainment. Serious articles on the proposed Bill of Rights and on tree grafting mixed happily with an "Anecdote on the Duke of Gordon," "Advice to Masons"—and advice to husbands with scolding wives, as well as to wives with "peevish" husbands.

Included, too, was Webster's inevitable essay "On Education"—one of fourteen he would write in less than a year. Six concentrated on reform of education and the rest on reform of the English language. In effect they refined, improved upon, and expanded the lectures from his 1785–86 tour of the states.

Few of the ideas were original, but Webster coalesced into a single document the educational theories of Jefferson, Madison, Rush, Franklin, Washington, and himself; their ideas, in turn, owed much to Locke, Rousseau, Plato, and other educational philosophers. Webster, Washington, Jefferson, Madison, and Rush had all favored a provision in the Constitution for universal public education. Madison had actually proposed a provision "to establish an University."[37]

Webster's essay renewed the call for universal public education. "The only practicable method to reform mankind is to begin with children," he wrote. "Education should therefore be the first care of a legislature—not merely the institution of schools, but the furnishing of them with the best men for teachers. A good system of education should be the first article in the code of political regulations."

He criticized several states for establishing colleges and academies for the sons of the rich while failing to teach the states' other children even to read or write. "Yet in these same states every citizen who is worth a few shillings annually is entitled to vote for legislators. This appears to me a most glaring solecism in government. The constitutions are *republican,* and the laws of education are *monarchical.* The former extend civil rights to every industrious citizen; the latter deprive a large proportion of the citizens of a most valuable privilege."

Educational deprivation, he pointed out, would leave the majority of Americans intellectually unable to govern themselves and, by default, cede the reins of government to an educated aristocracy. Throughout history, he said, illiteracy had invariably proved the most effective weapon for sustaining tyranny—more effective than prison cells, torture, or death.

"In our American republics, where government is in the hands of the people, knowledge should be universally diffused by means of public schools," Webster declared. "Of such consequence is it to society that the people who make laws should be well informed that I conceive no legislature can be justified in neglecting proper establishments for this purpose."

In addition to more schools, Webster's essays called for better instruction. Many communities, he said, entrusted their children "to worthless fellows—even English and Irish convicts who had been exiled to America for their crimes. Gracious heavens! Must the wretches, who have forfeited their lives and been pronounced unworthy to be inhabitants of a *foreign* country, be entrusted with the education, the morals, the character of *American* youth?"

Another defect in American schools—he called it "inexcusable"—was

the want of proper books. The collections which are now used consist of essays that respect foreign and ancient nations. . . . But every child in America should be acquainted with his own country. He should read books that furnish him with ideas that will be useful to him in life and practice. As soon as he opens his lips he should rehearse the history of his own country—he should lisp the praises of liberty and of those illustrious heroes and statesmen who have wrought a revolution in his favor.

A selection of essays respecting the settlement and geography of America—the history of the late revolution and of the most remarkable characters and events that distinguished it—and a compendium of the principles of the federal and provincial governments should be the principal school book in the United States.

Webster was aware of the deep-seated opposition to universal public education among Americans: farmers, Northern manufacturers, and Southern plantations all depended on child labor. To alienate as few readers as possible, Webster proposed the simplest form of public education possible.

"Every small district," he wrote, "should be furnished with a school at least four months in a year, when boys are not otherwise employed. The school should be kept by the most reputable and well-informed man in the district. Here children should be taught the usual branches of learning—submission to superiors and to laws, the moral or social duties, the history and transactions of their own country, the principles of liberty and government."

Anticipating the feminist movement that was about to begin in England and America, Webster reiterated a theme of one of his essays at college, in which he had urged that every girl attend school. Presenting the same argument that Horace Mann and Henry Barnard would echo a half century later, Webster pointed out that as caretakers of the nation's children, women ultimately had greater "influence in controlling the manners of a nation" than men. "Their own education should therefore enable them to implant in the tender mind, such sentiments of virtue, propriety and dignity, as are suited to the freedom of our governments."

"Americans," he exhorted,

unshackle your minds and act like independent beings. You have been children long enough, subject to the control, and subservient interest, of a haughty parent. You have now an interest of your own to augment and defend—you have an empire to raise and support by your exertions, and a national character to establish and extend by your wisdom and virtues. To effect these great objects, it is necessary to frame a liberal plan of policy and build it on a broad system of education. Before this system can be formed and embraced, the Americans must *believe* and *act* from the belief that it is dishonorable to waste life in mimicking the follies of other nations and basking in the sunshine of foreign glory.[38]

Webster's articles on education would be reprinted for decades to come—he himself published much of the material in a pamphlet the following year—and they would influence such nineteenth-century educators as Mann and Barnard, who founded public school systems in Massachusetts and Connecticut based on Webster's principles.

The first issue of the *American Magazine* was a success—of sorts. Although it lost money, it won the plaudits of scholars and political leaders whom Webster admired most—in Charleston, Philadelphia, Boston, Hartford, and, of course, New York. On January 2, as he posted the first issue, Georgia ratified the Constitution, and within a week, his home state of Connecticut followed suit. Webster believed his pamphlet *An Examination into . . . the Federal Constitution* had been at least partially responsible for these early successes for ratification—and many members of Congress, which was then meeting in New York, agreed.

From the moment he had arrived in New York, Webster had found himself in demand by the city's most influential members of society and government. He attended theater, teas, and dinners, had his portrait painted, and took up the latest popular fad—social dancing. The aristocracy had always danced minuets and such, but new types of folk dances, such as hornpipes, had captured the public's imagination. What had been an occasional pastime became a nonstop occupation. Urban American women, seemingly in full rebellion against Puritanism, had turned dancing into a national craze. Brissot de Warville, the French journalist and Revolutionary leader, on a visit to Hartford's new dancing school, where sixty women had enrolled, had been stunned by the contrast between chaperoned French maidens and the uninhibited American girls "galloping boldly" and "hazarding themselves alone, without protectors . . . a stranger takes them by the hand and laughs with them, and they are not offended at it."[39] Oliver Wolcott's younger sister wrote her brother from Hartford that she had danced all morning and would dance again all night.

It was much the same in New York, where Webster could not resist the lure of dancing with so many women. While his heart remained in Boston with Becca, his feet "danced till fatigued" in New York at a society ball attended by "60 brilliant women,"[40] according to his diary.

Although Webster plunged wholeheartedly into New York's social whirl, by the end of January 1788, as he prepared the second issue of *American Magazine* for the printer, both he and his venture began to falter. He was physically exhausted from overwork and could no longer maintain his pace. Many literary contributions simply never arrived, and he had to write far more of the magazine himself than he had anticipated—nearly one-third of the first issue and half of the second.

Like the first, the second issue of the *American Magazine* drew plaudits. His father was pleased with his son's success:

> I have rec'd your monthly magazines, two of them which I Read with Pleasure, as do others, I think they are well written and will increase in credit as they are more known and read in future, but such things must have time to operate to the advantage of the Publick, and consequently to yours. . . .
>
> If you can help me to ten pounds of money by the 25th of next month and not embarrass your affairs, you will greatly help me. I mean not as a

gift, for I hope to pay it at a future day with interest. Your mamma says
if you miss any stockings supposed to be carried with you, they are here.
. . . No more at present. Wishing you return to Hartford as soon as may
be consistent with your interest, I remain your

Effectionate Father[41]

Despite acclaim from friends and family, Webster's magazine did not attract the wide national readership he had anticipated. Booksellers in almost
every city but New York were left with unsold copies, for which he was
never paid. The average American was uninterested in the schoolmaster's
lessons, and Webster's first two issues produced nothing but financial
losses.

It was also a critical failure in some respects. Webster wrote on so many
topics himself that his voice dominated the magazine and made it increasingly monotonous and uninteresting. His opinions colored everything from
freedom of speech to his friend Timothy Dwight's poetry. After publishing
Dwight's *Triumph of Infidelity*,[42] he accused Dwight of plagiarizing Pope.
Dwight never again contributed to the magazine. Although Webster's articles on education and ratification earned praise, his efforts in other areas
drew criticism, some of it humiliating. In his first issue, he wrote an absurd
"Letter to Dr. Stiles [of all people!], Accounting for the Fortifications West
of the Allegany."[43] His article claimed that the ruins of old forts on the
Muskingum River in Ohio were remnants of Hernando de Soto's expedition in 1539–40. The noted historian and clergyman Jeremy Belknap responded in the rival *Columbian Magazine*, published in Philadelphia, that
neither de Soto nor, for that matter, Webster had ever ventured into or
knew anything about Ohio, much less the forts along the Muskingum.

By the end of January, Webster was clearly discouraged and longed for
the comfort of Rebecca's attention and affection.

"Becca," he wrote,

> I could speak a thousand things which I cannot write and yet I speak
> but little. I wish to see you every day, and yet I know not whether you
> would add to my happiness. I sometimes think of retiring from society
> and devoting myself to reading and contemplation, for I labor inces-
> santly and reap very little fruit from my toils. I suspect I am not formed
> for society; and I wait only to be convinced that people wish to get rid
> of my company, and I would instantly leave them for better companions:
> the reflections of my own mind. Mankind generally form a just estimate
> of a man's character, and I am willing to think they do so with mine.
> And if I find that they think less favorably of me than I do myself, I sub-
> mit to their opinion and consent to a separation.
>   You will see by the tenor of this letter that I am in the dumps a little
> and will require the reason. Why, Becca, I have been asked the question
> so often that it really displeases me. To satisfy such enquiries, it would
> be necessary to relate the history of my life, which you have heard be-
> fore, and to enumerate a thousand things which ought to be forgotten.

I suspect that I have elevated my views too high, that I have mistaken my own character and ought to contract my wishes to a smaller compass.[44]

Although Webster later admitted that he had been too "vain and inexperienced," at the time he had no doubt that his editorial power and love of country gave him the right and obligation to write and dictate national opinion on every conceivable topic. He sought to be "monarch" of public thinking, according to Ebenezer Hazard, a leading New York historian and essayist of the period.[45] Webster was literally what one nineteenth-century Webster biographer called "a busy body,"[46] involving himself in every aspect of American life.

Among other things, Webster plunged into the growing debate over adding a bill of rights to the Constitution to guarantee certain liberties in perpetuity against infringements by Congress. Massachusetts, Virginia, and North Carolina, among others, threatened not to ratify the Constitution without a bill of rights. Webster took the opposite view, calling the Bill of Rights "absurd" and asserting that it would "shut the door to improvements [of the Constitution]. . . . No constitutions in a free government can be unalterable. The present generation have no right to say what the next generation shall deem a privilege. . . . If our posterity are bound by our constitutions, and can neither amend nor annul them, they are to all intents and purposes our slaves."[47]

For reasons that remain unclear, Webster decided to alienate the powerful former governor of Virginia, Thomas Jefferson, whom he needlessly assailed for his advocacy of the Bill of Rights. In addition, Webster alienated the nation's press. Citing widespread publication of salacious and libelous articles, he called for restrictions on press freedoms.

Weary of his constant complaining, the readership of Webster's magazine slipped badly, and the flow of contributions all but dried up. As he was preparing his third issue in mid-February, he wrote to Becca once more:

> It is one of the greatest misfortunes to me that a severe attention to business will hardly allow me to think of those I love, much less to write to them. The eyes of America are upon me, and, having made my appearance upon the stage, I must act my part well or lose both my reputation and my prospects. I do not doubt of success, but success depends on my unremitted exertions, and exertions which few men of my age have ever made. I can, therefore, only steal a few moments, once in a few weeks, to indulge my wishes and tell you my thoughts. I sometimes enjoy your company in dreams; a few nights past I was with you and passed a few happy hours with your smiles and your conversation. Would to heaven every night might be so happy. But, Becca, I cannot command my *waking* thoughts, much less my *sleeping ones*. Yet your happiness is among the first objects of my attention; and tho I do not write you so often, yet I am striving harder to promote your felicity than any person on earth. . . .

I sometimes go to dances and other parties, where I see ladies, and good girls, too, they are. But there is not a Becca Greenleaf among them; no such tenderness, such delicacy, such sentiment, such unaffected goodness. Adieu, Becca, your merit will certainly be rewarded, if heaven will grant the prayer of Your cordial friend and unalterable Admirer.

N. Webster[48]

7

AT THE END OF FEBRUARY, a two-day visit by his old friend Joel Barlow brightened Webster's somewhat somber winter. Barlow's fortunes had soared over the previous year, and he had come to New York to arrange passage to Europe later that spring. A year earlier, Barlow had published his fervently patriotic epic poem *The Vision of Columbus*.[49] He could not have timed its publication more perfectly—in May 1787, as the Constitutional Convention began its deliberations. A fanfare of publicity accompanied its publication, including an anonymous letter to newspapers—written by Barlow himself—that called "the writings of the Poets now living in Connecticut . . . equal to any which the present age can produce."[50] It was an instant best-seller, in large part due to Barlow's own promotional skills. Always the clever opportunist, he dedicated it to the king of France, Louis XVI, America's ally against Britain, and to the "gallant" French and American armies. The king immediately bought twenty-five copies, and Barlow placed his name on the top of the subscription list. Lafayette had little choice but to follow suit, with ten copies. George Washington ordered twenty, and naturally, Hamilton, Livingston, Burr, Pickering, and Paine, along with twelve obsequious generals, thirty-three colonels, seventeen majors, and fifty-two captains, subscribed as well. Together they bought one-fourth of the first printing. "It was their greatest exhibition of patriotism since the siege of Yorktown,"[51] noted one historian. Barlow reaped more than $1,500 from the first printing, of about sixteen hundred copies. Four months later, demand was still strong enough to warrant a second edition.

Barlow invested his profits in the Ohio Company, a huge land speculation by a group of slick former Revolutionary Army officers who talked Congress into selling them 5 million acres of wilderness along the Ohio River for about $1 an acre—and to let them pay for part of it in certificates worth less than ten cents on the open market. In addition, they talked Congress into cutting the price per acre by one-third to allow for "bad land" that might be uncultivable. In the end, Barlow and other insiders (including many congressmen) bought land worth $1 an acre or more for six and two-thirds cents. As company agent in Connecticut, Barlow used his fame as a patriot poet to sell thousands of acres and amass a small fortune. He was so gifted a salesman that the Ohio Company sent him to Europe to sell land to would-be emigrants. What Barlow may or may not have known—he was a glib, slippery fellow by then—was that the Ohio Company had already sold more acreage than it had bought from Congress and that he would be selling land that did not exist. Barlow offered Webster an opportunity to invest in the Ohio Company, but as an avowed foe of speculation, Webster wisely refused.

8

CHASTENED BY the humiliating inaccuracies in his de Soto story, Webster decided to leave nothing to guesswork in a historical sketch he was about to write on the decisive battle of Yorktown for Jedidiah Morse's expanded geography book.[52] He turned to George Washington:

> Sir:
>
> Having engaged to write, for Mr. Morse's Geography a sketch of the History of the late war, I take the liberty of making an enquiry respecting a fact which I am told is commonly misrepresented, and which perhaps no person but the Commander-in-Chief of the late armies in America can set right. An opinion, Sir, is very general that the junction of the French fleet and the American armies at Yorktown was the result of a preconcerted plan between yourself and the Comte de Grasse; and that the preparations made at the time for attacking New York were merely a feint. But the late [that is, former] Quarter Master General [Timothy Pickering] has assured me that a combined attack was intended to be made upon New York, and that the arrival of the French fleet in the Bay of Chesapeake was unexpected and changed the plan of your operations. A true state of the facts is all I have to request of your Excellency. . . . in writing history it is of infinite consequence to know the springs of action as well as the events; and a wish to discover and communicate the truth is my sole motive for writing. Please, Sir, to accept this as an apology for giving trouble to a gentleman who must be oppressed by a multitude of attentions of more consequence, and be assured that with perfect respect for yourself and family, I am, Sir, Your Excellency's most obliged and humble Servant.
>
> N. Webster[53]

Washington's immediate and detailed reply reflected his respect for and warm feelings for Webster, and it provided an important historic document from a future president. In a letter dated July 31, 1788, he said he had planned the combined sea-and-land attack with de Grasse's French fleet a year earlier, although they had not chosen the exact site "because it could not be foreknown where the enemy would be most susceptible." In the meantime, Washington admitted, he had sent out false dispatches to all high-ranking American military officers and civilian officials, including Pickering, to induce the Eastern and middle states "to make greater exertions in furnishing specific supplies than they otherwise would have done, as well as . . . rendering the enemy less prepared elsewhere. . . . It never was in contemplation to attack New York."

Washington wrote that the only choices as targets had always been Virginia and Charleston, South Carolina, and that he waited to see where the British had concentrated their forces before deciding and alerting de Grasse.

"That much trouble was taken and finesse used," Washington wrote,

to misguide & bewilder Sir Henry Clinton in regard to the real object by fictitious communications, as well as by making a deceptive provision of Ovens, Forage & boats in his neighborhood is certain. Nor were less pains taken to deceive our own Army; for I had always conceived, when the imposition did not completely take place at home, it could never succeed abroad.—

Your desire of obtaining truth is very laudable, I wish I had more leisure to gratify it: as I am equally solicitous the undisguised verity should be known.—Many circumstances will unavoidably be misconceived & misrepresented.—Notwithstanding most of the Papers, which may properly be deemed official are preserved; yet the knowledge of innumerable things, of a more delicate & secret nature, is confined to the perishable remembrance of some few of the present generation.

I am—Sir

Your most obedient
H'ble Servt.
G. Washington.[54]

9

BY MIDYEAR 1788, the states were falling into line in support of the new Constitution. It seemed certain that a strong federal government would replace the crumbling Confederation. In May, Webster wrote in his diary that he "rejoice[d] that Maryland has acceded to the Constitution,"[55] and he left for Hartford to vote for Connecticut's electors: the men who would choose the first president of the United States. In June, New Hampshire produced "great joy [as] the Ninth,"[56] and decisive, state to ratify the Constitution. On July 2, the president of Congress announced that the Constitution had been ratified by the requisite nine states and appointed a committee to prepare the change in government. On July 4, Virginia became the tenth state to vote for ratification, and according to Webster's diary, New York celebrated with "public rejoicings . . . the memorable aniversary [*sic*] of Independence."[57]

On July 23, New York City held a "Grand Procession . . . to celebrate the Adoption of the Constitution by 10 states. Very brilliant but fatiguing," Webster wrote in his diary. The procession was to be the richest, most elaborate pageant in American history, and the Committee of Arrangements asked Webster to write the official account for the city's archives. All New York turned out to cheer beneath thick clouds of bunting along the route down Broadway.

On the day before the procession, the *Daily Advertiser* published this plea: "The inhabitants . . . are requested to sweep their respective streets this evening and early to-morrow morning for the accommodation of the Federal procession."[58]

Webster marched in the parade himself and wrote this account for the *Daily Advertiser* of August 2: "The line of procession containing nearly five thousand people, extended upward of a mile and half. The march was slow and majestic, and the general appearance of the scene as far surpassed every one's expectation, as mere description must fall short of it. While numberless crowds were pressing on every side, the doors and windows of houses were thronged by the fair daughters of Columbia, whose animated smiles and satisfaction contributed not a little to complete the general joy."[59]

Webster went on to describe each group that marched, along with its banners and floats. The tailors carried a flag "ten by eleven feet" with "Adam and Eve represented naked, excepting fig leaves for aprons," and the motto "And they sewed fig leaves together." Aboard the float, the figure of George Washington "stood in full stature, holding a parchment in his hand, with this inscription, 'The federal constitution.'"

Webster listed the other elaborate floats that passed by before him: the Tanners & Curriers, the Skinners, Breeches Makers & Glovers, the Cordwainers, Confectioners, Upholsterers, Block and Pump Makers, and even a float carrying a "Federal Horse Doctor"—one Walter Gibbons, who was "dressed in an elegant half shirt . . . with a bailing iron in the horse's mouth, putting a ball of physic down the horse's throat."

Most other floats were less earthy, preferring to carry patriotic banners and exhibits symbolic of the nation's independence and newfound unity. "By union we rise to splendor," said the slogan on the Tanners & Curriers' float; "Americans, encourage your own manufacturers" was the motto of the Skinners, Breeches Makers & Glovers. Webster described the Cordwainers' float as

> a stage, drawn by four white horses, with two postilions in livery; a shop on the stage, with ten men diligently prosecuting their business, emblematic of ten states that have adopted the constitution, with colours extended over the whole length of the shop, representing, in front, his Excellency General Washington coming out of the state house at Philadelphia, and presenting the constitution to Fame; she receiving it standing in her Temple, and ready to proclaim it to an astonished world!

Another float carried the motto "May the Federal Constitution be supported by Liberty and Justice."[60]

The long march and the struggle to finish the July issue left Webster "not very well," and on August 8, he decided the cure lay with Rebecca Greenleaf in Boston. He sailed to Providence, then rode to Boston, and was reunited with "the dear girl" on August 12.[61] Two days later, he asked and received her father's consent to their marriage, after pledging to abandon his editorial ventures and return to the practice of law.

He spent the next two weeks meeting members of the Greenleaf family and their distinguished in-laws, the Dawes and Appleton families. Like the Greenleafs, the Appletons were prominent merchants. Nathaniel, a doctor who was cofounder and secretary of the Massachusetts Medical Society, had married Rebecca Greenleaf's sister Sarah. Thomas Dawes, the husband of Rebecca's sister Peggy, was a Harvard graduate and a prominent Boston lawyer who would serve on the Massachusetts Supreme Court from 1792 to 1802. Both Dawes and Appleton, who were about three years older than Webster, joined Rebecca's brother James in the circle of Webster's closest lifelong friends.

Despite his new familial ties, Webster did not forget to visit Boston booksellers to sell his *Institute*. To his dismay, he found interest beginning to sag and realized the time had come to abandon his failing magazine and concentrate on shoring up sales of his *Institute*. Part I of the *Institute—The American Spelling Book*—remained a huge success. Though less popular, parts II and III, the grammar and reader, were inextricably tied to the speller in a three-for-the-price-of-one offering. The success of the speller, however, had invited competition, and Webster recognized that he would have to revise it before events left its passages on history and geography out of date. Edes of Boston and William Young of Philadelphia were each printing at least five thousand copies of the *Institute* a year, and Samuel Campbell was publishing twenty thousand copies a year in New York—enough to have made Webster a wealthy man if he had been collecting the usual penny-a-copy royalty. Instead, he had traded away the prospects of all New York and Philadelphia royalties for cash in hand to found the *American Magazine*. Although the magazine had enhanced his reputation as an essayist, it had produced a net loss of about £250 pounds, or about $500, in less than a year—about a year's income for the average American of the era.

Despite the unfortunate contracts with printers in New York and Philadelphia, sales of *The American Spelling Book* by his original printer, in Hartford, were at least providing Webster a steady stream of income—about £300 a year. But as he recognized after visiting Boston booksellers, demand would almost certainly decline if he did not update its history and geography lessons to include ratification of the Constitution and American territorial expansion into Tennessee, Kentucky, and Ohio.

After two weeks in Boston, he returned to New York—by way of Hartford—to see his parents. His mother was not well, and Webster was concerned. He nevertheless set to work revising the speller, and in early September he sent the new edition to Hudson & Goodwin, his Hartford printers, with this covering letter:

New York, September 4th, 1788.

Gentlemen,

When you advertise the improved editions of the *Institute* . . . it may be useful to notify the public that it is the wish of many leading men in America that all the children in the different States should learn the language in the same book, that all may speak alike. . . . The University of Georgia, preferring this to Dilworth, Perry, Fenning or any other, have determined that this alone shall be used in all the schools in that state. The publishers flatter themselves that the northern states will heartily concur in the design of a *federal language.*[62]

10

AFTER WRITING TO JAMES GREENLEAF of his betrothal to Rebecca, Webster sailed to New Haven to attend Yale's commencement before riding to Hartford to see his parents. Reassured that his mother was well again, he returned to New York determined to sell his magazine and move to Boston, where he hoped the influence of his future in-laws would help him establish a law practice.

Upon his return, despite the worst hurricane season New Yorkers could remember, Webster found the implementation of plans for the new government progressing like a juggernaut. Congress had established New York as the site of the new government and fixed January 7, 1789, as the date for each legislature to appoint members of the electoral college. The college would cast ballots for the presidency on February 4, and the first Congress of the United States under the new Constitution would hold its inaugural session on March 4. On October 10, the last session of the Continental Congress adjourned officially, and the Confederation of the United States came to an end.

Webster's Federalists had triumphed, but for the first time in two years, Webster found himself ignored by government policy makers. His magazine had all but disappeared from bookstands, and he himself had run off to Boston at the very time that the nation's most influential men (along with those seeking influence) were huddling together to plan and organize a new form of government. Having absented himself from the initial deliberations, he found it all but impossible to influence them after their results had become faits accomplis.

To make matters worse, Webster suffered an abscess after his return to New York and had two teeth extracted—one by mistake. "This is hard indeed," he noted in his diary.[63]

On October 16, 1788, Webster turned thirty, having experienced a lifetime that would have satisfied most men. He commented in his diary: "30 years of my life gone, a large portion of the ordinary age of man! I have read much, written much, & tried to do much good, but with little advantage to myself. I will now leave writing & do more lucrative business. My moral conduct stands fair with the world, & what is more, with my own Conscience. But I am a bachelor & want the happiness of a friend whose interest & feelings should be mine."[64]

In November, he received a letter from his future brother-in-law James Greenleaf, who had moved to Amsterdam, Holland, and had established a profitable trading venture:

> My Dear Friend
>
> I have recd your favors . . . the affectionate stile in which you write me claims my warmest acknowledgements—'tis not sufficient to say . . . I am indeed made happy by the assurance that you have gained the affections of a Sister who is exceedingly dear to me. the manner of your proceeding in Boston I am much pleased with, & as you have gained the consent of my parents & friends, if mine is necessary or acceptable, you have it in the fullest manner, & may God Almighty bless you many, *many* years in the enjoyment of each other. . . . with respect to the time of your union taking place, I rely much on your prudence, & if my advice is of any weight you will not urge it until you have some fixed plan & until that plan produces sufficient for your maintenance comfortably. My Sister has never yet known the want of the little comforts of life & it would afford me a very painful reflection were she ever placed in a situation to want them. . . . my dear Webster, I do not hesitate to say that you will possess a treasure in my Sister which few would know sufficiently how to value.[65]

At the same time, Webster received warm wishes from Becca's brother-in-law Dr. Nathaniel W. Appleton of Boston. "If you make this fine Girl your Partner for Life," Appleton wrote, "you will have acquired the most amiable & all accomplished Lady for a Man of Sentiment & Taste for domestic Life, which this metropolis affords. You cannot prize her too highly."[66]

Just before Christmas, Webster swallowed his financial losses and turned over the *American Magazine* to Ebenezer Hazard, but it was never published again. Webster sailed for New Haven and the road to Hartford, writing in his diary that he was "happy to quit New York."[67] He spent Christmas with his parents and arrived in Boston in time to celebrate New Year's Eve with Becca and her family.

As the year turned, the state of Maryland agreed to cede ten square miles of its land to Congress for a new federal capital on the banks of the Potomac River.

CHAPTER SIX

Public Servant

I

SEVENTEEN EIGHTY-NINE was a year of firsts for the United States—the year the federal government began to take shape in its present form.

On January 7, the states that had ratified the Constitution selected presidential electors, and a month later, the electors cast ballots for the nation's first president. Each presidential ballot, as the Constitution then prescribed, contained two names. The man with the most votes would become president, and the runner-up, vice president. This ensured that the two chief candidates would hold executive office.

America's First Congress convened for the first time in April—the House of Representatives on April 1, and the Senate five days later, with only nine of its twenty-two members present. Congress counted the ballots of the presidential electors: all sixty-nine had named George Washington—and John Adams, with thirty-four votes, had come in second. The new nation had its first president and vice president.

Neither belonged to a political party. There were none—only factions (Federalists and antifederalists) that disagreed over the division of power between the states and the central government. Both Washington and Adams were Federalists, but both were patriots pledged to the common good. The government was apolitical and pledged to national unity—exactly the system Webster and other Federalists had worked so hard to create.

On April 16, Washington left Mount Vernon, and fourteen days later, he took the oath of office on the balcony of Federal Hall in New York, at the corner of Wall and Broad Streets.

Webster was lodged comfortably in Boston by the time Washington took his oath of office. Far from the political maelstrom, Webster had spent the winter sharing long walks and tête-à-têtes with Rebecca, and teas and dinners with her family and their in-laws, the Appletons and Daweses. He also converted his lectures on language into a 410-page book, *Dissertations on the English Language*, which Isaiah Thomas published in Boston.[1] With political unity seemingly assured, Webster was focusing his attention on building cultural unity. He set out to refine and simplify his new national language, so as to enable American children to learn to read, write, and speak alike as easily as possible. His original speller had only simplified learning methods—not the words and phrases to be learned. Webster had asserted in his earlier lectures on language that new, simplified spellings were needed "to render the pronunciation . . . uniform," so that "all persons of every rank, would speak with some degree of precision and uniformity. Such a uniformity in these States . . . would remove prejudice, and conciliate mutual affection and respect."[2]

Like most books of its day, *Dissertations* produced profits for no one but the printer. Almost all authors absorbed losses from books because they had no effective way of selling enough books to cover publishing costs and produce a profit. Unlike many other authors, however, Webster could not afford such losses.

Completed in May, *Dissertations* added another $400 to his losses from the *American Magazine*. *Dissertations* was, nonetheless, a landmark in the development of the American language. It opened with a flowery dedication to Benjamin Franklin and ended with an enormous appendix on spelling reforms that ignored Franklin's alphabet with its new characters and relied entirely on the existing alphabet. It simply changed spellings to read the way the words sounded when spoken. Webster proposed three broad categories of spelling reforms.

First was the omission of all superfluous or silent letters—for example, by respelling words like *bread, head, give, breast, built, meant, realm,* or *friend* as *bred, hed, giv, brest, bilt, ment, relm,* and *frend*. Webster also expanded the rule, introduced in his earlier speller, that eliminated doubling the final consonants of verbs with unaccented final syllables—*travel* simply became *traveled* instead of the British *travelled, cancel* became *canceled,* and so on.

The second category of spelling reform replaced letter combinations having ambiguous sounds, such as *ie* and *ea*, with combinations whose pronunciations were unmistakable, such as *ee*. Webster himself, three years earlier, had started introducing a few such phonetic spellings—*executiv* for *executive*, for example—in his personal letters and essays. Now he broadened their use into a major spelling reform, proposing to spell words such as *mean, grieve, speak,* and *zeal* the way they sounded: *meen, greev, speek,* and *zeel*. Similarly, he respelled words such as *grief, key, believe, laugh, daughter, plough, tough, prove, blood,* and *draught* phonetically, and they became *greef, kee, beleev, laf, dawter, plow, tuf, proov, blud,* and *draft*. He respelled words with the hard *ch* sound, such as *character, chorus, cholic,* and *architecture,* with a *k*; they became *karacter, korus, kolic,* and *arkitecture.* The soft *ch* in *machine, chaise,* and *chevalier* was respelled *sh—masheen, shaze,* and *shevaleer.* That left all other *ch* words uniformly pronounced *tch,* as in *chapel, cherish,* and *charge.*

Webster's third broad reform was the addition of pronunciation symbols, or diacritics, over vowels to indicate their pronunciation as long or short—a point (.), for example, just above an *a* to indicate it should be pronounced as in the word *father,* or a macron (-) over it to indicate its pronunciation as the long *a* in *same.*

"The advantages to be derived from these alterations," he wrote,

> are numerous, great and permanent. . . . The simplicity of the orthography would facilitate the learning of the language. It is now the work of years for children to learn to spell; and after all, the business is rarely accomplished. . . .
>
> Such a reform would diminish the number of letters about one sixteenth or eighteenth. This would save a page in eighteen; and a saving of an eighteenth in the expense of books is an advantage that should not be overlooked.

Apart from the savings in paper, Webster said, his new language would create differences between English and American orthography that would benefit American printers economically. "The English," he said, "would never copy our orthography for their own use . . . the same impressions of books would not answer for both countries." Because it would be uneconomical for British printers to print separate editions, American printers would necessarily have to print books for the American market in the United States.

Of far greater importance than its economic benefits, however, were the political and cultural benefits of a uniquely American language. "A *national language,*" Webster said, "is a band of *national union.* Every engine should be employed to render the people of this country *national;* to call their attachments home to their own country; and to inspire them with the pride of national character."

Webster felt that, despite their newly won independence, Americans had not severed their cultural ties to their parent countries. "The continued reading of the literature of one's homeland and the perpetuation of its customs prevent the development of respect for one's new land," he wrote. "Let us then seize the present moment and establish a *national language* as well as a national government. . . . As an independent people, our reputation abroad demands that, in all things, we should be federal, be *national;* for if we do not respect ourselves, we may be assured that other nations will not respect us. . . . Nothing but the establishment of schools and some uniformity in the use of books can annihilate differences in speaking, and preserve the purity of the American tongue."[3]

Webster's *Dissertations* had little immediate impact. Franklin studied it carefully for several months and, toward the end of the year, thanked Webster with a long letter suggesting even more reforms. Yale president Ezra Stiles acknowledged receipt of the book by writing, "We glory in a Son of this Alma Mater that can be the author of such a learned production."[4] He did little to encourage adoption of Webster's reforms, however. Nor did any of Webster's other friends. They had heard and read his material before and were uninterested in changing their ingrained habits—or forcing their children to do so. Without the support of influential men of letters, his reforms stood little chance of success in a nation of largely poor, illiterate farmers and laborers who seldom thought about or cared how they pronounced their words.

2

WEBSTER'S SEARCH FOR OPPORTUNITIES in the Boston legal establishment were no more fruitful than his writing venture, and by the end of April, he and his prospective in-laws reached the inevitable conclusion that he should return to practice law in Hartford, where he was better known.

Leaving Becca behind until he could afford to support her, Webster went to Hartford in mid-May 1789. By then, the growth of trade along the Connecticut River had made Hartford a center of commerce and culture, the equal of Boston, Philadelphia, and New York. In addition to resident cultural icons such as Timothy Dwight, John Trumbull, and Oliver Wolcott, artists and authors such as Benjamin West and Joseph Dennie were frequent visitors. Of Webster's personal friends who had settled in Hartford, the only absentee was the poet-turned-realtor Joel Barlow—also a celebrity, of course, but one who was comfortably settled in Paris, selling phantom Ohio Company land to panicky French aristocrats anxious to flee an incipient revolution.

Webster's friends welcomed him home to Hartford with an uninterrupted schedule of "festivities" that left him "little time for business."[5] Oliver Ellsworth, who had gone to New York as Connecticut Representative in the First Congress, welcomed Webster with a note:

> I congratulate you and the City of Hartford on your settlement there in the practice of the law. Should you like . . . my house, by and by, when you can see what accommodations will be, I shall be glad to engage it to you.
> The business of Congress progresses slowly, but not unfavorably.
> I hope in a month or two more, to see the judiciary and revenue departments organized, when the Government will begin to live and move and have its being.[6]

By the end of summer, Webster was earning about £300 a year in royalties from the *Institute* and handling enough cases in his law practice to convince Rebecca's parents to allow him and Rebecca to make marriage plans. James Greenleaf, his future brother-in-law, made things easier for the young couple by sending Rebecca a lavish wedding gift of $1,000 from Amsterdam.

Webster replied:

My Dear Friend,

 . . . By your kind assistance, your lovely Sister is enabled to furnish a house, and our union is not far distant. I have taken a house in the center of the town & of business, where I hope to find a home & domestic happiness. . . . If there ever was a woman, moulded by the hand of nature to bless her friends in all connections, it is your sister B[ecca]. . . . To be united to her is not mere pleasure, bliss, felicity, it is more, it is a union that blends pleasure and delight with social advantages, it is a *blessing*. The man who loves her, loves the temper of saints, and by associating with her, must become a better man, a better citizen, a warmer friend. His heart must be softened by her virtues, his benevolent & tender affections must be multiplied. In short, he *must* be good, for he would be in some measure, like her. It is vain to keep us asunder. Our hearts are inseparably united, & could you be a witness to our attachment, you would wish our hands united also. While health will permit I will exert myself with unceasing anxiety, to support your sister in easy circumstances. . . . You will hear of us often & we shall often be wishing for you[r] presence to make us happier.[7]

Although Webster had obviously idealized Rebecca as a paragon of wifeliness, she was, in actuality, a somewhat naive product of a rich Boston home, where she had learned all the social graces and ornamental arts—singing, piano, and the like—but few of the skills needed to be self-sufficient and administer a household efficiently. Long before her marriage, she carelessly spent her brother's $1,000 for expensive bedroom furniture, china, and mirrors—and saved none to furnish the living room and kitchen, or even to buy a wedding gown. When Webster told her the condition of her account, "she cried as if to break her little heart," and Webster thereupon paid for the gown himself.[8]

On October 16, Webster turned thirty-one and set out for Boston on what he called "an important errand"[9]—his wedding. The day after he arrived, he came down with the flu—then a serious disease—and he could not join Rebecca as "all the world collected" to see President Washington stopping in Boston on his first tour of the nation. Ten days later, Webster recovered, and on Monday, October 26, he married Rebecca Greenleaf.

"This day," he wrote in his diary,

I became a husband. I have lived a long time a bachelor, something more than thirty one years. But I had no person to form a plan for me

The only known portrait of Rebecca Greenleaf Webster, the wife of Noah Webster. Engraving from an 1832 portrait by Jaret Flagg.[10] (Yale Picture Collection, Manuscripts and Archives, Yale University Library.)

in early life & direct me to a profession. I had an enterprising turn of mind, was bold, vain, inexperienced. I have made some unsuccessful attempts, but on the whole have done as well as most men of my years. I begin a profession, at a later period of life, but have some advantages of traveling and observation. I am united to an amiable woman, & if I am not happy, shall be much disappointed.[11]

Rebecca's brother James wrote to Webster from Amsterdam: "I am indebted for a flood of happiness. my dear Becca married! & married to a dear friend who is happily among the few who know her worth, & her virtues! That you may live *long* & *enjoy* every *day*, every *hour* of your lives is my hearty prayer."[12]

3

WEBSTER RENTED A LARGE, appropriately elegant house in the center of Hartford. Rebecca's maiden sister, Priscilla, accompanied the young married couple to their new home to help Rebecca settle in and provide companionship during her first separation from her family. At the end of November they celebrated the nation's first federal Thanksgiving Day—a two-day holiday for which the vivacious Rebecca demonstrated her domestic skills by making "eleven pumpkin puddings, three plum puddings, & seven apple pyes." In a letter to her brother John, in Boston, she wrote that "Webster & Priss have demolished all the pumkin puddings & begin to make a hugh & cry after more. but they shan't have any till the other things are eaten, & I dont find myself dispos'd to help them eat. Pastry is my aversion. I can eat roast oysters, & potatoes with any body."[13]

The next day, they went by carriage for her first visit to Webster's family at his boyhood home, in West Hartford. Her husband's country relations stared in wonder at Rebecca, who wore her most elegant dress, a thick green brocade, flowered with pink and red roses.

"Mr. Webster's mother shed tears when she saw me for the first time," Rebecca wrote in her letter to John. "Most of the family were together; the little children crouded round their new aunt & admird her cloaths (for you must know I had on my green brocade)[.] we past an agreable day, return'd as we went—in a close carriage and caught no colds notwithstanding the storm which was very violent."[14]

The visit was not without its awkward moments. Webster's mother "was quite shocked to find that Noah had married a Boston lady who did not know how to knit,"[15] while Webster's young bride was so disgusted by "one custom" that Webster threatened his father never to bring her on visits again. There were any number of customs (including belching and blowing wind) that might have evoked the disgust of a proper city girl from Boston, although spitting on the floor seems the likeliest. The spittoon was not invented until 1823.[16]

Whatever it was that disgusted her, however, it was changed "at once," according to Webster's daughter Emily, "and though the neighbors grumbled at first at the 'Boston fashion,' it was finally followed by all of them, much to the improvement of their comfort."[17]

The following day the Websters held an elaborate and joyous house-warming dinner for "a large company of the most respectable Citizens" to meet Noah's bride.[18] Only Oliver Wolcott was missing. At Washington's request, he had gone to New York to help organize the new government. John Trumbull wrote to him after the housewarming: "Webster has returned and brought with him a very pretty wife. I wish him success, but I doubt in the present decay of business in our profession, whether his profits will enable him to keep up the style he sets out with. I fear he will breakfast upon Institutes, dine upon Dissertations, and go to bed supperless."[19]

Trumbull's fears proved unfounded. Hartford County had just reorganized its government, and Hartford became an incorporated city. The reorganization expanded the amount of legal work and tripled the number of official appointments. Webster profited immediately and was away working so much that Rebecca wrote to her brother John, "Yesterday, I was terrible homesick, & did nothing but baul the whole day—it was disagreeable weather—& husband was out the whole day. Today the sun shines clear, & the world wears a different appearance. what wavering mortals we are! the very winds & clouds are masters of our chearfulness."[20]

Webster joined two clubs—a legal club and a literary group—each of which produced additional legal referrals. In addition, Rebecca's family in Boston were unfailing in referring their Connecticut-bound clients. Thomas Dawes, who had married Rebecca Webster's sister Peggy Greenleaf, was particularly helpful. A prominent Boston attorney and jurist, he was part of a Boston intellectual elite that included the Adams and Quincy families, and he was able to funnel a great deal of important legal work to Webster.

Webster also attracted a good deal of important legal work on his own. To his delight, the merchants in Hartford turned to him to lead their fight for repeal of a hated state import tax. He gleefully unsheathed his pen and produced a biting eighteen-page pamphlet, with a typically provocative Webster title, *Attention! or, New Thoughts on a Serious Subject: Being an Enquiry into the Excise Laws of Connecticut.*[21]

Webster was his usual, blunt self, accusing the state government of threatening commerce and acting "contrary to the spirit and letter of the federal Constitution. . . . Excise duties are in themselves odious to a free people, unfriendly to morals, and productive of infinite frauds."[22] His pamphlet led to repeal of the tax and whetted his appetite for writing political essays again. He plunged into the growing conflict over slavery. Although he had agreed to overlook the Constitution's shortcomings when he agreed to campaign for its ratification, he no longer felt he could ignore the issue of slavery after his friend Dr. Benjamin Rush became the target of vicious attacks in Philadelphia for urging a constitutional amendment to emancipate the

The great physician Benjamin Rush became a close friend and supporter
of Webster. A champion of universal public education and emancipation,
he strongly supported Webster's efforts in both areas and provided considerable data for Webster's historic work *A Brief History of Epidemic and
Pestilential Diseases.* (Library of Congress.)

slaves. Webster sent Rush a letter of support and received this reply just
before the end of the year:

> Your acceptable letter shall be laid before the Abolition Society at
> their next meeting. I am sure it will meet with their most cordial thanks.
> It is en'o to reconcile a man to censure & redicule for *present* unpopular
> opinions & enterprises, to see the progress of justice & humanity towards

the poor Africans, for in the year 1772 it was as much a mark of a distempered imagination to advocate their claims, as it is now to defend the claims of criminals to the rights of humanity, or to the means of reformation. The most virulent attack that ever was made upon me was in the year 1772 for publishing a pamphlet in favor of a law to emancipate the slaves in Pennsylvania.

That man will be egregiously disappointed who expects the rewards of his patriotism or successful enterprises on this side of the grave. . . .

Accept my congratulations upon your marriage, & best wishes for your health & happiness.

Continue to do all the good you can by enlightening our country. *Expect* to be persecuted for doing good; & *Learn* to rejoice in persecution.[23]

Buoyed by his happy marriage and prospering law practice, Webster poured unimaginable energy into his writing, which, as he had told George Washington five years earlier, remained "a happiness I cannot sacrifice."[24] He began the new year of 1790 by producing a simplified, abridged edition of his grammar for five-year-olds[25]—to accompany the simplified speller he had produced at Pickering's urging in 1786. To these two, he added an abridged reader—*The Little Reader's Assistant*,[26] with a "Federal Catechism" that taught youngsters the basic elements of the Constitution.

In January 1790, Rebecca's father arrived from Boston—"to our great joy," according to Webster's diary.[27] A week later, he left with Priscilla in hand—and the news that Rebecca was pregnant with her first child. A few days later, Webster took possession of "my pew" at church and hired a maid to help Rebecca.

Rebecca's pregnancy capped what had been a complete turnaround in Webster's fortunes since his wedding. His law practice was thriving, and he had resumed the writing he adored. He responded to his good fortune with a gift to Yale College of 1 percent of his annual royalties from the *Institute* in Connecticut, for the duration of his copyright, to be awarded as prizes for the best essays on ethics, moral philosophy, and literature. At the same time, he established reading and writing prizes for boys and girls at Boston academies, with each of six annual winners receiving a leather-bound, gilt-lettered edition of his 372-page reader, which he renamed *An American Selection of Lessons in Reading and Speaking*.[28] Designed to teach U.S. geography, history, and politics, it also included "Rules in Elocution, and Directions for Expressing the Principal Passions of the Mind."

In April 1790, Noah Webster's father sold his farm, and the historic Webster property that John Webster had carved from the wilderness 155 years earlier passed out of the family's hands. At sixty-eight, with no sons to help, the elder Webster was not strong enough to work the fields. Moreover, he had accumulated debts with unwise land investments in Pennsylvania. Noah paid the interest on his father's debts, and the elder Websters went to live with one of their daughters, who was still living in Hartford.

4

ON APRIL 19, 1790, Benjamin Franklin died, and Webster immediately picked up his old friend's mantle by pressing ahead with the cause of spelling reform. Webster had grown appalled at the variations in spelling evident in letters from some of the nation's most outstanding scholars and political leaders. All had different ways of spelling. George Washington and Benjamin Franklin had the excuse of being autodidacts, but Yale president Stiles and Webster's close friend the poet-lawyer John Trumbull also spelled words inconsistently. Each had his own way of spelling and was often inconsistent in his own spellings. Even Webster's wife had her own peculiar, inconsistent ways of spelling. There simply was no standard orthography for the English language.

He sent the *American Mercury* the first of thirty essays to promote spelling reform, along with a copy of the letter Franklin had written the previous year, commending Webster's *Dissertations*. In June, he published all thirty in book form as *A Collection of Essays and Fugitiv Writings*.[29] Far wittier than his *Dissertations,* the *Essays and Fugitiv Writings* drew more public attention—if only because of its spelling of the word *Fugitiv.*

"The following Collection," Webster began,

> consists of Essays and Fugitiv Peeces, ritten at various times, and on different occasions, az will appeer by their dates and subjects.
>
> It haz been said that coquettes often looze their reputation, while they retain their virtu; and that prudes often prezerve their reputation, after they hav lost their virtu. . . . During the course of ten or twelv yeers, I hav been laboring to correct popular errors, and to assist my yung brethren in the road to truth and virtue; my publications for theez purposes hav been numerous; much time haz been spent, which I do not regret, and much censure incurred, which my hart tells me I do not dezerv. . . .
>
> In the essays, ritten within the last yeer, a considerable change of spelling iz introduced by way of experiment. This liberty waz taken by the writers before the age of queen Elizabeth, and to this we are indeted for the preference of modern spelling over that of Gower and Chaucer. The man who admits that the change of *housbonde, mynde, ygone, moneth* into *husband, mind, gone, month* iz an improovment, must acknowledge also the riting of *helth, breth, rong, tung, munth* to be an improovment. There iz no alternativ. Every possible reezon that could ever be offered for altering the spelling of *wurds,* stil exists in full force; and if a gradual reform should not be made in our language, it will proov that we are less under the influence of reezon than our ancestors.[30]

In fact, Webster had not yet worked out a formal plan for reform, with the result that he applied many phonetic principles in *Fugitiv Writings* inconsistently. He changed *is* to *iz,* for example, but left *would* and *offered* untouched. What he was doing, however, was thinking about reforms, playing with them, and testing them. His daring—and humor—went unappreciated in what was still a Calvinist America. Even among his closest friends, his only reward was stinging criticism, and the book was another financial loss.

Even his longtime champion Yale president Ezra Stiles, who gladly accepted a free copy for the Yale library, could not help carping, "I suspect you have put in the pruning Knife too freely for general Acceptance."[31] Historian Jeremy Belknap, still scornful over Webster's misidentification in the *American Magazine* of de Soto's forts in the West, wrote to Ebenezer Hazard, who had failed in his attempt to revive that publication: "I join with you in reprobating the new div-is-ions of words, as well as the new mode of spelling recommended and exemplified in the *fugitiv Essays ov No-ur Webster eskwier junier*, critick and coxcomb general of the United States."[32]

At least one anonymous reader seemed to understand what Webster was trying to do. Admitting he was "pleasingly astonished" with the *Essays*, he urged Webster to compile a dictionary with the new orthography, adding that "illiterate persons . . . spell *wrong* now, and they will do no *worse* (but probably better) in the improved orthography."[33] Webster responded with thanks, but opined that it was "doubtful whether the public mind is prepared for a reformed plan of spelling."[34]

Just after publication of *Fugitiv Writings*, Rebecca, in her eighth month, took a turn for the worse, and Webster asked his brother-in-law Dr. Nathaniel Appleton to come to Hartford. Appleton was unable to come but sent Webster these words of comfort and medical advice:

> Give my Love to Becca & tell her that 5 of her Sisters have been repeatedly in the same predicament & that there can be no reason why she, who has always led a rational & regular Life & enjoys good Health, should not do as well as they. I hope your Obstetrical Gentry whither Male or Female, practice on the modern plan of allowing their patients free air & moderate Exercise to the very last, & allow Nature to do her own Work. if it is customary with the Ladies at Hartford to have Females & there is any male practitioner in whom you confide in that department, do not let Custom but Reason prevail. I never yet knew a Lady who had ever had a female practitioner upon such occasions & afterward a male, that would ever permit a Woman to assist her again, & who did not always recommend a Physician to all her acquaintance.[35]

To distract himself from worries about his wife, Webster undertook another costly, albeit historically valuable, publishing venture—the first complete transcription and publication of the journals of John Winthrop, first governor of the Massachusetts Bay Colony. Webster had seen the original journal in Gov. Jonathan Trumbull's library and, in the flush of his prosperity, had hired the governor's secretary to decipher and transcribe the cramped Elizabethan handwriting. Webster then edited and published the work in two volumes at his own expense, but aware of the controversies his name might provoke, he omitted his name from the title page. To this day, for whatever reasons, historians and reference works—including *Webster's American Biographies*[36]—fail to mention Webster's role in preserving one of the most important historical documents of the American colonial period. Up to that time, American leaders had been careless about preserving records of early American history. Webster was the first American scholar to recognize the significance of this failing and begin remedying the situation with the Winthrop journal.

Even Webster's constant critic the historian Jeremy Belknap was impressed, and wrote a letter that was unusual for its humility toward Webster: "I beg you would send it to me as soon as you have it in your power. If I can be serviceable in any other way to the production of this much desired work, I will readily perform what you shall desire—& am with much respect. . . ."[37] At the time, Belknap was organizing the nation's first historical society, in Massachusetts, but had found little financial or intellectual support. In a typical display of generosity, Webster gave Winthrop's journal to Belknap to republish, at no cost and with no credit to Webster.

5

EMILY WEBSTER, Noah and Rebecca Webster's firstborn, arrived on August 4, 1790, after Rebecca spent forty-eight hours in labor. Emily's grandparents from Boston and West Hartford were there to greet her. Fortunately, as his law practice prospered, Webster was able for the first time in his life to absorb the financial losses from his publishing ventures. Indeed, his income was enough for him to invest $200 in a law library of his own.

Publication of *The Little Reader's Assistant*[38] inspired Webster to begin writing a series of homespun essays designed to educate adults who had not had the benefit of instruction by his *Institute*. Once again picking up bits of Benjamin Franklin's—or at least Poor Richard's[39]—mantle, he wrote a total of twenty-eight articles signed "The Prompter." They appeared weekly in the *Connecticut Courant*, beginning in December 1790. He reissued them as a book, *The Prompter*, which became one of the most popular and widely read books of its time, with more than one hundred editions printed over the next sixty years, in England as well as America.[40] Webster again left his name off the title page because, as he explained to his friend Colonel Pickering, who arranged for its publication in Philadelphia, "should it be known among my enemies that Noah Webster wrote it, I am confident both the writer and the book will be abused."[41]

Similar in style to Franklin's *Poor Richard's Almanac*,[42] it was a collection of moralistic stories and essays that entertained as well as taught essential lessons. Mixing humor and satire, Webster used his teaching skills to instruct readers in practical ways of conducting business as well as their daily lives.

"A Prompter," he explained in the preface,

> is the man who, in plays, sits behind the scenes, looks over the rehearser, and with a moderate voice, corrects him when wrong, or assists his recollection, when he forgets the next sentence. A Prompter then says but little, but that little is very necessary and often does much good. He helps the actors on the stage . . . and enables them to go forward with spirit and propriety.
> The writer of this little Book took it into his head to prompt the numerous actors upon the great theater of life; and he sincerely believes that his only motive was to do good.[43]

Among the Prompter's essays[44] were "Green wood will last longer than dry," "The Fidgets," "The Grace of God in Dollars," "It is better to borrow than to buy," "When a man is going down hill, every one gives him a kick," "Carpe diem, Take time by the forelocks," "A stitch in time saves nine," and "I told you so," which is reprinted here.

The Prompter
Number XX
I told you so.

What a wise man is this *I*! He foresees all evils and tells when and how it will happen. He warns *every* one of *every* misfortune that ever falls upon him after the mischief is all done, he struts and says with a boasting superiority, *I told you so,* tho perhaps he never said a word about it, until the thing happened.

It is warm weather—a man buys a quarter of veal or mutton—he deliberates whether he had better hang it up in the buttery or the cellar—he does not know whether the heat *above* stairs, or the damp air *below,* is most injurious to fresh meat—finally he puts it in the buttery—his wife knows nothing of this but the next day the meat is spoiled—the husband says; "My dear, the meat is spoiled." "Where was it put?" says the good woman. "In the buttery." "Aye, I told you so," says the wife.

"My dear," says the wife, one very pleasant day, not a cloud to be seen; "I shall visit Mrs. Such a one today; will you come and drink tea and wait on me home?" The husband pouts a little—but the woman makes her visit—in the afternoon a shower comes over, and the earth is covered with water—in the evening the woman comes in, dripping with water—the husband meets her at the door, exulting, *Aye, I told you so,* but you are always gossipping about.

A young man is going to take a ride—it is fine weather, and he thinks it useless to take a great coat—a shower comes about him suddenly and he gets wet—he comes home at evening and is met at the door with the consoling address, *I told you so.*[45]

The Prompter also included letters from readers:

> Sir,
>
> In your last number, do you mean me?
>
> A.B.

And Webster replied:

> To A.B.
>
> Sir,
>
> I *do,* and all that are like you between A and Z, and you have not on earth a better friend than the
>
> Prompter.[46]

For the first time as a mature author, Webster was clearly having fun, as Franklin had. The Prompter—and Webster—kept his mind off national political affairs. Neither his diary nor *The Prompter* mentioned that the Bill of Rights, which Webster had opposed so earnestly, had been ratified by the eleventh state and added to the Constitution.

Just as Webster was publishing his charming *Prompter,* Congress passed a national copyright law, which superseded the state copyright laws that Webster had pioneered. The new law gave authors copyrights to their works for fourteen years and the right to renew once for an additional fourteen years.

By the end of 1790, nearly four hundred printers, in every area of the nation, were producing Webster's spelling book, and it was used in almost every school. Competing spelling books had emerged, but the quality of Webster's speller precluded their ever gaining a toehold in the market.

His publishing enterprise was not without problems, however. Some printers extended their reach into other printers' areas and ended up in lawsuits with one another—and often with Webster. Webster had carelessly signed a loosely worded contract with Samuel Campbell in New York in September 1788, to raise capital as quickly as possible for his *American Magazine.* The contract now came back to haunt Webster by allowing Campbell to print an extra hundred thousand copies—a five-year supply—just before his rights expired. Campbell's huge stock precluded any other printer from entering his market. Webster sued Campbell, but the case dragged on for years, and Webster collected only a few hundred dollars.

To avoid paying royalties, many printers understated the number of copies they published. Others were simply careless and produced so many typographical errors as to preclude the uniformity that was the premise of Webster's standardized national orthography. It was impossible for him to supervise quality at dozens of different presses in cities across the nation.

For a complex, one-man enterprise spread across a nation linked only by dirt roads and rivers, the publication of his books progressed well enough. Webster was smart enough to get as much help as possible from friends and relatives. He convinced them it was their patriotic duty to over-see printers in their areas to ensure universal education and the linguistic unity of the American people.

Colonel Pickering, who was named postmaster general in the Washington administration, served as Webster's representative in Philadelphia; Dr. Nathaniel Appleton, Rebecca Webster's brother-in-law in Boston, constantly read page proofs from printers in that city; and all of Webster's friends and relatives became the equivalent of a nationwide sales force of volunteers, who ultimately convinced every college president, teacher, and minister to make Webster's speller the foundation of elementary education and national unity.

6

FROM THE MOMENT the Websters had arrived in Hartford in the autumn of 1789, their home had been a center of the city's social life and the destination of many distinguished visitors, including Yale president Stiles, Chief Justice John Jay, the artist Benjamin West, and an endless parade of friends and relatives, regardless of rank. Even the most distant cousins were always welcome, as were any of the acquaintances he had made on his travels through the now–United States.

Each of Hartford's most elegant homes, of course, took its turn as a site for teas, dinners, balls, and assemblies, to which the Websters were always invited. Noah and Rebecca broke the routine of their lives with occasional visits to Boston to see Rebecca's parents, to whom Webster formed such close bonds that they addressed him as "Son," while he called them, with all sincerity, "Father" and "Mother." The same bonds applied to Webster and Rebecca's brothers and sisters and their spouses; they addressed one another as "Brother" or "Sister."

Apart from social functions, Webster's description in his diary of life in Hartford at the time of the nation's birth displays nothing more startling than a litany of deaths, births, illnesses, fires, snowstorms, downpours, droughts, heat waves, and holiday celebrations. One holiday featured the ascension of a balloon that "took fire and fell." Webster's diary noted a near epidemic of crimes that included the sale of "cantharide" (cantharis), the aphrodisiac known as Spanish fly. Other entries noted:

"Mr. F. Bull's house broke open, & 300 dollars stolen."

"Grand Jury sit on the Windsor man charged with the murder of his child."

"Powder Mill blown up, 3 persons killed."

"Ledyard Seymour & Mr. Timons tried on a Complaint for firing a gun in the night near a School."[47]

After considerable, often bitter, debate, Connecticut established a lottery, which "commenced drawing" on January 7, 1791, with the "highest prize 1000, drawn by No 2069."

The entire town turned out in April 1791 to witness an eclipse of the sun—"the whole body of the moon immersed in the sun's disk, left a circular ring of light, bright day turned into half night." A month later, townsfolk again rushed into the streets—to tremble collectively in the aftermath of a mild earthquake.[48]

To his surprise, Webster discovered that "there is a Webster among the Onandagoes, who was taken an infant the last French War (about 1758, probably) son of a Mr Webster of New London. Bred a savage, he will not leave that life, altho his father brot him away at 13 years of age & put him to school, yet he staid but two years at Dartmouth College; he ran away, married & still lives among the natives. He must be of our family."[49]

Webster planted a large kitchen garden—potatoes, beets, carrots, parsnips, cucumbers, peas, and lettuce. He rejoiced over his first serving of fresh home-grown lettuce at the table, with Ezra Stiles, who had traveled to Hartford to see his former student and his bride. Webster was no amateur gardener. He had learned his craft growing up on a working farm and knew how to get the most from the land. By mid-June, he planted his third crop of potatoes—"in rows, 2 N rows, 7 or 8 inches apart." Unable to get enough cow manure to fertilize his garden, he studied all the books he could find on husbandry and began experimenting with plant materials, or compost, as manure: "Experiment, lay 3 square yards of mellow earth with seed potatoes about 8 inches apart, cover them with half rotten hay & straw, cover 1 yard with shoots broken off from the potatoes."[50]

After a series of additional experiments, Webster, ever the writer-teacher, published his findings in a pamphlet he called *The Farmer's Catechizm,*[51] with "Lessons for the Husbandman." He sent a copy to President Washington, a recognized authority, who had conducted agricultural research and pioneered composting at Mount Vernon. Webster suggested that the president create a national agricultural society to educate farmers and improve American agricultural output, but Jefferson blocked the proposal. Webster had so alienated Jefferson that the latter was suspicious of even the most innocent Webster suggestion, fearing it was motivated by Federalist ambitions to concentrate more power in the president's hands—and by Webster's ambition for a cabinet post to organize a farmers' voting bloc.

Unwilling to get caught in the line of fire, Washington sent Webster this reply:

> I think your train of reasoning in general good, and that the application of the principle in practical husbandry may be of considerable utility. This opinion is derived in part from facts; for your theory respecting vegetable manure has formed a part of my system of experiments for several years past. Buck-wheat, sowed expressly for the purpose of ma-

nure, and, when in its most luxurious state, turned into the earth by ploughing, has been found beneficial to the Crop, but not fully to answer my expectations. I cannot now give details of the Causes which I conjecture operated in rendering the effect less visible than I had concluded it would be; and I fear I shall not have leisure myself to repeat the experiments.

I cannot suppose there would be anything improper in bringing your observations on so interesting a matter to the consideration of some agricultural Institution. But, in truth, I have so many objects which claim my attention that I must hasten to conclude, with sentiments of regard and esteem,

Sir,

Your most Obed & Hum Servt
G. Washington[52]

The following spring, Webster solved his manure problems by buying a cow, which later calved, and then by adding a third cow for good measure.

7

THE HARTFORD YEARS saw Webster become an indefatigable community leader as well as a loving husband and father. His influence in Hartford expanded with his law practice, and on October, 22 1790, six days after his thirty-second birthday, he was admitted to practice before the United States Supreme Court by Chief Justice John Jay. Four days later, his diary noted with a tone of happy relief, came the "Anniversary of our marriage—one year past & no quarreling."[53]

Widely traveled by the time he returned to Hartford, Webster was an authority on urban problems and the efficacy of efforts to solve them. A wave of immigration had doubled the populations of Baltimore and increased the population of New York, Philadelphia, and Hartford by one-third. The population increases inevitably brought increases in crime and prostitution, housing shortages and soaring rents, and overwhelming waste disposal problems. Farmers usually agreed to clean streets of small towns and carry off the waste to use or resell as manure, but they had no incentive to do so on anything approaching a regular basis. As cities grew too large for farmers to clean, many streets accumulated huge heaps of garbage and horse manure. "Dead dogs, cats, fowls and offal from the market place . . . [were] the cleanest articles to be found," according to reports in the *Pennsylvania Gazette*.[54]

Webster threw himself into the task of solving Hartford's public health problems, proposing such projects as the paving of Hartford streets, which in Webster's day meant "covering them with hard rock stone."[55] He won strong support from merchants. They even agreed to pay taxes to underwrite the project after he convinced them that paving would eliminate mud, make street cleaning easier, and render stores more accessible, which would lead to increased sales.

In the spring of 1792, a mild epidemic of smallpox swept through Hartford. Webster urged the Common Council to authorize physicians to inoculate willing subjects—including Webster's own daughter. Experimental inoculation with pustule from patients with mild cases had been effective in lowering the incidence of the disease, although its effects on any given individual were unpredictable, and it could prove fatal. Webster's daughter's inoculation, however, was successful.[56]

Webster's effectiveness as a community leader reflected his skills as both teacher and writer. He used his pen to explore, expose, and explain Hartford's needs, and he then educated the public about the benefits of the projects he proposed. In March 1791, he wrote three articles for the *Courant* entitled "On the Utility of Banks." At the time, Hartford's merchants conducted trade by barter, buying single barrels of rum, for example, in exchange for similarly small quantities of grain or cloth. Philadelphia, meanwhile, had established a state-backed bank, which allowed that city's merchants to trade in larger quantities and capture an ever increasing share of the nation's trade.

Calling barter "a public and private calamity . . . the father of fraud and the instrument of knavery," Webster warned Hartford's citizens that the scarcity of paper money made it more valuable than actual commodities. "The consequence," he said, "is that . . . articles acquire two prices, a cash price and a barter price."[57] Webster urged formation of a bank as a depository for private and public funds, and a source of loans to spur the growth of commerce.

He followed up his article with a series of newspaper columns entitled "The Patriot." Each examined one broad community need or problem. In one article, the Patriot called for establishment of a publicly funded society for promoting arts, sciences, husbandry, and domestic manufactures. The society would help establish or improve local industries and reduce dependence on costly imports. As an example, he suggested that planting flax and hemp and improving sheep management could expand the spinning industry and keep workers employed during the winter season, while reducing the need to import expensive cotton and wool fabrics from England. "We are not in reality independent," he continued, "whilst we are obliged to look to [Great Britain] for our necessary clothing, or even superfluous ornaments."[58]

Webster's Patriot urged dredging the Connecticut River and digging a canal across Cape Cod from Buzzards Bay to Boston Bay to speed shipments between Hartford and Boston—a visionary proposal that would not be translated into actuality until 1914. He also called for construction of roads "with a hard, impenetrable foundation, to admit the transportation of loads at any season of the year."[59]

His Patriot articles were startlingly effective. In March 1792, the Connecticut legislature created the Hartford Bank, with Webster, John Trumbull, and a third attorney as shareholders. In March 1792, the people of Hartford rewarded him with his first elective office, as a member of the Common Council.

He, in turn, rewarded the people of Hartford. Ever the compulsive "busy body," he involved himself in every aspect of public affairs. He forced encroachers on valuable public riverfront property to return the land to the city. Then he expanded the program to pave city streets, adding sidewalk pavements for pedestrians, with gutters to drain rainfall into the river and prevent flooding. To reduce the swelling number of disputes between neighbors—and the consequent increase in court cases—he pushed through an ordinance requiring all property lines to be surveyed and marked. No detail seemed too small to draw his attention, and he approached each issue with the discipline of a scholar. When the council voted to build a new courthouse, Webster insisted on a thorough examination of brick manufacturing to ensure the use of the longest-lasting construction materials.

Webster was troubled by the city's social problems—particularly the plight of the poor and disenfranchised. "Examine the situation of most of the large towns in this state," he wrote in an article for the *Courant,* "and you will find an abundance of poor children wandering about the streets, clothed in dirt and rags."[60]

He continued to be outraged by slavery. He had seen the plight of blacks on his travels in the South and had expressed his disgust to Washington at Mount Vernon. In 1791, he spurred the founding of the Connecticut Society for the Abolition of Slavery and he delivered the principal oration at its first annual meeting, on May 12.

Every man, he thundered, has "a sacred right of freedom. No time, no circumstance, no human power or policy can change the nature of this truth, nor repeal the fundamental laws of society by which every man's right of liberty is guaranteed. Justice and Humanity require [abolition] . . . Christianity *commands* it."[61] Later published as *Effects of Slavery, on Morals and Industry,* his lecture cited Washington as having told him that "from the northern to the southern states, the agricultural improvements are in an inverse proportion to the number of slaves"—to which Webster added, "There is not an owner of slaves in Europe or America, the value of whose estate might not be doubled in a few years by giving liberty to his slaves and assisting them in the management of their farms."[62]

Webster adopted a politic approach to emancipation that appealed to selfish interests rather than emotions. Indeed, he frequently clashed with rabid abolitionists, who, he argued, so alienated slaveholders as to preclude any possibility of compromise and eventual abolition. "I endeavor to show by arguments and facts that the labor of slaves is less productive than that of freemen. A doctrine of this kind, if clearly and incontrovertibly established will perhaps go farther in abolishing the practice of enslaving men than any declamation on the immorality and cruelty of the practice."[63]

"The industry, the commerce, and the moral character of the United States," he said, "will be immensely benefitted by the change." Pointing out that the economy of Northern free states was advancing more rapidly than that of the South, he asked,

> What has produced this difference in the productiveness of labor in the Northern division? Peace and good markets have been common to both divisions; and the laboring people in the Northern States were as free before the year 1791 as since. What, then, has stimulated the industry of the free laborers since that period? The answer is obvious. An augmentation of capital operating upon their free labor. . . . It is of little consequence to a slave whether his master . . . gets four dollars or two for a hundred of tobacco . . . he plods along at his task with the same slow, reluctant pace. A *freeman,* on the other hand, labors with double diligence when he gets a high price for his produce; and this I apprehend to be a principal cause which has in the last two years occasioned such a surprising difference of exports in favor of the Northern States.[64]

While a councilman, Webster also pioneered the nation's first all-inclusive social insurance system, to provide welfare, unemployment, pension, and survivors' benefits to the poor, the widowed and orphaned, the handicapped, and the disadvantaged and homeless. He organized what he called a Charitable Society to operate the program and financed it by asking each merchant to contribute at least $1 a year for every worker in his employ. The society, in turn, would "give relief to honest, industrious, and frugal people, especially mechanics and other laborers who may be suddenly reduced to want." As he had done in founding the abolition society, Webster, always the consummate teacher, educated those who might oppose the Charitable Society by proving that poverty was inimical to Hartford's economic interests and would impede growth—in other words, that it was in the best interests of the business community to combat such social ills. Calling their contributions "a pittance," he said merchants would benefit by reducing poverty and resultant crime and by attracting "honest, industrious tradesmen and other laborers to settle in the town; it cannot fail to operate as a premium for industry; it will do honor to the town."

Webster rallied public support for his revolutionary concept with a moving plea, "To the Inhabitants of Hartford," in the *Connecticut Courant* in September 1792.

"The merchant," Webster wrote,

can insure his ship and goods against the hazards of the sea, and the citizen can insure his house and furniture from the risk of fire; but no insurance is found for the poor man who climbs the shrouds in a gale of wind, who risks his limbs and life upon a plank or scaffold in the air, or who exposes himself at the bottom of deep wells or trenches. Yet the poor *must* live, and to furnish the means they *must* labor; not only so, but they cannot always choose their employment—they must do such work and in such places as their employers direct, and the price of hazardous occupations is not always, perhaps not generally, proportioned to the danger.

He said that most nations "think it just to maintain their disabled soldiers for life" but make no provisions for a civilian worker "in case he loses a leg or an arm; nor *for his family,* when he loses his life by falling from a building or a ship's round-top, or by being buried by earth in digging a well." Webster said that "humanity" demanded more than sympathy for families "stripped of their principal means of support . . . it demands the helping hand of the charitable placed in more favorable circumstances." Pointing out that the poor were "the most numerous class of people," he admitted that many had invited their own misfortunes by "idleness and vices." But, he insisted, the majority of the poor were victims of misfortune.

Although most churches provided help for the occasional poor family, Webster's scheme was the first to establish such a far-reaching, publicly supported social security system, and he introduced it in an age—and in a society—that believed in rugged individualism. Not until 1935, more than two centuries later, would the United States put a similar program into effect. His Charitable Society provided a remarkable social safety net. It covered all family expenses of workers disabled by illness or accident, and if they died on the job, it took care of their widows and orphans. It provided supplemental food and clothing for children in large families of working parents who did not earn enough to provide such assistance. It provided aid to care for the handicapped children of the poor, and food, clothing, and money to "old poor people as have been honest and industrious, but by reason of infirmity are disabled from securing subsistence and who are unwilling to be placed in a common poor house." To forestall objections to his scheme, Webster pledged that his Charitable Society would limit all aid to poor people "whose poverty is not the effect of their *own vices.*"[65]

On October 16, 1792, Webster celebrated his thirty-fourth birthday— "one year more," he noted, "will make half the *three score years and ten*"[66]— and on November 29, Thanksgiving Day, he realized what had become one of his most cherished goals: "At evening, a number of Gentlemen convened at the Court House & formed themselves into a 'Charitable Society.' "[67] A few days later, Webster voted to elect George Washington to a second term—

then returned home to attend to mundane but pleasurable family affairs. Rebecca had been weaning Emily, who responded with a rain of tears that only Webster seemed able to stem by playing funny little melodies on his flute or by taking her in his arms and singing to her, ever so softly.

8

THE WEBSTERS' SECOND CHILD, Frances Juliana—Julia—arrived on February 5, 1793. The Websters and all of Hartford were at peace and experiencing their greatest prosperity in decades. At church, the Sunday before Julia's birth, Webster "preached for the Charitable Society" and collected $100—a large sum then.[68] Bitter cold engulfed the town, and violent snowstorms drove the Websters and their neighbors into hibernation during the rest of February. With Julia's baptism the only event of consequence, Hartford seemed frozen in time.

The world beyond Connecticut's ordered boundaries, however, was in chaos. Europe was a tumultuous battlefield, with no clear battle lines. Six armies warred a common foe but were in such disarray that they fired at one another as often as at their enemy—France. On February 1, Europe's conflict had spilled into the Atlantic Ocean, as France declared war on Great Britain and the Netherlands.

France had already been at war with Europe's other monarchies, whose crowned heads feared the French Revolution would spread to their lands and topple their thrones. With Britain drawn into the conflict, the huge British and French fleets were added to the military mix, along with colonial armies in the two nations' Canadian or West Indian territories. Americans were quick to take sides. Independent for barely a decade, many Americans remained fierce Tories, with deep emotional, familial ties to the former motherland and a longing for reunion. Others, still bitter toward the British, felt almost as strong an allegiance to France, the first nation to recognize American independence and to send its men to fight and die alongside Americans in the war against King George's tyranny. To these Americans, the French Revolution was a logical extension of their own overthrow of despotic monarchy.

As war fever infected North America, pro-French and pro-British mobs marched and rioted in Charleston, Philadelphia, and New York. Jefferson deliberately courted the "Gallomaniacs," whom he hoped would support his bid for the presidency in 1797. An admirer of all things French, Jefferson had been American minister to the French court and a decidedly undiplomatic spectator at the original Bastille Day, in 1789; and through the bloodiest days of Revolution, he would continue to issue apologias for French massacres.

"The liberty of the whole earth," he proclaimed, depended on the success of the French Revolution. He called France the "true mother country [of Americans] . . . since she has assured to them their liberty and independence."[69]

Initially, Webster and many other American leaders echoed Jefferson's sentiments. "When the States General first assembled in France, for the dignified and glorious object of reforming the abuses in the French government and raising the people from their degraded state of vassalage to the rank of freemen, I exulted in the joyful event, and my heart felt the liveliest interest in the success of their measures," Webster would explain several years later.[70]

Like Washington himself, Webster hailed Lafayette, who had fought in the American Revolution and led the French army to victory over French king Louis XVI's forces. Only a few years earlier, Webster had dined with Lafayette in the very house he now occupied with Rebecca in Hartford. For Webster and the nation, the key to the Bastille that Lafayette gave George Washington after the French Revolution began locked the two nations in brotherhood and united their two revolutions. A year after the storming of the Bastille, the French king signed the Declaration of the Rights of Man, which made France a constitutional monarchy. The French Revolution seemed to have ended as liberally as the American uprising.

In August 1792, however, the Revolution resumed when a mob stormed the king's palace in Paris and massacred his Swiss guard. When Louis and his family took refuge in the legislative Assembly, the Assembly suspended and confined him. A month later, the government rounded up and summarily executed more than one thousand suspected royalists. Ever the dissimulating French apologist, Jefferson excused the September Massacres, saying, "Rather than it [the Revolution] should have failed, I would have seen half the earth devastated."[71] Webster echoed Jefferson's sentiments. Although shocked by the massacres, he convinced himself that the French were only "creating some evils to correct enormous abuses." He predicted that the Revolution would still yield "an improved system. . . . My faith in the goodness of the cause and the purity of the intentions of the reformers continued unabated."[72]

And then, to his amazement, the words of Joel Barlow, of all people, appeared in American newspapers to sustain Webster and Jefferson. The farm boy–turned–Calvinist chaplain–turned–lawyer and real estate speculator did not just apologize for the Revolution; he was leading it. Two years earlier, an angry mob of would-be émigrés had run Barlow out of Paris after he had sold them phantom land in Ohio and his aides had embezzled all of their (and his) money. A desperate plea to Oliver Wolcott back in Hartford had brought a loan of £100 to flee to London, where, within months, he reemerged on the crest of opportunism as Tom Paine's replacement essayist. After stealing their money, Barlow had the audacity to lecture his aristocratic French victims in an essay he called *Advice to the Privileged Orders in the Several States of Europe Resulting from the Necessity and Propriety of a General Revolution in the Principle of Government.*[73]

The essay joined Paine's *Rights of Man* as the most widely read work of the Revolution. It earned Barlow French citizenship (with Paine) and a seat as a delegate at the French National Assembly, where he read "A Letter to the National Convention," outlining a form of republican government. Asserting that "kings can do no good," he urged direct popular rule based on universal suffrage, a lower age of majority, and frequent elections. Barlow called for an end to capital punishment, to debt prisons, to colonization and standing armies, and he called for complete separation of church and state.[74] His letter won America's applause—from Jefferson, Webster, Yale president Stiles, and all his old Yale friends.

But only two months later, on January 15, 1793, the National Assembly voted to try the king for treason. It found him guilty the next day, sent him to the guillotine a week later, and declared war on Britain ten days after that. Barlow not only approved, he gleefully galloped away to claim control of a vacant seat in Savoy, even as King Louis XVI's hooded head still bobbed in the basket at the guillotine.

In Philadelphia, the Tory *Porcupine Gazette* assailed Barlow as a man with such "passion for murder, that the sacrifice of Louis and his Queen, on the scaffold, was made the theme of his exultation, and bacchanalian orgies."[75] The newspaper claimed the poet Barlow had commemorated the king's execution by penning these words to the British anthem "God Save the King":

> God save the Guillotine,
> Till England's King and Queen,
> Her Power shall prove;
> Till each appointed knob
> Affords a clipping job
> Let no vile halter rob
> The Guillotine.
> When all the sceptered Crew
> Have paid their homage to
> The Guillotine,
> Let Freedom's flag advance,
> Till all the world, like France,
> O'er tyrants' graves shall dance,
> And peace begin.[76]

Webster was now truly appalled by the succession of bloody events. Along with other American Federalists, he condemned the French Revolution as a vehicle of irreligion, anarchy, and mass slaughter. Barlow's light-hearted opportunism disgusted him. "No man on earth not allied to me by nature or by marriage had so large a share of my affections as Joel Barlow,"

Webster later wrote to Barlow. "The principles of irreligion you avow . . . form the partition-wall which has separated you from many of your old friends."[77]

<h1 style="text-align:center">9</h1>

AS THE SPRING OF 1793 invited Americans into the streets, groups gathered outside newspaper offices to read the papers—or rather to hear them read by the most literate of their number. Emotional comments by Gallomaniacs erupted into angry debates with anti-Gallicans who favored neutrality. By late spring, the debates deteriorated into brawls that spread down the alleys and streets of major cities and exploded into rioting.

No one in government seriously favored America's entry into the war. Hamilton, a Federalist, and even Jefferson, despite his populist rhetoric, knew the nation could not afford war—either financially or militarily. Interest on the national debt was consuming more than 40 percent of the nation's revenues. The country had no navy, and its tiny army was too busy fighting Indians in the Northwest Territory to defend frontiers in the Northeast and South, against the British in Canada and the Spanish in Florida.

The French government, however, was eager to draw the United States into the war—to weaken the English and the Spanish by forcing them to fight a war on two fronts. The French sent squads of agents to America to infiltrate a network of Democratic Clubs that Jeffersonians had organized to build a political party that would carry him to the presidency. Eleven clubs were flourishing by the beginning of 1793,[78] and at least twenty-four more were being organized. By the spring of 1793, French agents had infiltrated them all and converted them into Jacobin organizations similar to those that had fomented revolution in France.

Their goal, Webster later explained in a newspaper article, was "to gain a controlling influence" over the United States by fomenting revolution, overthrowing the Washington government, and eventually uniting the two countries in war against England.[79] "The most effective means of carrying their point in this country was . . . gradually and secretly to acquire numbers and strength till they were able to bid defiance to the constitutional authorities. The moment this project was announced in 1793, I was persuaded of its fatal tendency, and set myself to unmask the views of the founders of private clubs and to expose their dangerous effect on my unsuspecting fellow countrymen."[80]

Webster said the clubs formed "a league of societies, disciplined to the orders of chiefs, whose views were concealed, even from the members themselves, and which must be crushed in its infancy or it would certainly crush the government." It was, he said, one of "the most daring projects of throwing the world into confusion that have been exhibited since the incursions of the Goths and Vandals."[81]

The mastermind of the project was Edmond-Charles-Edouard Genet, the French Republic's first minister plenipotentiary, or ambassador, to the United States. Genet arrived in the United States on April 8, 1793, with secret orders to overthrow the United States government and extend French hegemony over North America by linking the United States, Canada, Spanish Florida and Louisiana, and the French West Indies into a new, French-ruled American federation.

The secret orders he carried instructed him to begin by negotiating a "national pact in which the two nations should amalgamate their commercial and political interests . . . in order to assist in every way the extension of the Kingdom of Liberty [France]." The pact was to ensure "the emancipation of Spanish America . . . the deliverance of our ancient brothers of Louisiana from the tyrannical yoke of Spain, and the addition, possibly, of the beautiful star of Canada to the American constellation."[82]

"In order to make your representations more effective," his orders went on,

> [you are] *to direct opinion by means of anonymous publications.* The Boston and Baltimore gazettes will be the best ones to use for distributing such publications in order to turn aside suspicion of authorship from you; but the more you contrive to influence public opinion indirectly, the more your official discussions with the President and with the Senate must be kept secret so as not to arouse alarm and give them time to cabal against you. Your mission requires of you the greatest astuteness, but in order to be effective it must be secret.[83]

Instead of following normal diplomatic procedure by presenting his credentials to the American president in Philadelphia, Genet sailed to Charleston, South Carolina, the heart of the secessionist-minded South, aboard a gunboat, the *Embuscade*. Abhorrence for the federal government had reached explosive levels in the Carolinas, where a popular majority had opposed the Constitution and the establishment of a strong federal government.

"French agents," Webster explained in a newspaper article, had preceded Genet and "spread pamphlets and other papers tending to alienate the minds of people from the government of their country and . . . labored zealously to effect a revolution in the United States and to overthrow the government."[84]

Charleston greeted Genet not simply as the representative of the French Revolution but as a leader of their own budding insurrection against the federal government. The handsome young Frenchman said nothing to discourage them. A fiery orator, the thirty-year-old Genet was a brilliant, if arrogant, strategist, with experience, as French chargé d'affaires, of maneuvering among the intrigues of the court of Catherine the Great in Saint Petersburg. His role in organizing Jacobin clubs in her capital city had so infuriated Catherine that she expelled him. His orders now gave him the opportunity to try again in America.

South Carolina governor William Moultrie led the raucous crowd of greeters at dockside, where Genet responded in a mesmerizingly attractive French accent. "In the United States," he cried out, "men still exist who can say, 'Here a ferocious Englishman slaughtered my father; there my wife tore her bleeding daughter from the hands of an unbridled Englishman' [and] those same men can say, 'Here a brave Frenchman died fighting for American liberty; here French naval and military power humbled the might of Britain.' "[85]

The crowd exploded with cheers and spontaneous choruses of "La Marseillaise." They adopted Genet's cause as their own. Night after night, Charleston's leading citizens smothered him with adulation at banquets, public receptions, and concerts.

"This man," Webster later wrote in a newspaper article, "began his mission by telling a croud [sic] of people a most daring lie. He declared the French government did not wish the United States to engage in the war, when his instructions, afterwards published, expressly charged him to use all his endeavors to induce us to become a part in the war and join France."[86]

Within ten days, Citizen Genet, as he was called in Jacobin France, turned Charleston into a base of sedition, fitting out four privateers that sailed out to raid British and Spanish shipping. He dispatched agents to Canada to prepare the French-speaking islands of Saint-Pierre and Miquelon for recapture by a French fleet from the West Indies. Other agents went to Georgia to organize angry residents against neighboring Spanish forces in Florida. For years, the Spanish had lusted for Georgia's lush agricultural heartland and had sent Indian raiders to attack American settlers.

Genet, Webster fumed, did not have "the civility to call on the Executive and show his commission . . . his first acts of commissioning privateers and enlisting men for an expedition against the Spanish colonies were the grossest insults to our government and to the people; for it was assuming the right of sovereignty without the authority of the American people."[87]

In the West, Genet had secretly engaged a force of mercenaries to strike at the Spanish in Louisiana, under George Rogers Clark, a bombastic inebriate who had risen to brigadier general in campaigns against the Indians and the British in the Revolutionary War. Crushed by debt—and drink— Clark lusted desperately for the booty that would be his if he and his ragtag mercenaries raised the French flag in Spanish-held Louisiana and the Floridas.

News of Genet's activities plunged the capital, Philadelphia, into crisis. Washington himself exploded with anger, for at any moment Britain might use Genet's activities as an excuse to declare war on the United States.

Washington knew another war would shatter his fragile young nation and leave it prey to foreign conquest, with France, despite her pretense of friendship, as likely a predator as any other nation.

Jefferson defended Genet: "It is impossible for anything to be more affectionate, more magnanimous, than the purport of his mission."[88] Jefferson hoped that if America tacitly supported French conquest of Spanish Florida and Louisiana, France would cede Florida to the United States and grant American vessels navigation rights on the Mississippi.

Buoyed by Jefferson's support, Genet left Charleston for Philadelphia on April 19, convinced that Americans would rise to support his cause. At every town, the people cheered, church bells rang, and French flags waved as the Frenchman rode by. Aides traveled ahead "to announce me to the people"—and distribute free rum.[89]

On April 22, President Washington tried to blunt the effects of the Frenchman's procession by issuing a proclamation of neutrality. Although it did not contain the word *neutrality,* the proclamation prohibited American citizens from "aiding or abetting hostilities" or participating in non-neutral activities in the United States.[90] Far from calming the nation, however, the proclamation enraged street mobs even more. "The cause of France is the cause of man, and neutrality is desertion," cried Jefferson's power-hungry republican Democrats.[91]

Along Genet's march to Philadelphia, the crowds damned the proclamation. His journey became "a succession of civic festivals," with Genet "clasped in the arms of a multitude that had rushed out to meet me."[92] On May 2, Genet's frigate, the *Embuscade,* which had been sailing up the coast parallel to Genet's overland route, arrived in Philadelphia with huge banners streaming from her mastheads. *Enemies of equality, reform or tremble!* trailed from the foremast. *Freemen, behold we are your friends and brothers!* flew from the mainmast. *We are armed for the defense of the rights of man!* waved from the mizzen. Thousands gathered to cheer its arrival and greet its sailors at dockside.

"The bosoms of many hundreds of freeman beat high with affectionate transport," Genet wrote, "their souls caught in the celestial fire of struggling liberty."[93]

Demonstrations extended through the night and grew more tumultuous the following day. John Adams described "the terrorism excited by Genet . . . ten thousand people in the streets of Philadelphia, day after day, threatened to drag Washington out of his house and effect a revolution in the government or compel it to declare war in favor of the French Revolution and against England." Adams said he "judged it prudent and necessary to order chests of arms from the war office" to protect his house.[94]

Washington received Genet with icy formality. The president reiterated his deep resolve to keep America neutral, but after bowing obsequiously, Genet showed his utter contempt for the American leader by converting eight more American ships into French privateers. Public adulation had convinced the arrogant young Frenchman "that a very distinct party had risen against Washington."[95]

"Instead of respecting our independence," Webster wrote angrily in a newspaper article, "he began his infernal intrigues by sowing sedition and taking steps that would force us from neutral ground."[96]

On June 5, with the British threatening war against the United States, Washington ordered Genet's privateers out of United States waters, but with no American navy to enforce the order, Genet again defied the president. He bought newspaper advertisements urging "Friends of France" to enlist in the French service to fight the British.[97] As Genet's ships sailed in and out of American ports, raiding British ships, the British retaliated by seizing American vessels and impressing or imprisoning American crews. War with Britain seemed inevitable unless Genet was stopped.

Washington's impotence was frighteningly evident in Boston when the Websters arrived to visit James Greenleaf, Rebecca Webster's brother, who had just returned from Holland. What they saw in the harbor shocked them: a banner flew from the masthead of a French ship listing names of eleven prominent Americans as "aristocrats" and enemies of France. Most were friends of the Greenleafs and the Websters.[98]

An infuriated Webster returned to Hartford to organize Connecticut in support of the president's stance on neutrality. He drew up an "Address from the Inhabitants of Hartford to the President of the United States" for the Common Council to sign and send to the president.

"Warmly attached to our government, both by interest and affection," Webster wrote, "we take the liberty to assure you, that we shall ever stand ready by our utmost exertions, in every legal and constitutional way, to support the just measures of your administration; and to lend the assistance in maintaining the peace and harmony of the States, and in opposing the insidious designs of those persons, if there be any so deluded, who may wish to subject the country to foreign influence, and involve it in the horrors of war."[99]

By late July, the French Reign of Terror was slaughtering thousands at guillotines in every city in France. By then, Genet's influence in America had evolved into an ominously powerful political movement that threatened full-scale revolution. His privateers had captured more than eighty merchant ships, some within United States territorial waters. French consuls routinely flouted American laws by bringing captured British ships into American ports for condemnation and sale. The American government was powerless to interfere. As Webster prepared his message to Washington, Genet's sailors were running riot in every port. The British consul in Philadelphia reported to his government: "The French seamen ranged the streets by night and by day, armed with cutlasses, and committed the most daring outrages when they met any of our seamen . . . wounded and abused

them, and even took some on board the frigate where they were de-
tained."[100] The Washington administration was unable "to enforce any measures in opposition to the . . . French faction." Genet seemed ready to raise
the tricolor and proclaim himself proconsul.[101]

Genet called for nothing less than revolution. Day after day, night after
night, he whipped the Philadelphia crowds into a frenzy, encouraging them
to unite with their French brethren in "the Revolution of the World." He
spoke nonstop. His voice was heard everywhere. The Jeffersonian press fueled the conflagration with wild accusations that Washington, Hamilton,
and Vice President John Adams were plotting to establish a hereditary
monarchy, with Washington as king. The ardently pro-Genet *New-York Journal* charged Vice President John Adams with subversion: "Were he to embrace a stinking prostitute, and endeavor to palm her on the people of
America for an unspotted virgin, [Adams] would not . . . act a more infamous part than he has done."[102] Antigovernment newspapers elsewhere accused Adams, Treasury Secretary Hamilton, and Chief Justice John Jay of
joining a royalist plot to restore the British king to power. The *Journal* went
a step further by publishing cartoons portraying Washington's head falling
into a guillotine basket on Market Street. "The President was much in-
flamed,"[103] wrote Jefferson, who had now grown thoroughly disenchanted
with Genet and accused him of being "hot-headed . . . disrespectful & even
indecent towards the President."[104] He had defended Genet as a friend of
the United States, and Genet's activities had thoroughly embarrassed and
humiliated him. Jefferson submitted his resignation as secretary of state, to
take effect at the end of the year.

A group of twelve of Washington's advisers feared the government would
fall unless they could break the hold of the Jacobin-controlled press over
public opinion and disperse the street mobs. The group, which included
Treasury Secretary Hamilton and Chief Justice Jay, agreed to invest $150
each to fund a new progovernment newspaper that would expose Genet
and his Jacobins as spies and urge Americans to rally behind the president.
With Webster's letter of support for the president in hand, Watson, Wolcott, Pickering, and King suggested that Webster, an experienced magazine
editor and publisher, whose essays had consistently encouraged national
unity, head the new publication.

They selected New York as the logical city because it had no progovernment newspaper, and its port made it a logical distribution center for a
national newspaper. Moreover, if Genet continued his northward procession, New York would be his next destination. The group asked James Watson, the partner of Rebecca's brother James Greenleaf, to enlist Webster.
Chief Justice Jay agreed to serve as liaison to Webster in New York.[105]

Already infuriated by the French fleet in Boston Harbor, Webster could
not resist Watson's summons to the national stage to help save the union.
He agreed to meet with Chief Justice Jay in New York on August 16.

Genet's ineluctable ascent to power reached a peak on August 1, with an arrogant ultimatum he sent directly to President Washington demanding that the president call Congress into special session to choose between neutrality and war. Believing the adoring street mobs were ready to overthrow Washington, Genet warned he "would appeal to the people . . . [the] decisions of the President."[106]

His audacity knew no bounds. He asked Treasury Secretary Hamilton for money to finance Clark's militia in the West and then asked Secretary of War Henry Knox for cannons. Hamilton rebuffed him out of hand, while Knox responded angrily that the United States would not lend him even a pistol, let alone a cannon.

On August 2, Washington issued a formal demand to the French government for Genet's recall. The French ignored it, believing Genet's dispatches that the imminent overthrow of the American government would make the recall meaningless. An infuriated Washington ordered his cabinet to prepare a bill of "verifiable incidents" that would justify deporting the French envoy.

Genet responded by carrying out his threat to appeal directly to the American people to revolt against the United States government. He boarded his flagship, the *Embuscade,* the frigate that had brought him to Charleston, and sailed out of Philadelphia at the head of a flotilla of privateers, destined for New York, where he planned to begin his revolution. On August 7, his fleet arrived flying red-white-and-blue banners with incendiary slogans.

A huge crowd greeted his arrival with a chorus of "La Marseillaise" and led him on endless parades through Manhattan's narrow streets. Adoring mobs wearing Revolutionary cockades cheered his every step with cries of "Genet to power," "Down with Washington," and pledges to follow the young Frenchman into battle against Britain.

"Americans are ready to mingle their most precious blood with yours," one newspaper assured Genet. Even New York governor George Clinton marched with Genet and invited the French envoy to the governor's mansion to dine with him and his daughter Cornelia, whom Genet immediately began to court.

On August 12, Secretary of State Jefferson sent Genet a letter of rebuke for violating "the established course for the diplomatic characters residing here" by engaging in "direct correspondence" with the president. He told Genet that "the Secretary of State is the organ through which their correspondence should pass" and that the president would ignore Genet's message.[107]

As Genet read Jefferson's message, Noah Webster arrived in New York. It had been "one of the most excited days" in the city's history, according to Webster's diary. The papers and diaries of Webster, Genet, and Genet's aides, along with newspaper reports, paint a vivid picture of the day's events.

Swirling mobs had captured the streets of Manhattan when Webster's coach reached its terminal on South Street. As he made his way to his lodgings up the slope of Maiden Lane, the city's streets echoed with cries of *"Vive la France!"* and "Down with King Washington!" Fireworks crackled everywhere. Mobs sang, *"Allons enfants de la patrie,"* and menaced passersby with threats of "King or country?" And beneath the staccato of shouts, the steady, irritating chant *"Vive Ge-net, Vive Ge-net, Vive Ge-net, Vive Ge-net . . ."* droned on and on throughout the day. Webster tried his best to understand the anger in the faces of his countrymen.

"The people of this country are deceived," he concluded, in retrospect, in a newspaper article. "They believe the French to be fighting for liberty. This opinion is not well founded. They began the revolution with honest views of acquiring their rights, but they have overleaped this limit and are contending for plunder and empire. The people of America must be undeceived—they will be undeceived."[108]

As he shut the door behind him at the tavern, it may have muted the chorus of *"Vive Ge-net"* from the mob outside, but a clatter of voices inside resounded no less harshly than those in the street. "Americans love you," one voice called out. "They are your brethren—ready to die with you."[109] Webster poked his head into the barroom and identified the unmistakable face at the center of the idolatry as the minister plenipotentiary of France to the United States, Edmond Genet.

Although Webster knew a confrontation was inevitable, he had not intended to cross paths with Genet so soon. The unexpected coincidence of both of them lodging at the same inn gave him little time to calm himself and gather his thoughts.

The Frenchman was so intoxicated by mob adulation, so confident of victory over Washington, that he paid scant attention to the former schoolmaster settling in at the tavern. Asked the purpose of his visit to New York, Webster said simply that he had come to supervise the printing of his textbooks, which were well known nationally. Webster was not telling an untruth. Wherever he set foot, Webster obsessively promoted additional printings and sales of his spelling books.

Genet invited Webster to dine with his party but quickly regretted his decision. The New England teacher's well-practiced classroom stratagems of innocuous *hows* and *whys* gradually annoyed the Frenchman and evoked aggressive, seditious responses. Thinking the Connecticut schoolmaster would not understand, Genet uttered angry asides in French to his aides, arrogantly predicting that the mob outside would sweep Washington from power and lift him, Genet, to leadership.

To the Frenchman's surprise, Webster understood every word and exploded angrily at Genet's "insolence and insults to the nation and its leaders." He called Genet "a madman"—and as he later admitted, much worse.

"I cannot with propriety state all I said myself." At one point, however, Webster thundered, "Do you think the Cabinet is made up of fools?"

Genet lost his temper and responded in "severe language," declaring that only "Jefferson is no fool." Genet then charged that "Mr. Washington makes war on the French nation" and that "the Executive of the United States was under the influence of British gold and the officers of our [American] government were in the British interest." Genet seemed possessed and "uttered other seditious condemnations" of the American government.

"Sir," shouted Webster, rising to quit the table, "there are a million people in the Eastern states whom you have not seen. I am acquainted with those people: they are a free and intelligent people; they know their rights perfectly, and are able to defend them—and be assured, Sir, that it is no more in the power of General Washington or Mr. Hamilton to bring them under the government of Great Britain, or to change the government, than it is to make a world."[110]

He had heard enough, and he left the room to calm himself and await his meeting with Jay four days later. Still seething with fury at Genet, Webster dined secretly at John Jay's on August 16, intent on using the new newspaper to destroy Genet. In a city teeming with French agents and their American hirelings, Jay felt it important to keep plans for the newspaper hidden as long as possible. After they worked out details for the publication, Webster described his meeting with Genet. The chief justice related Washington's need for evidence of a "verifiable incident" to force Genet's recall. Washington, Jay told Webster, would need "direct proof" of Genet's comments.

Webster spent the next two days in New Jersey, looking at printing facilities—again under the pretense of publishing expanded editions of his books. After his return to New York, he dined with James Watson and the Federalist New York senator Rufus King, holding more secret discussions about the new newspaper, in which both King and Watson were investors. On August 30, according to his diary, Webster formed "a partnership with G. Bunce to carry on the Printing business in N York."[111]

After returning to Hartford, Webster rode to Westdivision to tell his heartbroken parents that, once again, he planned to abandon his successful career in Hartford and move to New York. Three days later, he sold his precious law library and sent a letter detailing his confrontation with Genet to Wolcott, who by then was controller of the Treasury and trusted adviser to Alexander Hamilton and President Washington. Wolcott had agreed to invest in the Federalist newspaper venture that Webster was to head.

On September 19, Wolcott replied that the legalities of diplomacy would require a formal affidavit attesting to Genet's transgressions. Webster complied:

Noah Webster jun of Hartford in the State of Connecticut of lawful age,
testifies and says, that on or about the twenty sixth day of August last
past, the deponent with Mr. Timothy Phelps of New Haven, & Mr Hax-
hall of Petersburg in Virginia, dined in company with Mr Genet, the
French Minister, Capt Bompard, & Mr Genet's Secretaries, at the house
of Mr Bradley, in Maiden Lane, New York. After dinner, but before the
Gentlemen rose from table, the deponent related the report from Boston, which had that day been circulated that "the Governor of Massachusetts had taken measures to secure a prize or two which had been
sent into that port by a proscribed privateer, (so-called) for the purpose
of restoring said prizes to the owners; that in consequence of this the
Commander of the Concord, frigate, had taken prize or prizes under his
protection, & determined to resist by force any attempt to take possession of the said prize or prizes for the benefit of the owners." When the
deponent related this story, Mr Pascal, one of Mr Genet's Secretaries,
immediately replied in French "Mon[sieur] Washington fait la guerre à la
nation Française," or in words to that effect; to which Mr Genet and
Capt Bompard both assented by saying *Yes*. Mr Genet proceeded & said
that the Executive of the United States was under the influence of British Gold—the deponent asked him if he meant the President of the
United States; he replied No—Mr Genet further said that the officers
of our government were in the British interest, or words to that effect.
& further that a plan was formed to subject us to Great Britain, & that
we should soon be slaves of that Kingdom. Mr Genet declared he had
very good letters which gave him this information. The deponent representing to Mr Genet that it would be impossible to subject the independent freemen of America to British or any other foreign power, & that
the Executive officers of our national government knew the people too
well to harbor a thought of effecting any such purpose, asked Mr Genet
whether he believed our Executive Officers, the President, Mr Jefferson,
Mr Hamilton, & Gen. Knox to be fools; to which Mr Genet replied,
Mr Jefferson is no fool.

The Deponent says further that in another conversation, Mr Genet
railed ag[ains]t some of the measures of Congress & particularly of the
funding system, in very severe language. And further the Deponent says
not. Dated at Hartford the twenty fifth day of September, 1793.

Noah Webster jun.[112]

Webster's affidavit mistakenly set the dinner with Genet "on or about
the twenty sixth day of August."[113] In addition, it omitted many details of
the conversation. Webster had lost control of his temper as never before,
and as a Calvinist, he was too embarrassed to report many of the angry
words and epithets he hurled at Genet.

As Webster confirmed in his covering letter to Wolcott, "I cannot with
propriety state all I said myself, but I felt no small degree of resentment
that Mr Genet should suppose our Executive *weak enough* to believe it possible to subject us to G Britain. The *wickedness* of a plan for that purpose

did not excite my indignation so much as the *weakness* of it; this circumstance called forth my blunt enquiry, whether he tho[ugh]t our *Executive officers to be fools,* as stated in the affidavit."[114]

Webster said his affidavit contained "the charge of corruption" necessary to expel Genet, including the latter's characterization of the nation's executive officers as "fools." Webster had no way of knowing—and Hamilton's Federalists did not share the information with him—that the administration had obtained copies of Genet's original orders from his government, along with other affidavits, including one from Pennsylvania's secretary of state, Alexander Dallas, who swore that Genet "had declared that he would appeal from the President to the people."[115] They knew, however, that Genet's recall would not bring peace to the streets. French agents still controlled nearly three dozen Jacobin clubs, and the pro-French Jeffersonian press was not about to ease its attacks on the president. Only the reasoned voice of Webster calling for national unity would be able to restore calm.

10

IN ADDITION TO ASKING for Webster's affidavit, Wolcott sent Webster details of a yellow fever epidemic that was raging in the capital:

> This dreadful malady which has raged for some time in the City, has prevented me from writing before—business of all kinds is nearly suspended, my imagination could never have conceived that a short time could have effected such an alteration in Philadelphia as has taken place—every face is sad, all conversation is avoided except at a distance, a great part of the houses are shut up—& the Citizens fled, the Streets in the buisy [*sic*] parts of the City where I now write are as silent as at midnight. For the last two days the malady has much abated, but few are taken sick—it will be some time however before the panic is over & business reassumed. Mrs. Wolcott & part of my family are in the Country. I am here no more than absolute necessity requires. In a few days we shall begin to operate in an Office, which I have concluded to open near the falls of Schuylkill.
> This account which I have given is not a highly coloured one, but it is meant only for *your self.*
>
> From your friend,
> Oliver Wolcott[116]

Although Webster had every intention of leaving Hartford to publish the new government newspaper, he was still a Hartford councilman, with a deep concern for the public health of his city, and the news from Philadelphia made him fear for Hartford's future. Philadelphia's yellow fever epidemic had already claimed more than four thousand lives—10 percent of that city's population. Dr. Benjamin Rush reported treating as many as eighteen hundred patients a week. Five of his students had died helping him.

Wolcott's letter stunned Webster. "The melancholy accounts rec[eived]d from you & others of the progress of a fatal disease in Philad excite commiseration in every breast," he wrote Wolcott. "An alarm is spread over the country. God grant that the disorder may be checked & Philad restored to its former state."[117]

As he had done with the smallpox epidemic the previous year, Webster investigated ways to prevent yellow fever from spreading to Hartford. He devoured every text he could find at the Yale library. With epidemiology in a preconceptual stage, the data he collected—a century before Walter Reed's discovery of the mosquito as the carrier of the disease—was a mixture of superstition and nonsense couched in pseudointellectual syntax. Webster nevertheless sensed correctly the dangers of bad air, city filth, and undrained swamps in high-population areas, and he proposed cleaning the city streets of its filth—another important pioneering venture by Webster as civic leader.

In mid-October, Webster turned his attention to Philadelphia's plight and sent more words of commiseration to Wolcott—along with suggestions for improving Philadelphia's public health:

> By the last accounts from Phild we learn that the raging malady still spreads & is more fatal. . . . We all feel most sensibly affected with the calamity & public prayers are offered up every day in one of the churches of this town. The meetings are unusually full, all classes of people uniting on these solemn occasions. We are not apprehensive here, & no measures to restrain travellers have been taken. Tho in Boston such measures are taken. It is the wish of our citizens & efforts have been made to procure a sloop & load it with vegetables & livestock for the suffering Philadelphians. Hitherto in vain, as there is no vessel in the river at present to be chartered. Should the distresses of the people be continued for any time, we shall have an opportunity of affording our mite of charity. . . .
>
> It is no time not to devise ways of rendering the City more healthy, but a word on the subject can detain you but a moment. . . . By what means shall Philada (or indeed any other great town) be rendered more healthy? I have an idea that a large stream of fresh water may be bro[ugh]t from the falls of Skuylkill along the west side of the city, & thence poured into all or most of the streets. I do not recollect the ground from the falls well enough to determine on the practicability of this, but if practicable at almost any expense, what an important acquisition to that city![118]

CHAPTER SEVEN

Editor

I

As THE SUMMER OF 1793 CAME TO AN END, Webster made a decision that would ultimately condemn him to political oblivion and, but for his dictionary, to relative obscurity in the history of his nation. He decided to found a newspaper in New York City and abandon his work in Hartford. His diary and letters reveal little of the thinking that went into his decision other than his ever-present determination to do good "by fighting disunion." Genet now stood as leader of the forces of disunion, and Webster was determined to join those in combat against the Frenchman. Webster's sketchy *Memoir*,[1] written in 1832, when he was seventy-four, cites financial reasons for the move to New York, but that document often contradicts his diary at the time of the event. Webster was too experienced an editor and publisher not to know his venture would produce nothing but financial losses, but he could not resist what he saw as an opportunity to become the voice of the federal government and influence national policy.

As he had done with the *American Magazine,* however, he overestimated the importance, popular appeal, and potential audience of his new publication, and his Federalist friends said nothing to dissuade him. There was no easier way to convince Webster to do anything than to tell him it was essential to the good of the nation—and that is what they all told him.

At the end of August, he rode his horse to West Hartford to tell his parents of his plans to quit Hartford. They were heartbroken. The only reason he offered to them and most of his friends was that "it seems necessary to superintend my own publications, which are now become of value."[2] The reason did not ring true to many in Hartford, and his plan to leave caused much consternation in the light of his achievements there—with the abolition society, the Charitable Society, the new Public-School Board, and the

Common Council—which made him a probable gubernatorial candidate. Hartford had expected Webster to remain in his native state and build on his already formidable achievements in law and public service. Connecticut, along with his family in Hartford and Boston, expected him eventually to assume leadership of the state his forefathers had helped found, leadership to which he seemed destined and entitled to succeed by blood and deed. Hartford saw his decision as nothing less than an abdication of his obligations and a violation of the trust the citizens had placed in him.

On September 3, three days after seeing his parents, he sold his precious law library. Even Rebecca's family in Boston was dumbfounded by the move. Webster's brothers-in-law lawyer Dawes and Dr. Appleton offered to finance a publishing venture or even a farm for him in the Boston area, but Webster politely declined, writing only that "his business [in Hartford] . . . was not adequate to the support of his family" and that he needed to "contemplate a change of business."[3] Webster kept details of his August visit to New York secret, along with his deal with George Bunce and the plans for a progovernment newspaper. There were spies everywhere, and he believed it essential to the survival of the government that the new journal and its editor appear independent and nonpartisan—that is, pro-American rather than pro-Federalist or anti-Jeffersonian.

Except for Rebecca, Webster told no one about the new venture. He carried on his normal routine in Hartford for another six weeks, trying a murder case in mid-September—his client was "acquitted on ground of insanity"[4]—attending the city's Common Council meetings and, of course, the meetings of his beloved Charitable Society. Then, on October 26, he abandoned to others the civic institutions that he had helped found and that could have catapulted him to state and national political leadership. He and Rebecca packed their furniture for New York and, two days later, put their belongings aboard ship. On the thirty-first, they left their puzzled and distraught friends and family, their beautiful home, and the city they loved.

Emotionally it was not easy for Noah and Rebecca Webster to leave Hartford. Both were exceptionally happy there. His children were secure in the comfortable Webster home, and he was content socially and professionally alongside friends he had known for much of his life. He was also intellectually fulfilled—both at work and at play. He regularly updated his various textbooks, which were yielding a steady income of more than $800 a year, and he had developed a myriad of exciting hobbies, in which he was deeply engrossed. He experimented with seeds, soils, and fertilizers; recorded meteorological data; investigated the then mysterious phenomenon of dew; and experimented with damp and dry soils, wood and brick walls, wet and dry cellars. Aside from the joys of his life in Hartford, his parents needed him emotionally and financially.

But the rioting in New York, the confrontation with Genet, and the arguments of his Federalist friends had convinced him that disunion threatened the nation and that it was his duty to defend his country. As Webster's granddaughter explained, "He felt the crisis of affairs and believed that his federalist pen which had already helped to defeat the enemies of his country, had no right to draw back from the new conflict. His little wife, fondly as she loved her Hartford relatives and happy as she had been in her domestic life, was willing to renounce her pleasant home, where her first two children came to her, to start life anew in a precarious enterprise."[5]

2

IN PARIS, the Reign of Terror had turned France into a slaughterhouse. Before Webster's affidavit denouncing Genet reached Washington's desk, Secretary of State Jefferson informed Genet that his activities in America "rendered it necessary in the opinion of the President to lay a faithful statement of them [Genet's activities] before the government of France" and to insist on the appointment in America of a French minister "disposed to respect the laws." In the meantime, Genet would be permitted to continue "your functions so long as they shall be restrained within the limits of the law."[6]

Genet showed no inclination to relent, however. Perhaps encouraged by Cornelia Clinton's letter charging that his expulsion was "a Federalist plot," Genet had the audacity to send Jefferson this reply on September 18:

> Persuaded that the sovereignty of the United States resides essentially in the people and its representation in the Congress; persuaded that the executive power is the only one which has been confided to the President . . . persuaded that this magistrate [the president] has not the right to decide questions the discussion of which the Constitution reserves particularly to the Congress; persuaded that he has not the power to bend existing treaties to circumstances and to change their sense . . . I will suffer no precedent against the rights of the French people while there remains within me a breath of life. . . . It is in the name of the French people that I am sent to their brethren—to free and sovereign men; it is then for the representatives of the American people and not for a single man to exhibit against me an act of accusation if I have merited it.[7]

Genet continued his original mission, sending more agents to whip up anti-British sentiment in French-speaking Canada and Louisiana. He commissioned George Rogers Clark "citizen general" of the Independent and Revolutionary Legion of the Mississippi and ordered the French fleet in the West Indies north to recapture Saint-Pierre and Miquelon, burn Halifax, return south to capture the Bahamas, and then sail to the mouth of the Mississippi to support Clark's invasion of Louisiana. As the first of the French ships raised sail, however, a mutiny aboard the frigates immobilized the entire fleet, and Genet had to postpone implementation of the grandiose scheme.

Genet's agents in the United States continued to whip up the street mobs. Everywhere but in New England, church bells rang as the Jacobins marched, firing guns in the air for the French. Genet continued to believe Congress—the representatives of the people—would not force his recall.

Webster was eager to get to New York and put his newspaper on the streets to combat Genet's Gallomaniacs, but he ran into interminable delays. The Websters reached dockside on the Connecticut River on October 31, but gales kept them at anchor for days on end, and it took two weeks to reach New York. When they arrived, the house they had rented wasn't ready for them to move in, and they stayed at James Watson's in the interim.

On November 22, Webster bought the Elizabeth Town printing company to produce his newspaper—only to be interrupted by family problems. Rebecca's brother James Greenleaf had joined the land grab along the Potomac River swamps, hoping to profit from the transfer of the U.S. capital from Philadelphia. Webster had exhausted his own savings moving to New York when he received a plaintive letter from his brother-in-law Dr. Nathaniel Appleton, in Boston:

> Our good friend & Bro James [Greenleaf] has in the goodness of his Heart & in the Assiduity of his business, made a proposition to me, by the last mail, with which it is not impossible you may be already acquainted. It is for me to quit all my business, family & other connexions & remove with my Wife & Children to the New City of Washington, where, as you have doubtless been informed he is a very great proprietor, probably the largest of any man in the U.S. he wishes me to reside there as his Agent & is willing to *guaranty* to me a certain sum for a certain term of years. Such a proposition from most men would appear to me to be visionary, but relying on his judgment I do not conceive this to be so. In so important a concern as you may easily conceive this to be I am desirous of the best judgment of my best friends, among these I rank you as one very dear to me. Y[ou] will therefore please by the *return of this Mail,* give me your friendly advice on the subject.[8]

Land speculations had left many investors bankrupt in Pennsylvania and Ohio. Webster wanted to warn Appleton away from the Greenleaf venture, but dared not do so. To begin with, Noah and Becca loved brother James dearly. Generous to a fault, James had shared his earnings with them to help them get their own start, as he had happily done with every member of the family. Greenleaf believed that because of his partner James Watson's close ties to the Federalists in government, they would profit handsomely by investing in land in Washington, and he wanted his entire family to participate. Webster was an avowed foe of speculators, however, and as much as he cared for Greenleaf, he also cared deeply for Appleton; in a carefully worded letter he warned Appleton of the risks of speculation without specifically advising him to reject Greenleaf's appeal for funds.

3

ON DECEMBER 5, 1793, President Washington told Congress, "It is with extreme concern that I have to inform you that the proceedings of a person whom they [the French] have unfortunately appointed their minister here have breathed nothing of the friendly spirit of the nation which sent him" and that "their tendency on the contrary has been to involve us in war abroad and discord and anarchy at home."[9]

To Genet's shock, Congress agreed with the president. "Congress has met," Genet wrote to a confederate. "Washington has unmasked himself, America is befouled." For the French government, Genet's recall symbolized "the ruin of our cause in America" and "the triumph of the English."[10] In effect, Genet would have to sail home in disgrace to a government that was chopping off heads for indiscretions far less than the failure to consummate official orders to conquer a continent.

On December 9, four days after Washington's message to Congress on Genet, Webster published the first, four-page issue of the *American Minerva*[11] as the "Patroness of Peace, Commerce and the Liberal Arts," to be published "every day, Sundays excepted, at four oclock, or earlier if the arrival of the mail will permit." The first issue carried Webster's pledge to make his newspaper "chaste and impartial," while remaining the "Friend of Government, of Freedom, of Virtue and every Species of Improvement."[12]

Webster was true to his word, carrying not only the progovernment essays his Federalist backers expected but articles addressing every ill the country faced: slavery, poor sanitation, epidemics, uncompensated job injuries, abandoned children, and other social problems.

To ensure inexpensive dissemination of his views beyond the city, Webster developed a novel idea of issuing a lightweight, single-sheet semiweekly he called the *Herald: A Gazette for the Country*,[13] which he began distributing the following June. The pioneering little sheet did away with almost all advertising and carried only a selection of news items from the daily newspaper; it could be printed at little cost, without resetting type, and mailed to booksellers everywhere. Webster sent it not only to subscribers across the nation but to readers in Britain and Europe, who had no other easy access to American news. True to form, Webster ensured that both his *Herald* and the daily *Minerva* always carried prominent notices and advertisements for his *Institute* and new editions of the speller. His newspapers thus brought his books to the attention of numerous literate persons in

America, including schoolmasters and clergymen who taught children to read and write.

As anticipated, Jacobin anarchists flooded the newspapers with criticism of the *Minerva,* to which Webster replied,

> I have defended the administration of the national government, because I believe it to have been incorrupt and according to the Spirit of the Constitution. I have advocated the Constitution because if not perfect, it is probably the best we can obtain, and because experience teaches us, it has secured to us important rights and great public prosperity. . . . I have cautioned my fellow-citizens against all foreign intrigues, because I am aware of the fatal dissensions they would introduce into our councils, and because I hold it proper for us to attach ourselves to no foreign nation whatever, and be in truth and spirit *Americans.*[14]

On December 26, with Genet still French minister while awaiting his replacement, Webster published an open letter to the French envoy and to his Jacobin supporters in the streets:

> British influence in America is extremely limited and feeble. Almost every man who espoused the cause of America in her struggle for independence is now friendly to the Revolution in France. It is a general wish in America that the Revolution might be effected and a *free Republican* government be established. There is a general abhorrence of the combination of tyrants against France, which is intended to crush the rising genius of freedom in Europe, and which aims to establish the feudal despotism and tyrannical hierarchies of the 12th century.[15]

The following day, Webster received word that Thomas Paine had been imprisoned in Paris two days before Christmas for having advocated exile instead of execution for Louis XVI the previous January. On the night before his arrest, he was denounced on the floor of the Convention and expelled.[16]

On December 31, Thomas Jefferson left the office of secretary of state and returned to his home in Virginia. Genet would never see his "friend of France" again.

4

ALTHOUGH JEFFERSON'S SUCCESSOR, Edmund Randolph, was also a Virginian, he did not share Jefferson's fervor for France. As a result, Jefferson's departure left Democratic Societies without a leader, although the pro-French press continued to stir discontent on the streets. As Federalists had hoped, Webster's essays helped educate the public and combined with the flow of events to calm New York. The daily demonstrations that had so disrupted city life came to an end. Webster's articles provided a history of the French Revolution and explained how, despite a few superficial similarities, it not only differed from the American Revolution but espoused principles antithetical to those of the United States.

"Our government is a government of universal toleration," he wrote.

The freedom of America, its greatest blessing, secures to every citizen the right of thinking, of speaking, of worshiping and acting as he pleases, provided he does not violate the laws. The only people in America who have dared to violate this freedom are the democratical incendiaries, who have proceeded to threaten violence to tories and aristocrats and federal republicans; that is to people not of their party. Every threat of this kind is an act of tyranny; an attempt to abridge the rights of a fellow-citizen. If a man is persecuted for his opinions, it is wholly immaterial whether the persecution springs from one man or from a society of people,— when men are disposed to persecute. Power is always right; weakness always wrong. Power is always insolent and despotic: whether exercised in throwing its oppressors into a bastille; burning them at the stake; torturing them on a rack; beheading them with a guillotine; or taking them off, as at the massacre of St. Bartholomew,[17] at a general sweep. Power is the same in Turkey as in America. When the will of man is raised above the law, it is always tyranny and despotism, whether it is the will of a bashaw or of bastard patriots.[18]

Webster was careful not to disparage the original goals of the French Revolution, with which he said he agreed. "But the mission of Mr. Genet to the United States compelled me to abandon my faith," he wrote. "The bold and insulting attacks of that minister on the independence and government of the United States left no room to question that the insidious views of French republicans extended to gain a controlling influence over all nations and countries where they could obtain a footing, either by force or intrigue."[19]

Webster explained that the leaders of the Revolution had mimicked the Romans by flattering conquered nations as "allies . . . and this honorable appellation almost reconciled the vanquished people to a state of vassalage." France, Webster said, had violated the "most formal stipulations by treaty and, instead of respecting the rights of other nations . . . has invaded, conquered, and annexed to France the little helpless republic of Geneva. She sent an army to Holland [and] Holland is enslaved; Venice has been annihilated—divided and sold! So much for the promised respect which France was to pay the independence of other nations, as far as it respects Europe."[20]

Webster outlined the atrocities of the Terror—the beheading of the queen, Marie Antoinette, and of sixteen French patriots who had led the original Revolution against the French monarchy; tens of thousands beheaded without trials; even the languishing in prison of America's Tom Paine.

French agents in New York were furious at Webster's articles and incited Democratic clubs to demonstrate outside Webster's newspaper office. "The French Democratic Party consisting of American citizens," Webster wrote in his memoir, "was numerous and violent; and to those were added great numbers of French refugees from France & from Haiti. When animated . . . [they] often assembled, & formed a procession which passed through the streets of N[ew] York, singing *ça ira* or the Marseillaise hymn; and at times so violent were their proceedings that NW was apprehensive for the safety of his printing office. But he steadily pursued his business without interruption."[21]

Webster reprinted his articles in pamphlet form as *The Revolution in France,* and sent one to President Washington with a covering letter:

New York, April 20th, 1794.

Sir,

At the present critical juncture of our political affairs, it appears to be the duty of every good citizen to use his influence in restraining the violence of parties and moderating the passions of our injured fellow-citizens. . . . The enclosed is intended to aid the cause of government and peace. Should it have the least influence for this purpose, I shall be satisfied. Be pleased to accept it as a proof of my attachment to you and the Constitution of the united States, and believe me, with sincere wishes for your personal happiness and a firm resolution to support your administration, Your most obedient and most humble Servant,

Noah Webster Jun.[22]

Webster's pamphlet delighted his friend Oliver Wolcott, who predicted it would cool American ardor for the French Revolution. "It is precisely the thing which I have long wished to see published," he wrote to Webster from Philadelphia, where he remained controller of the currency,

and [it] will eminently serve to fix publick opinion on rational opinions & to tranquilize those passions which have threatened the peace of this country.

Whether the governments of Europe have arrived to that maturity in wickedness, which renders it necessary . . . that the people should revert to barbarism, I pretend not to determine. . . . I am certain the modern French principles are inconsistent with the present state of society in Europe.

Wolcott charged that the French were attempting to overturn every government in Europe and wreak "signal and compleat" destruction. "During this interesting period," he said,

we ought carefully . . . to be prepared for defence against invasions & intrigues, and, above all, to come to an absolute determination, that we will on no account become a party in the War.

With these principles you will believe that I read the book you sent me with pleasure & with a sincere wish that it may produce the good effects for which it is calculated.

Mrs. Wolcott has lately brought us a fine daughter, she desires to be remembered affectionately to Mrs. Webster.

With much sincerity I remain
Your friend[23]

Webster's essays proved remarkably prescient. In them, he predicted that "the combined powers would never conquer France"—and almost immediately, Prussia and Spain withdrew from the coalition and sued for peace. Webster predicted that Robespierre's head would fall—and it did—and he predicted that the turmoil of the Revolution would culminate only with the arrival of "some popular man, who can attract around him a military superiority."[24] Five years later, Napoleon came to power.

The savagery of the Terror in Paris during the autumn of 1793 and winter of 1794 cost the French Revolution most of its sparkle in America. "An American now openly espousing the cause of liberty by joining a French army," lamented one of Genet's supporters, "is branded with the epithet of traitor—his body accordingly is seized and thrown into jail, his locks are forced and the most private recesses are searched for papers . . . to convict him."[25] Although Genet retained his official position, his future seemed insecure at best, and he sent a plea to Cornelia Clinton, the New York governor's daughter. He addressed her as "my dear friend" and asked her to "consider me as a man who has consecrated his life to you, and who looks upon you as the best reward which Heaven could confer upon him."[26]

By the end of January 1794, the toll of writing an entire daily newspaper by himself began to wear on Webster. He was up one-half hour before sunrise to get to his desk in time to use all the natural light the day provided. From then until it was too dark to see the page, he wrote editorials, political essays, read English and French newspapers to report foreign intelligence, and wrote letters incessantly to Americans and foreigners abroad to obtain their insights on events overseas, which he could then print. As he himself admitted, "his strength was exhausted; in two instances, his pulse was scarcely perceptible."[27]

5

THE WORLD WAS STILL AT WAR, and America was hovering uncertainly between the huge French and English juggernauts, either one of which might crush the tiny new nation at any time. Moreover, Genet and his agents were still hard at work fomenting revolution in America and trying to force the

United States into war against Britain. "During the heat of the French Revolution," Webster later wrote, " . . . I was carefully watched by the partisans
of France, as these [news]papers were established for the purpose of vindi-
cating and supporting the policy of President Washington, which those partisans alleged to be unfriendly to the French interest. When conversing
with gentlemen in the Coffee house, I sometimes turned round suddenly
and found a Frenchman just behind me standing with his ear as near me,
as convenient, listening to the conversations."[28]

On January 20, the president sent Congress a letter saying, in part, "I
now communicate to you that [Genet's] conduct has been unequivocally
disapproved [by the French], and that the strongest assurances have been
given that his recall should be expedited without delay."[29] The marching for
Genet did not stop, however, and he prepared to send six ships to blockade Saint Augustine, in Spanish Florida. He had a two-thousand-man force
in the West and another fifteen hundred on the Spanish frontier in southern Georgia prepared to attack the Floridas and Louisiana on April 10. On
February 7, officers of the Pennsylvania militia refused to lift their glasses
to President Washington at their banquet. Instead, they drank to "Citizen
Genet, victim of so much persecution—may his country reward his pure
civism; may the shafts aimed at him, come back on those who fire them."[30]

Then a frigate arrived from France with a new ambassador, Joseph
Fauchet, who relieved Genet. On March 6, the nation's press, including
Webster's *Minerva,* printed the new envoy's proclamation: "In the name of
the French Republic: every Frenchman is forbid to violate the neutrality of
the United States. All commissions . . . tending to infringe on that neutrality are revoked and are to be returned."[31] The proclamation sent shock
waves across the United States. What nearly a year of President Washington's proclamations could not do, the new French ambassador was able to
accomplish in a single day. French agents along the Spanish border were
stunned—in tears, according to some reports. "Success was never so near,"
said a French minister in retrospect, "and if [Genet's] orders had been
obeyed this brilliant revolution would undoubtedly have been achieved."[32]

France thus relinquished its ambitious plan for American conquest and
repudiated Genet's orders—as well as Genet himself. Indeed, as new ambassador, Fauchet demanded "the delivery of Genet in order to send him
to France by the return of the ships of war in which he arrived."[33] Genet
pleaded with Washington that the ship on which he was to return had "a
brand new guillotine" aboard to effect his immediate execution.[34] Washington showed the young Frenchman more kindness than the latter had
ever demonstrated to the president. "We ought not to wish his punishment," said Washington about Genet, and he refused to hand Genet over
to the new French envoy.[35] For several weeks, Genet surrounded himself
with an armed guard to prevent his being kidnapped and put aboard the
French ship.[36] The ship finally left for France in May, without Genet.

Two months later, to Webster's astonishment, the arrogant Frenchman who had tried to overthrow the American government marched with Governor Clinton in the July 4 Independence Day parade in New York, singing American hymns of independence. By the end of August, substantial funds materialized to permit his purchase of a farm in Jamaica on "longisland." A month later, he assumed the title of "American cultivator" and began working his new farm. In November, he married Cornelia Clinton, the governor's daughter, who had used her dowry to buy the farm. He became an American citizen and disappeared from public life. Genet died on Bastille Day, July 14, 1834, at the age of seventy-one.[37]

The new French ambassador's proclamation put an end to street demonstrations in American cities, and Webster and his newspaper were cast adrift with no purpose for existing. The Federalist leaders who had backed the newspaper—especially Alexander Hamilton—no longer needed it to retain power. Jefferson had resigned from the cabinet and returned to his country home in Virginia, leaving Hamilton as the dominant force in the cabinet and among the Federalists. He needed and wanted no direct help or interference from Webster himself, and indeed, used Webster's newspaper only as an occasional vehicle for his own self-serving articles.

With Webster's loss of influence in government, his newspaper threatened to become a financial and professional disaster. In less than a year, he had sacrificed a thriving law practice and political leadership of his state to run a newspaper with limited reader appeal and ever-diminishing political influence. It was too late, however, to retrace his steps, and he had little choice but to try to save his newspapers, the *American Minerva* and the *Herald*.

He shifted the focus of the *Minerva*. He began writing abstracts of French books and pamphlets, along with a wider variety of editorials, which touched on every conceivable topic of public interest. He had no more time for his diary, and he abandoned this valuable historic record on May 12, 1794, although he added an occasional monthly summary for a few years more.

On June 5, 1794, Congress enacted President Washington's neutrality proclamation into law, thus forbidding U.S. citizens from enlisting in the service of a foreign power and banning the fitting out of foreign armed vessels in U.S. ports. Although this did not end tensions with Great Britain, it ended the threat of war. Webster explained that the new act was based on the principle that "Free ships make free goods" and that ships of warring nations have no right to seize cargoes on ships from neutral, or "free," nations—regardless of the origin of those cargoes. "Neutrals," he insisted, "have a better right to trade than nations have to fight and plunder."[38]

His articles attracted little reader interest, coming, as they did, after the fact rather than before or during. For the first time in his writing career,

Webster seemed no longer to be anticipating events, and his essays were not written to alter the course of events as much as to explain them. He struggled to find enough material to fill his newspaper. In early June, he resurrected his essays on emancipation and published a thousand-word treatise proving, in dollars and cents, that the "labour of slaves is less productive than that of freemen."[39]

As readership slowed, he doubled his efforts and pushed himself to near exhaustion. Finally, at the end of June, he all but admitted defeat and published a letter "to the Friends of the Minerva." He intended it as much for the Federalists who had lured him into the venture as for the general public.

> Gentlemen:
>
> More than 6 months have elapsed since we began the publication of this paper. I have done everything in my power to render it acceptable to an impartial public, but it has not received the encouragement I had reason to expect. The subscribers scarcely amount to 250, a number not equal to the support of the paper, and it does not appear to be increasing. There is not a daily paper in town that has not double the number of subscribers, and double the number is requisite to make it worth while to continue it. The *Herald* or country paper will succeed if it has a daily paper to support it, but not otherwise; for a thousand subscribers would not defray the cost of the *Herald* if printed *alone*. If the *Minerva* fails, the *Herald* must fail also. Unless we can obtain much more support from merchants, grocers, and shopkeepers, the paper cannot be worth printing.
>
> I would only state further that in addition to the obstacles which the *Minerva* must encounter from several established and now well conducted papers, it has to encounter a determined host of enemies, who feel some alarm at its circulation and who have already influenced some subscribers to withdraw their names.
>
> I think it proper to state these facts for the consideration of my friends, for the business will not enable us to keep a clerk; and unless I can get some relief from my present drudgery, my health will not long sustain my application to business.[40]

The letter had little effect. Readership continued falling. To compound his trouble at work, the exhausted essayist was beset with a new set of family problems, generated by his hitherto problem-free in-laws, for whom life had always seemed swathed in success. For some time the Websters had not heard from Rebecca's normally cheerful, superloquacious brother James Greenleaf. Webster guessed correctly that he was suffering reverses in his land deals. Soon a letter from Nathaniel Appleton confirmed his suspicions. Against Webster's advice, Appleton had abandoned his Boston medical practice to join Greenleaf in real estate speculation in the new city of Washington.

City of Washington 26 July 1794

Dear Webster

. . . You know that I was never so sanguine as to the speedy settlement of this place & the ease with which a City might be built, as some of our family, nor did I ever expect that the business i had undertaken would be free from troubles. . . .

All the difficulties you have narrated may occur; *some* of them doubtless will; the slow & *inefficient* . . . conduct of the Commissioners hitherto, has greatly retarded the public operations & I am suspicious deranged the finances, & the public may have been defrauded by unprincipled Agents & Undertakers [as contractors were then called], by dilatory & unskillful Workmen. . . .

I knew that Bro. J. has been very sanguine & appears at times to be impatient of advice, but . . . he makes large & bold Speculations.[41]

As Webster had feared, the same type of corruption that had undermined most land speculations in the United States seemed to be undermining Appleton's and Greenleaf's investments.

6

IN NOVEMBER 1794, Chief Justice John Jay temporarily revived Webster's journalistic fortunes by sending him, exclusively, documents that again made the newspaper a platform for influencing public opinion for at least a few months. Webster and Jay had remained close personal friends since the two had worked out details for publishing the *Minerva* a year earlier. Moreover, they had become political allies, and unlike Hamilton and other Federalist backers of the *Minerva,* Jay refused to abandon Webster.

After Genet withdrew from the political picture, President Washington had named Jay special envoy to Great Britain to resolve as many outstanding differences as possible between the two nations. Britain was still seizing American ships and impressing American sailors. In addition, the British army was violating the Treaty of Paris of 1783 by refusing to withdraw from the Northwest Territory and cede the valuable fur trade. The British had even helped establish an Indian barrier state that effectively blocked the western advance of American settlers. The effects on the United States were disastrous. A tidal wave of European immigrants had packed East Coast cities with unemployed men, women, and children. Sanitation had deteriorated to intolerable levels, and epidemics of smallpox, yellow fever, malaria, and influenza had erupted for three successive years, claiming 10 percent or more of the population in major cities such as New York and Philadelphia.

Opening the West for settlement was essential for absorbing immigrant growth and dispersing the population, and it became a top government priority when Jay left for Britain. The British refused to make any concessions or to relinquish the West until the United States provided full compensation for British and loyalist properties seized during and after the Revolutionary War.

On November 19, 1794, Jay signed a treaty with England and forwarded the terms to Webster for publication in the *American Minerva*. As the first American paper with details of the treaty, the *Minerva*'s circulation soared. The Jay Treaty called for British withdrawal from the Northwest over a period of eighteen months in return for repayment of debts to British subjects, as determined by an arbitration commission. The British made no other concessions, however. They refused to stop seizing ships and impressing American sailors or even to return slaves stolen from plantation owners in the South.

The treaty pleased no one. It outraged Southern planters as well as Northern and Southern merchants whose property the British were still seizing at sea. Even Jay's closest Federalist allies seemed opposed, with President Washington cool at best. The treaty was the subject of debate for the next seven months. Webster's ties to Jay made the *Minerva* New York's most widely read newspaper, and his editorial voice echoed through Congress, with moderates citing his contention that Jay had wrung every possible concession from the British. Good or bad, Webster's essays insisted, the treaty was all that was possible for the moment, given America's bargaining position as a weak neutral trying to profit from trade with all participants in a world war.

"I am of opinion," Webster wrote in a letter to Wolcott, "that the Treaty . . . makes no sacrifices, which are dishonorable to us as a nation & none which are very prejudicial to the United States. The objections raised ag[ains]t it are many of them at least totally unfounded. I believe in the present state of America, it would be good policy to carry it into effect as a temporary agreement."[42] Webster succeeded in convincing Wolcott and the Federalists to support the treaty. Wolcott wrote Webster, "I have rec'd your letter . . . & I thank you for your remarks. . . . I have since that time carefully examined [the treaty], and compared it with other Treaties, and am satisfied that it is as favourable as . . . we had a right under all circumstance to *expect*."[43]

Webster published a series of twelve essays of "Vindication" for the Jay Treaty, under the pseudonym "Curtius." New York senator Rufus King later told Jay that "the papers of 'Curtius' had operated more powerfully than any other publication in calming the public mind and restoring confidence in the administration, being from their style and structure peculiarly adapted to the comprehension of the great body of the people."

From the hills of Virginia, Jefferson wrote angrily to his friend James Madison: "I send you by post . . . one of the pieces, Curtius, lest it should not have come to you otherwise. . . . For God's sake, take up your pen and give a fundamental reply."[44]

The only significant reply to Webster, however, came from Benjamin Franklin Bache, a grandson of Benjamin Franklin and the editor of the *Aurora*, a fanatical Jeffersonian newspaper that opposed all ties to Britain. Bache used every imaginable epithet he could invent to discredit Webster for supporting the Jay Treaty with England: a "self-exalted pedagogue," "base and uncandid," "utter enemy of the rights and privileges of the people," "quack," "incurable lunatic," "pusillanimous, half-begotten, self-dubbed patriot," "scribbler of British faction," "dunghill cock . . . alias Squire Webster."[45]

The viciousness of the attacks shocked Webster, and he struck back in a dignified fashion that carefully avoided all hints of vituperation:

> I am persuaded that . . . public papers have been the direct and principal means of all the civil dissensions which distract this country and have threatened it with civil war. I have defended the administration of the national Government, because I believe it to have been incorrupt and according to the spirit of the Constitution. I have advocated the Constitution, because, if not perfect . . . it has secured to us our important rights and great public prosperity. I have vindicated neutrality, because there has appeared no occasion for war, but great advantages for peace. . . . Impartial truth has been and will continue to be my aim.[46]

Many years later, Webster was still seething from years of absorbing such libelous barbs when he wrote to his younger cousin Rep. Daniel Webster to seek passage of federal libel laws: "The freedom of the press is a valuable privilege, but the abuse of it in this country is a frightful evil. The licentiousness of the press is a deep stain upon the character of the country; and in addition to the evil of calumniating good men and giving a wrong direction to public measures, it corrupts the people by rendering them insensible to the value of truth and reputation."[47]

Congress ratified the Jay Treaty the following June, and Webster's pen had restored his influence on the course of national events. Readership of his newspapers—especially the widely circulated *Herald*—continued to increase throughout the summer and early autumn, and Webster worked nonstop. His brother-in-law the Boston attorney Thomas Dawes visited the Websters and asked:

> How do you get thro' the cleaning all the Augean stables in the manner you do? translating, transcribing, composing (tho the last I know you can do when asleep) correcting other peoples' blunders, answering other people's absurdities, in short finding brains for people who, when they've got them don't know what to do with them. Mercy on me (or rather on *you*) how do you produce so many columns a week, and so good ones? I don't believe you have kissed Beccy these six months. . . . Well, drive on. "Youth is the time to serve the Lord." To be serious, I am highly

gratified at the success of your paper. It is my duty to tell you that I hear it spoken of in the most flattering terms in all companies. I suppose, tho' you can tell best, it has the greatest currency on the Continent.[48]

7

JUST AS WEBSTER'S BUSINESS FORTUNES were recovering, however, those of his and his wife's families took terrible turns for the worse. On October 4, 1794, two weeks before his thirty-sixth birthday, his mother died. He had last seen her eleven months earlier, before his departure for New York, when he had left her grief-stricken by quitting Hartford.

Then, shortly after his mother's death, his brother-in-law Nathaniel Appleton, whom both Webster and his wife adored, contracted malaria in the Potomac swamplands and was forced to return to Boston, devastated physically as well as financially from his land speculations with brother-in-law James Greenleaf. The following April, he died. His death devastated the Websters. He was a young man—only forty years old—a longtime friend of the most elegant and prominent Boston families, including the Adamses and the Quincys. He had amassed a fortune as one of Boston's most outstanding physicians—only to die bankrupt after following his brother-in-law Greenleaf's siren calls promising unlimited wealth and power in Washington.

Soon after his brother-in-law's death, James Greenleaf returned to New York but was of little consolation to the Websters. He had lost most of his own fortune in Washington land speculations and moved in with the Websters. A fun-loving bachelor who enjoyed his drink and gaming, Greenleaf came and went at all hours, often with equally boisterous friends, whose sudden appearances added tensions to a home already under stress because of Webster's crushing workload. Greenleaf tried to recoup some of his real estate losses by gambling and amassed such huge debts that he ended in debtors' prison. Although he lived to be seventy-three—he died in 1843— he never again drew close to the Websters, who held him responsible, in large part, for Appleton's misfortunes and death.

8

IN JANUARY 1795, two of Webster's closest friends joined Washington's cabinet: Oliver Wolcott Jr. became secretary of the Treasury to replace Alexander Hamilton, who left to practice law in New York; and Timothy Pickering became secretary of war, succeeding Henry Knox, who retired to his farm. Webster was certain the appointments of his friends to the highest levels of government would make the *Minerva* the voice of the American government, as well as its eyes and ears, and give Webster himself considerable influence in policy-making decisions.

"At this important crisis of our public affairs," he wrote to Wolcott, "a free & confidential intercourse between the friends of peace & good order appears very necessary. I will therefore freely communicate my opinions & information to you & I make no doubt you will render the communications mutual."⁴⁹

Both Pickering and Wolcott were amenable. Indeed, just after his appointment, Pickering told a friend, Federalist senator Theodore Sedgwick of New York, to consult Webster for a successor to Pickering as postmaster general. Sedgwick also asked Webster to look over a speech he planned to deliver to the Senate urging tighter immigration laws.

Webster strongly supported such laws and told Sedgwick his "speech on naturalization . . . does you much honor. I consider as a matter of infinite consequence the cautious admission of foreigners to the rights of citizenship. Numbers of them who have within the past year arrived and settled in this city come with violent prejudices against arbitrary government, and they seem to make no great distinction between arbitrary government and a government of laws founded on free elections."

Webster warned Sedgwick that Jefferson's Democrats had organized an emigration society that served ostensibly to welcome foreigners as they arrived at dockside but gradually and insidiously converted them into Democrats. "If . . . that system of raising a multitude of isolated private clubs over the nation as its guardians—should spread into the country, we may bid adieu to our Constitution. Our safety is in the country people, who, more scattered and more independent, are out of the reach of demagogues."⁵⁰

As he intended, Webster became the government's eyes and ears in New York, reporting every effort to undermine the Washington administration. In March, he wrote to Wolcott warning that at a meeting of opposition leaders in New York, "one of the gentlemen in the heat of conversation uttered this expression: '*We must prostrate the government.*' 'Where will you land then?' was asked by a person present. The answer was, 'We shall land where France has landed.' From these expressions," Webster's letter continued, "I collect the meaning to be, 'We must dissolve the present Senate and Executive, and reduce all to *one branch*' . . . there is no doubt, Colonel [Aaron] Burr's aim is, if not to dissolve the Senate, at least to change the whole administration of the government the first moment it shall be practicable."⁵¹

Webster told Wolcott that Gen. John Lamb, a Jefferson appointee at the New York Custom House and an ally of Burr, had also attended the meeting. Lamb, he wrote,

> is a most inveterate and avowed enemy of the government. He declaims against it boldly on every occasion. His influence is considerable, and it

is much augmented, perhaps, by his connection with the government. His commissions, &c., amount consistently to 10,000 dollars a year, perhaps more. His office is a mere *sinecure*, for he never goes to the Custom House. It is even said he does not enter the house from year to year. He spends his time and his money in entertainments which, in some instances at least, can have no object but to multiply partizans.[52]

Several months later, Webster sent Wolcott another warning, along with the startling prediction—sixty-five years before the event—that the South would secede from the Union. Jefferson's Democratic Societies, Webster wrote, "are secretly extending their force, & in my apprehension some decisive legislative remedy *must* be speedily applied to extirpate the evil, or we must ultimately be governed by irregular town-meetings . . . in the Southern states the danger appears to be more real. . . . The opposition to our govt then is general—& to me it bodes an ultimate separation between us & them."[53]

In mid-1795, Edmund Randolph resigned as secretary of state, and Pickering added the foreign affairs portfolio to his job as secretary of war. He immediately canceled the State Department subscriptions to Bache's inflammatory, antigovernment *Aurora,* which had been sent to each of America's five ambassadors abroad. Pickering asked Webster "to furnish six copies of the Herald to the department of State to our ministers abroad, to present them, in a small compass, a correct detail of domestic intelligence and just ideas of our public affairs. . . . My predecessor furnished our ministers with Mr. Bache's 'precious' memorials and descriptions of our public concerns: but feeling no inclination to continue this department as the vehicle of our country's opprobrium, I have dropped the five papers that used to be sent abroad."[54]

At the end of July 1795, the debate over the Jay Treaty subsided suddenly. New York's normally busy streets emptied and turned still. Even marchers from Jefferson's Democratic Societies stayed at home, while those who ventured out did so furtively and quickly. For the third successive year, yellow fever was infecting the city. It arrived aboard the brig *Zephyr* from Port-au-Prince on July 20. According to one account, "Dr. Treat, then health officer of the port of New-York . . . found the crew sickly; that several men had died on the passage; that a boy had died the morning of her arrival; that Dr. Treat had incautiously opened the dead body; that it was very generally tinged with a yellow colour; and that it was extremely offense to the smell. . . . A few days after Dr. Treat visited the brig *Zephyr,* about the 20th of July, he was seized with fever."[55]

By August, the fever had spread down the East Coast, first to Baltimore, and eventually to Norfolk, Virginia, and into the Carolinas. The epidemic exacted its heaviest toll—often 10 percent of the entire population—along a huge swath that stretched down the coast from Boston to the Carolinas, then broadened dramatically across the entire South, incorporating all of

Georgia and reaching west to the Mississippi River, into Louisiana. Although the incidence of the disease declined in the inland areas of the North, no one in the United States was safe, with the pestilence claiming some victims as far west as Ohio and Kentucky.

As the toll mounted, Webster decided to act. He had studied epidemic diseases in 1793, when yellow fever had infected Philadelphia. He had been frustrated by the widespread ignorance—and conflicting opinions—among physicians about such common diseases. He found it hard to believe that, with so many thousands of case studies, modern science had been unable to identify a common cause. Indeed, the 1793 fever epidemic had left Philadelphia's most prominent physicians bitterly disputing the causes and proper treatments. Dr. Benjamin Rush, the hero of the epidemic, had resigned from the College of Physicians and organized a new Academy of Medicine after a bitter dispute with Dr. William Currie. A professor of chemistry and author of the first U.S. chemistry textbook as well as many medical studies, Rush reported that he had cured himself of the disease by profuse bloodletting and two doses of mercury. Currie called Rush a "bloodletter" and "charlatan" and said the disease was nothing more than "fall fever," which affected only influenza victims. A war of medical pamphlets ensued that left physicians as divided over the causes and treatment of epidemics as the Federalists and antifederalists were over governing the nation.[56]

Webster grew as enraged at the factionalism in medicine as he had over political factionalism. He decided to organize doctors in a crusade to determine the causes of the disease and to eradicate it. He called for a massive effort by doctors that was unique in medical history. "The world is a book of instruction," he wrote in the *Minerva*, "and he who will not profit by the lessons before him, must be unfaithful to himself and his fellow citizens." With the exception of the Indians and their herbal remedies, he said, Americans had contributed nothing to advance medicine. "Theories are of little use, but facts are of infinite importance; and we conceive every new fact of observation on the subject of pestilential diseases to be well worth attention."[57]

As the epidemic reached its peak in late October, Webster's *Minerva* became the first newspaper ever to lead a campaign to improve public health. Readership surged. To the consternation of his competitors, Webster's newspaper had become New York's largest, with a total circulation one-third greater than that of its closest rival. With the companion *Herald* mailed all over North America and Europe, everything Webster printed reached the most influential men in the Western world.

On October 31, 1795, he launched the world's first epidemiological study with a letter in the *Minerva* and the *Herald* addressed to "the Physicians of Philadelphia, New York, Baltimore, Norfolk, and New Haven"—cities that had all suffered epidemics during each of the previous three years. In effect, he asked them to respond to a questionnaire to determine whether "the bilious remitting fever, commonly called yellow fever, is of foreign or domestic origin; whether it is always imported or may be generated in our own country; whether it is an epidemic or depends for propagation on specific contagion; or whether it partakes of the nature of both an epidemic and a contagious disease." Webster recognized that no single doctor was likely to know the answers to all the questions, but he believed that "collecting the fragments of knowledge that lie scattered in various places and arranging them and publishing them" would produce answers that would permit government "to make such regulations as to guard our commercial towns from a repetition of the calamities they have once suffered. If the disease has been imported, more effectual measures must be taken to prevent its introduction; if generated in our own country, it is absolutely necessary for our populous towns to suffer most decisive amendments in their docks, houses, streets, &c."

His remarkable questionnaire, the first in scientific history—indeed, perhaps the first questionnaire of any kind in history—asked each physician to respond by detailing

> the *origin* of the yellow fever in the respective places to which you belong; the time of its first appearance and disappearance; its symptoms and the most successful mode of treatment; what proportions of persons seized with decided symptoms of this fever who have died; how far the fever has been attended with specific contagion, and the proofs of this; in what situations as to free air, water, streets, and buildings this disease has been most fatal; what descriptions of people have suffered most, and their mode of living; what malignant complaints have, for two or three seasons, preceded the yellow fever; how it differs in symptoms from the ordinary bilious fever [hepatitis] of the country; whether or not you have known a fever, with the same or similar symptoms, to occur in scattered instances in other seasons than that in which the yellow fever has prevailed; and whether such cases can be traced to any known cause—and in short, please communicate any other information which, in your opinion, may throw light on the origins, nature, and care of the disease.

"I cannot but hope, gentlemen," Webster ended his letter, "that you will be of opinion that this subject is of great and universal concern to the United States; and that you will consent to aid a plan which has the health of our fellow citizens and the happiness and prosperity of our country for its object."[58]

After running the letter in his *Minerva*, Webster asked other newspapers to join the campaign—even the Jeffersonian papers that had abused him for his political views. In a knee-jerk response, the vicious Benjamin Franklin Bache published a long, rambling diatribe in the *Aurora*, addressed to "Noah Webster, Esq., *Author and Physician General* of the United States":

When men of your eminence condescend to turn bookmakers for Physicians . . . when a man who can recite the etymology of words with as much facility as a child can recite its alphabet, deigns to step forward in behalf of the faculty, it would be the extreme of rudeness and brutality not to lend an attentive ear to him, and to furnish him a ladder to mount to fame and genius. . . . To the author of the *Institutes,* the Editor of the *Minerva* . . . which has "dashed whole conspiracies with his single pen," is reserved the honor and glory to triumph over a malady, dire as the conspiracies which he vanquished.[59]

Instead of answering Bache directly, Webster sent a letter to the editor of the *Argus,* another of the abusive Jeffersonian newspapers:

You omitted my Letter to the physicians several times "for want of room," as you informed the public; but as soon as the *Aurora* had furnished an abusive answer, you had room for *both.* To this I have no objections, for *abuse* conveyed through the *Aurora* and the *Argus* are considered as the highest commendations of honest men. But I would just apprize you that your abuse extends to censure some of your friends and some of the most respectable of the faculty in this city. . . .

Humanity is a common cause and one that should level all distinctions of party. The investigation of the causes of disease and the means of alleviating the calamities of life is the business of every good citizen, whatever be his profession. In doing this I encroach not on the proper business of medical gentlemen. I undertake only the part of a compiler and publisher; and no man whose heart is not hardened by party prejudices can wish to throw cold water on the undertaking.[60]

Webster's landmark campaign produced a torrent of correspondence from around the world, from which he gradually collected millions of bits of data. His proposal encouraged doctors in Philadelphia, New York, and other major cities to produce carefully detailed studies of the history, theoretical causes, and various treatments of the disease in their cities. Ministers in churches kept daily tallies of the number of deaths. In New York, James Hardie produced a massive list of thousands of names "of the dead, arranged in alphabetical order, with their professions or occupations, and as far was practicable to obtain information, the names of the countries of which they were natives."[61] Benjamin Rush in Philadelphia produced a study showing the disease to be the result of contagion.[62]

Webster printed many of the doctors' responses—only to discover that the theory of one doctor inevitably provoked bitter contradiction from the doctor's rival colleagues. One prominent doctor, Joseph Browne, ascribed yellow fever to atmospheric imbalances of "animal vital air" and "vegetable vital air," with excess summer heat causing a deficiency of animal vital air, "the grand corrector of putrescency." The cure for yellow fever, he said, lay in cleanliness, abstention from meats, avoidance of crowds, and "the planting of trees to absorb vegetable vital air and to evolve animal vital air."

Dr. Alexander Hosack disagreed, saying inhalation of camphor was all that was needed to cure yellow fever, along with frequent enemas, cold water showers, and frequent perspiration. Hosack, along with Dr. William Currie, warred continuously with Benjamin Rush, who favored bloodletting. But Hosack and Currie had their share of enemies. One called Currie's theories "absurd and untenable," while Dr. Samuel Latham Mitchill at Columbia College insisted that camphor applications were dangerous because they "stimulated the absorbents of the nostrils and promoted the ready inhalation of the morbid effluvia."[63]

Throughout 1797, Webster printed the doctors' letters—until he could take no more of the senseless bickering. Instead of providing him with data on disease to collate for the good of the nation, they were trading childish insults with one another. "It has often been noticed by medical gentlemen," Webster wrote in a *Minerva* editorial, "that the yellow fever and plague have a most powerful effect on the brain. Is not this effect very visible in the violent contentions among the faculty in Philadelphia? Is not a partial delirium discernible in their writings and challenges? It seems to be nearly time for the police of the city to think of the strait-jacket for some of them."[64]

Webster nevertheless made the study and the eradication of epidemic diseases his overriding mission for the next three years, extracting what he considered the most salient points of each doctor's findings and combining these with materials gathered from medical texts he studied himself. In July of the following year, he published a compilation of the responses he had received in a volume called *A Collection of Papers on the Subject of Bilious Fever, Prevalent in the United States for a Few Years Past*. He would later republish it as part of a massive two-volume work on epidemic diseases.

Webster's summary ended the book with an appeal for improved city planning and sanitation of the type he had promoted in Hartford as a city councilman. "Sources of disease and death," he wrote, "may be found among [the people] themselves created by their own negligence . . . until they learn this, they will never attend to the means of preserving life and health. They will still wallow in filth, crowd their cities with dirty houses and narrow streets; neglect use of bathing and washing; and live like savages, devouring in hot seasons undue quantities of animal food at their tables, and reeling home after midnight debauches." A century would pass before the identification of the mosquito as the carrier of yellow fever. Although Webster's work did not eradicate the disease, it encouraged better sanitation in almost every major city in the northeastern United States.[65]

The *Minerva* called for massive sanitation measures in New York City, including the draining or filling of swamps and the construction of water channels to clean the streets. By the end of 1796, Webster's campaign produced new sanitation laws in New York, and a year later, on October 14, 1797, at the end of the usual epidemic season, he was able to exult in the pages of *Minerva*, "The cleansing of the city has diminished the mass of autumnal diseases of a lighter kind, and therefore cleansing has had a great and obvious influence in lessening the number and severity of autumnal fevers. . . . our public health depends on ourselves."[66]

Convinced that filthy, overcrowded city streets spread epidemic diseases, Webster moved his family out of the city in 1796. They moved to "a pretty cottage and garden in the country at Corlear's Hook," a spit of land that jutted into the East River a half mile north of the city. Years earlier, it had been a Dutch farm, and had been converted into a community of "detached villas with land about them."[67]

While the Websters may have escaped the city's filth, they did not escape its crime. As Rebecca Webster waited alone with her babies for her husband's return from work one evening, four masked men pushed their way into the house next door. Rebecca described what happened:

> The lady . . . had a very young infant. . . . They came and demanded her money and jewels—not silver—"as it was too cumbrous to carry." She parleyed, but one man caught up her babe and threatened it, and she then gave up some hundred dollars that she had concealed. They . . . found her diamonds. By this time the delicate invalid trembled in spite of her courage, when the one who was evidently the leader, carried an armchair to her, begged her to seat herself, and taking a footstove from the hearth filled it with coals and placed it at her feet. In doing this he bared his white hand, which both the lady and the maid noticed was that of a gentleman, and had a handsome diamond ring on it. The thieves then left, "hoping that the lady would not be harmed by the fright they had given her." They were—or at least the leader was evidently—a man conversant with the polite forms of life. In spite of this clue they were never discovered.[68]

Just as the Websters had settled into their new home, Webster heard from his older brother, Abram, whose ineptitude at farming had left him perennially dependent on Noah for supplementary income. Noah never failed to send money and practical gifts, such as clothes, for the children. The promise of cheap land in the wilderness had lured Abram and his family and other equally foolish farmers to Hamilton, in central New York State, where a slick speculator gave them worthless deeds to vacant lands. Abram wrote that he was having "a very tight summer," which was aggravated by legal problems over the title to the land. Things were not going well.

> Provisions are very dear and difficult to be bought even by those who can make ready pay, but Harvest is near and affords a prospect of plenty-full crop. I have been unlucky in many things since I have been in this country amongst other misfortunes I have lost three large swine by the Bears and sickness besides two litters of pigs. Bears are plenty here, and have killed numbers of hogs. You must not think from what I write that I am Discouraged—this is not the case but quite the contrary—we are in

good spirits and all my family are exerting themselves to the utmost of their abilities to assist me in getting a living in the woods. . . .

I wish you to make further inquiry respecting Kirkland's title to this land, the stories circulating that he is not able to procure good title hinders settlers from comeing on and is a damage to us that are here. I wish [you] could certify me that he has a good title. . . .

Rachel and Sophia are not at home. I have often heard them mention your Gifts and Kindness and sensibly express their Gratitude to their Uncle and Aunt.

My wife unites with me in Love to you and Sister with the little ones.

Believe that I am Effectionately Your Brother[69]

9

ALTHOUGH EPIDEMICS RAGED in Boston and other Massachusetts ports in the summer of 1796, they spared New York and opened the streets again to Democratic Society protesters against the Washington administration. At the end of summer, Washington announced he would not stand for election to a third term, and he issued a Farewell Address to the American people. Never delivered orally, it appeared in Philadelphia's progovernment newspaper the *Daily American Advertiser* on September 19. Washington warned the American people against the dangers of division by political parties. He advised the nation to avoid *permanent* alliances with foreign nations and to resort only to "temporary alliances for extraordinary measures."[70]

With the election three months away and the streets free of disease, Jefferson's Democratic Societies filled the streets of New York and Philadelphia with unemployed immigrant marchers to rally for Jefferson's elevation to the presidency. As they had done earlier, French agents called for America to join France in war against Britain.

Infuriated by the renewal of mob demonstrations and fearful they might steal the election for Jefferson, Webster wrote to Secretary of War Pickering:

Permit me to ask you, as a private man and a friend, how long the *delicacy* of our government will suffer every species of indignity from the agents of the French nation in this country? Our people *do not know* the extent of their intrigues nor the base treatment our government receives and has received from them. Could not the French minister, in case of a civil disturbance, command force enough in the City and County of Philadelphia to drive every honest man away and lay waste the city? I firmly believe it. Are we then to be split into parties to become convenient tools of foreign intrigues? For mercy's sake, let the government assume a decided tone. We had better surround our country with a wall of brass than to be thus torn into factions by the agents of powers in whose rivalries we have not the slightest interest.[71]

Although Webster's concerns were not unwarranted, John Adams nevertheless squeaked to victory on December 7, and Jefferson was forced to settle for four years of political impotence as vice president. Webster was anticipating the Adams inauguration when he received a desperate plea from his brother Abram. Abram's land had yielded nothing but destitution and hunger, and his children were suffering. "Kind Brother," Abram wrote,

> I have received so many favours from you that I have not the face to ask for more still if you will write by the Mail to Whitestone and enclose a bill of 30 dollars you will do a great kindness to me, for it will furnish my family with bread corn & meat & then I can attend to my farm in the spring I was unable to do a great deal last summer on account of my eye sight being not able to distinguish a man from a stump at 10 rods [fifty-five yards] distance this difficulty is in a great measure removed so that I read without spectacles. I did however, sow 2-1/2 acres of wheat last fall and have more land clear to sow spring wheat & to plant.
>
> The Dispute about the land we are on render it not safe paying money for it at present, still I have a mind to try another summer and I think I have a prospect that I shall be able to raise my own provision, I keep my family as small as I can but cant always find work abroad for my Daughters who are willing to work and anxious to assist me as far as they are able. we live as frugal as possible purchasing nothing but what is of absolute necessity. . . . it is hard beginning on a new farm. my paper is full and must subscribe myself
>
> Your Effectionate Brother
>
> My wife and children Join with me in love to you Sister and the little girls.[72]

Worried that Abram and his children might starve, Noah immediately sent money to buy them food, along with clothing for the children. With all his other responsibilities, Noah Webster now had to provide for his brother and his brother's family—and track down a thieving speculator who had absconded with his brother's savings.

10

THE INAUGURATION OF JOHN ADAMS as America's second president, in March 1797, was remarkable for its serenity—it was a transfer of power with no rancor or turmoil, a triumph for the American Constitution and the democratic process it had created. Adams wrote that many in the audience were "moved to tears" as he assumed the reins of office from Washington—

an event the new president described modestly as "the sun setting, full-orbit, and another rising (though less splendid)."[73]

A stream of libelous statements in the antigovernment press, however, tarnished the occasion. Benjamin Franklin Bache's *Aurora* called Washington "the man, who is the source of all misfortunes of our country." Bache exulted that Washington would be

> reduced to a level with his fellow-citizens, and is no longer possessed
> of power to multiply evils upon the United States. If ever there was a
> period for rejoicing this is the moment—every heart, in unison with the
> freedom and happiness of the people, ought to beat high with exultation,
> that the name of Washington from this day ceases to give a currency to
> political iniquity, and to legalize corruption. . . . When a retrospective
> is taken of the Washingtonian administration for eight years, it is a sub-
> ject of the greatest astonishment, that a single individual should have
> cankered the principles of republicanism in an enlightened people, just
> emerged from the gulph of despotism, and should have carried his de-
> signs against the public liberty so far, as to have put in jeopardy its very
> existence.[74]

Appalled by the attack on a man he revered as a national hero, Webster struck back firmly and viciously, not only with an emotional defense of Washington but with charges bordering on treason against Bache's hero Thomas Jefferson.

"During the whole period of President Washington's administration, & amid the most perplexing difficulties," Webster wrote,

> that great man maintained the most rigid impartiality toward the bel-
> ligerent nations; his integrity, firmness, justice & love of his country re-
> mained unshaken. But his prudence could not shield him from incessant
> abusive attacks in the democratic papers. He was charged with partiality
> to Great Britain, & his cabinet, with enmity to republican principles.
> He bore the calumnious charges with astonishing magnanimity; but his
> sensibility was at times so wounded that he vented complaints. "I won-
> der," said he, "why I am so much abused; I do as well as I can."[75]

Then, hoping to crush the credibility of the anarchic republican Democrats, Webster exploded a bombshell that resounded across America and the Atlantic to Britain and Europe. "We have," he declared, "a specimen of the charges of the democratic party against President Washington's administration in a letter of Mr. Jefferson to his Italian friend Mazzei."[76]

Webster then published an English translation of what he called a "treasonable letter" that the former secretary of state had written in French a year earlier—when Washington was still president—to his Italian friend Philip Mazzei, a sometime wine merchant and foreign agent. Webster had obtained a copy of the original "Letter to Mazzei" from the French newspaper *Moniteur* and translated it into English.

"Our political state has been prodigiously altered since you have left us," Jefferson wrote to Mazzei.

> Instead of that noble love of liberty & of republican government, which enabled us to pass triumphantly through the dangers of war, an Anglican, monarchical, aristocratical party has arisen. Their avowed object is to impost on us the substance . . . of the British government. . . . We republicans have against us, the Executive power, the judiciary power, two of the three branches of the legislature; all the officers of the government, all those who aspire to offices; all timid men who prefer the calm of despotism to the stormy sea of liberty; the British merchants & Americans who trade with British capitals; the speculators, the people who are interested in the bank, & in the public funds; establishments invented for the purpose of corruption, & to assimilate us to the British model of corrupt parts.
>
> I should give you a fever, if I should name to you the apostates who have embraced these heresies, the men who were Solomons in council & Samsons in combat, but whose locks have been shorn by the harlot of England.
>
> These men would ravish from us that liberty which we gained by so many labors & dangers. But we shall preserve it; our mass of weight & of wealth is too great to suffer us to fear that our opposers will employ force against us. It is enough that we are awake & that we shall break the lilliputian ties with which they have bound us, during the first slumbers which succeeded our toils. It is sufficient that we arrest the progress of that system of ingratitude and injustice toward France, from which they would alienate us, to subject us to British influence.[77]

Webster published the letter in two parts—a clever marketing scheme to stimulate readership. Between the two issues, he received another letter from his brother Abram, who was becoming a heavy financial burden:

> Dear Brother:
>
> I have this Day Rec'd . . . £20. You[r] unbounded generosity is of so Great service to me and my family that I know not how to express the sence I have of it has enabled me to supply my family with a good store of provision for the Summer and has changed the countenance of my family from maloncholy to Sprightliness. there is still one thing wanting which you cannot remedy that is the title of our land it is in such situation that no body purchases there which is of great Disadvantage to the few that are there. Kirkland has no Deed of the land. He is been gone to New England six or seven months and reports are not favorable about him. some say the land belongs to A Coll Walker of N. York if you please you may enquire for your own satisfaction.
>
> Our Honoured Father made me a visit last fall which was very agreeable to me. I find he is failing very fast especially in his mental powers, indeed the morning he set off home he was so lost in his mind (I suppose it was the thoughts of the journey) that he could not remember

what was him one minute. I therefore accompanied him to uncle Steels
who was his company to N England.

My wife Joins with me in Love to you and Sister and the girls their
Duty to their uncle and aunt whom we all acknowledge as our kind
Benefectors.

    I am kind Brother your effectionate
        Abram Webster[78]

Webster sent his brother more money, but had no time to chase land
swindlers. He had to publish the second part of Jefferson's letter to Mazzei.

Publication of the letter infuriated Jefferson and raised the mutual distrust he and Webster felt for each other to a level of bitterness that would
eventually end Webster's influence in national politics. Jefferson complained that Webster had mistranslated the letter from the original French,
but Webster, who was nearly as fluent in French as Jefferson, rechecked
every word and could find only one error—*form* had been written in the
plural, *forms.*

The letter to Mazzei cost Jefferson all influence he might have had in
the Adams administration, and France all hope of obtaining military support from the American government. With all hopes of alliance shattered,
France broke relations with the United States and expelled the American
ambassador, Charles Pinckney. France also stepped up seizures of American
vessels and began hanging Americans impressed aboard captured British
ships. American ships captured with British cargo aboard were seized and
confiscated without compensation. At the same time, the French were trying to reacquire Louisiana from Spain, and with it control of the Mississippi and the power to block American expansion in the West. Suddenly,
war with France seemed as imminent as or more so than it did with Britain.

For several months before publishing the letter to Mazzei, Webster had
assailed the French in the *Minerva,* warning that the French had begun the
Revolution

> with honest views of acquiring their rights, but they overlapped this
> limit and are contending for plunder and empire . . . the warm admirers
> of French policy, who *rejoiced* and *exulted* to see French armies overrun-
> ning, laying waste, and plundering Germany, Italy, and Holland, no sooner
> *feel the same evils themselves* than convictions break in on their minds and
> they acknowledge *they have been deceived* as to the views of the French.
> The seizure of one hundred and fifty sail of vessels has done what the
> insults of French ministers here could not do; it has *brought Americans
> to their senses.*[79]

President Adams called a special session of Congress to denounce
French depredations of American shipping and the treatment of Ambassador Pinckney. He urged Congress to build an American navy, arm merchant vessels, and modernize the militia. He fell short of a declaration of

war, however, and called for "a fresh attempt at negotiation" with the French.

Neither Jeffersonians nor Federalists were ecstatic. The former sought alliance with France; the latter wanted war. Although he favored neutrality, Webster believed war with France was inevitable, and he wrote a brilliant policy paper urging negotiation of a treaty with Britain. It was one of the most dazzling displays of Webster's ability to analyze complex international problems, and had Adams adopted it, the United States might well have averted the War of 1812. Webster wrote:

> . . . as we are probably approaching a rupture with France, I sincerely wish the British Ministry could be convinced of the utility of conciliating the attachment of Americans. . . . The tide is turned, and the current is setting strong against the French Government. The northern states wish peace as much as ever, but the losses of property already sustained and the insolent conduct of the French government toward ours has united them in the opinion that war is probable, and they are ready to meet it with firmness.
>
> Never was there a more favorable moment for the British Government to . . . regain the confidence of our citizens; and what extreme ill policy in the Ministry not to embrace it.[80]

Webster pointed out that Britain's naval strength, commerce, and manufactures had made her the world's most powerful nation, militarily and economically, but that the European war would gradually erode that strength by cutting export sales to Europe. America's growing population and expanding frontiers, he said, would provide a marketplace of "immense magnitude" for British goods "and one . . . which of itself in a few years will be sufficient to give employment to all the manufacturers in England and *alone* will maintain the whole naval force of Great Britain."

With a population that was doubling every twenty to twenty-five years, America, said Webster, would need "all the goods the British Empire can furnish" within the next thirty years. Britain could, in other words, compensate for all other market losses by simply building its trade with America. "In addition," Webster wrote,

> the vicinity of the United States to the [British] West Indies, and the abundant supply of cattle, horses, lumber and provisions which the Islands may always receive from these [United] States, renders the intercourse between the two countries extremely convenient for both parties. The West Indies cannot be furnished with the foregoing articles from any other quarter at the same low rate; and *all* their lumber and livestock must be supplied from this continent. The trade, at the same time that it is beneficial to the Islands, is highly advantageous to the United States and to Great Britain, as the cargoes shipped to the West Indies furnish our merchants with bills to make remittance to England for her manufacturers.

Webster said the mutual interests of both nations demanded "a system of regulations for the mutual encouragement and protection of trade. The United States have no navy, but in point of tonnage are probably second only to Great Britain. Great Britain has a navy . . . and the value of the American trade to Great Britain makes protection of that trade as useful to Great Britain as to the United States."

Webster suggested that the two nations form "a maritime league, like the famous Hanseatic Confederation, in which the two most considerable commercial nations should guarantee mutual protection to trade." Failure to do so, he warned, would permit unfettered French expansion of

> colonial establishments on the southern borders of the United States. It is now believed that Spain has surrendered to France Louisiana, if not the Floridas. The possession of these countries and of course Mississippi by the French will place that nation in a situation to annoy, if not to endanger, the British possessions in the West Indies. Louisiana is a world of itself, and the export trade of the Mississippi hereafter will be equal to that of half Europe. With these advantages of trade, the ship timber, iron, and naval stores in abundance at hand, and perhaps the mines of Spanish America in the hands of France, France hereafter may become formidable to all the commercial nations of Europe.
>
> To oppose this formidable nation and her gigantic strength, a *new* and formidable power *must* be created, or Europe and the trade of the Atlantic will be at her mercy.

All that Britain has to do to prevent that eventuality and "reap the utmost advantage from us," Webster said, "is to desist from vexing our trade and to protect our vessels and seamen on the high seas as she does her own. By such protection, Great Britain immediately derives a benefit to herself by saving the property of her best customers and thus enriching herself . . . the commercial interests of Great Britain and the United State are so closely interwoven that . . . the party that wishes to impair commerce of the other aims a blow at its own."[81]

Although Webster's policy paper appealed to King, Pickering, and Wolcott, it had little impact on President Adams. Rejecting Webster's recommendations, he named a three-man commission to go to France to negotiate a new treaty of commerce and amity. French foreign minister Talleyrand, however, insulted the Adams commission by sending three agents—known infamously as agents X, Y, and Z—to demand a bribe of $240,000 as the price for opening negotiations. In addition, they demanded U.S. government loans and an official apology by President Adams for his anti-French remarks to the special session of Congress.

The XYZ Affair, as it was called, set off political turmoil in and out of government in the United States, with some Federalists displaying the same ferocious bellicosity toward France that antifederalist Jeffersonians had shown toward England a year earlier. Once again, the street mobs joined the debate, but this time they were Tory mobs, led by Federalist rabble-rousers demanding war with France on the side of Britain.

Adams tried to steer a neutral course and postponed any immediate reply to French insults. He called on Congress to strengthen national defenses in the event France declared war. Congress created a standing army of fifteen thousand men, strengthened the state militias, built three frigates, and authorized merchant ships to arm and defend themselves. It imposed new taxes to pay for military expansion and granted the president discretionary war-making powers. Washington was named commanding general, with Hamilton second in command, as inspector general. Hamilton, in effect, became leader of the Federalist war faction.

In contrast to their demands for war against Britain the previous year, the Jeffersonian republicans became apostles of peace, saying a navy was more likely to cause war than prevent it. By late 1797, bitter congressional debates erupted into violence. When Connecticut Federalist Roger Griswold insulted the pro-French republican Matthew Lyon of Vermont, Lyon crossed the House chamber to Griswold's desk and spat in his face. Griswold lashed out with a pair of fire tongs; the two fell to the floor in a scuffle that ended only when other representatives dragged Griswold by his legs and forced him to release his opponent. Federalists moved to expel the "Spitting Lyon" from the halls of Congress. One representative called him a "kennel of filth" that ought to be removed the way "citizens remove impurities and filth from their docks and wharves." One Boston representative noted that Lyon had immigrated from Ireland as a young man and added, "I feel grieved that the saliva of an Irishman should be left upon the face of an American & he, a New Englandman."[82]

In the end, the Adams commission accomplished nothing but provoke an undeclared naval war with France, deepen the divide between pro-British and pro-French factions in the United States, and split the Federalist party between those who favored war on the side of Britain against France and those who, like Adams, favored neutrality and noninvolvement in foreign affairs. Through it all, Webster believed it his patriotic duty to remain loyal to the president. "I know no party, but that of my country," he explained.[83]

His position earned him nothing but vicious assaults by both the pro-British Tory press and pro-French Jeffersonians. With no libel laws to dissuade him, William Cobbett, the English editor of *Porcupine's Gazette,* fired a volley of invectives at Webster—"cameleon-like editor," "dictatorial newsman," "spiteful viper," "base creature," "rancorous villain," "contemptible creature," "great fool and a barefaced liar," and "prostitute wretch."[84]

It was all too much for Webster. By the end of 1797, he was exhausted—physically, emotionally, and mentally. The rejection of his policy proposal and the breakdown in political civility had left him and his newspaper politically impotent. Adding to his dismay was the discovery of missing company funds. He reorganized his company and renamed the daily newspaper the *Commercial Advertiser* and the weekly paper the *Spectator*.

Webster began to think seriously of retirement. His third child, Harriet, had been born on April 6, 1797. With his oldest daughter, Emily, approaching seven and his middle girl, Julia, already four, Webster realized that his obsession with work had cost him the joys of watching them grow and learn. He needed their love—as they did his—and he missed being with Rebecca. And all of them missed their many relatives in Hartford and Boston.

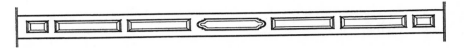

CHAPTER EIGHT

Philosopher

I

$\mathbb{A}$T THE BEGINNING OF 1798, Webster conceded defeat in his effort to influence national political affairs and promote national unity. Federalism was dying. Its leaders—even George Washington, America's revered patron saint—had been unable to generate broad-based popular allegiance to a strong, apolitical central authority acting in the best overall interests of the nation. To Webster, national political unity seemed no closer under the Constitution than it had under the Articles of Confederation. He sat helplessly in his newspaper office as political anarchy seemed to grip the nation. Congress had split irreparably into two political parties, and each had divided along so many fault lines it was difficult to identify the position of each member clearly. Debates raged between Northerners and Southerners, pro-English, pro-French, prowar, antiwar, proimmigration, anti-immigration, protax, antitax . . . positions overlapped; the bickering went on and on—and intensified every day.

Webster's closest friends, Wolcott and Pickering, had grown increasingly distant from President Adams, and the materials they sent Webster grew less reliable as indications of administration policies. In any event, Webster had tired of long hours of daily journalism. The sameness of it, day after day—the half-hour walk to work before sunrise, through icy winter snows and unrelenting summer heat; the full day at his desk, writing, rewriting, editing; rushing materials to press; policing production and distribution—it was all too much, and, worse, it was all for nothing. In the end, the performance of his duty had accomplished little for the country and earned him only a constant barrage of vicious epithets by the opposition press.

Before entering journalism, Webster had always enjoyed hard work, but he also enjoyed the great variety in his life—writing grammar rules one minute, history the next, guidelines for a constitution after that, all the while traveling about the nation, to Philadelphia, Boston, Mount Vernon, visiting Washington, Franklin, Rush, and the like, debating everything from agricultural science to phonetic alphabets to Socratic methods of instruction. He loved being a "busy body," but his editorship in New York had reduced his life to impotent boredom. Even worse, it was depriving him of the pleasures of home.

Webster loved being with his wife and children. He adored his wife. Holding his little girls in his arms, watching them squirm away to run and spin and dance, filled his very soul with joy. He rejoiced at their squeals and songs and laughter, and loved nothing more than playing with them, piping on his flute to them, singing to them, teaching them to sing, to count, to spell, to speak and write and draw.

When he began his newspaper, he deprived himself of many of these pleasures for the sake of his country. He had not only failed to bring political leaders together, he had not even convinced doctors to stop bickering long enough to unite in common cause. As Webster put it, he was quitting because he had tired of relating "the absurdities of man."[1]

On April 1, 1798, Webster found a new editor, turned management over to the printers, packed up his family, and moved to New Haven to pursue a new life, of diversified scholarship and public service. He was particularly eager to pursue his study of epidemic diseases, which he saw as a great humanitarian project that would benefit not only his countrymen but all mankind.

"No sober reflecting man," he said, "can cast his eye over the world, and see the miseries of man, without a humane wish to alleviate them."[2]

Webster was certain the answers lay buried in the mountains of data that scientists and physicians had accumulated in the course of dealing with the ill—data he believed he simply needed to gather and sort to find answers. "This removal," he wrote to Pickering, "is the accomplishment of a purpose of many years standing—that of having an income which will enable me to pursue, with little interruption, my taste for science."[3]

In quitting New York, he retained majority ownership in his newspapers, which ensured a steady income to supplement the comfortable royalties he now collected from his speller and other textbooks. His two newspapers—especially the semiweekly *Spectator*, which reached out across the nation—had promoted his speller so successfully that no school in the nation failed to stock it among its basic supplies. He planned to continue using his newspapers to promote his books. Moreover, he also retained editorial control of the political columns in the papers and planned writing occasional essays when current events inspired him to do so.

Rufus King, in London, was devastated by Webster's plan. Fearful that Webster's departure would mute the voice of Federalism, King tried to dissuade him. "I have no remaining Hope that we shall come to a friendly settlement with France," he warned Webster.

> All that we hear . . . serves to show the ascendancy of France, and the dissolute Principles which influence the House of Austria.
> If England shall be unable to resist, Europe will be again thrown into a state of Barbarism, worse even than that of the dark ages. . . .
> I with others have earnestly hoped that we should escape the war; but since no alternative is allowed us, I feel persuaded that we shall [be unable to] resist the power, as well as the injustice of France. What we have done on a former occasion, and under Circumstances less favorable, should give us confidence as well as Energy in the conflict.
> You have done much Sir, by the constant publications with which you have labored to disabuse the public; but a great deal will remain to be done, and no one among us is better able to assist in the very important Department of the Press than you are.[4]

Webster, however, had made up his mind. "A newspaper," he wrote,

> is common property in which all parties claim a right to utter their venom; and . . . I found myself exposed to so many personal indignities from different parties that retirement was essential to my happiness, if not to my life. I found in more instances than one that my best endeavors to please those whose esteem I valued gave offence. To a gentleman of my education and standing in society this treatment became intolerable. It wounded me to the soul that the purest motives were often misinterpreted into the basest designs; the worst possible construction was put on paragraphs; articles and opinions laid to my charge which were easily known to come from other quarters; and any little mistake was laid hold of to injure my feelings, and as an excuse for exercising revenge. . . . A property of this kind is hardly worth the purchase, and in the collision of hostile passions in our country few men of honour and feeling can consent to take charge of public papers—they must generally be superintended by men who are callous.[5]

Although Webster said he intended to continue to "communicate my opinions on political and literary subjects,"[6] he spent much of the first three months of 1798 organizing his affairs for the move and collecting additional data from New York hospitals, churches, and medical practitioners and faculties for his study of epidemic diseases. On March 17, he ran an advertisement in his newspaper to make his study self-supporting by asking for subscriptions for "An Inquiry into the Origin of Epidemic Diseases," at $2 each, bound. "As the compilations will not only cost great labor but considerable expense, no more copies will be printed than to supply subscribers."[7] Two weeks later Webster quit New York's tumult and moved to New Haven.

2

UNQUESTIONABLY ONE OF the nation's prettiest cities of that era, New Haven was a peaceful port community of four thousand. Its broad avenues threaded tall archways of stately old elm trees that stretched across a broad gentle slope to the green. From the green, the gleaming white steeple of the Congregational church reached out from among the elms to guide the graceful sailing ships that dotted Long Island Sound. And above the green, crowning the city's landscape, stood Yale College and its beautiful chapel, the nation's last citadel of the old Calvinist Puritanism.

Webster and his family settled "in a large, old fashioned mansion," built by Benedict Arnold, for which Webster paid $2,666.66. The house had "a great old-fashioned garden attached where," according to his granddaughter, "his children reveled. The cherries and peaches were particularly fine. . . . Peaches then grew freely in New England and great pear trees with fruits of the richest flavors, stood in every garden of any pretension." His granddaughter recalled Webster's bounding out of the orchard "bringing a great basket of fresh apples or plums, saying, 'Now children, eat your peck of fruit to-day.'"[8]

Webster's daughter Eliza, the sixth of eight Webster children, later described the joyful home she remembered as a little girl:

> My honored father's study was over the living room, the east parlor . . . [which] was used as a dining room. . . . The house was open to the sound and with a large space about it for orchard and garden. These my Father delighted in and his recreation was found in their cultivation and adornment. It was a lovely home. My very earliest recollections of this dear Parent, when I was about five years old were of his leading me among his flower beds, when the tulips were in bloom. He plucked one of variegated hues and placed it in my hands, pointed out its beauty and told me that "our heavenly Father made them all beautiful to make us happy." His lesson then of God's goodness was never forgotten.[9]

Webster turned forty during his first year in New Haven. He was a "tall, slender, graceful" man, according to one neighbor, "with keen gray eyes and sharply cut features . . . remarkable for his erect walk and perfection of and neatness in dress. He was never seen on the street without a broad hat and long cue." He was delighted to be "home" in New Haven, where he had gone to college and had evolved from adolescent to student to patriot soldier to scholar.[10]

He explained his reasons for the move in his diary: "My attachment to the State of Connecticut, my acquaintances, my habits, which are literary & do not correspond with the bustle of commerce & the taste of people perpetually inquiring for news & making bargains; together with the cheapness of living, are among my motives for this change of Residence."[11]

New Haven was as happy to welcome its renowned son of Yale as he was to be there. His speller was the best-selling book in America after the Bible, and the eponym *Websterian* had gained as much currency as *Johnsonian* among scholars and educators in discussions of the English language. He was also a Calvinist and a defender of Federalism in a citadel of both beliefs. Calvinism remained the official state church, and the same old Federalist families—the Ellsworths, Wolcotts, Trumbulls, Dwights, and other sons of Yale—still governed the state, its cities, and its college, as they had for generations. The Reverend Timothy Dwight, Jonathan Edwards's grandson and Webster's friend and tutor at Yale, had assumed the presidency of the college three years earlier—just after the death of Ezra Stiles.[12] And Josiah Meigs, the distinguished mathematics and science professor, who had been Webster's college classmate, was also still at Yale. Indeed, of the state's oldest family names, only Webster's had been missing, and he now returned—triumphantly. Few communities in America would have greeted Webster and his family as warmly as New Haven, and with the exception of Hartford, there was none in which he could have felt more at home. Almost immediately after his arrival, the City Council invited him to be its orator for the city's Fourth of July celebration, one of the most prestigious honors a community could offer each year.

From the moment Webster set foot in his huge garden and looked out across Long Island Sound, a spasm of comfort and joy swept through his huge frame and reignited his spirit. He attacked the suckers on his fruit trees with his pruner, then thrust his experienced hands into the earth to plant seeds—while his adoring girls surrounded him with gaiety and laughter. He enrolled his two oldest in "the best day school in the neighborhood," taught by Miss Eunice Hall, whose superstitions dissatisfied the science-oriented Webster from the day he first met her.[13] After a few years, he withdrew his girls from school abruptly, after Miss Hall refused to let them view an eclipse of the sun through pieces of smoked glass their father had given them for that very purpose. "I would not have you see it for the world," she told them and their mates, and kept them all in school until after sunset to prevent exposing them to the evil phenomenon.

The Websters compensated for poor common-school instruction by teaching their daughters at home. Rebecca Webster taught the girls to sew, knit, and cook, while Noah taught them reading, writing, spelling, ciphering, and science, and gave them lessons in singing and on the harpsichord and flute.

The Websters joined the Congregational church on the New Haven green and took over direction of its musical activities, with Webster himself leading the choir. In early May, less than a month after he settled in New Haven, he went to vote, and a few days later he wrote a joyful letter to Pickering to report that Jeffersonian Democratic Societies had mustered a mere five hundred of the more than seven thousand votes cast. "I rejoice also that every man of reputable character in this state appears well informed on the subject of the ultimate views of France. People appear to have correct ideas of the intentions of the French Government and the tendency of their principles to destroy all the *pillars* of public peace and private safety."

With a burst of energy he had not experienced since his Hartford days, Webster again became the quintessential "busy body." At home both socially and politically, he accepted a City Council invitation to serve on the school board. Dissatisfied with Miss Hall's school, Webster organized parents and raised money to build a new school, a charming two-room brick structure called the Union School, with one classroom each for girls and boys. Webster enrolled his three daughters, and within a year enrollment swelled to fifty-two boys and sixty-three girls. In June 1799, the city's overwhelmingly Federalist landholders elected him to the Court of Common Council, or City Council, a post he held for five years. A year later, Webster became school board president, and after he helped found the Connecticut Academy of Arts and Sciences, the city's voters sent him to the state legislature, where he served until 1807, while also holding the appointive position of justice of the peace in New Haven.

The amazing range of his activities filled his life with joy—and Rebecca quickly grew as enraptured with social life in New Haven as she had been in Hartford. According to her daughter, the Websters were "very happy in New Haven and had a large circle of congenial friends. Father worked assiduously but with many interruptions. His large family were growing up about him. He was very hospitable."[14] As in Hartford, Rebecca Webster was "remarkable for her hospitality," according to her daughter Emily. "Her doors were open as wide as her heart. . . . She was an excellent housekeeper and my Father was a generous provider, and she presided over the affairs of the household with a gentle dignity which was lovely."[15]

Much of their New Haven social life centered around Yale and the church. "Dr and Mrs Webster were the most noticeable people that walked the streets [of New Haven]," according to their neighbors, "both for their beauty of face and great elegance of carriage."[16] In addition to their myriad of friends from New Haven, Hartford, and the rest of Connecticut, Rebecca's brothers and sisters and their families from Boston were frequent house guests, as was the elder Noah Webster, who made regular visits from West Hartford.

Along with his many civic activities, his rich social life and church life, his gardening, and his family life, Webster carried on with his writing, including work on his massive opus *A Brief History of Epidemic and Pestilential Diseases; with the Principal Phenomena of the Physical World, Which Precede and Accompany Them, and Observations Deduced from the Facts Stated.*[17] He scoured the Yale Library, darted up to Cambridge to do the same at Harvard, and went to Philadelphia to gather materials at the University of Pennsylvania library. He gathered materials from churches, ship captains, and anyone else who had witnessed the course of epidemic diseases. He wrote to America's and Europe's most eminent physicians. Many scholars and scientists eagerly cooperated. Even historian Jeremy Belknap put aside his old—and irrational—antipathy for Webster by extracting the account of Governor William Bradford, Webster's forebear, of a plague among the Indians:

> In New England the Indians are afflicted with pestilent fevers, plague, black-pox, consumption of ye lungs, falling sickness, King's evil, & a disease called by ye Spaniard the plague in the back, with us Empyema. Their Physicians are the powans or Priests who cure sometimes by charms & medicine, but in a general infection they seldom come among them therefore they use their own Remedies which is sweating. Their manner when they have *plague* or *small-pox* is to cover the Wigwam with bark, so close that no air can enter, and make a great fire. They remain there with a stewing heat, till they are in a top sweat, & then run into the Sea or a River & presently after they are come into their huts again, they either recover or give up the Ghost.[18]

Benjamin Rush was particularly helpful, providing Webster with a continuous flow of materials and letters. In one letter he complained that despite his own and Webster's articles relating pestilence to poor city sanitation, Philadelphia had made no effort "to clear a single gutter of its filth. I fear nothing but another visitation by the yellow fever will cure us of our infidelity upon this interesting Subject. Go on—go on with your inquiries. Cause Physicians to blush, and instruct mankind to throw off their allegiance to them. Posterity will do you justice. The man who produces truth upon the origin of pestilential fevers, and persuades the world to conform to it, will deserve more of the human race than all the heroes or statesmen that ever lived."[19]

Rush believed that yellow fever was imported from the West Indies, and he petitioned Congress to prohibit ships from the Mediterranean and the West Indies from landing in the United States during summer months. Webster disagreed, saying that the diseases were produced locally. Scottish-born Samuel Latham Mitchill, a doctor who held the chair of natural history, chemistry, and agriculture at Columbia College, agreed with Webster.

"When every hour almost brings News of the Sickness or Death of some of one's acquaintance or friends," Mitchill wrote to Webster, "it is a matter of no small difficulty to preserve calmness and tranquility throughout.

"New York this time has got a plague indeed," Mitchill continued.

> The Scourge is applied severely and cuts deep. I am satisfied more if possible than ever, of its local origin. Nobody now talks of importation. It seems to be admitted on all sides to be a home-bred Pestilence. The Inhabitants have really poisoned their City by the accumulation of Excrement, putrid Provisions and every unclean thing. There is besides this, however, certainly another cause which is the predisposition

to this Disease induced by gross animal diet, and long use of strong malt liquors, Wines and distilled Spirits. I have witnessed so many instances of it, that I am satisfied, if some our citizens breath an Air pure and balmy as the breezes of Eden, they would engender this Sickness by their way of Life. They would breed it within them. To get the better of these Visitations, will therefore require more than municipal regulations. An alteration and a considerable one too, of Housekeeping and modes of Life will be necessary.[20]

Webster's two-volume work — 712 pages — was the world's first study of epidemic diseases and became the standard text on the subject in medical schools around the world for much of the nineteenth century. Volume I provided the first detailed history of epidemics, from biblical times to 1799, and then offered a compilation of medical opinion on the causes of pestilence (none of which included rats, fleas, or mosquitoes). Volume II was divided into a huge statistical section listing mortality rates and a section of inconclusive theories about the causes of epidemics. Still noteworthy as a great historical compilation, the work emerged too early in the history of epidemiology to have any scientific or medical value.

On the cause of the fever, Webster himself concluded that electricity produced "carbonic gas vapors" in the air, which, when inhaled, led to influenza and catarrh, which he said were the precursors of yellow fever.[21] There was, he explained in a letter to Rush, a basis,

stronger than I could have imagined, for believing our atmosphere to be much influenced by vapor from the earth — occasioned by subterranean heat. The mortality or sickness among fish, during pestilence is a strong fact in favor of the idea. I have facts on this point, that will surprize those who never thought on the subject. Every medical man knows that earthquakes *always* attend the plague in countries subject to them, & *usually* in countries not subject to them; And will you believe it, all the *great* plagues of the earth have been attended with the eruption of volcanoes. I could have no conception of the uniform testimony of history to these facts, without a careful examination of *all* the books I can find. But there *must* be something in the suggestion of subterranean heat.[22]

Webster's theories were no more far-fetched than those of other scientists of his day. In an era when every scientist claimed indisputable access to scientific truth, Webster was at least modest enough to conclude his work by writing, "The reader will consider these opinions rather as *conjectural* than *positive*. No certain conclusions can be drawn from an interrupted and imperfect series of facts. More materials are necessary to enable us to erect a theory of epidemics which shall deserve full confidence." Webster proposed "that all medical and philosophical societies undertake to register facts and reciprocally to communicate them by means of general correspondence."[23]

Scientists around the world hailed Webster's work, but few were willing to pay for it. Dr. Joseph Priestly, the famed English scientist who discovered oxygen ("dephlogisticated air"), called Webster's work "a most important publication" deserving of "the thanks of all mankind."[24] The editors of the *Medical Repository,* in New York, wrote, "In our judgment Mr. Webster has performed a great work," which was so "astonishing" that it advised every layman as well as doctor to purchase it.[25]

On the other hand, William Currie, a doctor with perhaps more prescience than most, but an enemy of Rush, could not resist insulting Webster, whom he knew to be Rush's close friend: "The doctrine of Mr. Webster on this subject, notwithstanding his elaborate researches, appears . . . to be as much the creature of the imagination as the tales of the fairies."[26]

Webster himself had contracted yellow fever during the epidemic that claimed more than six thousand lives that summer in New York and Philadelphia. Sick for about ten weeks after visiting New York in August, he had nevertheless continued writing and had managed to finish his *History of Epidemic and Pestilential Diseases* by the end of the year. In February 1799, he wrote to Benjamin Rush that "after all my labor, I see no prospects of publishing the work; for people will not subscribe to it, and I have bestowed so much money and labor on it that I am determined to stay my hand."[27] A year later, Webster believed he had accumulated enough subscriptions to warrant publishing it, but as he had done so often before, he misjudged the market. Late the following year, he wrote to Rush, "I shall never print another [edition.] not more than 200 copies are sold in this country, & I am 700 or 800 dollars out of pocket on account of it, with all my previous expenses, my labor & toil. I wish the Physicians in New York & Philad. would take the remaining copies, about 700, at a dollar in Sheets, the first cost,—& distribute them over the country, among young students. The young are susceptible of truth—the old are incorrigible."[28]

3

ON JULY 4, 1798, Webster again delivered the annual Independence Day oration in New Haven, Connecticut. Once a reverent student of Rousseau, Webster now warned his fellow citizens that Rousseau and republicanism posed a threat to American liberty. "At no period since we became a nation," his voice boomed out,

> have our political affairs been so critical as at this moment. Ambition, under the specious cover of republicanism, and infidelity, under the deceptive title of reason, have assumed the scepter and the sword, and are stalking over the earth with giant steps . . . dragging from seats of

justice the wise and venerable, and replacing them with bullies and cox-
combs; encouraging violence and robbery . . . plundering states under
the name of taking pay for protecting them; dethroning God and tram-
pling on man. . . . Such are the inevitable consequences of that false
philosophy which has been preached in the world by Rousseau, Con-
dorcet, Godwin and other visionaries. Never, my fellow citizens, let us
exchange our civil and religious institutions . . . or the sober industrial
moral habits of our country, for experiments in atheism and lawless
democracy. *Experience* is a safe pilot; but *experiment* is a dangerous
ocean, full of rocks and shoals![29]

Three days after his speech, the Federalist-controlled Congress abro-
gated the Franco-American alliance and prepared for war. In addition to
twenty defense initiatives against the enemies beyond American shores,
Congress also acted against its enemies within. Reacting to rumors that
French agents were ready to burn Philadelphia and massacre its inhabitants, Congress passed four Alien and Sedition Acts to protect the nation
against aliens in America who acted against the nation's interests. In addition to extending from five to fourteen years the period of residency required for citizenship, the acts authorized the president to imprison or
expel citizens of an enemy power or any other aliens he considered dangerous. The fourth law, or Sedition Act, passed on July 14, France's Bastille
Day, made it a crime for anyone—alien or American—to aid "any insurrection, riot, unlawful assembly, or combination."[30]

To Webster's delight, the Sedition Act made it illegal to "write, print,
utter, or publish . . . any false, scandalous and malicious writing or writings
against the government of the United States."[31] Although the act undermined constitutional guarantees of press freedoms, the nation had no libel
laws, and Webster believed the nation needed to curb the freedom of a
newspaper editor to libel those with whom he disagreed.

"The falsehoods and calumny propagated by means of public papers,"
he declared, "have been the direct and principal means of all the civil dis-
sensions which distract this country and have threatened it with civil war."[32]

Some of the Jeffersonian editors who had abused Presidents Washington and Adams and had libeled Webster were not American citizens. Three
days after passage of the Sedition Act, Webster demanded retribution. He
wrote to his friend Secretary of State Timothy Pickering asking for strict
enforcement of the new law—especially the prosecution of William Cobbett, the English editor of Philadelphia's *Porcupine's Gazette,* who had so insulted Webster for supporting President Adams's policy of neutrality.

"The violence of the resentment of the English . . . knows no bounds,"
Webster wrote to Pickering.

They are determined to overbear all other influence but their own. They
are intolerably insolent, and strive, by all possible means, to lessen the
circulation of my papers, and my influence, which I believe to be consid-

erable in the interior of our country. I am told that the columns of Porcupine's [Cobbett's pseudonym] paper are filled with abuse against me. . . . This is uncivil and perfidious. . . . One thing I know, I have been faithful to my principles and to my country, and I have a subsistence by my labors.

But the time is come when *aliens,* in the interest of foreign nations, are taking a lead in our politics, which to me is alarming. The English are determined to ruin my influence, if possible; for no reason, unless that I do not love England better than my own country: for I have never treated their nation with disrespect.

But I will not long submit to be thus abused by the subjects of foreign nations. I shall withdraw my exertions for the support of government, and as I shall be its advocate in private, I shall only support it by my single suffrage. When *aliens,* assume such a tone and abuse honest faithful men, it is time for native citizens to retire and seek peace and quietness in more private occupations.[33]

Pickering responded immediately, indicting fifteen editors and printers. He won ten convictions, with each of them fined and several sentenced to prison for as long as nine months. Cobbett was fined for libel and, to Webster's delight, returned to his native England and, as he put it, "left Americans to govern themselves."[34]

The first person prosecuted under the Sedition Act was the Irish-born Vermont congressman Matthew Lyon, the fiery Jeffersonian "Spitting Lyon" who had brawled with Connecticut Federalist Roger Griswold on the House floor. Sometime in 1798, he obtained a copy of a letter from "Citizen" Joel Barlow in Paris to Barlow's brother-in-law Georgia congressman Abraham Baldwin. Barlow's letter assailed President Adams in the harshest terms for the XYZ Affair and for ending America's alliance with France. Lyon printed the letter in pamphlet form and distributed it nationally, hoping to provoke a political crisis. He succeeded.[35]

Newspapers everywhere reprinted Barlow's letter. Connecticut's *Courant* was first to reprint it. With shock and chagrin, Webster responded with a scathing attack on his old friend in the *Spectator,* Webster's own nationally distributed weekly. He called Barlow "fundamentally wrong" for supporting the French Revolution and urging an alliance between the United States and France. "The friendship of France," he charged, "instead of being a blessing, is to be dreaded by the citizens of the United States as the most dangerous mischief. Her *enmity* alone can save us from ruin."

Webster said France was interested only in conquest and charged that

the French government professes to be pursuing *liberty* while it is extending its *territories.*

In the face of formal declarations and of the most formal stipulations by treaty, instead of respecting the rights of other nations, the French government has invaded, conquered, and annexed to France the little helpless republic of Geneva. She has conquered a part of the Swiss Cantons . . . sent an army to Holland . . . and with portfolios filled with French promises to respect the independence of that country. Yet look to the event: Holland is enslaved; a tributary nation, its money gone, its trade ruined, saddled with the maintenance of a French army and rulers chosen by the Dutch people seized in their beds by French orders and sent to prison!!

Genoa, also a neutral state which had as far as possible avoided giving France cause for offence, has been revolutionized and in fact placed under the direction of France.

Venice has been annihilated—divided and sold!! So much for her promised respect which France was to pay to the "independence of other nations," as far as it respects Europe.

Webster called it inexcusable for the French to have sent its ambassador Genet to the United States with secret orders to foment rebellion and lure Americans into war with Britain.

The people of America, Sir, will not be *tricked* out of their independence in the mean, dastardly manner by which the French extend their conquests. That sneaking mode of sending spies and emissaries into a neutral country to spread dissatisfaction and turn one half of the people against the other, planting sedition in the peaceful regions of harmony and good neighborhood, is held in such abhorrence by all patriotic and high-spirited Americans that we do not wish for friendly intercourse with a nation which practices such cowardly acts on our national happiness.

He called the French policy of "secretly and silently" trying to undermine governments of other nations "more dangerous to society than war, famine, and pestilence. . . . Against this system, Sir, we rise in mass.

"One more word, Sir," Webster added,

from an old friend who once loved and respected you. The contemptuous manner in which you speak of the President and Senate of America is a striking proof of the effect of atheism and licentious examples on the civility of a well-bred man. You went from America with a good character for talents and for good breeding. Your charging the President with *stupidity* is not excused by its being intended for a private letter. Good breeding would have blushed at the charge and suppressed it. No, Mr. Barlow, in divesting yourself of religion, you have lost your good manners, and like the French by the same process you have commenced a rude, insulting, dogmatical egoist. When you left America, you left many men of acknowledged superior talents to your own. Do not believe, Sir, that *all* your countrymen who support their government have become idiots, that our councils are guided by "stupidity" or "madmen." Distant as you are from this country, it becomes you to speak of yourself with modesty and of your native country and her councils with more moderation and respect.[36]

Instead of signing the letter to his old friend with his usual full signature, Webster simply and contemptuously ended it with his initial: "W."

Webster's bitter letter temporarily ended an intimacy of more than twenty years. Secretary of State Pickering— "Old Pick," as he was called by then—could not arrest Barlow in France, but he did prosecute Lyon for publishing Barlow's letter and libeling President Adams. The court fined Lyon $1,000 and sentenced him to four months in prison, where he became something of a martyr, running for reelection to Congress from his cell—and winning. At the same time, Lyon made the Alien and Sedition Acts a central issue that helped defeat the Federalists in the next presidential election.

Barlow's letter cost him all his old friends in America. After he learned of the furor his letter had provoked, he wrote to Wolcott, "I understand . . . that you and Meigs are the only friends that remain to me in Connecticut."[37] In fact, only Meigs, who had become a staunch Jeffersonian, remained his friend, but his views so alienated Yale's Calvinist and Federalist president, Timothy Dwight, that Dwight forced Meigs to resign. He went to teach in the open air while construction began on the University of Georgia, which Barlow's brother-in-law Abraham Baldwin had just founded.

Barlow, meanwhile, had become a traitor in the eyes of his former Yale classmates and Connecticut friends. James Watson wrote to Wolcott of Barlow: "Although there are few men I loved so much, there are few whose present conduct I detest more."[38]

4

ON JANUARY 7, 1799, Rebecca and Noah Webster's fourth child, Mary, was born. From the moment of her birth she became Noah Webster's favorite— she was blue eyed, with long dark lashes, chestnut brown hair, and fairer skin than the others. Cheerful and sweet tempered, she riveted her eyes lovingly on her father as he sang to her, played the flute, recited poetry, or read from the scriptures. "She was a sunbeam everywhere," her younger sister Eliza recalled later.[39]

The year of Mary's birth, however, ended with sadness for Webster and the many others who had served in the Revolution. George Washington, whom Webster had revered since his boyhood at Yale, died at his home, Mount Vernon, on December 14, 1799, two months short of his sixty-eighth birthday. Congressman Henry (Light-Horse Harry) Lee, the Revolutionary War hero and three-time governor of Virginia, eulogized the former president as "first in war, first in peace, first in the hearts of his countrymen."[40]

Webster sought permission from Washington's heirs to write the official Washington biography, but the honor went to Virginia representative John Marshall, whom President Adams would later name chief justice.

5

BY STRENGTHENING AMERICA'S DEFENSES at sea and silencing its enemies at home, the Federalist Congress accomplished exactly the opposite of what it had originally intended: instead of war with France, it got peace. America's small navy and newly armed merchant ships exacted so steep a price for French attempts to plunder American commerce that the French government sued for peace. With his bargaining hand strengthened, President Adams sent a new negotiating team to France and won French recognition of American neutrality.

The mission, however, irretrievably split the Federalist party and the Adams cabinet. Inspector General of the Army Hamilton, a strong advocate of war, resigned and challenged Adams for Federalist party leadership. Adams dismissed disloyal cabinet members, including Hamilton's ally Secretary of State Timothy Pickering. In 1800, the split produced a second Federalist candidate for president, Hamilton's puppet Charles Pinckney, who ran against incumbent president John Adams. The Democratic-Republicans also split, along regional rather than political lines, with the South favoring Thomas Jefferson and the North backing New York's Aaron Burr Jr.

Although pleased by the division among Democratic-Republicans, Webster was incensed at Hamilton for his disloyalty to the president and for dividing the Federalists. Although Hamilton had been one of his original financial backers at the *American Minerva,* Webster sent Hamilton a long, scathing letter, saying that his opinions and essays were no longer welcome on the pages of that newspaper. He warned Hamilton that if "an Antifederal man" is elected "to the chief magistracy, the fault will lie at *your* door and that of your supporters."[41]

Webster called Adams "a man of pure morals, of firm attachment to republican government, of sound inflexible integrity and patriotism, and by far the best read statesman that the late Revolution called into notice." Webster said that if Hamilton's opposition to Adams produced a Jefferson victory, "your conduct on this occasion will be deemed little short of insanity."[42]

The Democratic-Republicans patched up their regional differences enough to permit Jefferson and Burr to defeat both Adams and Pinckney, but the ballot count in the Electoral College in January 1801 gave the two winners an equal number of votes and forced the Federalist-controlled House of Representatives to break the tie. After thirty-six ballots, Hamilton, who had long-standing personal differences with Burr, asked his Federalist allies in Congress to vote for Jefferson. Neither Burr nor Webster ever forgave Hamilton, the former because of Hamilton's disloyalty to the North, the latter for Hamilton's disloyalty to the president and the cause of Federalism. Jefferson's victory signaled the end of the Federalist party and the influence of its leaders—including Webster—in national political affairs.

As much as Webster despised Jeffersonian republicanism, he believed that loyalty to the Constitution and the nation remained essential to national unity and the survival of the nation. "It is the duty of good citizens," he wrote in the *Spectator*, "to acquiesce in the election and be tranquil. It is proper that Mr. Jefferson be made Chief Magistrate."[43] At his inaugural— the first in the nation's new capital, Washington, D.C.—Jefferson pleased Webster with a call for national unity, saying, "We are all Republicans—all Federalists."[44]

Federalists scorned Jefferson's appeal, however, and Webster rebuked them for their quickness to assail the new president before he had even taken office or had a chance to fulfill his inaugural pledge. "The Federalists," Webster wrote in the *Spectator*, "chagrined at the triumph of their opposition, wish further to irritate their opposition. . . . They are now . . . descending to the baseness of supporting their cause by railings, abuse, and scurrility. Nothing can be less politic or honorable."

Humiliated by Webster's attacks on him, Hamilton, the man responsible for Jefferson's election, turned on Webster and plotted to silence him as the official voice of Federalism. In 1800, Hamilton fanatics in Boston launched a new hard-line Federalist paper, the *Palladium*, to compete with Webster's *Spectator*, and a year later, Hamilton personally established the *New York Evening Post* as the new voice of Federalism in that city. He appointed a Federalist extremist, William Coleman, as editor, with instructions to drive Webster out of the Federalist party and his newspaper out of business.

"As soon as I have a spare column," Coleman pledged, "[I will] give that pedant . . . Webster a rousing box on the ear. i can never forgive this man for his infamous & unprincipled attack on the great & good Hamilton, & tho' nothing shall lead me to attack him unjustly, yet whenever I have to speak of him I shall take no pains to soften my expression."[45]

When Webster had moved to New Haven, he had appointed Samuel Bayard editor of the *Spectator*. A moderate Federalist and a New York judge who much admired Webster, Bayard had assumed the editorship as an interesting pastime. With too many other obligations to become involved in a vicious press war, Bayard warned Webster of Hamilton's plot and urged him to return to assume personal charge of his newspaper in the emerging press wars:

> You are aware, I doubt not of the extraordinary patronage which a new daily & halfweekly paper, to be edited by William Coleman, & designed to supplant the Commercial Advertiser & the Spectator, has received

from the Federal interest of New York. The feeble manner in which your papers have been conducted of late, owing to your absence have led to this result. . . . That some extraordinary caution is necessary to prevent your papers from sinking under the weight of a rival interest, is the general opinion here. You have strong claims on federalism for past exertions, but further services are necessary to retain & insure its support. . . . Not a day is to be lost. Your rivals subscription-list is rapidly increasing. Where *his* paper is taken, *yours* will be discontinu'd in general. Your own presence or that of a *competent* editor, will be indispensibly necessary to rescue your papers from neglect, & yourself from loss.[46]

On September 15, 1801, however, Webster's first son, William Greenleaf, was born, and he was not about to trade the joys of raising a son for the abuse he would receive as a newspaper editor. The letter from Bayard nevertheless provoked enough anxiety to warrant a visit to New York. His visit gave him little hope for saving his newspaper, the Federalist cause, or even the nation. After he returned to New Haven, he sent Bayard an extraordinarily prescient letter. Written sixty years before the Civil War, it said, "I have no hope of the duration of the Union, but I am sorry to see and hear men talk of *blood*. It is the language of rashness and madness. Let the evils work their own cure. Be calm. Suppress passion. We have on former occasions emerged from equal gloom, and we may do it again, if we will keep our passions bridled."[47]

Webster wrote Oliver Wolcott that the visit to New York confirmed

what I before suspected, that a secret enmity to me for the part I took in the controversy between Mr. Adams and General Hamilton is among the influential causes of the patronage given to Mr. Coleman. . . . No man in America has labored so incessantly to oppose anarchy as I have done. . . . I have spent the best portion of my life without honor and with little pecuniary reward, and an attempt to deprive me and my family at this period of life, too late to renew my profession, is a proof of an unfeeling heart in any man who can deliberately make the attempt.[48]

With Webster unwilling to return to New York to supervise his publications, Hamilton's editor systematically reduced Webster's newspapers to relative insignificance, although the editorial quality of the papers remained far higher than that of the *Post*. It was Webster, for example, who was first to publish a legitimate criticism of the Jefferson administration. Not long after his inaugural pledge to promote national unity, the president broke faith by turning Federalists out of administrative and judicial positions and replacing them with Democratic-Republicans. In what marked the beginning of the political spoils system in America, Jefferson replaced a particularly able and popular collector of the port in New Haven. City Councilman Webster responded to merchant protests by writing to Rufus King, who was still American ambassador in London, and to James Madison, whom Jefferson had named secretary of state.

"The best officers are displaced," he railed to King, "to make room for the supporters of Mr. Jefferson, and some of them worthless men."[49] To Madison he wrote,

> We all expected that the chief magistrate [Jefferson] would gratify a number of his friends and especially place about himself men in whom he has particular confidence; and be assured, Sir, that not a complaint was uttered until the appointment of foreigners to the highest offices. But when we found that the principle was adopted of *making vacancies* in subordinate departments to gratify or reward partizans; and more especially when it was seen that the most meritorious officers were dismissed to make room for characters less meritorious as men and as citizens, and some of them ignorant, unprincipled, and even contemptible; what do you imagine must have been our sensations!
>
> I submit these facts and reflections to you, with a frankness that proceeds from a sincere and honest zeal, in hopes that your influence may be exerted to heal the divisions of our country.[50]

When neither Madison nor Jefferson replied, Webster issued in the *Spectator* a barrage of eighteen thunderous "Letters to the President of the United States" assailing the spoils system.

"Your measures, Sir," Webster wrote,

> invert the whole order of society. The natural sentiment of man is, to respect virtue, religion, grave manners, eminent talents, the wisdom of experience, and the hoary head. Your practices tend to depress eminence of talents, to point the finger of scorn at a veneration for religion; to exalt the young over the head of the old; to discard solid worth, and to dignify with the honors and emoluments of government, the departed, the licentious and profane . . . the illiterate, the debauchee, the blasphemer, the infidel. . . . On the event of this experiment, depends the fate of your official character, and of your administration.

"No, Sir!" Webster exploded, "no individual or party has a *claim* or *right* to any office whatever."[51]

Webster published his articles continuously throughout the autumn and republished them in book form early the following year, but they earned him nothing but abuse from Jeffersonian newspapers and Democratic-Republicans hungry for political sinecures. They assailed him as a "capacious squirt of federal calumny" and a "political Leviathan . . . as immortal as is Monsieur guillotine." For Jefferson, Webster's essays were more of a nuisance than anything else. As he told Madison, "I view Webster as a mere pedagogue of very little understanding and very strong prejudices and party passions."[52]

As Jefferson's scornful words implied, he had little to fear from Webster's attacks. Clearly, Webster's ability to influence national political affairs had come to an end. He was out of touch with the mood of the nation, living by a garden in a small citadel of conservatism, one or two days distant from his New York newspaper, and by the summer of 1801, even more remote from the nation's capital, which was now situated in Washington, D.C.

Across the nation, Americans were rejecting the old ways of Puritanism. Only Connecticut's Federalist legislature still limited the right to vote to property owners, and it was one of only a handful of states that still had an official church — Webster's Calvinist church — and continued to collect property taxes to support it. But even in Connecticut, Methodists, Baptists, and other non-Calvinist Protestant groups were growing in number and demanding an end to what they saw as infringements on their rights as citizens. Ironically, Webster, who once championed church-state separation, led the opposition.

By 1802, Webster recognized that his political views were not only losing popular appeal but were beginning to hurt the sale and use of his textbooks. It was clear that Jefferson was in office to stay and would easily win reelection. Indeed, he had carried all the states but Webster's Connecticut. The Alien and Sedition Acts had lapsed, and newspapers once again returned to printing libel. Webster had little choice but to admit defeat. On October 15, 1803, his last article appeared in the *Spectator,* and he traveled to New York for a few weeks to negotiate the sale of his newspaper, bringing a close to his career as a journalist.

If he had any second thoughts once in New York, they quickly vanished after a bundle of charmingly silly little notes arrived to make him long for the nearness of his wife and children. Included was a letter from Rebecca, who was sixteen days shy of giving birth to their sixth child:

Dear Husband

Our pens are worn out & the ink is dry, the large ink bottle is not to be found, what shall we do? I think it all owing to your care lest the botle of ink shou'd freeze. Your kind favor came to hand on thursday, & made us all happy, but we shoud have been better pleasd, if a time had been set for your return it is now three *long* weeks since you left us; everything goes on well, the weather is uncommonly pleasant, & I should have ventured to meeting to day, if I did not fear to take so long a walk. The last walk I took made me lame for a week, & I can scarcely take exercise enough to keep me in health, or spirits, yet I am as well, on the whole as I can *reasonably* expect to be. Our children are gone to meeting. William is helping Ruthy [a servant] make apple-sauce, for we are going to have a roast spare-rib for dinner, it is a favorite dish of yours, & I wish you could partake with us.

I have promised to write but one page.

Adieu
Yours[53]

On the same page, Webster's oldest child, Emily, thirteen, wrote:

Dear Papa

As my Mama has said nothing about the children & I am in a writing humor, & can find nonsense enough to fill up the blank paper I will take her place. Mary [four years old] is learning a piece & Harriot [Harriet, six years old] is preparing for meeting, & both intend to surprise you, on your return with their little acquirements.

You mentioned my dear Papa going to church & their singing in the old manner, indeed I should be happy to have any kind of music here, there has been no singing at the brick meeting house since my Dear Papa left us & on thanksgiving day Doc Dana reprimanded the singers— I make a great many mistakes—the children make such a noise in the Room. William [two years old] grows fat & *very* funny as well as *very* mischievous & grows *very* fond of his sister Emma [Emily]. some times we speak a hard word on purpose to hear his little blunders for he repeats every word we say.

The Children are stuffing with hard sour apples which Mama bought yesterday to the great joy of us all, for we were quite distitute.

I hope you will return soon Papa and bring some apples with you that are good & sweet. My pen is poor & I have promised to leave the other page to Julia, & must now subscribe myself your Affectionate[54]

Julia, ten, added,

I don't think it fair my dear papa, that Mamma & Emily should write first, & tell you all the news & to leave me to make up a letter out of my own noodle. I go to school very steadily & pass 8 or 9 hours there every day, there are 68 schollars. Miss Hall remains in tolerable health. I have began ciphering & have got to Multiplication. & I have almost finished a little Cap—*for somebody*. I have a good mind to tell you what *Em* has been doing to surpriz you on your return but I have promised not to.

Mama desires me to tell you she finds it very difficult to procure Butter which is 15d a pound & salt as brine. I long to have you come home for 2 reasons—the first is I want to see my dear papa. The 2d that we may have Buckwheat cakes for breakfast & Puddings for dinner. These are trifles I know, but of great consequence to me after fasting 5 hours. Good night my dear father it is quite dark & mama will add a postscript.

Your most dutiful daughter[55]

Rebecca Webster added a postscript:

I will thank you to purchase for me a few groceries (if convenient) some young hyson [tea], loaf sugar, a quarter of pound of Nutmegs, & the same quantity of Cloves & Cinnamon, & if you think it worth while some rice for puddings—milk is now plenty.

good night[56]

The Websters' fifth daughter, Eliza, was born two weeks later, on December 21, 1803.

The following July, Aaron Burr shot and killed Alexander Hamilton in a duel. Hamilton's *Post* survived him and, indeed, remains on New York City's newsstands to this day. Webster sold the *Spectator* to a group led by Bayard. It eventually became the *Globe,* whose name survived until its merger into the *Sun,* in 1923.

Although Webster continued writing occasional unsolicited political essays for newspapers in New England, they had little or no impact in stemming the popular tide of republicanism and usually provoked nothing but abuse from Democratic-Republicans. Even Federalist Connecticut was considering a new constitution to extend voting rights to non–property owners. Webster, however, was out of concert with the national mood and drew on Plato instead of Rousseau for his political thinking.

"It would," he wrote, "be better for the people, they would be more free and happy, if all were deprived of the right of suffrage until they were 45 years of age, and if no man was eligible to an important office until he is 50, that is, if all the power of government were vested in our old men, who have lost their ambitions chiefly and have learnt wisdom by experience."[57]

Calvinist New Haven again honored Webster by naming him the city's orator for July 4, 1802, and he continued his losing battle against expansion of voting rights: "If all men have an equal right of suffrage, those who have *little* and those who have *no* property, have the power of making regulations respecting the property of others; that is, an equal right to control the property with those who own it. Thus, as property is *unequally* and suffrages *equally* divided, the principle of *equal* suffrage becomes the basis of *inequality* of power. And this principle, in some of our larger cities, actually gives a majority of *suffrages* to the men who possess not a *twentieth of the property.*"[58]

A few months later, he wrote, "The admission of too many persons to the right of suffrage who have no settled habitation . . . has been the ruin of all popular governments," and a few days after that, "The very principle of admitting every body to the right of suffrage, prostrates the wealth of individuals to the rapaciousness of a merciless gang who have nothing to lose, and will delight in plundering their neighbors. . . . Our laws principally respect property . . . and it is very improper that it should be at the direction and disposal of those who have little or no interest in it."[59]

6

WEBSTER'S WITHDRAWAL FROM JOURNALISM left him entirely dependent on the sale of his books to support his family. By 1804, more than 1.5 million copies of *The American Spelling Book* had been sold, and Webster's fourteen-year copyright was about to expire, along with contracts with more than fifty printers and booksellers around the United States.

Many printers had been cheating him, often publishing unauthorized editions or paying him for fewer copies than they actually printed and sold. As his newspaper fortunes were declining, Webster had begun revising his speller. In 1804, he issued a new and vastly improved edition that made previous editions obsolete, and he refused to grant licenses to print the new edition unless all copies of older editions were destroyed.

He wrote new contracts giving each printer sole and exclusive rights to publish and sell the book within a specific geographic area. The contract stated the number of copies that the printer could publish, with a special license to exceed that number. Webster had the right to examine each printer's records of paper purchases to verify the number of books printed—twenty-two quires of paper were needed to produce one thousand spellers. The contracts called for strict accounting procedures, with a statement of account to be issued each June. Webster was to receive one cent from the sale of each copy, whose retail price was fixed at twenty-five cents. The printer's selling price was set at no less than "ten cents for each copy in quires or sheets [unbound, uncut pages], and sixteen cents five mills for each copy in common binding with scaleboard, covered with blue paper."[60] The blue paper became a distinguishing characteristic of Webster's speller, which quickly became known as "The Blue-Back Speller," or "Old Blue Back."

To assure consistent quality, each printer was to publish the spellers from "standing type." In other words, the type for the speller, once set, was to remain in place and untouched for the duration of the contract. The stipulation ensured that the last spellers printed were identical to the first. To ensure national uniformity, Webster specified type sizes (pica, large enough for children to read) and style (*roman*). He specified the variety of paper to be used and told binders, "I wish that all books . . . may be sewed."[61]

The new books represented a vast improvement, with larger type, better printing, and new, more interesting reading selections. Webster added original stories of his own, including exploits of his own four daughters. In one of these, Pa tells daughter Mary, "Your little fingers are very handy with the needles. Very pretty; very pretty work. What small stitches. You shall hem and mark all your Papa's handkerchiefs, and very soon you shall work a muslin frock for yourself."[62]

Renegotiation of his contracts forced Webster to travel from city to city about the Northeast and separated him once again from his family, sometimes for a week or more at a time. The trips were profitable, however, because he often received royalties in the form of sheets of his own books, which he sold to booksellers for cash. Webster nevertheless grew desperately lonely on his trips, and only Rebecca's and his children's notes sustained him.

Dear Husband

Emily is at work by my side. She intends to write you a few lines on
this sheet, the other girls are at School & they have all been good children & have strove hard to improve that Papa on his return may applaud
them. dear little Dumps [a nickname for Mary] told me this morn'g that
She dreamed Papa had come home & brought a *proper sight* of little
books & a *buss gee* for William; the little dog is trying to get my pen—
I believe I must let him scribble a little—[in little William's writing:]
Dear Pappa come home see Willy—[in Rebecca's writing again:] I know
you will admire the little scrawl! Your darlings all wish much for your
return & I will tell them that you will certainly keep Christmas with us.
Take good care of your self, my dear husband, & remember that on your
welfare depends the happiness of a large family.

Yours with unabated affection[63]

Rebecca continued the letter the following day:

Emily has not succeeded in buying a bonnet. if it is convenient for you
to purchase a split straw, or leghorn bonnet for her, the price will be
about 3 dollars. Mrs. Leffingwell will probably be in N Y & can tell you
what is worn. I am sorry to trouble you with such trifles, but there are
none here.[64]

His daughter Emily wrote on the same sheet of paper:

Dear Papa,

I am now going to write a letter to my Dear Papa without making
one apology, but I have a great deal of news, & don't know how to begin, & which to tell first.

We have had a mighty wedding here. Miss Sally Bradly & Mr. Lewis
are married & they have had a deal of company. Mr. Buddington has sent
4 barrels of fine apples, but the Barrels are very small. we opened one
and the Apples were good, indeed, & taste very much like ours.

Little Willy says pow aw waw deffy & I assure you dear Papa he
grows very fat, & weighs 30 pounds, & he is *far* the handsomest of the
bunch. Doc Dana called to see mama the other day, & appeared to be
quite pleased with William, & gave him a great many kisses.

It is quite dark, & I must leave off & finish to morrow Morning.
Mama has heard that straw bonnets are very high in New York & Mrs
Leffingwell is not going till January, that it is not worth while to get
one, there, for we will make our old ones do *for the present* & there will
probably be enough in the Spring. Adieu, my dear Papa[65]

Rebecca added a postscript to the same letter:

. . . don't purchase a split straw bonnet for Emily as I'm told they are
very high. perhaps you can get some Lady to purchase a leghorn which
are much cheaper, but you need not give yourself much trouble. . . . We
are well. I suffer a good deal for want of sleep—the rats, & mice, disturb

us very much, & multiply fast. the punkings which you put in the Celler are eat intirely hollow, & a ham which Ruthy took up to cook (but for some reason delayd) was eat so that it was reduced to half its weight, & I find that the fish in the garret does not escape altogether. . . . I am anxious to have the passage clos'd up, for the cows come into the garden every night, and destroy my flower-roots, the buds are eat off of the pink-roots and I fear they will not bear the next season. the neighbours begin to enquire when *Squire* W—— will return. I tell them all that you will be at home at Christmas . . . but you need not be anxious about us, for (bating a few trifles) everything goes on as well as if you were here.

Yours with unabated affection[66]

In addition to tight supervision of his printers, Webster also took direct charge of promoting his new edition of 1804. As he had done with the original *Institute,* he contacted leading educators for endorsements. Yale president Timothy Dwight replied, "You are perfectly welcome, Sir, to make use of my name . . . if you imagine it will be of the least service to your design."[67] At every school Webster never failed to present the principal with specially bound copies of *An American Selection* as prizes for outstanding students.

In addition to improving the speller, Webster wrote new textbooks to improve education at every level in American schools. As president of the Union School in New Haven, he lamented the lack of American texts for advanced instruction in the arts and sciences.

"In the highest branches of literature our learning is superficial to a shameful degree," he wrote to the English scientist Joseph Priestly. "As to classical learning, history, civil and ecclesiastical, chymistery, botany, and natural history—excepting here and there a rare instance of a man who is eminent in some of these branches—we may be said to have no learning at all, or a mere smattering."[68]

To remedy the situation, Webster produced four new textbooks from 1802 to 1812, giving them the collective title *Elements of Useful Knowledge.* The first two volumes were a "Historical and Geographical Account of the United States," from the beginning of the colonial era to 1789, and included summaries of each state constitution and the U.S. Constitution.[69] Volume three was a "Historical and Geographical Account of . . . Europe, Asia and Africa." The fourth was a simplified biology text, a "History of Animals."[70]

By 1804, sales of his speller reached an astounding two hundred thousand copies a year—in a nation with a total population of only about 6 million. Recognizing the limited range of vocabulary in the little book, Webster decided to produce a small dictionary to supplement it and to expand the scope of his American spellings. The speller was too small to provide pronunciations and meanings for more than a few hundred words, and students and teachers had to use dictionaries from England to expand their vocabulary. It galled him that schoolmasters continued to use the dictionary by the English actor and elocutionist John Walker as the ultimate guide for correct pronunciation.[71] Walker's approach to pronouncing the word *garden*, for example, stated: "When the *a* in this and similar words is preceded by G or K, polite speakers interpose a sound like the consonant *y* which coalesces with both, and gives a mellowness to the sound; thus *a Garden* pronounced in this manner is similar to the two words *Egg* and *Yarden* united into *eggyarden*, and *a Guard* is almost like *eggyard*." Such passages infuriated Webster because he believed they would encourage Americans to perpetuate speaking with English affectations instead of adopting Americanisms.[72]

Walker's, however, was not the only dictionary in use in American common schools and academies. The standard dictionary in use in America was another English work: teacher John Entick's *New Spelling Dictionary of the English Language*,[73] which was first published in London in 1764 and revised in 1787. Unlike Dr. Johnson's dictionary, which limited itself to definitions and etymology, Entick's added spelling rules and encyclopedic information, including a "List of all the Cities, Boroughs, Market-Towns and Remarkable Villages in England and Wales."

Two Americans had also written dictionaries for schoolchildren by the time Webster began work on his dictionary. Ironically, the first American to do so was named Samuel Johnson Jr.; he was, however, unrelated to England's Dr. Samuel Johnson, the author of the great *Dictionary of the English Language* of 1755.[74] Although Dr. Johnson's dictionary was the standard in England—and Webster had, of course, seen and studied it—it did not arrive in the United States in large enough quantities to have any direct impact on American education until 1818.

The son of the first president of Columbia College, Samuel Johnson Jr. was a schoolteacher and a Yale graduate. His dictionary was published in 1798 and was called, quite simply, *A School Dictionary*.[75] It contained forty-one hundred words selected from "preceding authors of established reputation." A slim, 198-page volume, it was designed as a "sizeable cheap book . . . to furnish schools with a dictionary which will enable youth more easily to acquire knowledge of the English language." Unfortunately, it omitted more than one definition of many words and left other definitions vague beyond understanding. It defined *bemused* as "overcome with musing" and *chymistry* as "the act of separating bodies with fire." In addition, its pronunciation guides were often dreadful, and Johnson inconsistently spelled words with the same roots and suffixes—*arbor* and *fervor*, for example, but *honour* and *odour*. In addition, Johnson's choice of words was puzzling. He included *cap-a-pie*, for example, but omitted *newspaper, ocean*, and *population*.[76]

In 1800, the American Johnson had collaborated with the Reverend John Elliot to improve his earlier dictionary by publishing *A Selected Pronouncing and Accented Dictionary*, the first dictionary ever to include American Indian words such as *tomahawk* and *wampum,* along with American place-names and the unique American usages of certain English words, such as *federal.* Although the book offers corrections for "some vulgar errors in pronunciation"—such as *chimbley* for *chimney* and *widder* for *widow*—it too had inconsistent spellings of such suffixes as *-or/-our* and *-tion/-xion.*[77]

The second dictionary by an American was Caleb Alexander's *The Columbian Dictionary of the English Language,* also published in 1800.[78] Like Samuel Johnson Jr., Alexander was a Yale graduate. He had gone on to be headmaster at several academies, one of which evolved into Hamilton College, in Clinton, New York. A more substantial work than Samuel Johnson Jr.'s, the *Columbian Dictionary* listed 25,700 words in its 556 pages (although the tally of words includes multiple listings of the same word, because each meaning was listed separately). The *Columbian* omitted words ending in *-ly* and *-ness,* to reduce printing costs, but it did offer far more Americanisms than Samuel Johnson Jr.'s work, including *dime, dollar, Congress,* and *minuteman.* Although it listed a few local American spellings, such as *check* alongside the English *cheque,* it retained most traditional English forms.

In contrast to Johnson Jr. and Alexander, Webster planned an *American* dictionary with *American* spellings, to enlarge the scope of *The American Spelling Book* and create a complete *American* language. Webster originally planned his new work as a small dictionary for children, but because he had already suffered too many financial losses from books with limited market potential, he decided to broaden the appeal of his dictionary to as wide an audience as possible—adults as well as children. On June 4, 1800, Webster issued a press release that he hoped would convince teachers, college professors, and businessmen to postpone buying other dictionaries until his came off the press:

> Mr. Webster of this city, we understand, is engaged in completing the system for the instruction of youth, which he began in the year 1783. He has in hand a Dictionary of the American Language, a work long since projected, but which other occupations have delayed till this time. The plan contemplated extends to a small Dictionary for schools, one for the counting-house, and a large one for men of science. The first is nearly ready for the press—the second and third will require the labor of some years.
>
> It is found that a work of this kind is absolutely necessary, on account of considerable differences between the American and English language. New circumstances, new modes of life, new laws, new ideas of various kinds give rise to new words, and have already made many material differences between the language of England and America. Some new words are introduced in America, and many more new significations are annexed to words, which it is necessary to explain. It is probable that the alterations in the tenures of land and the ecclesiastical polity, will dismiss from the language in America several hundred words which

belong to the English. The differences in the language of the two countries will continue to multiply, and render it necessary that we should have *Dictionaries* of the *American Language*.[79]

Although Webster admired Dr. Johnson's great English dictionary, he used the English lexicographer as a public whipping boy in publicizing the benefits of his own forthcoming work, pointing out correctly that Johnson's work lacked legal, medical, scientific, and technical terms.

Webster's announcement provoked a torrent of ridicule and abuse from his traditional journalist enemies—inspired somewhat by publishers of dictionaries then on the market. Assuming Webster's new dictionary would use phonetic spellings from his 1790 *Essays and Fugitiv Writings*, Benjamin Franklin Bache, the vicious editor of Philadelphia's *Aurora* and Webster's longtime enemy, wrote a venomous, calumnious essay, headed, simply, NOAH WEBSTER.

"There are some beings," the essay began,

whose fate it seems to be to run counter from reason and propriety on all occasions. In every attempt which this oddity of literature has made, he appears not only to have made himself ridiculous, but to have rendered what he attempted to elucidate more obscure, and to injure or deface what he has intended to improve. His spelling-book has done more injury in the common schools of the country than the genius of ignorance herself could have conceived a hope of, by his ridiculous attempts to alter the *syllable* division of words and to *new model* the spelling, by a capricious but utterly incompetent attempt of his own weak conception.

After involving the question of the yellow fever in deeper obscurity, and producing nothing but the profit by the sale of the work, he now appears as a legislator and municipal magistrate of Connecticut; writes nonsense pseudo-political and pseudo-philosophical for his newspaper at New York, and proposes to give to the American world no less than three dictionaries!

This man, who ought to go to school for the regulation of his understanding, has, it appears, undertaken a *system of education*, and as a part of these, we are told, is to give us a dictionary for *schools*, a dictionary for the *counting-house*, and a dictionary for the *learned!*

His motives, for they are truly *Gothic*, it appears are that a number of English words have been misapplied, new words introduced and a considerable number exploded in America; for this reason he says it is necessary to make a new Dictionary. The plain truth is, for the reason given is preposterous, that he means to *make money* by a scheme which ought to be and will be discountenanced by every man who admires the classic English writers, who has sense enough to see the confusion which must arise from such a silly project—and the incapacity of a man who thus undertakes a work which, if it were at all necessary or eligible, would require the labor of a number of learned and competent men to accomplish it.[80]

Not to be outdone by a Jeffersonian, Joseph Dennie, who succeeded the expelled British editor Cobbett at the Tory *Gazette of the United States*, published endless columns of letters from fictional readers:

To Mr. noab Wabstur

Sur,

by rading all ovur the nusspaper I find you are after meaking a nue Merrykin Dikshunary; your rite, Sir; for ofter lookin all over the anglish Books, you wont find a bit of Shillaly big enuf to beat a dog wid. so I hope you'll take a hint, and put enuff rem in yours, for Och 'tis a nate little bit of furniture for any Man's house so it 'tis.

Pat O'Dogerty

As I find der ish no Donder and Blixsum in de English Dikshonere I hopy your put both in yours to oblige a Subscryber

Hans Bubbleblower

Masa Webser plese put sum HOMMANY and sum GOOD POSSUM fat and sum two tree good BANJOE in your new what-you-call-um Book for your fello Cytsen

Cuffee

Mistur Webstur

being told as how you wants a word maker to help you fil a new diksonery, with the consent of my good man, I offer my servis, please to let me know whether you buy words by the hundred or by the dozen, &c your price, I unclose your a certificat from my husband of my billyties.

and am at your servis

Martha O'Gabble

I heeby certify that my wife martha has the best knack at coining new words of any I ever knew—& with the aid of a comforting drop she'll fill you two dictonerys in an hour if you please,—before she had work out the drum of my ear with her tongue you might have had it for nothing, but as I am now quite deaf & she a useful body in other espects I shall expect something for service in her way

Dermot O'Gabble

Brother Noab

Instead of *I keant keatch the keow,* and English man or *a town bred american* would say, *I cannot Catch the Cow,* but you being a *brother Yankey* will be sure to spell right in your new Yankey dictionary

yours, &c.
Brother Jonathan[81]

Hard-line Federalists, whom Webster had alienated by defending Adams against Hamilton, also attacked. The Boston *Palladium,* which had displaced Webster's *Spectator* as New England's official Federalist newspaper, called Webster "vain and presumptuous" and assailed his "absurd orthographical doctrines." Assistant editor Warren Dutton, a former Yale tutor, wrote, under the pseudonym "Restorator": "I turn in disgust from the pert hypercritic whose pages . . . are never illuminated with a single ray of genius. . . . A language, arrived at its zenith, like ours, and copious and expressive in the extreme, requires no introduction of new words. . . . Colloquial barbarisms abound in all countries, but among no civilized people are they admitted with impunity into books." Dutton condemned the "foul and unclean things" in Webster's projected dictionary.[82]

The remarks infuriated Webster, and he replied:

When the design of an improved paper, to be denominated the *New-England Palladium,* was destined to protect our moral, political and religious rights was first announced, it was little suspected that, in less than one year, from its first publication, it would be permitted to degenerate into a vehicle of personal abuse. Much could it be supposed that the assistant editor of the paper, a man of reputation and letters, would become accessory to an attempt to vilify a fellow citizen, who has never been charged with a crime, and whose whole life has been devoted to promote the honor, and defend the rights, of his country. . . .

In two or three late numbers of the RESTORATOR, many illiberal remarks have appeared upon my proposed dictionary. Whether that work, if ever published, will have merit or not, is a point about which the gentleman may make himself easy. . . . If the work should be a real improvement on those before published, my fellow citizens will find it useful. If not, the loss would rest on myself or the printer, and the work would descend quietly into oblivion, accompanied perhaps by the RESTORATOR.

But what connection has this subject with a general charge of "dullness" against all my writings, which, it seems "are not illuminated by a single ray of genius"?

Wishing by all means, to improve my mind, I have regularly read the RESTORATOR; and although I have not been able to discover in it much elegance of style or originality of remark, yet this may be ascribed to my want of capacity, than the author's want of genius. . . . Some beauties, I think I *have* discovered; such, for instance, as *"hitting the taste"* — the *"scanning of dishes"* — *"a brace of vixens"* — *"fires and darts, flames and arrows* played off in fearful *corruscations"* — *"elegant* and substantial *food,"* & c., which are probably specimens of the sublime or "rays of genius."[83]

A bit later, Webster wrote a short piece using his old title "the Prompter":

An American Dictionary! Impossible! Who has effrontery to attempt such a thing!

But perhaps some improvement can be made —

Improvement! What, improvement on Bailey, Johnson, Walker, Sheridan, Ash, Kenrick, and other English authors! Ridiculous! None but a blockhead would ever think of such a project! An American, a native of this God-forsaken country, where horses degenerate to palfrey, and man dwindles to a pigmy—An American harbor the audacious opinion that he can improve upon the works of British authors! I turn from the wretch with disgust and contempt!

But be quiet a little. Perhaps we have a few words not used in England.

Not used in England! Then banish them from the language. They are corruptions and must be rejected.

But suppose we have some new ideas, originating from new objects, new laws, new customs, new inventions; must we not use new words to express them?

New words! New ideas! What, Americans have *new* ideas! Why the man is mad!

But suppose the continent is peopled with a hundred millions of inhabitants, must they have no ideas, nor words, nor books, but what come from Great Britain? Perhaps the British nation may hereafter learn something from America.

Pshaw! What nonsense. No, no. Keep to the authorities; never try to mend them. Let us have none of your improvements.[84]

7

THE RIDICULE HEAPED on his spelling reforms affected Webster more than he ever admitted. He recognized that the rain of mockery could well destroy any chance of his dictionary's success and, in all likelihood, fatally damage sales of his speller, which the dictionary was meant to accompany. In the end, he tempered his patriotic zeal and modified his goal of a phonetically spelled, uniquely American language to coincide with the realities of what the public could and would accept.

Priced at $1.50, *A Compendious Dictionary of the American Language* contained about 40,600 words, most of them spelled in traditional English fashion.[85] Webster's preface stated that the 408-page work (about six and a half inches tall by four inches wide) represented no more than "an enlargement and an improvement of Entick's spelling dictionary which public opinion, both in Great Britain and the United States, has pronounced the best compilation of the kind. . . . To his list of words . . . I have added about *five thousand* others, which have been mostly collected from the best writers, during a course of several years reading. The purchasers of the Compendious will therefore find the list of words by far the most complete of any vocabulary extant."

To the embarrassed surprise of his mean-spirited critics, Webster's first dictionary contained far fewer phonetic spellings than they had anticipated, and the reforms he introduced did not differ radically from spellings that were commonly in use. It was, nevertheless, the most innovative and comprehensive dictionary ever produced up to that time—and it was uniquely American. It contained more than spelling reforms. There were five thousand words more than Entick's dictionary, and all (except for a few American Indian words) were new Americanisms that no other dictionary had ever included and with which his critics could not find fault. His dictionary not only muted his critics, it won praise from many of the nation's most eminent scholars—even some who disagreed with his reforms but recognized the validity of his effort.

In introducing reforms, Webster had the good sense to examine the aesthetics of spelling as well as phonetics. The universal elimination of silent letters that he had suggested in his earlier *Essays and Fugitiv Writings* produced too many words that either were aesthetically unappealing (*giv*, for example) or produced confusion (*bred* instead of *bread*, *meen* instead of *mean*, *speek* instead of *speak*).

In the end, he limited spelling reform in the *Compendious* to a handful of words. Almost all involved changes that American children—and adults—eagerly embraced because of their logic and aesthetics. Americans quickly adopted his change of *-ce* in *defence*, *offence*, and *pretence* to *-se*. They gladly abandoned, also, the second, silent *l* in verbs such as *travel* and *cancel* when forming past-tense or participial endings. (Webster's rule stated that verbs ending in a single consonant but not accented on the last syllable do not double the final consonant in derivatives.)

Phonetic spellings had mixed success: *gaol* became *jail* and *mould* quickly turned to *mold*, but Americans rejected *ake* for *ache*, *hainous* for *heinous*, *soop* for *soup*, *sley* for *sleigh*, *cloke* for *cloak*, and *spunge* for *sponge*. Efforts to eliminate silent letters had similarly mixed results. His abbreviated spelling of *though* as *tho* was already in common use,[86] but the public refused to adopt *ax*, *imagin*, *medicin*, *doctrin*, or *wo*, and Webster restored the final *e*'s in his subsequent dictionaries. Similarly, *catcal*, *etiquet*, *farewel*, *benum*, *thum*, *crum*, *fether*, *lether*, and *wether* would recapture their silent letters in Webster's later works.

Other reforms he tried to introduce included phonetic spellings such as *epitomy*, *castastrophy*, and *apostrophy*, and the introduction of the adjectival *-y* ending for nouns. The first reform failed. The second succeeded in part—with *soap* and *soapy*, *squall* and *squally*, but not with *hail* and *haily*, *stream* and *streamy*, *straw* and *strawy*, or *doze* and *dozy*.

To his critics, Webster argued that his reforms simply represented a continuation of the trend that had started several centuries earlier. Various editions of Shakespeare, for example, dropped the *u* from some *-our* endings, while many poets and playwrights reversed the French-origin *-re* ending in *sceptre* and similar words to facilitate delivery of lines such as "His Scepter shewes the force of temporall power"[87] and "This royal throne of kings, this scepter'd isle."[88] It was simply too difficult for even the finest Shakespearean performer to enunciate *sceptre shewes* or *sceptred isle* as spelled, without slurring. Milton, Pope, and other poets adopted similar reforms, although somewhat inconsistently. Even England's Dr. Johnson had introduced some reforms by changing the *sk* beginnings of Greek-origin words such as *skene* to *scene*, but he left *skeptic* unchanged. As in Johnson's dictionary, most earlier reforms had been applied inconsistently, and Webster said his dictionary merely standardized them.

Webster did indeed apply spelling reforms more consistently than any previous lexicographer, and many became new American standards. His first dictionary reconfigured all Norman-origin words ending in *-re*—*centre, theatre, metre,* and so on—with the phonetic *-er* ending. Similarly, he dropped the *u* from most *-our* endings—for example, in *humour* and *rumour.*

He also incorporated as standard many spellings that, by custom, had crept into American writing. Many Americans were already substituting *-k* for the *-que* ending in words such as *risque* and *masque,* and Webster adopted the simpler spelling. Similarly, he dropped the *k* from words such as *musick* and *publick*—something many Americans (and some English) were already doing. Americans had not, however, abandoned the *k*'s in *traffick* and *almanack,* and Webster temporarily left them intact. His inclusion of popular American spellings produced some duplicate spellings: *ake* and *ache,* for example, along with *croud* and *crowd, tung* and *tongue, wimman (wimmen)* and *woman.* He eliminated *croud* and *wimman (wimmen)* in later editions of his dictionary because the spellings had no etymological basis other than the phonetics of incorrect American pronunciation. The spelling of *tongue* as *tung,* however, had an etymological as well as a phonetic basis, which Webster traced to the Saxon word *tunga,* and he retained the alternate spelling in later dictionaries. Indeed, given its origin, Webster insisted, "the common orthography, *tongue,* is incorrect."[89]

Webster published his *Compendious* in 1806. In addition to new American words, he added a host of terms used in medicine, law, chemistry, botany, geology, agriculture, and other sciences. "A living language," he explained, "must keep pace with improvements in knowledge, and with the multiplication of ideas."[90] Webster also included new political terms—*caucus,* for example, as well as *Federal* and *Federalist* (which he defined self-servingly as "a friend to the Constitution of the U. States"). He also included many words that were peculiar to specific regions or towns—for example: "*yux* v.i. To hiccough."

Unlike the American Samuel Johnson Jr., Webster was careful to eliminate Anglicisms that had disappeared from American speech, such as *fishify, jackalent, parma-citty, jeggumbob, conjabble, fourtra,* and other words that Dr. Johnson's great dictionary had included. Ever the Calvinist, Webster also excluded all "vulgar words and offensive ribaldry"[91] found in Dr. Johnson's work, such as *fart, turd,* and *cullion,* and he omitted other terms associated with excretion or sexuality.

Defenders of Dr. Johnson's dictionary and Tory purists assailed the changes, but he had a ready reply, charging that "Johnson has transgressed the rules of lexicography beyond any other compiler; for his work contains more of the lowest vulgar words than any other now extant. . . . Alas, had a native of the United States introduced such vulgar words and offensive ribaldry into a similar work, what columns of abuse would have issued from the Johnsonian presses against the wretch who could thus sully his book and corrupt the language."[92]

As Entick had done, Webster expanded the scope of his dictionary to include useful encyclopedic material, but he Americanized it as much as possible. He included tables of moneys, weights, and measures, of time changes around the world, of U.S. post offices, of American population figures, of the value of U.S. exports, and other "new and interesting chronological tables of remarkable events and discoveries."[93]

Although the dictionary was conceived as a supplement to his speller, Webster had the foresight to recognize the marketing potential among adults and the economies of producing a larger edition first and issuing a smaller, abridged version for children later, rather than the other way around.

Just after publication of his *Compendious,* Webster's second son, Henry Bradford, was born, on November 26, 1806, but he survived only nine weeks. His death sent the family into deep mourning through the Christmas season. With the new year, Webster returned to work. He published his abridged version of the *Compendious,* with thirty thousand words, at a price of $1.00, under a new title: *A Dictionary of the English Language; Compiled for the Use of Common Schools in the United States.*[94]

In preparing both dictionaries, Webster simplified the pronunciation rules of previous dictionaries by first testing them at home to see if his own children found them too difficult to learn. He developed a new system that used accent marks with dual meaning. An accent after the vowel of a syllable, as in *vo'cal,* indicated the stress on the first syllable, and a long vowel; an accent after the consonant after a vowel, as in *hab'it,* also indicated stress, but a short vowel.

Webster's first two dictionaries were the most successful dictionaries published in America until then. Actual sales were minuscule in comparison to sales of his speller, and they yielded him little additional income. Although virtually every schoolmaster bought the dictionary for his classroom, he would carefully preserve its condition by forbidding the children to use it, looking up words they needed to know himself. Ultimately, the financial success of Webster's speller—and of any speller, for that matter—lay in each child's wearing out his or her copy (and sometimes two) in the course of the school year by thumbing through its pages over and over, which prevented the development of a market for used volumes.

In general, the public reacted to the Webster dictionaries with disinterest. Dictionaries seldom have enormous impact. They are not narratives, and for once, Webster had not included an essay accusing anyone of treason to the nation. His dictionaries simply took their place on bookshelves as standard references and provoked little controversy.

Historically, the first Webster dictionaries were monumental triumphs of scholarship for their era. There were faults to be found, but they were few in number—and insignificant compared to those in the works of his predecessors.

Webster, of course, sent his *Compendious* to all his friends in and out of politics and academe. Most scanned the first paragraph of the preface and thumbed through the microscopically small type of the dictionary proper. Only a few scholars actually studied the work. One was the eminent Columbia College scientist Samuel Latham Mitchill, who had helped Webster with his *History of Epidemic Diseases*.

"I heartily wish you both fame and emolument from your Labors," Mitchill wrote.

> To convince you that one of your Readers, at least has proceeded beyond the Preface, I would ask why the following Aboriginal words may not be considered as naturalized, and worthy a place in the dictionary, to wit, *Esquaa*, a woman, *Pappoos*, a child, *Terrapin*, a tortoise . . . as likewise, the following popular words . . . *stall*, to stop when the Team is unable or unwilling to draw . . . *Yellow fever*, a malignant fever, but uncontagious and of local origin . . . *Catbird*, a fine musical bird resembling the mocking-bird. . . .
>
> These I merely give you as proofs of my having turned over your pages with some Care.[95]

Webster added *terrapin* and *yellow fever* to his next dictionary, but omitted the other suggestions.

Webster also received a beautiful letter from Lindley Murray, the grammarian whose *Murray's English Grammar* and *English Reader* had been in universal use in American classrooms in the 1780s until Webster's texts displaced them. Exhibiting no rancor, Murray wrote to Webster in the polite, formal, third-person form, asking the recipient to

> do me the favour to accept a copy of the new edition of my grammar, as a small testimony of my respect for his talents and character. At the same time, I hope he will permit me to thank him for the pleasure and improvements, which I have derived from perusing [your] ingenious and sensible writings.
>
> If, on looking over the grammar, anything should occur to him, by which he thinks the work may be further improved, I will take the

communication of it, as a particular favour; and will give it an attentive and respectful consideration.[96]

David Ramsay, the eminent Charleston, South Carolina, physician and scholar, also complimented Webster but warned that "prejudices against any American attempts to improve Dr. Johnson are very strong."[97]

The first prominent scholar to display such prejudices was Sen. John Quincy Adams of Massachusetts, a Harvard graduate and trustee, who revered Dr. Johnson and the scholars of old. When Webster sent Harvard a complimentary copy of his dictionary, Adams objected to Webster's "undertaking to compile a large Dictionary to supersede those which come to us from England." The future president criticized Webster's "introduction into your dictionary of local vulgarisms" and the alteration of spellings and pronunciation on "the authority of a single writer." Adams objected to standardization, maintaining that the lack of agreement on spelling standards among English lexicographers

> is undoubtedly a strong argument to dissuade an unqualified submission to any *one* of them. . . . I would neither adopt nor reject a mode of spelling or of pronunciation. . . .
>
> With respect to the Introduction into your Dictionary of new words . . . where we have invented new or adopted new senses to old words, it appears but reasonable that our dictionaries should contain them. Yet there are always a multitude of words current within particular neighborhoods or during short periods of time, which ought never to be admitted into the legitimate vocabulary of the language. A very large proportion of the words of American origin are of this description, and I confess that I should prefer to see them systematically excluded, rather than hunted up for admission into a Dictionary of classical English.

Adams said he was not certain whether Harvard officials "would deem it advisable to pledge our University to support your system of spelling, pronunciation, or of departure from the *English* language."[98]

Webster's brother-in-law Thomas Dawes, the prominent Boston attorney, who was a close friend of John Quincy Adams, was less circumspect: "I ain't quite ripe for your *Orthography*," he wrote. "Still, I dare not make up my judgment in a matter which has never been my study, against a learned, laborious, ingenious investigator."[99] Webster sent Dawes a reply, knowing it would also reach Adams:

> Dear Brother,
>
> I am charged with an attempt to innovate, by changing the orthography of words. To this charge I plead not guilty. . . . In the few instances in which I write words a little differently from the present usage, I do not innovate but *reject innovation*. When I write *fether, lether,* and *mold,* I do nothing more than reduce the words to their original orthography, no other being used in our earliest English books. . . . I write *hainous,* because it is the true orthography from the French *haine, haineux.*

Webster said many of his other spelling changes represented corrections of misspellings that had converted many words (such as *controller*)
"into palpable nonsense" (*comptroller*). Far from being innovations, Webster
wrote, such changes were "guided by fixed principles of etymology" and an
endeavor to call back the language to the purity of former times, supported
by the authority of Isaac Newton, Alexander Pope, Jonathan Edwards, and
a host of other writers.

> I do not write *publick, republick,* because the introduction of *k* was ori-
> ginally a useless innovation wholly unknown to primitive English, and
> because the prevailing practice in Great Britain and America has revived
> the primitive etymological orthography, from *publicus.* I do not write *hon-
> our, candour, errour,* because they are neither French nor Latin. If we fol-
> low the French, the orthography ought to be *honneur, candeur, erreur;* if
> the latin, as we ought because they are Latin words, then we ought to
> write *honor,* &c., and this is not the best and most common usage.

He called John Quincy Adams's criticism of Americanisms and vulgarisms

> one of the most extraordinary charges which my opposers have ven-
> tured to suggest. I have indeed introduced into our vocabulary a few
> words, not used perhaps in great Britain or not in a like sense, such as
> . . . *decedent,* for deceased, on the authority of the laws of New Jersey
> and Pennsylvania; and a few others, probably not twenty, noting them as
> *local* terms. And is this an offense never to be forgiven? Such local terms
> exist, and will exist, in spite of lexicographers or critics. Is this *my* fault?
> And if local terms exist, why not explain them? Must they be left unex-
> plained, because they are local? This very circumstance renders their
> insertion in a dictionary more necessary, for as the faculty of Yale Col-
> lege have said in approbation of my work, how are such words to be
> understood, without the aid of a dictionary?

Webster was clearly hurt and insulted by John Quincy Adams's criticisms, asking his brother-in-law, "But what have I done that others have not
done before me? Has not Johnson admitted . . . *tup,* 'a ram,' upon the authority of local usage in England? Has he not inserted many such words?
And why does *he* escape the censure of our fastidious American critics? . . .
and what are Johnson's *fishefy, jackalent, jiggumbob* and *foutre!!* Let the admirers of Johnson's Dictionary be a little more critical in comparing his
vocabulary and mine and blush for their ill treatment of me!"

Webster pointed out that he had rejected between two and three thousand obscene or archaic words found in Johnson's dictionary. "On the other
hand," he wrote,

> I have enriched the vocabulary with such words as *absorbable, accompa-
> niment, acidulous, achromatic, adhesiveness, adjutancy, admissability, amend-
> able, animalize, aneurismal, antithetical, appellor, appreciate, appreciation,
> arborescent, arborization, ascertainable, bailee, bailment, indorser, indorsee,*

prescriptive, statement, insubordination, expenditure, subsidize and other elegant and scientific terms now used by the best writers in Great Britain and America. The number of these is not exactly known; but of the terms now well authorized, Johnson's dictionary is deficient in five or six thousand words, or about a seventh part of the English vocabulary.

But I will trouble you and the public no farther. Enough has been said to satisfy the candid and liberal, and more would not satisfy men of a different character.[100]

At the beginning of 1806, Webster sent a leather-bound presentation to his nemesis Pres. Thomas Jefferson, but he received no personal acknowledgement.

By the time Webster completed his *Compendious*, he was so enraptured by etymology, orthography, orthoepy, and lexicography that he decided to compile a new, larger, more complete work. Indeed, he envisioned the creation of the largest, most complete dictionary of the English language ever compiled, larger even than Dr. Johnson's massive two-volume work. But it would be *An American Dictionary of the English Language*,[101] and it would be the foundation of the "Federal Language" he had long envisioned as America's "band of national union."[102]

Webster wrote to the most influential people he knew in America—personal friends, college presidents, political leaders, and so on—to solicit subscriptions to underwrite his new dictionary. Common in England, the subscription approach to funding the writing and printing of major works was relatively unknown in America. Dr. Johnson, according to Webster, had found a patron among his booksellers "who advanced him the whole copyright of his Dictionary, *fifteen hundred pounds Sterling*, before the manuscript was completed."[103]

Webster mailed a long, esoteric circular to "the Friends of Literature in the United States." In it, he described the etymological shortcomings of previous scholars, saying that

> Johnson's Dictionary and other lexicons in use, which are deemed the highest authorities, contain material errors. . . . Were these errors a few mistakes only . . . the evil might be permitted to exist without essential injury to literature. But they are very numerous and important. . . .
> To this ill consequence it may be added that the origin and progress of language, one of the noblest gifts of God to man, the instrument of most of his social enjoyments and all his improvements, lie covered with darkness.[104]

Webster said it would take him eight to ten years to prepare his new dictionary—to which "are to be added the expences of a numerous family and the cost of many books. My own property is not adequate to these expenditures. Similar undertakings in Great Britain have been supported by contributions; and can there be a question whether the lovers of learning in the United States will aid by like means any design which promises to enlarge the sphere of knowledge?" Webster asked "friends of this undertaking" to assist him "by contributions in money and by extending the use of the books which I have published for use of schools, which would augment my own resources.[105]

The response was dreadful. Harvard's Anglophiles rejected the project outright. The faculties of Yale, Williams College, Middlebury, and Nassau Hall (Princeton) and Pres. John Wheelock of Dartmouth College all gave Webster's dictionary "unqualified approbation of the design" but contributed nothing other than the promise of free access to their libraries.

In the end, his appeal produced only seventeen subscribers and a mere $1,050, of which Webster eventually refunded $150 to impatient subscribers. Yale president Timothy Dwight contributed $50, Oliver Wolcott, $100, and Eli Whitney, the inventor and Yale graduate, $50. Webster received more subscriptions later—$100 in 1811, $200 in 1812—and a continuing flow of contributions from John Jay beginning in 1813, but these were hardly enough to support so huge a project, whose costs he estimated at about $15,000, but which eventually grew to $25,000.

Even those who backed Webster warned of the dangers of embarking on so costly a project. Oliver Wolcott, by then president of a New York bank, said, "I cannot encourage you to expect success."[106] Former ambassador to England Rufus King, who had retired to his farm on Long Island, warned Webster of American "prejudice against learning," adding, "I am sorry to remark that I am able to discover but little probability of your receiving adequate encouragement to continue to devote your time and talents to the important and laborious investigation in which, for so many years, you have been engaged. Neither learning, morals, nor wisdom seem any longer to be regarded as objects of public esteem and favour."[107]

A few months later, Webster, ever the Yankee peddler, tried a broader approach, aimed at raising large numbers of small contributions rather than a few large contributions from a small number of institutions and wealthy friends. He sent out a mass mailing to every preacher, schoolteacher, bookseller, and printer, every relative, and, of course, every newspaper editor— foe as well as friend—asking each to contribute a small amount. The circular was addressed to the common man—the "yeoman" he had admired so much as a young man—and promised that "every gentleman advancing *ten dollars* on subscription shall be entitled to a copy of the Dictionary on fine paper and in elegant binding. Booksellers advancing money for ten copies or more shall have a discount of twenty-five per cent."[108] The response was encouraging but not lucrative enough to support the project, and Webster knew he would either have to abandon his great American dictionary or find a way of doing it on his own. He was too stubborn to consider the first choice and did not earn enough for the second, so he temporarily set aside his plans.

8

IN THE ELECTIONS OF 1804, Thomas Jefferson and his Jacobins retained power, in a near sweep. Jefferson won 162 of 176 electoral votes and carried every state but Connecticut, where Federalists retained most local and state offices, including the governorship. New Haven voters returned Webster to the City Council and his judicial posts. His reelection gave him the opportunity to establish a charitable society in New Haven, similar to the one he had founded in Hartford. The New Haven society went on to found New Haven's first hospital.

In Washington, however, Jefferson followed up his election victory by increasing the implementation of the spoils system. Jefferson's policies had provoked Col. Timothy Pickering, who had been elected senator from Massachusetts in 1802, to propose secession of Northern states from the union. "Massachusetts, as the most powerful . . . should take the lead," wrote Pickering.

> At a word from her, Connecticut would instantly join. There can be no doubt of New Hampshire. Rhode Island would follow of necessity. There would be no great difficulty in bringing in Vermont. But New York should also concur, and as she might be made the center of the Northern union it can hardly be supposed that she would refuse her assent. New Jersey would assuredly become an associate, and it is to be wished that Pennsylvania, at least east of the Susquehanna might be induced to come into the Confederacy. At no distant period, the British provinces on the north and north east would probably become part of the Northern Union. . . .
>
> While thus contemplating the only means of maintaining our ancient institutions in morals and religion and our equal rights, we wish no ill to the Southern states, and those naturally connected with them.[109]

The appeal of Pickering's concept grew in popularity throughout New England during Jefferson's second term. Even Noah Webster, once the outspoken champion of union, flirted with Pickering's ideas after Jefferson's outrageous appointments of unqualified Democratic-Republican loyalists to federal posts throughout the North.

9

EARLY IN OCTOBER 1805, as Webster approached his forty-seventh birthday, he was astonished to see Joel Barlow at his door. After seventeen years, Barlow and his wife had returned to New England. They had left in their early thirties, and Barlow had now turned fifty-one, branded a traitor to his nation and to his religion by most of the Calvinist and Federalist Yale community. He did not look well.

"I have seen our friend Barlow," Webster wrote to a classmate. "He is a little convalescent, briefly by means of Bonaparte's *harsh remedies* for new philosophy, but I think his constitution so much impaired that a radical cure is impossible. He feels himself in an awkward situation: a downcast look, at least when I saw him, marks great depression of mind or consciousness of something wrong at bottom."[110]

The Barlows had left France for England eighteen months earlier, after French doctors seemed unable to identify, let alone treat, an illness that had laid Ruth Barlow low for more than two years. After an equally fruitless year in London, the Barlows left on what turned out to be the stormiest trans-Atlantic crossing imaginable. After fifty-two days amid riotous waves, they landed in New York in August and needed a month to recuperate before traveling to New Haven to try to reforge broken links to family and friends. Barlow immediately sought out Noah Webster, his oldest and dearest friend, who had publicly branded him near treasonous and an atheist. By avoiding all discussions of politics and religion, Barlow, still the charming poet and land swindler, succeeded in restoring a semblance of their old friendship. Barlow was enthusiastic about Webster's *Compendious Dictionary* and his plans for an even larger American dictionary. The reconciliation reached a point where Webster and a group of his Yale classmates even spent an evening at a joyful reunion for the Barlows, although Yale's orthodox Calvinist president, Timothy Dwight, refused to attend or even see his former student.

Boston's Federalist newspaper was even more unkind, attacking Barlow as an atheist and reprinting the words to "The *Guillotine*" the bloodthirsty verse Barlow allegedly wrote after the beheading of the French monarchs. Although Jeffersonian republicans welcomed him, New England's hostility so discouraged him that Barlow quit his native region forever and moved to the friendlier climate of Washington, D.C. He went directly to President Jefferson to seek a job. The two had become friends in Paris in the summer of 1789, when Jefferson was ambassador and Barlow was selling phantom American lands to the French aristocracy. They had celebrated the storming of the Bastille together.

When he arrived in Washington, Barlow met with Jefferson and suggested an interest in working on the establishment of a federal system of education similar to one that leaders of the French Revolution were considering. Jefferson had long supported a scheme of James Madison's to build a national education system, with a common school in every town, an academy in every county, and a college in every state. Derived from Plato's *Republic*, the system was to be crowned with a university in the nation's capital, from which all those seeking public office would have to graduate in order to serve. It was the only national issue about which Webster and

Jefferson had always agreed—from the time they first met outside the Continental Congress in Philadelphia twenty years earlier. Later, Franklin, Rush, Madison, and Washington had supported the scheme at the Constitutional Convention, and ten years later, George Washington left a bequest in his will to establish the national university in the new capital.

Barlow suggested converting Washington's bequest into reality. Jefferson approved, and Barlow began working on a *Prospectus of a National Institution, to Be Established in the United States.*[111] He sent Webster details of his project, along with warm thanks for the pleasant visit in New Haven and the opportunity to see Webster's *Compendious Dictionary*. He asked Webster to outline a curriculum for the new university.

Webster replied in an equally warm letter that reinforced the reconciliation that had occurred between the two old friends in New Haven. They had been as brothers at Yale, and Webster was genuinely happy about their reunion:

> Dear Sir,
>
> Your favor of the 12th has given me much pleasure, not merely on the score of former friendship, but because it informs me of your favorable opinion of my Dictionary and my further design. The approbation of classical scholars is the most flattering reward I can receive. . . .
>
> A few gentlemen of this character like yourself duly appreciate the merit of my labors, but the number is small; my hope and expectations are that it will increase. You will recollect that Judge [John] Trumbull and yourself were the only friends who in 1783 ventured to encourage me to publish my *Spelling Book*. The attempt to correct English books was thought a rash undertaking; yet more than 200,000 copies now sell annually.

Webster went on to describe his other textbooks and his plan for a new, larger dictionary:

> My views comprehend a *whole system,* intended to lay the foundation of a more correct practice of writing and speaking, as well as a general system of instruction in other branches. It is time for us to begin to think for ourselves. Great Britain is probably in her wane. . . .
>
> I agree with you that we ought to correspond and understand each other. Dr. Mitchill [the Columbia College scientist] often suggests this union as important. I will cheerfully accord with any scheme of this kind that shall be deemed prudent and advantageous. . . . My plan is to correct rather than innovate, for this is a subject of extreme difficulty. I, however, will be accommodating. I endeavor to unite other opinions with my own on many points, and shall be happy to take the advice of my friends. . . . I shall be happy to receive your opinion on any subject favorable to American literature and to be of any service to you in the pursuit. . . .
>
> Assure Mrs. Barlow of my respect and accept the same from your old friend.[112]

In January, Barlow finished writing his *Prospectus* and showed it to the president, who approved it and asked Barlow to draft a law that would turn the proposal into a reality. Barlow published his *Prospectus* in pamphlet form to distribute to Congress and the public, and he sent copies to friends around the nation, including Webster. It was the most detailed and forward-looking proposal ever presented for a university.

Barlow envisioned bringing together the nation's finest scholars and scientists to teach all branches of the arts and sciences and to conduct research in mineralogy, botany, chemistry, medicine, mechanics (engineering), hydraulics, and mathematics. In addition to schools of arts and sciences, graduate schools would train students for careers in government, law, and medicine. His prospectus, in effect, outlined a plan for a great university that would combine basic research, graduate studies, and undergraduate education in the arts and sciences in a single institution.[113]

Barlow's vision anticipated the modern university press—"a printing facility to publish scientific and scholarly reports and to supply inexpensive text books for elementary schools throughout the nation." Every element of his vision made Webster's participation as a central figure essential to the new institution—as an educator, a formulator of curricula, and an experienced author and book publisher. To prepare the curriculum for the new institution, Barlow asked Webster for details of his "general system of education," which would, in effect, precede and be a requirement for admission into the university.[114]

His friendship with Barlow renewed, Webster saw the *Prospectus* for a national university and Barlow's close ties to Jefferson as an opportunity to realize his life's dream of establishing American English as the U.S. government's official federal language.

He wrote to Barlow, calling it "derogatory to us as a nation" to depend on England for books, saying dependence on English books "checks improvement" in the American arts and sciences.

> Our people look to English books as the standard of truth on all subjects, and this confidence in English opinions puts *an end to inquiry*. Our gentlemen, even in the colleges and professions, rarely question facts that come from English authors of reputation; hence we have no *spirit of investigation*, and numerous errors are daily propagated from English presses which become current in this country. . . . I can affirm that the standard English books abound with errors which nothing could have kept in countenance in this country but a blind veneration for English authorities.

Webster said his solution was "to furnish our schools with a tolerably complete system of elementary knowledge in books of my own, gradually substituting American books for English and weaning our people from their prejudices and from their confidence in English authority." He told Barlow what he considered an essential curriculum for every child: it would include grammar, selected American readings, the history and geography of the United States, world history and geography, and the sciences. He described his own texts for each and went on to show how the huge dictionary he was contemplating would serve as a foundation for all American studies.[115]

Webster was confident that Barlow's national university would be a vehicle for establishing a federal language and that it would ultimately provide him a chair from which to produce his great American dictionary of the English language. And if, as anticipated, the university required every incoming student to have studied American textbooks, then Webster's books, his American system of instruction, and the American language would at last become the bands of national unity he had spent his adult years trying to create. Barlow, his old friend, was about to realize all of Webster's dreams and ambitions for his native land.

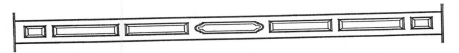

CHAPTER NINE

Lexicographer

I

A MONTH AFTER WEBSTER AND BARLOW had worked out plans for the new educational institution, President Jefferson abandoned Barlow's national university project[1] and turned his attention to the deteriorating situation at sea. Both the British and French were seizing American cargo ships with impunity and impressing or imprisoning American seamen. To protect American cargoes and lives and to punish both nations, Congress passed the infamous Embargo Act, which effectively ended virtually all foreign trade on December 22, 1807.

The embargo, however, accomplished the opposite of what Jefferson and Congress had intended. It prevented American merchant vessels from competing for international cargoes and left the British merchant fleet with a lucrative monopoly on trade to and from England. English merchants who had traded with American suppliers turned to new sources in South America. The French compensated for losses of American trade by seizing all American ships and cargoes in French ports—a plunder valued at about $10 million.

The Embargo Act did punish Americans, though, and wreaked its worst havoc with the economy of Northern states. The act idled the shipbuilding industry and the merchant fleet, which were mainstays of the New England economy, and it crippled the huge barge and wagon transport industries that carried imports and exports between Atlantic ports and inland destinations.

The embargo did stimulate some increases in domestic manufacturing, but not enough to offset shortages of imports and the inflation those shortages produced. Unemployment soared, with fifty-five thousand sailors and a hundred thousand merchants and laborers idled in port cities. Although smuggling prevented the embargo from stifling all trade, exports of American goods plunged nearly 80 percent and imports about 60 percent. American shipping companies lost millions, and U.S. government revenues from customs collapsed from $16 million a year to just a few thousand dollars.

The economic crush sent the cost of living soaring in New England, where Noah Webster's straitened finances did not permit him to stand for reelection as city councilman in 1807. Public service had simply become too costly for a father of six with another child on the way and a dysfunctional older brother in constant need of financial assistance. In addition, his eighty-six-year-old father had also become a burden.

> West Hartford June 9th 1807
>
> Effectionate Son.
>
> it is a Considerable time Since I saw you but I have heard from you often. it was sometime Before I recevd your letter that Mentioned the loss of your Child. by what I heard from you I have expected to see you at Hartford Before this time but I Suppose you was hindred by Publick or private Business. I am in want of Some money if you can help me Consistent with your own interest you will oblige an aged Parent. I have Been at great Cost . . . if you can help me to about ten Dollars or twenty . . . I have had Sickness which has Cost me much the winter past but now in Comfortable Health. I intend to have better ink before I write another letter.
>
> I remain your
> Effectionate Father[2]

The embargo (or "damn-bargo," as some called it) divided the nation along regional lines. Indeed, the depression in the North began to unite Federalists and Northern Democratic-Republicans against Jefferson's policies, while the agricultural South, which was less dependent on foreign trade, remained loyal to the president. In Boston, former secretary of state Timothy Pickering, who had won election to the Senate, proposed a convention to nullify the Embargo Act. The veteran Federalist continued to call for secession by the New England states, New York, and New Jersey to form an independent Northern confederacy.

By May 1808, the economic hardships provoked violence in the streets as well as in state legislatures, and Webster could no longer stand by silently and watch the nation deteriorate. Echoing his friend Pickering's sentiments, he called for Federalists and Democratic-Republicans "to unite the *northern* or *commercial* interests of the United states against a *non-commercial* administration." He said that party divisions had cost the Northern states

> that weight in the national councils to which their wealth, number, and resources entitle them. . . . The present struggles of parties are of no use . . . and I think both parties wrong in attempting to crush each other.

Neither party can be crushed, nor ought it to be attempted. But if the substantial men of both parties can . . . be induced to renounce their present warfare, and unite on some *general points* of policy, we may succeed in taking the administration out of the hands of the southern or anti-commercial interest. Is not the *common commercial interest* of the northern states their rallying point?

Webster urged the two parties to unite behind a bipartisan ticket in the 1808 presidential elections. He suggested Vice President (and former New York governor) George Clinton as candidate for president, and Massachusetts governor Caleb Strong "or some Massachusetts gentleman" for vice president. He urged returning the seat of government from the South to Philadelphia.[3]

A few days later, Webster jumped back into the national political arena with a call "To All American Patriots," in the *Connecticut Herald,* to form a new political party based on geography and common commercial interests rather than the constitutional principles that had formed the basis of the existing parties. Addressed to all "Who Value National Character and Who Are Disposed to Assert the Rights, Promote the Interest, and Maintain the Honor, the Dignity, and the Independence of the United States," his essay gave a long, rambling description of the different and often competing economies of the North and the South. He said that the North provided "the *principal wealth, strength* and *resources* of the country" and demanded that its influence

> be in proportion to the numbers of its free, active, industrious citizens, and to the wealth, strength, and resources which spring from their numbers and their industry. The question then occurs, how shall we obtain that portion of influence? The answer is obvious—by UNION. By *disunion* we have lost the commanding influence to which we are entitled; by UNION ALONE can we recover it. . . .
>
> Citizens of the northern states, our condition is deplorable, and there is no resource but in UNION. This is the only remedy for our political evils; and the remedy must be speedy; we are upon the brink of a precipice. Our party dissensions *must cease*—we MUST UNITE—or our country is doomed to encounter calamities which in prospect appall the stoutest heart.

He urged both parties to end their bickering over which nation, Great Britain or France, was violating the rights of American shipping more. "Both have violated and continue to violate our national rights," Webster said, and both would continue

> till we UNITE under a firm, vigorous administration and *array a single phalanx of united opinions and united resources* against these encroachments on the laws of nations. Say not union is impracticable: every thing is practicable to men who are determined to effect their object.

We have a *common interest;* and this, when understood, will *unite opinion* and direct them to a *common object.*

Banish then forever the distinction and the names of the present parties: away with *Federalist, Democrat, Republican, Jacobin.* Take the nobler title of *American Patriots.* Elect to the principal offices in the national government men of both parties, and unite in measures which shall restore the *honor* and the *commerce* of our country.[4]

Throughout the spring and summer, New England towns held meetings to condemn the embargo. Federalists returned to power, and at the end of the year, New England governors united in refusing to provide militiamen to enforce the embargo. Massachusetts senator Pickering led a group of disunionists in a formal call for a New England convention to nullify the federal embargo.

2

THE WEBSTERS' SEVENTH LIVING CHILD, LOUISA, was born in April 1808, and shortly thereafter the two oldest Webster girls—Emily, seventeen, and Julia, fifteen—felt "God's touch" at a revival meeting and made public professions. Though it was alien to his Calvinist upbringing, the fifty-year-old Webster agreed to his daughters' pleas to attend the revival, where both he and Rebecca were overwhelmed by emotion and experienced what was then called conversion—akin to the emotional experience of today's evangelical Christians when they are "born again." The experience of conversion was unrelated to a particular sect, and Webster and his wife and children, like other Calvinists, continued attending their regular churches for the remainder of their lives. Conversion simply made their religious experiences more intense because they believed deeply that God was with them every moment of every day.

Conversion did, however, rupture the fragile ties Webster had reestablished with Joel Barlow in Washington. With the national university abandoned, Barlow returned to writing—and rewriting—his poetry. He revised and lengthened his *Vision of Columbus* into a new, secular epic he called *The Columbiad,* which substituted evolutionary concepts for the earlier poem's reference to biblical creation. He foolishly sent it to Webster to review. The unswervingly devout Webster was disgusted.

"I had intended to give to the public a short review of your 'Columbiad,'" he wrote to Barlow,

> but . . . [I] doubt whether I can execute the purpose in a manner to satisfy you and my own conscience at the same time. Of the poem, as a poem, I can conscientiously say all, perhaps, which you can expect or desire, but I cannot in a review, omit to pass a severe censure on the

atheistical principles it contains . . . you renounced the religion which you once preached and which I believe. But with my views of the principles you have introduced into the *Columbiad* I apprehend my silence will be most agreeable to you, and most expedient for your old friend and obedient servant.[5]

Barlow was as wounded by Webster's breach of friendship as Webster had been by Barlow's audacity in writing a work so antagonistic to Calvinism. Barlow did not answer Webster's letter, and the two old friends never saw each other or communicated again.

Shortly thereafter, Thomas Jefferson, under attack by his own as well as the opposition party, followed George Washington's example and declined to stand for a third term. With republicans split along regional lines, Northerners picked Vice President George Clinton, the former New York governor, as their presidential candidate, and Southerners backed James Madison, Jefferson's heir apparent in the "Virginia dynasty." On December 7, 1808, Madison won the overwhelming majority of the electoral votes, and Clinton returned for a second term as vice president. Madison appointed Joel Barlow minister to France, with instructions to negotiate directly with Napoleon for an end to French attacks on American ships and French recognition of American neutrality.

Discouraged by the Madison victory, Webster buried himself in research for his new dictionary and tried to distance himself from politics. He had always liked Madison personally. Madison had, after all, helped win passage of Webster's copyright laws and, like Webster, was a champion of universal public education. But he was, nevertheless, a Jeffersonian Democrat, with views and policies that Webster could not tolerate. Webster continued in public office only until his term in each post expired. He served as New Haven councilman from 1799 to 1804, as member of the Connecticut legislature from 1800 to 1807, as alderman from 1806 to 1809, and as judge of the County Court from 1806 to 1810. Convinced the Federalist movement was moribund, Webster gave up his last public office in Connecticut in 1810 to devote his time to his work.

To prepare for the etymological research his dictionary required, he restudied his college Greek, Latin, and Hebrew; perfected his French and German; and then studied Danish, Anglo-Saxon, Welsh, Old Irish, Persian, and seven Asiatic and Assyrian-based languages. Ultimately he learned twenty different alphabets and languages. At the same time, but to little avail, he continued soliciting private and public subscriptions, even appealing to the Connecticut state legislature.

In trying to prove the need for his new American dictionary, however, Webster took the wrong tack. From the time he had marched with his father against the British, he had always attacked enemies head-on, by direct assault. This time, Dr. Johnson's dictionary was the enemy—the last vestige of British rule in America, to be expelled with the Redcoats. Apart from its inclusion of English words that were unknown to Americans and its exclusion of American words that were essential for everyday American life, Johnson's dictionary was just plain wrong, according to Webster. "Not a single page of Johnson's dictionary is correct," he declared. "Every page requires amendment or admits of material improvement."[6]

Webster was unrelenting:

> Even the definitions, which constitute the whole value of *Johnson's* Dictionary, are deficient in precision beyond any thing I could have imagined without a minute attention to the subject. Nor could I have believed . . . that *Johnson* had given currency to between *two* and *three thousand words* which are not English, having never been used in conversation or writing. This is a very serious evil, for his authority sometimes misleads men into the use of words which are not known to readers; and what is perhaps worse, great numbers of these illegitimate words are copied into . . . small dictionaries for schools. This was one of my reasons for compiling small dictionaries in which our American children may find no words but such as are used and really form a part of our language. Equally important was it to omit some vulgar and obscene words which the English compilers have injudiciously inserted.[7]

Had he been less strident, Webster might have attracted more support, but instead, motivated by his attacks, an army of conservative historians, writers, patrons of arts and letters, publishers, and printers rose to defend literary orthodoxy with unquestioning fervor. "It becomes the duty of every one to exert his talents for the preservation of what exists, and the renewal of what is past," declared an essayist in the *Monthly Anthology and Boston Review*.[8] Members of the Anthology Society of Boston—largely men of letters at Harvard—lashed out at Webster's audacity in questioning the authority of Dr. Johnson and daring to introduce American words that "sprang from the mouths of the illiterate" in the United States rather than from English literature.[9]

To protect their hold on the market, printers of English dictionaries joined in the criticism. They feared Webster would drive their books from the market if his proposed American dictionary ever proved as successful as his American speller.

In the face of nearly universal rejection, and with limited financial resources, Webster remained defiant, driven as always by patriotic zeal: "I . . . rely upon my own resources, and am not without a belief that I shall be able with these alone, to accomplish my design. If I should succeed, my opposers will certainly regret their premature expressions of disapprobation. I ask no favors: the undertaking is Herculean, but it is of far less consequence to *me* than to *my country*. . . . I shall pursue [the task] with zeal—and undoubtedly with success."[10]

Defiance, however, was costly in an economic depression. On June 19, 1812, President Madison declared war against Britain and crushed the last vestiges of economic activity that the Embargo Act had not already destroyed in New England. In Congress, Federalist senators from every New England state except Vermont joined with New York, New Jersey, and Delaware in voting against the president and in favor of peace. On June 26, a week after Madison's declaration of war, Caleb Strong, the Federalist governor of Massachusetts, called for a public fast to protest the war, and the Massachusetts legislature issued an "Address to the People" urging that "there be no volunteers except for defensive war."[11] In early July, the governors of Massachusetts and Connecticut refused to furnish militia to the Federal government for the war. A month later, New Hampshire and Connecticut protested the "hasty, rash, and ruinous" war and hinted at disunion.[12]

Webster could no longer afford to work full-time on his dictionary and remain in the luxury of his New Haven home. Moreover, the vicious personal attacks he suffered—for his political views, for the books he had written, and for the books he was about to write—had taken their toll. He longed for the peace and anonymity of the rural life he had known as a child on his father's farm.

"My name has been so much band[i]ed about that I am quite willing it should be seen & heard no more at present," he wrote in early 1812 to Federalist congressman Josiah Quincy of Boston, the future president of Harvard.

> I am engaged in a work which gives me great pleasure; & the tracing of language through more than twenty different dialects has opened a new & before unexplored field. I have within two years past, made discoveries which if ever published must interest the literati of all Europe, & render it necessary to revise all the lexicons, Hebrew, Greek, & Latin, now used as Classical Books. But what can I do? My own resources are almost exhausted & in a few days I shall sell my house to get bread for my children. All the assurances of aid which I had rec'd in Boston, N York & c have failed & I am soon to retire to a humble cottage in the country.
>
> Adieu, Dear Sir . . . We must drink the cup of disgrace to the dregs!
>
> Yours in low spirits.[13]

In September 1812, Webster sold his New Haven home at a loss and moved his family to the less costly rural community of Amherst, Massachusetts, a tiny center of conservative Federalism and Calvinism reminiscent of Webster's boyhood community in West Hartford. The Webster children expressed the expected range of emotions: the oldest were devastated to leave their New Haven friends at Yale; the youngest found nothing but joyful adventure in the freedom of the fields and woods. Eliza Webster, the sixth of the seven children, was nine years old when her family moved. She recalled:

> I remember the parting with some much loved companions . . . my older sisters wept. They realized the great change coming. . . . I have vivid recollections of stopping in Hartford, at a small Hotel, the first night of our journey . . . and well I remember my delight and my brother William's,

as our stage coach rolled slowly through the South Hadley woods—then a long stretch where the boughs almost met overhead and we children could reach them as we went along. It was all new to us, but Emily and Julia felt as if going into a wilderness and our gaiety almost annoyed them.[14]

The move to Amherst tore the two oldest Webster girls, Emily, twenty-two, and Julia, nineteen, from a corps of lively, cosmopolitan—and eligible—Yale students. One of them, William Wolcott Ellsworth, the son of Webster's old mentor Chief Justice Oliver Ellsworth, had escorted Emily to the junior ball of his class at Yale. She attended in "a pink silk" gown as "lovely as a poet's dream," according to her niece. "It had drawing strings at the waist and neck, and was trimmed about the low neck and sleeves with fine English lace at twelve dollars a yard." After the ball, young Ellsworth asked for Emily's hand in marriage. For her, the move to Amherst and the separation from her fiancé proved particularly painful.[15]

Amherst proper was a tiny community of about twenty-five houses when the Websters arrived. "The common was a swamp of white birch and pasture land where each family, by the vote of the town, was allowed to pasture a cow for so many weeks every season," according to Eliza. "Mt. Pleasant Hill was an unbroken forest of chestnuts and walnuts, and the village lads and the squirrels alike enjoyed what Massachusetts Senator Rufus Choate called 'this jewel on the brow of Amherst.' There was a lovely grove . . . thick and unbroken, and full of spring beauties—princes pine and checkerberries, which was called lovers' Walk. Sidewalks and paving stones were quite unknown."[16]

The homes in Amherst were scattered along the town's two small streets, one on the north-south axis from Deerfield to Holyoke, the other on the east-west road from Worcester to the Hampshire County seat of Northampton. Northampton had drawn many wealthy people to its beautiful hills, and the rich soil of nearby Hadley produced substantial wealth for corn and tobacco planters. The county's two distilleries filled the church's pews with repentant sinners and its coffers with the wages of their sins. The county had 250 homes and about sixteen hundred residents.

Webster bought and finished, Emily recalled, "a large double house half finished on a gentle eminence opposite the 'green,'" on ten acres of meadowland that he soon transformed into a small farm and elaborate garden.[17] The minister's home stood nearby.

"The daughters of the Parsonage and my sisters used to read together the best books of English literature, and for amusement in the long winter evenings would act the simple plays of Hannah More[18] and others," Eliza wrote.[19] A neighbor, George Montague, remembered the Webster girls: "They had the sweetest ways . . . they would sometimes . . . go up and pick flowers in Mr. Sweetser's grove; and they were full of fun, but full of kindness. I remember them as angels."[20]

Once he finished the house, Webster set to work transforming his ten acres of meadow into a farm that would provide his family with vegetables, fruit, fowl, and milk the year round. "I remember . . . every nook and corner," Eliza wrote later, "even the pig pen—where 'Heliogabalus' grunted—and the white spots on the cows, 'Gentle,' 'Comfort' and 'Cricket,' who roamed in the pasture. Father's horse was named 'Rolla' by sister Mary, after reading a play or drama. . . . All our horses have been Rolla since. Ah, me! the old happy Amherst days."[21]

Webster planted a large orchard of hardy apple, pear, peach, and cherry trees, many of them the products of his own grafts. He also raised a grapevine "of a peculiarly large and rich sort of native growth" from his father's farm in West Hartford. "His garden was a great delight and resource to him," Eliza recalled, "and he cultivated fruits, vegetables and flowers with equal interest and success."[22]

For one of the few times in his life, he wrote a number of articles that insulted no one—agricultural essays for the *Hampshire Gazette,* describing his experiments with potatoes and fertilizers and recounting his success growing crops not normally produced in the area. He also wrote pioneering essays on forest conservation, which suggested careful thinning to harvest wood while preserving the integrity of the forest.[23]

Life in Amherst gave him more time to dote over his children. His daughters' wardrobes overflowed with dresses—he could not give them enough. Julia had seventeen dresses by the time she was married.[24] Mary was his favorite—and she knew it. "While the rest of us were often shy in his dignified presence," her younger sister Eliza wrote, "she gave way to her playfulness and it pleased him. She seemed to understand his nature and to know the deep currant of tenderness concealed in his heart and well up when circumstances overcame the habitual reticence of his manners."

Mary was also the brightest of the Webster children. As she reached her young teens, Webster read his essays and Fourth of July orations to her for criticism. Mary also shared Webster's musical gifts and his love for poetry and song. "She sang like an angel," according to her sister. "In the morning early, as soon as she was awake, she would sing the hymn, 'While thee I seek protecting power.'

"She would sing every verse and Father was usually in the next room, which was his study and for years after her death his eyes filled with tears when the hymn was sung at church or in the family. 'Mary's hymn,' he called it."[25]

Webster installed his study in a large, warm corner room on the second floor, facing south and east. He had already collected a library of encyclopedias and reference books on virtually every aspect of the arts and sciences, along with dictionaries in dozens of languages. He devised a semicircular table for his work, about two feet wide. Standing in the well formed by the semicircle, he was within arm's reach of twenty to thirty dictionaries and grammar texts in different languages, arrayed around him. He would thus trace the roots of each word to its origins, dictionary by dictionary, language by language, making notes with each bit of data he discovered.

"He would take the word under investigation," his granddaughter explained, "and standing at the right end of the lexicographer's table, look it up in the first dictionary which lay at that end. He made a note, examined a grammar, considered some kindred word, and then passed to the next dictionary of some other tongue. He took each word through the twenty or thirty dictionaries, making notes of his discoveries, and passing around his table many times in the course of a day's labor of minute and careful study. This was comparative philology which has given such great results to modern philologists."[26]

At four o'clock each afternoon, Rebecca climbed up to his study with fruit or nuts and cake, and he removed his eyeglasses and relaxed for a short while.

When Webster began compiling his dictionary in Amherst, he estimated it would take him about ten years to complete. He tried to follow a daily routine of rising just after dawn, and after organizing his work for the day, he awakened his children with the call of "Up, up, children!"

"We never lingered after that call," Eliza recalled. "We assembled for prayer in the common parlor and Father read the Scriptures, and then from a little book of his own composing he offered prayer."[27] Webster had tired of the conventional, impersonal prayers from church, and he composed his own—for weekday mornings, weekday evenings, Sunday mornings, Sunday evenings, and any other occasion that warranted an appeal to the divine. He wrote them in a small diary that he carried with him on his travels and shared with his family at home.

"Great & glorious Jehovah," one of his morning prayers began, "the author & righteous governor of the world, our creator, preserver & bountiful benefactor! our voice shalt thou hear in the morning—To thee will we direct our prayer. We thank thee, o thou preserver of men that thou hast guarded us in our defenseless moments, & brought us to behold the light of this day in safety. We have lain down, slept, & awakened, for thou, Lord, has sustained us.

"We confess, Lord, we have sinned against thee, & forfeited all thy mercies."[28]

Webster's routine was seldom free of interruptions. His and Rebecca's home became as much a center of hospitality in Amherst as it had been in New Haven and, before that, Hartford, with friends and neighbors often dropping in unannounced and sitting down to share the food at the Webster's large table. His huge library was a constant lure to the well-educated gentry in the area. Two sons of Massachusetts governor Caleb Strong and their families were neighbors—and admirers. In Franklinesque style, he

Ch & Syr.] J ℸ ✗, adone.

Adonists n. [Heb. ___ Low, a scriptural title of the Supreme Being.]
Among critics, a sect or party who maintain that the Hebrew
points ordinarily annexed to the consonants of the word Jehovah, are
not the natural ~~vowels~~ points belonging to that word, & that they do not
express the true pronunciation of it, but that they are the vowel-
points belonging to the words Adonai & Elohim, applied to the inef-
fable name ~~of Jehovah~~, which the Jews were forbid to utter, & the
true pronunciation of which was lost; they were therefore always to
pronounce the word Adonai, instead of Jehovah. These critics are
opposed to the Jehovists.   Encyc.

Adonéan a. Pertaining to Adonis. "Fair Adonean Venus". Faber. 2.32

Adópt' v t. [L. adopto, of ad & opto ... to desire or choose.] See option. To take a
stranger into one's family, as son & heir; to take one who is not a child,
and treat him as one, - giving him a title to the privileges & rights of a
child..

2 In a spiritual sense, to receive the sinful children of men into the
invisible church, & into God's favor, & protection, by which they become heirs of salvation by Christ.   Brown

3 To take or receive as one's own, that which is not naturally so,
as to adopt the opinions of another; or to receive that which
is new, as to adopt a particular mode of husbandry.
4 To ~~choose~~ to select & take; as, which mode will you adopt?

Adópted. ___ Taken as one's own; received as son & heir; selected for use

Adópt'édly adv. In the manner of something adopted.

Adópt'er n. one who adopts. In chemistry, a large round re-
~~Adop~~ ceiver, with two necks, diametrically opposite to each other,
one of which admits the neck of a retort, & the other is joined to
another receiver. It is used in distillations, to give more space to
elastic vapors, or to increase the length of the neck of a retort.

Adópting. ___ Taking a stranger as a son; taking as one's own.

Adóption n. [L. adoptio.] The act of adopting, or the state of being
adopted. - The taking & treating of a stranger as one's own child. The
receiving as one's own what is new or not natural. God's taking
the sinful children of men into his favor & protection. Eph. 1. 5

A page from Noah Webster's handwritten draft of his *American Dictionary of the English Language.* Webster was the last lexicographer ever to write an entire dictionary—a total of seventy thousand entries—with no help. (Webster Papers, New York Public Library.)

opened his huge library to them and eagerly engaged them in endless political and philosophical conversations.

The Websters' hearts were as open as their hearth, and like the minister and his wife, according to Emily, they "often took charge of the few stray waifs then left to the charity of the town and brought them up with charity and kindness." Webster himself could not tolerate idleness, and he confronted any boy he found loitering on the green or along Amherst's two streets. "Are you needed at home?" he asked them. If not, Webster ordered them to "go work in my garden for an hour" or "pick the stones up from the road in front of my house." The number of "idlers" multiplied quickly when they learned that the generous old scholar often paid a silver ninepence, or twelve and a half cents, an hour, a huge sum for a boy in that era.

"All the village boys grew fond of him," said Eliza. "They would go down on purpose to be hired, for they liked the instruction he would give them about plants and trees, and grafting and budding, and they liked his wages also. Indeed, in money matters, while most scrupulous to avoid debt, and to discharge obligations, he was very liberal."[29]

A year after moving to Amherst, Emily Webster, Webster's oldest daughter, married William Wolcott Ellsworth, the son of the U.S. chief justice, Oliver Ellsworth, who had been one of Connecticut's first senators before replacing John Jay on the Supreme Court.

Emily moved to Hartford. Only two months later, on November 9, 1813, her husband, a future Connecticut congressman and governor, had the duty to write to his father-in-law: "Though you will not get this letter in season to attend the funeral, I write you that you may know of your Father's death. . . . The funeral is to be to-morrow afternoon. We, in union with the other friends very much regret you could not be with us here. Emily, Julia and myself will attend. Yours sincerely and affectionately."[30]

3

AS WEBSTER STRUGGLED through the New England winter of 1812–13, he developed a new theory of the origins of languages. Influenced by his ever-deepening religious beliefs, he concluded that all the world's languages had a common origin, akin to the common origins of man described in Genesis. He attempted to explain his theory in a letter to his brother-in-law the attorney Thomas Dawes:

> The families of men which first peopled the earth migrated in diverging
> courses. Their progress from the center of *Asia* may be distinctly traced
> by their languages; and their progress or courses being radiuses of a circle,
> and the first races of families removing to the greatest distances as they
> were invited by the conveniences of hunting or impelled forward by suc-

ceeding tribes, their descendants and their languages are now to be found at the periphery of the circle in the north and west of *Europe,* &c. These languages retain many primitive words which are lost or disguised in the Greek and Latin; and an inattention to this circumstance has retarded the progress of this kind of enquiries more than any other circumstance.[31]

In the spring of 1813, when he had given up all hope of outside support for his dictionary, Webster received a subscription from John Jay, who had retired to his farm in Bedford, New York, in 1801 but had never forgotten Webster's loyalty during the long national debate over the treaty Jay had negotiated with Britain. Webster replied, describing the astonishing lack of support for his dictionary:

> Some few of my friends would do all in their power to encourage me, but literary men in the large towns appear to be opposed to *me* or my *design* and their pointed opposition has had no small effect in preventing me from receiving encouragement. If I live to finish my work, it is probable, I shall go to England to revise and publish it, and as my own country furnishes no patron, I may find one in Great Britain. I am so well satisfied that my researches will open an unexplored field and throw more light on the origin and history of language than all that has before been written as well as lead to important illustrations of ancient History, sacred and profane, that I think it my duty to pursue the subject, unless absolutely compelled to relinquish it.
>
> I thank you sir for the interest you kindly manifest in my success, and am,
>
> > With great respect,
> > Your obedient servant.[32]

Born to a wealthy family, Jay was a fiercely patriotic Federalist who genuinely liked Webster and began to send regular, generous donations to help underwrite Webster's great dictionary.

Despite Webster's intention of working full-time on the dictionary, events conspired to sound the call of public service, which he had never been able to ignore. Like many of his neighbors, Webster deplored conditions and teaching standards at the local common school—a "forlorn, unpainted, and unshaded building" on the edge of the village green, according to daughter Eliza. "There was an entry way where hats and cloaks were kept and then one large room with an open fire place at each end and in winter full of green logs with the sap oozing out of them. Two or three rows of hard benches before them were on each side and a tall desk in the centre of the room was for the teacher. There were no maps or pictures of any kind—no maps or equipments for the assistance of the teacher, but I remember that the children were happy and anxious to learn."

Within a year of his arrival in Amherst, Webster organized the townsfolk and raised the funds to build an academy, "where their sons could be fitted for college and their daughters taught the higher branches of education."[33]

Two years later, Webster was elected president of the board of trustees, and in 1815, he threw open the doors of the new Amherst Academy to ninety girls and more than a hundred boys, whom the Webster name had helped draw from all parts of New England, as boarders and day students.

4

BY THE END OF 1813, "Mr. Madison's War," as Northerners called it, had destroyed New England commerce. It had also cost Joel Barlow his life. In November 1812, Barlow had gone to Vilna, Poland, to meet Napoleon and negotiate peace with France. By the time Barlow arrived, the French—and Napoleon—were in full retreat from Russia. Barlow fled into the fierce winter snows and died of exposure trying to find his way back to Paris; he lies in an unmarked grave somewhere in Poland.

In America, even those New Englanders who had voted for Madison were bitter about the shortages of essential goods and soaring prices. After discussions with Webster and other Federalists, county judge Joseph Lyman of South Hadley called the "Friends of Peace & Union" in Old Hampshire County to "a free and dispassionate discussion touching our public concerns" on January 5.[34] They met that day and decided to organize "a convention of all the Northern and Commercial States by delegates to be appointed by their respective legislatures . . . for procuring such alterations in the Federal Constitution as will give to the Northern States a due proportion of representation."[35] The group appointed Webster to write a petition to other towns. Suddenly, Webster, who had sought rural retirement to write a dictionary, was in the national political maelstrom again, writing:

> By means of the representation of slaves the southern states have an influence in our National Councils altogether disproportionate to their wealth, strength and resources; and we presume it to be a fact . . . that for about twenty years past, the United States have been governed by a representation of about two-fifths of the actual property of the country.
> In addition to this, the creation of New States in the South, and out of the original limits of the United States, has increased the Southern interest, which has appeared so hostile to peace and commercial prosperity of the Northern States.[36]

Webster accused Jefferson's Virginia dynasty in Washington of having "repeatedly violated" the compromise whereby "the northern states acceded to the representation of slaves . . . upon the express stipulation in the constitution, that they should be protected in the enjoyment of their commercial rights." He called the embargo unconstitutional and "subversive of the first principles of civil liberty. . . . It arms the President and his Agents with complete control of persons and property."

Webster's petition called for "a convention of all Northern and Commercial States" to change the Constitution to give Northern states "a due proportion of representation, and secure them from the future exercise of powers injurious to their commercial interests;—Or if the General Court [Massachusetts legislature] shall see fit, that they would pursue such other course, as they, in their wisdom, shall deem best calculated to effect the objects"—including disunion, if necessary.[37]

Connecticut's chief justice, Zephaniah Swift, Webster's friend and classmate from Yale, strongly supported Webster's call for a convention, as did Webster's brother-in-law in Boston, the influential Federalist lawyer Thomas Dawes. "I am gratified with every sentiment in it," Dawes wrote Webster, "except that I despair of obtaining the political justice that is due to New England. To utter my conviction plainly to you, I have no hope. I consider that a tyrant's foot is upon our neck and we are undone: for his power is as great as his inclination is wicked. By the tyrant I mean, not merely Madison, but the Southern Policy."[38]

Chancellor (New York Supreme Court justice) James Kent wrote Webster:

My sentiments are in unison with yours on the great Points of national Policy, & I look upon the State of this Country as most distressing for the present time, & very cheerless in Prospect. It is probably best to hobble along as well as we can for the present & await the course of Events for the ensuing winter. Probably we may have Peace, & this will be some alleviation.

As to the Imperfections of the federal government I see & lament them, & they have been greatly aggravated by the accession of New Territory & above all by the weak & wicked Policy of the South. But I apprehend it is the lesser Evil to cling to the Ship as long as she can swim. . . . If I can be brought to believe that an Administration will continue the War rather than make Peace on what you & I deem just Principles of public law, that administration must be changed or the Union is gone forever. We shall certainly be ruined if things go on in this course much longer.[39]

In the spring of 1814, Webster won election as Amherst selectman and as representative in the Massachusetts General Court, where, in a speech published in the Boston press, he aggressively supported a convention to change the American Constitution. The Connecticut patriot who had started his political career as the scourge of conventions and disunion at Middletown thirty years earlier now became a standard-bearer for both.

By midsummer, the war with England had torn the nation apart. Resistance to the draft left the U.S. Army too weak to fight without support from state militias. New England's governors, however, refused to send their troops beyond their own borders. With unimpeded access to the nation's capital, the British marched into Washington and burned it to the ground on August 24 and 25, while President Madison and his government fled in panic to Virginia, along with the impotent U.S. Army.

A few months later, the war came home to Noah Webster in a letter from his older brother, Abram:

Dear Brother

God in his Holy and wise Providence has seen fit to take from me my only and beloved son under Circumstances peculiarly aggravating. He was called with the melitia to Sacketts Harbor the beginning of September . . . [and] Died November 21st aged 25 years, & 2 days.

Pray for your afflicted brother.[40]

On December 15, 1814, the convention that Webster helped organize met at Hartford, Connecticut. Only the five New England states sent representatives, all of them chosen from members of the state legislatures. The Massachusetts legislature sent only native-born delegates, thus preventing any participation by the Connecticut-born Webster.

After three weeks, delegates approved a resolution of "interposition," which Southern states would use for 150 years to defy federal government authority: "In cases of deliberate, dangerous and palpable infractions of the Constitution, affecting the sovereignty of a State and liberties of the people; it is not only the right but the duty of such a State to interpose its authority for their protection, in the manner best calculated to secure that end."[41]

The Hartford Convention passed other resolutions, to protect citizens against federal military conscription, reserve federal revenues collected within a state for the defense of that state, create an interstate defense force independent of the federal government, and recommend a series of amendments to the Constitution. In effect, the delegates sought changes that would reduce federal powers to levels midway between those granted by the Constitution and those of the innocuous Articles of Confederation. Although excluded from its deliberations, Webster forwarded eleven proposals to the convention by intermediaries; one was adopted—to apportion taxes and representation among states according to the number of free persons in each state. Other proposed amendments would have prohibited all federal embargoes of more than sixty days and would have required a two-thirds vote of both houses of Congress to declare war, to restrict foreign commerce, and to admit new states to the Union. The president would have been limited to one term.[42]

As delegates debated in Hartford, the Americans and British were negotiating a treaty that they signed on Christmas Eve, in Ghent, Belgium, establishing "peace without victory." News of the treaty, however, did not reach North American battlefields in time to forestall the violent and apparently decisive battle of New Orleans on January 8, 1815, when Gen. Andrew Jackson routed British forces. Although the battle came too late to affect the outcome negotiated at Ghent, the American public interpreted it as the battle that won the war. Their pride restored, they raised Jackson onto the pedestal of national heroism.

Although Federalists insisted the Hartford Convention had been responsible for forcing Madison to negotiate the end of the war, Jackson's victory turned public opinion against the convention, and its delegates, especially Zephaniah Swift, became objects of national scorn as conspirators and turncoats.[43] To his great good fortune, Webster had remained in the safety of his garden and his study in Amherst. Although he had been disappointed when the Massachusetts legislature refused to name him a delegate, the rejection proved a great service. Had he been at Hartford, he would have suffered a level of abuse that would almost certainly have ended all chances of success for his dictionary. As it was, he was reelected to the Massachusetts General Court in 1815. The Federalist party disintegrated, however, and in the presidential election a year later, James Monroe, another of Jefferson's Virginia dynasty, routed Federalist candidate Rufus King, Webster's old friend, who had come out of retirement. Zephaniah Swift was forced out as Connecticut chief justice and retired to write his monumental *Digest of the Laws of the State of Connecticut,* which became the basis of state laws throughout the nation.[44]

5

IN 1816, two more Webster daughters were married: Harriet married Edward H. Cobb, the son of a wealthy merchant in Portsmouth, New Hampshire, and Julia married the Reverend Chauncey A. Goodrich, who had graduated from Yale in 1810 with Emily Webster's husband, William Wolcott Ellsworth. Goodrich had been a tutor at Yale before becoming a minister at Middletown, Connecticut. A year after his marriage, he returned to Yale as professor of rhetoric and remained there until his retirement, forty years later. By the time Goodrich returned, Webster's old friend Timothy Dwight had died, thus joining Joel Barlow among Webster's contemporaries who had slipped away.

With two of his "angels" married and his father deceased, Webster had fewer mouths to feed, and his finances improved so dramatically that he ran for Congress. Although he was the overwhelming choice of his own district, too many other Massachusetts districts opposed him as a Connecticut outsider, and he lost the election. His friend Oliver Wolcott Jr., however, was elected governor of Connecticut, succeeding to the office once held by his father, Oliver Wolcott Sr., and his grandfather Roger Wolcott. Connecticut, at least, remained in the hands of the old Federalist families.

Webster was neither surprised nor terribly disappointed by his own election loss. With the copyright to his spelling book set to expire two years later, he needed to obtain a new copyright, and that would mean writing a new edition—the one-hundredth such revision of his remarkable little book. More than two hundred companies were publishing the speller, however, and Webster was in no mood to abandon his family for the six months of travel throughout the country that it would take to negotiate new contracts with so many printers. Spurning the $40,000 or more his trip might have earned him, he sold all rights to the 1818 edition for the fourteen-year life of the new copyright to his original Hartford printer, Hudson & Goodwin, for a flat fee of $23,000 in cash. As part of the deal, he apprenticed his son, William, then fourteen, to Hudson with the understanding that he would be groomed for a partnership when he reached twenty-one. Webster reasoned that, in a single transaction, he had eased his financial problems, eliminated tiresome and costly travel, and placed his son on the track to a successful business career.

By 1817, Amherst Academy was so successful that the trustees established a fund to train young men for the ministry. At the time, Williams College, in Williamstown, Massachusetts, was the only school preparing ministers for evangelical churches, but it lay some seventy-five miles away in the nearly inaccessible mountains to the northwest. As president of the board, Webster tried to convince Williams to combine with Amherst Academy. After Williams refused to move, Webster convened the Academy board in September of the following year to establish a ministerial college, and he agreed to lead fund-raising.

At about the same time, his beloved Mary, the fourth of his daughters, married a widowed lawyer with three children, Horatio Southgate, of Portland, Maine. Southgate was the nephew of Webster's friend former ambassador to England Rufus King, who had become a candidate for president. Shortly afterward, Webster turned sixty, which would have been cause for celebration had he not received an unexpected note from his son, William: "Hudson says that I take no interest in the business of the store, & that I am taken up with pleasure more than business." A few months later, William returned home prematurely from his apprenticeship, no wiser than he had been when he left.

For William and for his disappointed father, the dismissal from Hudson was another in an unbroken record of failures. William had never been gifted—or terribly happy, for that matter. Never the scholar his father was or had hoped that he might become, the boy lacked all his father's ambitions, had few of his own, and even confessed to "a native imbecility of mind."[45]

The boy's return marked the beginning of a succession of family tragedies. Webster's younger brother, Charles, died that year. Early the next year, on February 28, 1819, Mary Webster Southgate, Noah Webster's favorite "angel," died three weeks after giving birth to her first child. Heavy snows had delayed the mails, and the Websters had only just learned of the birth of Mary's child. Her younger sister Eliza, seventeen, ran from house to house in Amherst to tell Mary's best friends the good news. It took three more weeks before news of her death arrived, by which time she already lay buried in far-off Portland, Maine. Eliza recalled:

> Father opened the letter in our presence, turned pale, rose and left the room. Mother followed. Harriet, 23, and myself waited long. They did not return to us. I crept to the bed room door and knocked gently. I heard sobbing and at last opened the door. Father knelt by the side of the bed — Mother close beside him. There was no hope expressed in the letter — they could not reach their best beloved child, one who had never pained them by a word or a look in all her short, beautiful life. How could they bear it! I remember her unwearied kindness to me and tender love. I was six years younger than Mary and shared her room after the marriage of my three elder, gifted sisters. We were a changed household after this sore bereavement.[46]

Despite, or perhaps because of, his depression over the loss of his daughter, Webster plunged ever deeper into fund-raising for Amherst College, and he agreed to serve one last term in the state legislature, in Boston. He spearheaded a series of bold economic reforms, but, still considered the outsider from Connecticut, he met nothing but uncompromising opposition. He urged separating Maine from Massachusetts, but the legislature temporarily tabled his motion. He moved to reform government operations after presenting evidence of graft in the legislature, overcharges by the state printer, excessive fees by government contractors, excessive costs for supporting town paupers, and excessive military expenses. The legislature tabled each of his motions. He attempted to improve education by establishing a new, state-run system of public schools, and he moved to build a state hospital — but again the majority blocked his efforts.

He abandoned those efforts with an angry letter to the leader of the legislature saying:

> A State like this ought not to want the means of erecting and endowing hospitals, providing funds for seminaries of learning and for public schools, and for various other useful objects. . . .
> The State of Massachusetts possesses a great deal of talent, enterprise, and wealth, and individuals distinguish themselves by many noble enterprizes of great public utility. But, to be plain, Sir, I do not discover in this Commonwealth those comprehensive views of public interest and those prospective measures which tend gradually to augment the

resources, the dignity, and prosperity of the State, which characterize the proceedings of some other States. . . . But whatever may be my wishes, my efforts can have no effect. I have had so many intimations I am yet a stranger in the Commonwealth that I shall henceforth cease to concern myself with public affairs.[47]

Back in Amherst, Webster's indefatigable fund-raising yielded more than $50,000 for the new college. In July 1819, construction of the first building began. A year later, in August 1820, he delivered the keynote speech as the cornerstone was laid for the new educational institution.

"The object of this institution," Webster told the guests at the ceremonies,

is one of the noblest which can occupy the attention and claim the contributions of the Christian public. It is to second the efforts of the apostles themselves, in extending and establishing the Redeemer's empire—the empire of truth. It is to aid in the important work of raising the human race from ignorance and debasement; to enlighten their minds; to exalt their character; and to teach them the way to happiness and to glory. Too long have men been engaged in the barbarous works of multiplying the miseries of human life. Too long have their exertions and resources been devoted to war and plunder; to the destruction of lives and property; to the ravage of cities; to the unnatural, the monstrous employment of enslaving and degrading their own species. Blessed be *our* lot! We live to see a new era in the history of man—an era when reason and religion begin to resume their sway, and to impress the heavenly truth, that the appropriate business of men, is to imitate the Savior, to serve their God; and bless their fellow men.[48]

Following his speech, the college elected him president of the board of trustees.

Shortly thereafter tragedy once again struck Webster's daughters. After giving birth to a baby girl, Harriet and her husband, Edward Cobb, had gone to the West Indies, where they both contracted yellow fever and Edward died. By the time Harriet returned home, her only child had also died, and she returned in grief at the age of twenty-one to live with her parents. Toward the end of the year, when the infant daughter of the Websters' late daughter, Mary, had been weaned by the wet nurse, her widowed father, who had three children to raise from his previous marriage, sent the baby to the sixty-three-year-old Noah Webster and his wife to raise as their own. Her name was also Mary Webster.

In September 1821, Webster dedicated the first building of the new school. The following day, September 19, the first forty-seven students enrolled at Amherst College, and Webster resigned, assured that the college was on a firm financial footing and that his work was done.

With his resignation, he determined to devote the rest of his life to raising his little granddaughter and completing his magnum opus—*An American*

Dictionary of the English Language. His sixty-three-year-old body was tired and his heart heavy with the tragedies that had beset his family. He had helped found two academies and a college, and his books were teaching tens of thousands of American children to read, write, and speak. He had done enough for others.

"Experience," he wrote in his letter of resignation,

has long since convinced me that a faithful discharge of my duties as a member of the Board is not compatible with my private pursuits; and nothing but a sincere desire to assist in giving some stability to the collegiate institution and insuring its success has for a long time prevented a resignation of my seat.

I now resign my seat, and of course the Presidency, and request the Board to accept my sincere thanks for the confidence you have reposed in me, and my ardent wishes for the success and prosperity of the Institution under your superintendence.[49]

6

IN OCTOBER 1821, Webster received another generous gift from John Jay, who had remained interested in the great dictionary but had not heard from Webster in several years.

> Bedford. West Chester County. N. York.
> 29th. Octr. 1821

Sir

I understood from Col. Pickering about two years since that you were going on with your great work. Nothing further respecting it having come to my knowledge, I appreciate that either some new Obstacle, or the operation of former ones, may have retarded, tho' not terminated your Progress. Being desirous that each of my two Sons should have a Copy, I enclose a further Sum for that purpose. In no Event are my Subscriptions or any part of them to be refunded.

Whenever you come this way, it would give me pleasure to see you here. My House is only 15 miles from Stamford.

With my best wishes for the health and welfare of yourself, and Family, I am Sir. . . .[50]

Jay had been deeply interested in the project from its inception and now raised his status to that of a patron. Webster responded appropriately:

Sir:

I yesterday received your favor of the 29th *inst.* with another proof of your benevolence, for which please to accept my particular acknowledgements. As the mail returns this morning, I can only state that in a few days, I will write to you more particularly the progress I have made in my Dictionary and the reasons of delay, which I trust will be satisfactory. Please to accept my particular respects.[51]

A few days later, Webster again wrote to give Jay details and insights into his approach to the dictionary:

> When I began the compilation of a large Dictionary of the English Language, I limited my views chiefly to a correction of such errors as had escaped former compilers and the supply of such new terms as have sprung from modern improvements in science. But in searching for the originals of English words, I soon found the field of etymology had been very imperfectly explored: and one discovery succeeding another, my curiosity was excited to persevere in the pursuit. At length finding no safe clue to conduct me through the labyrinth, I adopted a new plan of investigation, that of examining and comparing the primary elements, articulations or consonants of words in 20 different languages or dialects, the vowels having been found so mutable as to be of no use. The result of this examination has been the formation of a synopsis of radical words in more than 20 languages which is complete or nearly so. This will probably form a Quarto, and be an appendix to the Dictionary.[52]

Webster later noted that his "Synopsis . . . was the fruit of ten years labor, but no bookseller will publish it, & probably I shall lose my labor."

Like many works in etymology that preceded his, Webster's synopsis was largely imaginative guesswork, which assumed that a similarity of sounds carried a similarity of meaning. Using his Bible as the source of all truth, he believed that language was "the immediate gift of God . . . bestowed on Adam, in the same manner as all his other faculties and knowledge."[53]

Webster maintained that all modern languages could be traced to a single tongue he called Chaldee, which the descendants of Noah developed on the plain of Shirat, at the foot of Mount Ararat. He accepted as historic truths the biblical accounts of the Tower of Babel and the linguistic anarchy that resulted. After all, he had witnessed the same phenomenon in the United States, at the Newburgh encampment following the American Revolution. Webster believed that each of Noah's three sons led a group into exile from Babel, and that Japheth's group eventually migrated to Europe and developed a family of "Japhethic" tongues. These, said Webster, were the linguistic ancestors of all European languages.

Webster's etymological techniques were as misguided as his ancient history. Noting the lack of vowels in the writing of ancient tongues like Hebrew, he developed a theory of "radical words" as the basis of tracing their etymological origins. He first eliminated all vowels from a word to obtain what he called its radical form—that is, a word made up exclusively of consonants. He then searched for similar-looking words in dictionaries of ancient languages. If the number of letters and the basic structure of a radical word seemed similar to one in an ancient language, he assumed he had found the origin of the modern English word.[54] Ironically—and astonishingly—he studied and learned to read and understand (and sometimes even to speak) more than twenty languages to pursue his studies: Chaldaic, Syriac, Arabic, Samaritan, Hebrew, Ethiopic, Persian, Irish (Hyberne, Celtic), Armoric, Anglo-Saxon, German, Dutch, Swedish, Danish, Greek, Latin, Italian, Spanish, French, and Prussian.

It took Webster about ten years to develop his theory of etymology and he was certain the world would not regret "the delay which this has occasioned, for if I am not deceived, the discoveries proceeding from this investigation will be quite important, and as *new* in Europe as in America." Unfortunately, he was appallingly deceived—and there are no documents to explain how so brilliant a scholar allowed himself to go so far astray and spend so many years developing so specious, and costly, a theory.

"Since my time has been almost exclusively occupied in this pursuit," he explained to Jay, "I must have expended about $25,000. This sum has been taken from my own income, except about $1000. My property . . . affords an income barely sufficient for my family expenses. Many books I have wanted which I have not had the means to purchase and I still want them. The work must be copied and revised, before it can be printed and at present there are not types enough in America to print the Appendix." Webster told Jay that he had reached the letter *h* in his dictionary but that there seemed little hope of publishing it in America; he would try to sell it in England.

"The evening before your letter arrived," the sixty-three-year-old Webster added with somewhat uncharacteristic emotion,

> I was conversing respecting you, Sir. I said to my family that there are few men whom I wish so much to see as Gov. Jay. If our lives should be spared till next summer, I will make an effort to visit you. I have a daughter settled in New Haven, little more than 50 miles from your residence, and I usually visit her at least once a year. However this may be, I shall never forget your public services, nor your private friendship for, Sir,
>
> > Your most obliged,
> > and obedient servant[55]

Jay immediately replied with a long letter of encouragement that said, in part, "Your dictionary will doubtless derive utility and Reputation from the extensive Investigation you mention. The assiduity with which you have for many years persevered, and still persevere in accomplishing this arduous Task, will I hope be followed by Results not only beneficial to the Public, but to yourself."[56]

7

IN 1822, Webster decided to sell his home in Amherst and move either to Boston or back to New Haven. A variety of factors precipitated his decision. One was financial. Massachusetts enacted a tax on all the personal property and assets of its residents. This would have included Webster's stock in the Hartford Bank (which he had helped found many years earlier), which was already taxed under Connecticut laws.

"This subjects my property to a double tax," he complained to his daughter Harriet Cobb. "This is unreasonable and appears to me illegal, or at least unjust. At any rate, the enormous taxes laid on me will compel me to sell my stock and convert it into some other property, or i must leave the town if not the state.

"There are other reasons for removal," he continued. "I have nearly given up thoughts of educating William for a profession. . . . I must then remove to some place where I can put him into business and inspect his management." In truth, Webster had all but despaired for the future of his only son, who, he admitted, only "studies a little and blows the flute."[57]

Still another reason for leaving Amherst was the completion of almost all the work on his great dictionary that he could do from the isolated Massachusetts hills. He needed access to major libraries at Yale, Harvard, or other large colleges. Although a move to Boston would have put the Websters close to Rebecca's family, they decided on New Haven and its proximity to their own daughters, grandchildren, and many friends from their previous years there. Life in New Haven would also be less costly than life in Boston and would allow the Websters to live in far grander style.

Revenues from the speller had increased substantially in the years following the War of 1812 because of a surge in the population. Annual sales averaged 350,000 copies, compared to 200,000 before the war. Webster bought an empty lot beneath the tall elms near the Yale campus, and he and his family squeezed into a rented house nearby while construction began on a new home.[58] Besides his wife and three youngest, unmarried children, Webster's family in New Haven included his widowed daughter, Harriet Cobb, and his granddaughter Mary Southgate, who replaced her mother, their beloved daughter Mary, in the Websters' hearts. Throughout her life, their granddaughter addressed them always as "Mother" and "Father" and signed her letters to them "Your affectionate daughter."

In 1823, Yale honored its son by conferring an honorary doctor of laws degree on the great lexicographer. A few weeks later, as a sixty-fifth birthday gift to her father, his daughter Harriet commissioned a more recent Yale graduate, the celebrated portrait artist Samuel F. B. Morse, to paint Webster's portrait (see the frontispiece). Morse was the son of Webster's old friend Jedidiah Morse, author of the great *American Geography*,[59] for which Webster had written a brief history of America.

8

AT THE END OF 1823, Webster finished extracting all materials pertinent to his dictionary from virtually every major American library. He had written to every library to ascertain what materials it had on hand and visited all those with books and manuscripts that were of value to him. He had progressed to the letter *r* but had been unable to determine the etymologies of so many words that he would either have to eliminate etymologies entirely or find other, older sources overseas to trace the origins and meanings of words farther back into antiquity. Unlike American colleges, both Cambridge and Oxford had renowned professors of linguistics, along with huge collections of dictionaries and encyclopedias dating back to the fifteenth and sixteenth centuries; the oldest available dictionary in America was Dr. Johnson's dictionary of 1744. Webster needed earlier etymological dictionaries: the *Etymologicon Linguae Anglicanae* of 1671, by Stephen Skinner; Thomas Bailey's *Dictionarium Britannicum, Urbanicum & Botanicum* of 1704 and *Universal Etymological Dictionary* of 1721; and the *Etymologium Anglicanum* of 1743, by Francis Junius. Webster also planned studying the Reverend George William Lemmon's *English Etymology, or A Derivative Dictionary of the English Language,* which was published in 1783 and traced every English word back to a Greek root. None of these works were available in America.

An equally important reason for traveling to England was to find a publisher for his great dictionary. He had all but despaired of finding subscribers in America but felt certain that Britain's more erudite academic community would support and even welcome a new, advanced, nineteenth-century dictionary to supplant Dr. Johnson's archaic eighteenth-century work.

By spring, Webster added France to his itinerary. He was fluent in both French and Latin and wanted to examine the great French encyclopedias to add the latest scientific terms to his dictionary. The famed Bibliothèque du Roi, or King's Library, in Paris, was one of the world's largest, with a trove of books and manuscripts that traced words to even earlier times than those at Cambridge and Oxford. The King's Library had not only remained intact during the French Revolution, but the leaders of the Revolution actually added to its collection by using it to warehouse some 250,000 books, 14,000 manuscripts, and 85,000 original prints that they had confiscated from the private collections of princes, émigrés, and clergy. After Louis XVIII and the ultraroyalists returned to power, restored calm in the streets, and made France safe for travelers again, they opened the library, with its expanded collection, to the public.

Webster again wrote to influential friends for subscriptions to finance his journey, but in the end, he had to raise most of the money for his trip himself. He sold much of his library and borrowed $1,000 from his daughter Harriet.

"If one thousand dollars will assist in affording aid to my dearest father in his contemplated journey to England," she told him, "he is at liberty to draw this sum in the name of his daughter, with the hope that should he succeed in his wishes, he may at some future time be able to repay it. But if otherwise and Providence should see fit that *disappointment* should be the result of the undertaking, then let this simply be considered as the *free* and *cheerful* gift of an affectionate child."[60]

On June 15, 1824, Webster boarded the packet *Edward Quesnel* with his twenty-three-year-old son, William, who was to serve his father as both companion and aide. Following his disastrous apprenticeship at fourteen, William had spent three equally disastrous years at Amherst Academy, where he embarrassed his family with his drinking. Although he enrolled successively at Yale and Middlebury Colleges, he had failed at each and was asked to withdraw. William further devastated his parents by quitting the church that all the Websters had embraced for more than two centuries and then accumulating debts that his infuriated father had to pay—just as he was trying to save enough to go to Europe. With William still a minor when he was at college, his creditors at Middlebury and New Haven had held the elder Webster personally responsible for the son's debts. "I hardly know which should excite most indignation, in my breast," the elder Webster railed, "the conduct of the debtor or of the creditors."

"Poor William," his mother said, "I wish he had more decision of character, what will become of him?"[61]

At twenty-three, William had no prospects for earning a living; and though he could barely afford the costs of his own trip, Webster thought it best to keep his son out of mischief by taking him to Europe and using him as a copier. Rebecca and her daughters Harriet and Eliza would be able to care for four-year-old Mary Southgate as well as the youngest Webster daughter, twelve-year-old Louisa. The Websters also had a maid and a serving girl working at the house. Julia's husband, Prof. Chauncey Goodrich, agreed to supervise Webster's publishing business.

As his family bowed their heads in their New Haven home, Webster read a prayer he had composed for his and his son's departure:

We entreat thee, Gracious God, to regard this family, in much mercy, during its approaching separation. May thy servants who are about to depart for a foreign land, be under thy constant guidance & protection. Wherever they may be, wilt thou be on their right hand & on their left, for their defence & their safety. Protect them from all dangers by sea & and from the influence of evil examples. Give them wisdom & prudence to guide them in all situations, & in due time may they return, rejoicing in thy goodness with thankfulness.

And may this family be the special case of thy kind protecting providence. Wilt thou watch over it & all its interests. Preserve all its members in safety. May our hearts be knit together in love to each other, &

may we all live in nearness to God, & enjoy the consolations of thy Grace.

Most gracious God, we commit our way to thee, trusting ourselves & all our interests, spiritual & temporal, to thy mercy in Jesus Christ.[62]

Webster wrote to Rebecca almost every day at sea:

Our company, consisting of bipeds & quadrupeds, is as follows—about 12 dozens of gallinaceous fowls, a dozen ducks, & about as many turkeys, half a dozen geese, about as many pigs, & sheep, a goat & three kids, one parrot, named Jaco, & a mongrel canary bird. Three French Ladies ["old and ugly as Macbeth's witches," according to son William], with one female servant, one English Colonel from Canada, an English Gentleman & Lady, with their son & a female servant. Eight or ten Frenchmen, three or four Americans, one German, one Swede, &c. Twenty one Passengers. The captain, crew & waiters, about twenty in numbers.

On Friday, the 18th, when in the Gulf-stream, we encountered a severe gale from the N E which compelled us to lie under a trysail or spenser, the whole day. This was to me a new scene, & extremely interesting. No person, who has been an eye-witness, can have an adequate idea of the awful grandeur of a tempest at sea. To see the ocean rolling in mountains, foaming & roaring, & the wind howling, is a scene that may well appall the stoutest heart. . . . William was sea-sick & lay in his birth all day. . . . I would not forget to mention, that in the midst of the storm we had a little comfort from the bird in the cage. . . . Indeed, we have a great variety of music & discords. The squealing of the pigs, the bleating of the sheep & goats, the crowing of the cocks, & the squalling of the Englishman's child, alternately or jointly salute our ears. These with the jabbering of the Frenchmen & with their humming & whistling, give us no little amusement.[63]

Although he spent most days playing whist, dominoes, and chess, Webster could not resist delivering an oration on July 4 to commemorate his nation's independence. After pointing out "the advantages that have actually accrued to both England and France since the separation of America from the old country," he closed with "an invitation to the ladies and gentlemen of both those nations to join us in celebrating the glorious event." Six days later, twenty-five days after they left New York, "a breeze . . . wafted us into Havre," at 8:30 A.M. on July 10.[64]

After settling in his hotel, Webster again wrote to Rebecca:

By the favor of divine Providence, I arrived here safely & in good health, this morning. . . . I am now writing in the Havre Hotel, but what a contrast a hotel here exhibits to one in America. . . . I cannot endure most of the dishes of French Cookery, but I generally find something that I can eat, & I have not yet lost a meal. . . . I believe the people of this town, who may be fifteen or twenty thousand, are generally poor, though there appears to be considerable trade. I have walked through the market, & it is to me a great curiosity, & thousand things, fish, vegetables & artificial things for food, for which I have no name. The market women sit bareheaded, some of them wear leather shoes, others clank about [in] their wooden shoes, with surprising ease. But the lower classes of people are a motley crew.[65]

Webster spared his wife descriptions of the army of rats that galloped through the streets of Le Havre—or the swarms of fleas that infested the mattresses and pillows of its hotels.[66]

Two days later, Webster and his son took the steamboat up the Seine River to Rouen, where after a night's rest they boarded a "diligence" for Paris. "This is such a thing as was never seen in America," Webster wrote excitedly. "It contains three apartments, that in front will carry four persons, the middle apartment, 6, & that behind, 4. On the top, is carried the baggage, perhaps half a ton or more, & a number of passengers. The vehicle is ten or twelve feet high, & looks as much like a Dutch hay rick as it does like a coach. It is drawn by four, five or six horses, three abreast, the driver or postilion rides one of them, & wears a pair of jack-boots which come above his knees, as in the days of Henry 7."[67]

William was less impressed, calling the coach "a large clumsy wagon," with six horses "not fit for a plough and with harnesses which would have disgraced the poorest beggars in America."[68]

The Websters took lodgings at 19, rue Bergère, "near the Boulevards at the house of Madame Riviere, who was several years in America, in Chancellor Livingstone's family & c." Webster complained that he had not seen "a carpet on a floor" in France. Although Webster's accommodations were only about ten minutes' walk from the rue de Richelieu and the Bibliothèque du Roi, they were

> not so good as I wish, the two rooms being small, only about 12 feet square, but I cannot afford the price of large apartments, & hope to make these rooms answer my purpose. I pay for board & lodging not quite 70 dollars a month, for both of us, which is considered here as a low price. Mrs Riviere is obliging to cook to my liking, as far as she can. Today she had an excellent piece of beef roasted *a l'Americaine,* without onions or garlic, & really I seem to be at home, but to wind up, we had a *plum pudding*—I believe the *first* her cook ever made, but it was very good. The French usually make their breakfast of bread & wine, and wine is their common drink at dinner, & even at supper, but I get good tea & *very good* coffee, such as I do not get anywhere except in France.[69]

At their first opportunity, Webster and his son went to the Bibliothèque du Roi, where they gasped as they stared up at the ribbed vaults that soared across the ceiling from their delicate perches atop a stand of exquisitely graceful columns. The walls carried more than a million books and eighty thousand manuscripts—twenty times the number of volumes in all of America's colleges combined.

Reconstructed interior (1851) Bibliothèque du Roi, Paris, where Noah Webster did research for his *American Dictionary of the English Language*. (From the author's collection.)

"I cannot give you a description of my feelings," Webster wrote to Becca. "To have an adequate idea of this collection of books, you must imagine rows of shelves 30 feet high, extending from the corner of my house to the Green, or public square [about three hundred yards]. If there is any exaggeration in this representation, there is not much."[70]

The Bibliothèque du Roi was one of the world's few truly public libraries. While most of the world's libraries were repositories that jealously guarded their treasures against wear and tear by the public, the King's Library in Paris was a public educative institution open to all twice a week. Its hospitable staff even offered free pens, ink, and paper to the five to six hundred readers who trooped in each day. Webster spent both days the library was open each week studying and copying from its extensive collection of encyclopedias. He pored over Antoine Furetière's original *Dictionnaire universel*, published in Rotterdam in 1690 after the Académie Française had banned it in Paris to protect their own, forthcoming dictionary from competition. Webster studied the original of that *Dictionnaire de l'Académie Française* of 1694, along with the updated edition of 1798. Here, too, was the twenty-eight-volume *Encyclopédie ou dictionnaire raisonné de sciences et métiers,* which Denis Diderot completed in 1772, after twenty years. It contained the knowledge of the world, compiled with the help of d'Alembert, Voltaire, Montesquieu, Rousseau, and other great French minds of the Enlightenment. The *Nouveau dictionnaire d'histoire naturelle,* which Georges Cuvier compiled and published in 1803 and 1804, added some of the world's most recent discoveries and scientific terms to Webster's lexicon. Webster also studied the three-volume *Dictionnaire étymologique de la langue française* of 1694, by M. Ménage. One by one, Webster verified questionable etymologies of words for his own dictionary and added terms and etymologies he had not found in America. He also pored over science texts, adding scores of scientific and technical words and definitions that might otherwise have remained unlisted.

Webster and his son spent six weeks in Paris, "as hard at work as ever I was at home. . . . I rise at six or soon after, & write two or three hours before breakfast, which is at about half past nine."[71] When not at the Bibliothèque du Roi, Webster transcribed the notes he had taken in the library, wrote new ones or rewrote old ones, and wrote long letters to Rebecca and the others at home. William divided his time between studying French and recopying the most heavily corrected of his father's entries into neat, legible form for the printer.

Occasionally, the two Websters strolled the great boulevards that lay but a block from their door. They crossed bridges on the Seine and visited the city's monuments and magnificent gardens. Ever the farm boy, Webster was enchanted by the spectacular Jardin des Plantes and its museum of natural history, which incorporated the world's first zoo. "These are magnificent establishments, & are sufficient alone to reward a man of taste for a voyage across the Atlantic," he wrote to Becca. "Every plant that will grow in the climate is here cultivated, & every species of animal from the whale, the camel & the elephant, to the smallest insect, is here found in a state of excellent preservation, the skins of all the larger animals being stuffed with care so as almost to present the real animal in life. The Cabinet of minerals is also very extensive." He was equally ecstatic about the gardens of Versailles, writing to Rebecca, "You would be delighted to ramble in the gardens of the palace. . . . But I perceive all the kinds of plants to be found in the large gardens in New York and Philadelphia."[72]

Webster stopped at the Chamber of Deputies, where he found that

members look better than the Country members of Massachusetts & Connecticut, as to dress, but not better than the more gentlemanly part of our legislatures. . . . I saw nothing of dignity in the proceedings of the house. The members were talking most of the time, & less order was observed than in the house of Representatives in Connecticut. . . . we visited the Hall of Audience or Council Chamber, where we saw most elegant portraits of the present King & his relations. The Duchess of

Angouleme has a bad face, & the most ugly eyes I ever saw. The King is a fat good-looking man.[73]

Webster was shocked by the spotty observance of the Sabbath in France. "The Catholics generally have no bibles, & the Sabbath is a day of amusement for the rich & the gay. The theaters are open every night, & one of the greatest inconveniences I experience is the noise of carriages at the breaking up of plays, about 12 at night." Webster scorned the theater: "Before I can believe the stage to be a school of virtue, I must demand proof that a single profligate had ever been reformed or a single man or woman made Christian by its influence. . . . I would caution you against the fascination of plays, novels, romances." The old Connecticut minuteman bristled at the "numerous guards of soldiers, *gens d'armes*. We meet them at every corner, & especially about the public buildings."[74]

Webster missed his wife and children more and more each day, and writing letters to them made him feel closer to home. "You may easily imagine how much I want to hear from home," he had written to Becca toward the end of a six-page letter to her on July 21, five weeks into his voyage. "I hope a few days now will relieve me. . . . Let me know, my dearest wife & children, how all things are at home. To know that you are well & happy will make me happy too."[75]

Finally, on August 9, a packet of letters arrived with cheerful news and "kindest love to William [and] dearest husband." On the same sheet, Harriet wrote that "after giving you the farewell kiss my dear Father, & brother, I remained in the cabin [of the boat back to New Haven] until all my tears were dry'd away."[76]

Webster answered tenderly: "This evening, my dear Becca, I have had the pleasure to see your hand-writing, your letter of June 23–26 having arriv'd. You may have some idea of the joy that this gives me. . . . I beg you to be less anxious about me, & Wm. We are in excellent health, & I think the climate more favorable to health than that of America."[77]

In mid-August, Webster learned that the Bibliothèque du Roi would close for the month of September, and he made preparations to go to Cambridge and Oxford. He had already written to various professors of linguistics at the two English universities, and in late August he heard from the Reverend Samuel Lee, a renowned professor of Arabic at Cambridge. A master of Coptic, Hebrew, Hindustani, Malay, Persian, Syriac, and ten other languages besides Arabic, Lee was author of many definitive works on languages and on translations of the scriptures from ancient manuscripts.

Lee described the costs of living at Cambridge and promised Webster, "I shall certainly be ready and willing to assist you in any way I can."[78] Webster thereupon made plans "to seat myself down at Cambridge" and wrote to Becca that he was confident "Dr Lee will lend me all the aid in his power."[79]

Late in August, Rebecca wrote to ask her husband's approval of Harriet's engagement to the Reverend William Chauncey Fowler, which Webster sent "most cheerfully" by return mail. "You know I have always chose to have my daughters please themselves & in doing that, they have hitherto pleased me. I sincerely wish them all the happiness of which the married state is susceptible. My love to both."[80]

Webster looked forward to leaving Paris. "The streets are incessantly thronged," he wrote to his daughter Eliza. "Carriages are running from three or four oclock in the morning till 12 at night without interruption, & they sometimes deprive me of sleep. The practice here is to breakfast from 9 o'clock to 11 or 12, & to dine at 5 or six. . . . These customs & the cookery are not pleasant to me, but by some sacrifices, on my part, & some accommodation on the part of the people where I live, I am pretty well supplied."[81]

Another batch of letters arrived before they left for England, with Becca telling Webster, "O, the Winter Squashes! perfect Mammoths, several of the largest have crept thro to Mr Sandford's & one poor squash (the largest I ever saw) in an attempt to emigrate is choked between the paling, the head on our side & body on Mr Sandford's. . . . Your letters my dear Husband make us as happy as we can be in your absence. Your picture [the portrait by Samuel Morse] is a great comfort to us."[82]

A letter from Harriet to William was also enclosed:

> I hope my dear brother you are constantly learning something in your new situation which will make you wiser & better, & that you will endeavor at all times to regard Pa's *interests* as well as his happiness. I long to have you back that you can assist me on the piano. . . . It is needless to repeat the pleasure your letters afforded. They perfectly crazed us with joy, and as to dear Mother, she hardly knew what she was about for many days. . . . Yesterday the newspaper was handed in which contained the account of the celebration of Independence on board ship. I felt in high glee & . . . read it to mother, forgetting not to mention what was undoubtedly omitted through carelessness, that this same *Mr. Webster &* *W. G. Webster* were the husband & son of *Becca Webster,* the Father & brother of *Harriet W. Cobb*—it sounded well & served for a laugh. Pity they should have forgotten this important fact, which would have clearly illustrated the reasons why they were such important personages. . . . Your account of the gale made us shudder.[83]

On September 8, Webster wrote to Becca, "I have obtained a passport for England & expect to leave Paris on monday next, the 13th & go by way of Rouen & Dieppe to Brighton, which is a shorter road than by Calais. . . . The [French] King's health is declining fast. He has now a kind of paralysis in the spine or back of the neck, which means he is unable to raise his head. He may live for weeks or months, but this is very uncertain. The Brother who will succeed him is about my age, but a man in good health."[84]

On the morning of September 16, the day before Webster left on the steamboat from Dieppe, King Louis XVIII died. "France is quiet," Webster wrote, "& the Kings brother comes peaceably into possession of the throne by the title of Charles X."[85]

9

AFTER A THIRTEEN-HOUR SAIL, Webster and his son reached Brighton, on England's south coast, and rode northward to London, where they spent two days before traveling farther north to Cambridge. On September 24, Webster wrote Becca that he had

> settled very snugly at lodgings for the winter. I have three rooms, a parlor & two bed rooms. The parlor, where I now sit, & where William & I write, & take our meals, is about 14 or 15 feet square. In this we have two little cabinets, two tables, a sofa & a few chairs, a handsome glass over the fire place, where we have a coal fire. . . . We board as well as lodge in the family, & Ann, the old servant, is very obliging. The expense is not greater than Paris. . . . The Colleges are mostly old stone buildings, which look very heavy, cold & gloomy to an American, accustomed to the new public buildings in our country.

Webster nevertheless found that "it is a pleasant thing to get among people that look & dress & eat & cook & talk like our own people."[86]

Dr. Lee's kindness gained Webster access to the volumes of the magnificent Wren Library at Trinity College, which housed the largest collection of books at Cambridge—nearly three hundred thousand volumes, including twenty-five hundred volumes of early manuscripts and two hundred seventy-five thousand printed books. Again, Webster concentrated on etymological dictionaries, scientific dictionaries, and encyclopedias, to ensure that he incorporated the widest possible vocabulary of words currently in use and provided the most accurate etymologies.

Although he had rented his lodgings for eight months, he needed only five months to complete his work. "I have nothing to do but to attend to my duties & my business," he wrote to Becca. "I want certainly the comfort & happiness of the presence of my dear consort & children. This thought sometimes chills me, but I am not distressed nor unhappy. I indulge the hope of meeting my family again in due time. I begin to grow uneasy that I do not hear from home."

Webster grew particularly lonely on October 16, his sixty-sixth birthday. "I think of you all very often with great affection," he wrote to Becca, "& sometimes my sensibilities are awakened in a degree to call forth a few tears. Still I am not unhappy. I have enjoyed very good health in Europe,

The exterior of the magnificent Wren Library, at Trinity College, Cambridge University, where Webster completed his *American Dictionary of the English Language*. (From the author's collection.)

& at no time for forty years past, have I been able to accomplish more business daily, than I have both in France & England."[87]

On November 11, Becca sent Webster a copy of a letter she had received addressed to him:

> New Haven, Novr 11, 1824
>
> Dear Sir,
>
> At a late meeting of the Phi Beta Kappa Society you were elected an honorary member of that Fraternity.
>
> The Society would be happy to be honoured with your attendance at future meetings and anniversaries of the members.

On the same sheet, Harriet appended this note: "I have taken this sheet of paper so full of honors, to fill up, because I wish you to know that you are remembered not only by your loving family & social circles, but also by the *literal* part of the community. When this letter was brought it gave mother great alarm—the sight of the black seal agitated her much. . . . We all miss you my dear Father very much, particularly after dismissing the tea table and arranging ourselves for the evening."[88]

Webster's work progressed at a faster rate than he had anticipated, and with time on his hands, he embarked on a daring new scheme to unify the English language not just in America but throughout the world. On December 20, with the Wren Library closed for Christmas holidays, he sent a letter to Professor Lee that should have been a landmark in the history of languages. He asked Lee to help organize a conference of linguists from Oxford and Cambridge Universities to unify the English language, with Webster himself representing American academe.

Webster predicted that, within two centuries, English would be "the language of one third or two fifths of all the inhabitants of the globe . . . [and] the instrument of propagating sciences, arts and the Christian religion." He called "the diversities of language among men . . . a curse and certainly one of the greatest evils that commerce, religion, and the social interests of men have to encounter." He said a conference of linguists could "resolve such points of difference in the practice of the two countries" and create a single unified language.[89]

Lee wholeheartedly embraced Webster's scheme, and he immediately recruited at least two other renowned English linguists at Cambridge who were equally enthusiastic: the Reverend Thomas Musgrave, professor of Arabic (who later became archbishop of York), and George Cecil Renouard, also a professor of Arabic, and like Lee one of the distinguished linguists of his day, with an intimate knowledge of French, German, Italian, Turkish, and Hebrew.

Both Musgrave and Renouard, along with several other Cambridge professors, met with Webster early in 1825 and became close personal as well as professional friends who would maintain a correspondence with Webster for the remainder of their lives. Although Lee and Webster each wrote to their peers at Oxford, the Oxford faculty, perhaps intent on remaining aloof from their Cambridge rivals, rejected the idea out of hand, and the conference—and the unification of the English language—never took place, despite overwhelming support at Cambridge. The rebuff by Oxford, however, did not end Webster's efforts at language unification, which he hoped his dictionary would facilitate.

Webster wrote to Becca:

> I lived very little known in Cambridge, till the last three weeks, when I was invited to dine with the Officers & Fellows of Trinity College. This introduction was followed by a visit from the Vice-Master, & two other invitations to dine in the same hall, & I took occasion, after retiring to the Combination-room, with the Officers & Fellows, to lay before the Gentlemen a general statement of what I have done & am doing, & what I wish in regard to the publication of my MSS. The Gentlemen take a great interest in my work, and some of them offered to subscribe for it. They also express great regret that they had not been made acquainted with me at an earlier period. From these Gentlemen & from several wealthy families in Cambridge, I shall receive very warm support.[90]

Late in January, after twenty years, Webster completed work on his great dictionary. The moment overwhelmed the aging scholar. "I finished writing my Dictionary in January, 1825, in my lodgings in Cambridge, England," he recalled a few years later. "When I had come to the last word, I was seized with a trembling which made it somewhat difficult to hold my pen steady for writing. The cause seems to have been the thought that I might not then live to finish the work, or the thought that I was so near the end of my labors. But I summoned strength to finish the last word, and then walking about the room a few minutes I recovered."[91]

On February 15, 1825, Webster completed his work at Cambridge and moved with his son to London, where letters of introduction from Professor Lee opened the doors to various libraries and the British Museum, for further research to refine his definitions. He also met with various printers, publishers, and booksellers but found little enthusiasm for a new dictionary. Most were burdened with a surplus of unsold copies of Henry Todd's 1818 edition of Johnson's dictionary, and Todd[92] was preparing a second edition that would add to their stocks. Webster nevertheless established a relationship with attorney John Miller, to whom he gave a power of attorney and instructions to continue the search for an English publisher.

After a short tour of southern England, Webster and his son sailed for America on May 18. They landed in New York a month later and were reunited with their family in New Haven the following day. By then, word had gone out from Cambridge University of the erudition of Webster's work, and the esteem with which that university's most distinguished scholars held it. Few could deny the grandeur of the dictionary—seventy thousand words, definitions, and etymological origins, all researched and written by hand over twenty years by a scholar now more than sixty-six years old, working entirely alone—the last lexicographer ever to do so. Even the great Dr. Johnson had relied on a staff of assistants to put together his dictionary of less than forty thousand words.

New Haven's most prominent citizens, along with the entire Yale faculty, turned out to greet and honor the great scholar. Family celebrations and reunions continued for a month, climaxing with the marriage, on July 26, of Webster's daughter Harriet to the Reverend Fowler, who had accepted a pastorship at Amherst.

At the end of the summer, Webster began the search for an American publisher, and shortly before the end of the year, he signed an agreement with Sherman Converse, in New York, who immediately sent to Germany for the unusual typefaces he would need.

Now assured that his magnum opus would be published, Webster saw absolutely no reason why anyone other than himself and his heirs should ever profit from a work to which he had devoted so many years of his life. He therefore renewed the struggle he had started a half century earlier for copyright protection—this time seeking a federal law granting authors copyrights to their materials in perpetuity. Noah Webster wrote to his cousin Daniel Webster, a Federalist who had been elected to the House of

Representatives from Massachusetts two years earlier. Pointing out that Britain had extended copyright protection to twenty-eight years, or twice the protection offered in the United States, Webster asked his younger cousin to propose new legislation in the House.

Daniel Webster replied, "I confess that I see, or think I see, objections to making it [copyright] perpetual. At the same time I am willing to extend it further than at present."[93] He took no immediate action, however, because he became engrossed in his campaign to win election to the U.S. Senate.

10

IN 1826, Webster's new son-in-law, Chauncey Fowler, resigned his pastorship and enrolled at Yale to prepare for a professorship at Middlebury College. At the same time, Fowler joined his father-in-law in the arduous task of preparing the gigantic manuscript and its seventy thousand entries for the printer. Before they were finished, however, Webster faced an annoying distraction: the sudden appearance of a number of new spelling books on the market, which threatened the near monopoly of *The American Spelling Book*. Far worse in his eyes, the new books used many of the English spellings that Webster had struggled for so many years to render obsolete. Unfortunately, he had changed his own spellings so many times in the more than one hundred editions of his speller that he had, in effect, never achieved his goal of standardizing American spellings. Depending on when they went to school and which edition of Webster's speller they had used, an entire generation of fathers probably learned many spellings that differed from those their children were learning. Moreover, his great new dictionary would undoubtedly render obsolete some spellings in the speller's latest edition, of 1818.

Many schoolmasters had grown confused by the constant changes. The old-fashioned, unchanging English spellings, as unpatriotic as Webster had portrayed them, had a good deal of appeal—a point made by a spate of newspaper articles assailing Webster's speller. As it turned out, most of the articles were written pseudonymously by Lyman Cobb, an obscure Midwestern schoolmaster who had written a speller of his own in 1821 and tried to compete with Webster's by pointing out its inconsistencies and errors.

Webster realized that he would have to prepare a new edition of his speller to conform with his new American dictionary, but he also realized that a new edition would render existing editions obsolete and leave printers with losses from unsold books. Each publisher had paid for the right to print a specified number of the old spellers and stood to lose huge sums if

AN

AMERICAN DICTIONARY

OF THE

ENGLISH LANGUAGE:

INTENDED TO EXHIBIT,

I. The origin, affinities and primary signification of English words, as far as they have been ascertained.
II. The genuine orthography and pronunciation of words, according to general usage, or to just principles of analogy.
III. Accurate and discriminating definitions, with numerous authorities and illustrations.

TO WHICH ARE PREFIXED,

AN INTRODUCTORY DISSERTATION

ON THE

ORIGIN, HISTORY AND CONNECTION OF THE

LANGUAGES OF WESTERN ASIA AND OF EUROPE,

AND A CONCISE GRAMMAR

OF THE

ENGLISH LANGUAGE.

BY NOAH WEBSTER, LL. D.

IN TWO VOLUMES.

VOL. I.

He that wishes to be counted among the benefactors of posterity, must add, by his own toil, to the acquisitions of his ancestors.—*Rambler.*

NEW YORK:

PUBLISHED BY S. CONVERSE.

PRINTED BY HEZEKIAH HOWE—NEW HAVEN.

1828.

The title page of Noah Webster's monumental *American Dictionary of the English Language,* first published in 1828. The book in this photograph was presented as a gift by Webster's only son, William Greenleaf Webster, whose signature is seen in the upper right-hand corner, along with the stamp of G. & C. Merriam & Co., which purchased exclusive rights to publish Webster's dictionary from the Webster family after Noah Webster's death, in 1843. (Beinecke Rare Book and Manuscript Library, Yale University.)

a new edition were introduced prematurely. Webster could not afford to alienate the printing industry.

He solved the problem by renaming the new edition of his speller *The Elementary Spelling Book* and postponing its publication and that of a new abridged school dictionary until after the great dictionary was published. He thus gave printers and booksellers time to sell their stocks of the 1818 speller, while promising standardization in future editions by ensuring that spellings conformed to those in the great dictionary.

In May 1827, printing of the dictionary got under way, and eighteen months later, in November 1828, a few weeks after Webster's seventieth birthday, the last pages of *An American Dictionary of the English Language* came off the press. The printer ran off twenty-five hundred copies and bound them in two bulky volumes in quarto (about nine inches wide by eleven inches tall), each about eight hundred pages, at $20 for the set, at retail.

For the first time in his life, Webster heard nothing but paeans from across the nation—indeed, from across the face of the earth—for his literary effort. Hailed by everyone from the president of the United States to the ordinary yeoman, Webster became America's literary hero. Even newspapers that had reviled him unremittingly as a "contemptible creature" and "prostitute wretch" referred to him reverentially as America's own Dr. Webster. College presidents, senators, and representatives hailed him; Congress and state legislatures issued congratulatory proclamations and, together with the courts, adopted Webster's dictionary as their official standard, thus making his the "federal language" he had spent his life attempting to create. Even foreign governments adopted it as their official English dictionary, relegating Dr. Johnson's dictionary to their stacks of rare and obsolete books. The *English Journal of Education* called Webster "the greatest lexicographer that has ever lived," while France's Royal Academy of Science in Paris awarded him its highest honors.

Webster, the patriot, took his place at last among America's founding fathers, as the father of the American language. His name and dictionary—"Webster's Dictionary"—entered the language, giving the phrase "Look it up in Webster's" a cachet of authority matched only, perhaps, by "The Bible says."

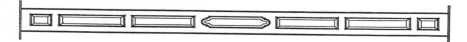

CHAPTER TEN

Elder Statesman

I

*A*N *AMERICAN DICTIONARY OF THE ENGLISH LANGUAGE,* "by Noah Webster, LL.D.," was a monumental work—the largest and best English dictionary ever before produced. With seventy thousand words, it was more comprehensive even than Todd's edition of Johnson's dictionary—by twelve thousand words—and it was recognizably better in every way, with a wider range of words, more precise definitions, easier-to-follow pronunciations, and far more complete etymologies. Webster traced the origins of some words back to the language that "God gave Adam." In addition to the body of words and definitions, the dictionary included an enormous "Dissertation on the Origin, History and Connection of the Languages of Western Asia and of Europe," an equally long "Concise Grammar of the English Language," and an extensive set of "Directions for the Pronunciation of Words."

In his preface, Webster dedicated the dictionary to God and offered it as a gift to the American people. "I present it to my fellow citizens," Webster wrote, ". . . with my ardent wishes for their improvement and happiness; and for the continued increase of the wealth, learning, the moral and religious elevation of character, and the glory, of my country." Then he added his "most grateful acknowledgements . . . To that great and benevolent Being, who, during the preparation of this work, has . . . given me strength and resolution to bring the work to a close. . . . And if the talent which entrusted to my care, has not been put to the most profitable use in his service, I hope it has not been 'kept laid up in a napkin,' and that any misapplication of it may be graciously forgiven."

From President Jackson to Webster's once-beloved yeoman, Americans accepted his gift and hailed him as a literary hero. Retired chancellor James

Kent, one of America's great judges and legal minds and a contributor to the *Federalist* papers, predicted that Webster's dictionary would outlive "obelisks, arches and triumphant arches"—even the pyramids and the Parthenon. He ranked Webster with Columbus and Washington, "among the most important men in American history."[1]

In England, the London *Times* wrote, "We can have no hesitation in giving it our decided opinion that this is the most elaborate and successful undertaking of the kind which has ever appeared."[2] The *Westminster Review* described the dictionary as "a work of admirable practical utility . . . that will enlighten and inform the most profound of our philologists."[3] German literary journals echoed the sentiments, and France's Royal Academy, as mentioned earlier, also paid him homage.

An elated Rebecca Webster, who had comforted her husband through years of constant abuse by the press, wrote to daughter Harriet on February 16, 1829: "And now, Dear Pod, I must tell a little about your Father and the babe which he has dandled twenty years and more. Mr. Converse writes that it is everywhere well received and the expectations of the public are fully answered. Letters are flowing in from every quarter to your father, praising the work with encomiums that amount almost to hyperbole."[4]

Webster, of course, was overjoyed—even overwhelmed—by the deluge of praise. To Becca's letter to Harriet he added, "I have just been reading Chancellor Kent's flights of fancy." Nevertheless, Webster was deeply grateful to those friends who, like Kent, had supported him during his many years of lonely travail. Indeed, the seventy-year-old lexicographer rode fifty miles by carriage through the cold November winds to John Jay's home in Bedford, New York, to present the aged jurist with the first two sets from the bindery. Jay died six months later.

A few Boston Anglophiles, of course, could not resist the occasional snide remark, but Webster's supporters quickly silenced them by quoting the patriotic preface to his dictionary: "In purity, in elegance, and in technical precision, [American writing] is equaled only by that of the best British authors, and surpassed by that of no English compositions of a similar kind." To crush his Anglophile enemies, Webster even quoted their revered Dr. Johnson. "The chief glory of a nation," Johnson had said, "arises from its authors." Webster then listed the names of Franklin, Washington, Adams, Madison, Jay, Kent, and Irving. "It is with pride and satisfaction," he wrote, "that I can place them, as authorities, on the same page with those of [the English] Boyle, Hooker, Milton, Dryden, Addison. . . . I may go further and affirm with truth that our country had produced some of the best models of composition." He cited "the style of the authors of the Federalist papers . . . of Chancellor Kent; the prose of Mr. Barlow . . . of Washington Irving; of the legal decisions of the Supreme Court of the United States and many other writings as unsurpassed by any works in English of a similar kind."[5]

His traditional critics were left with little they could, or knew how to, criticize. Originally a radical language reformer, Webster had settled on moderate reforms that only mirrored popular usage and had standardized English orthography by using etymology to determine the definitive spelling of every word. Where he included some of his own spelling reforms, he did so simply as an alternative to the traditional spelling—he listed both *fether* and *feather*, for example—without insisting, as he had in earlier years, that his was the only legitimate spelling.

In any case, even entries that merited scholarly criticism were too firmly wrapped in patriotic and religious bunting to attack. Americans were experiencing a widespread spiritual and patriotic revival, and only those with self-destructive instincts dared criticize God or country, which were the primary underpinnings of Webster's work. Webster made that perfectly clear. The first word in his title was *American*—*An American Dictionary*—and his introduction proclaimed language to be "of divine origin."

Even his least scholarly definitions were too often linked to the divine to risk criticizing:

> **Indebted,** *a.* . . . . We are *indebted* to our parents for their care of us in infancy and youth; we are *indebted* to God for life; we are *indebted to* the Christian religion *for* many of the advantages and much of the refinement of modern times.
>
> **Happy,** *a.* . . . . The pleasurable sensations derived from the gratification of sensual appetites render a person temporarily *happy;* he can be esteemed really and permanently *happy,* who enjoys peace of mind in the favor of God.
>
> **Love,** *n.* . . . . The *love* of God is the first duty of man.
>
> **Love,** *v.t.* . . . . The Christian *loves* his Bible. . . . If our hearts are right, we *love* God above all things.

Webster used patriotism just as blatantly:

> **Inestimable,** *a.* . . . . The privileges of American citizens, civil and religious, are *inestimable.*
>
> **Patriotism,** *n.* . . . . *Patriotism* is the characteristic of a good citizen, the noblest passion that animates a man in the character of a citizen.
>
> **Presidency,** *n.* . . . . The Office of president. Washington was elected to the *presidency* of the United States by a unanimous vote of the electors.
>
> **Witness,** *v.t.* . . . . To see or know by personal experience. I *witnessed* the ceremonies in New York, with which the ratification of the constitution was celebrated in 1788.

In addition to invoking God and country, Webster, for perhaps the first time in his life, infused his words with a gentle modesty instead of the didactic arrogance that had characterized some of his earlier works. "This Dictionary, like all others of the kind, must be left, in some degree, imperfect," he said softly. "For what individual is competent to trace to their source, and define in all their various applications, popular, scientific and technical, *sixty* or *seventy thousand* words! It satisfies my mind that I have done all that my health, my talents and my pecuniary means would enable me to accomplish."[6]

No author before or since has ever written a dictionary with so broad a purpose—and that is what made his work so remarkable. It was not just a list of words and definitions. It was a wellspring of truths that promised his countrymen an increase in "the wealth, learning, moral and religious elevation of character, and glory" of their country—a self-contained educative institution designed to serve as a secular companion to the Bible. If the Bible taught Americans how to live their spiritual lives, his dictionary would teach them how to live their temporal lives at home and in their communities.

It taught morality and child rearing:

> **Honor,** *n*. . . . *a distinguishing trait in the character of good men.*
> **Indulgence,** *n*. . . . How many children are ruined by *indulgence*! *Indulgence* is not kindness or tenderness, but it may be the effect of one or the other, or of negligence.
> **Instruct,** *v.t.* . . . The first duty of parents is to *instruct* their children in the principles of religion and morality.
> **Learn,** *v.t.* . . . It is much easier to *learn* what is right, than to unlearn what is wrong.
> **Parent,** *n*. . . . The duties of *parents* to their children are to maintain, protect, and educate them.

It lobbied blatantly for new laws and constitutional amendments:

> **Press,** *n*. . . . A free *press* is a great blessing to a free people; a licentious *press* is a curse to society.
> **Property,** *n*. . . . *Literary property;* the exclusive right of printing, publishing, and making profit by one's own writings. No right or title to a thing can be so perfect as that which is created by a man's own labor and invention. The exclusive right of a man to his literary productions, and the use of them for his own profit, is entire and perfect, as the faculties employed and labor bestowed are entirely and perfectly his own. On what principle, then, can a legislature or a court determine that an author enjoy only a *temporary property* in his own productions? If a man's right to his own *productions in writing* is as perfect as to the *productions* of his farm or his shop, how can the former be abridged or limited, while the latter is held without limitation? Why do the *productions of a manual labor* rank higher in the scale of rights or *property,* than the *productions of the intellect?*

It offered practical suggestions:

> **Sauce,** *n*. . . . *Sauce,* consisting of stewed apples, is a great article in some parts of new England; but cranberries make the most delicious *sauce*.

Scold, *v.i.* . . . . A *scolding* tongue, a *scolding* wife, a *scolding* husband, a *scolding* master, who can endure?

It often waxed poetic or entertained:

Modesty, *n.* . . . . Unaffected *modesty* is the sweetest charm of female excellence, the richest gem in the diadem of their honor.
Female, *a.* . . . Noting the sex which produces young; not male. . . . Pertaining to tenderness; as a *female* hand or heart. . . . "To the generous decision of a female mind, we owe the discovery of America." *Belknap.*[7]

Apart from their reticence to criticize God or country, few if any American scholars had the knowledge or education to criticize Webster's dictionary intelligently. Lexicography and etymology, especially, were relatively new areas of scholarship, and no one in America knew enough to question whether the root of a particular word stemmed from, say, an old Saxon, or Chaldean, or Syriac word. Much of Webster's etymology was indeed wrong, but who knew? He was America's *only* authority—George Washington, Benjamin Franklin, and the presidents of every American college had publicly attested to it—and no one, not even those who disliked him personally, dared question his authority.

In any case, the time was right for a new dictionary. More than seventy years had passed since the publication of Dr. Johnson's work. Two revolutions had shattered the political landscape of the Western world, and scientific advances had produced hundreds of new words and concepts. Although other English dictionaries had appeared, they varied little from Johnson's and offered few advances in orthography and few new words born of the scientific and industrial revolutions. The English-speaking world desperately needed a new, definitive dictionary, and Webster filled that need.

His dictionary advanced the limits of lexicography, adding elements that had never before been seen in a comparable work. Many of his definitions, for example, were careful to discriminate between American and English usages—something no lexicographer had ever done. He introduced colloquial and idiomatic, as well as proper, meanings, pointing out that the word *spell,* for example, also means "a short time" and that idiomatic usages of the verb *to make* include *to make a bed, to make amends, to make good, to make free with, to make light of, to make love, to make merry, to make suit, to make over, to make out, to make of,* and so on. No dictionary had ever included such comprehensive definitions. Some widely used American colloquialisms such as *whittle* earned separate listings, but unlike Dr. Johnson, Webster excluded vulgarities, obscenities, and eroticisms.

In addition, Webster's definitions were more precise than Johnson's. In effect, he was a more skilled instructor, able to *teach* as well as to *define* the meanings of words. For example, Dr. Johnson had contented himself to define *telescope* as "a long glass by which distant objects are viewed." In contrast, Webster wrote,

> An optical instrument employed in viewing distant objects, as the heavenly bodies. It assists the eye chiefly in two ways: first by enlarging the visual angle under which a distant object is seen, and thus magnifying that object; and secondly, by collecting and conveying to the eye a larger beam of light than would enter the naked organ, and thus rendering objects distinct and visible which would otherwise be indistinct and invisible. Its essential parts are the *object-glass,* which collects the beams of light and forms an image of the object, and the *eyeglass,* which is a microscope by which the image is magnified.[8]

The widespread acceptance of Webster's dictionary as the new standard necessarily discouraged classroom use of spelling books whose orthography did not conform to his. In 1829, Webster completed a new edition of his *American Spelling Book* that not only conformed to the spelling in his dictionary but bore his authoritative name. He published it in July under the new name of *The Elementary Spelling Book,* and it immediately recaptured the monopoly of his older spellers and pushed competitive spellers, such as Cobb's, out of most American classrooms.

Webster also issued a new small school dictionary with the new orthography to accompany his speller, and he published an abridged version of the great dictionary for sale to families and others who did not need as extensive a work as the two-volume edition. He hired Joseph Worcester, a Yale graduate of the class of 1810 and an author of geography and history texts, to do the abridgement for a fee of $2,000. Worcester, who had also taught school for five years, had recently finished editing Todd's *Johnson* for the American market and was, therefore, knowledgeable about lexicography.

Despite Todd's two revisions of Dr. Johnson's dictionary, even the English recognized that it was out of date. In February 1829, as Webster was reaping honors in America, the renowned British scholar, linguist, and editor Edmund Henry Barker of Thetford, Norfolk, decided to reprint Webster's dictionary in England and make it the new standard of the language there as well as in America. Under an agreement he signed with John Miller, Webster's London attorney, Barker agreed to give Webster one-sixth of the profits.

Of all scholars in England, few were more qualified to handle the project than Barker. Although he had no master's or doctor's degree, Barker was a Cambridge University graduate with a mysterious O.T.N. degree appended to his name. No one knew what it meant but no one questioned it, because he had edited and published so vast a number of scholarly works by Greek and Latin authors, ranging from Aesop and Demosthenes to Cato and

Catullus. He had compiled and published a definitive Greek-and-English lexicon and had edited and produced an edition each of Lemprière's *Classical Dictionary* and the ten-volume sixteenth-century *Thesaurus Graecae Linguae* of Henry Stephens.

In all of these and many other successful ventures, E. H. Barker, O.T.N., had the financial backing of the extraordinary Dawson Turner, who, like Barker, was a Cambridge graduate. A brilliant botanist, Turner abandoned science to take over his father's bank upon the latter's death but kept botany as an avocation, becoming one of Britain's preeminent field botanists and a renowned author on the subject. He used his wealth to accumulate one of the world's largest collections of books and manuscripts on natural history. Turner was also a patron of scholarly works. He had financed many of Barker's previous works, and in February 1829, Barker automatically turned to Turner to solicit support for an English edition of Webster's dictionary.

"This Webster," Barker wrote to Turner, "is a vast improvement on *Todd's Johnson*, & if the speculation answers, as I may well expect, I shall make a good thing out of it, & I can make it the foundation of a *national* work such as we all want. This book of Webster is a vast step in English lexicography. I reprint the book under his sanction. . . . It will add a splendid jewel to my crown, bringing this book into England."[9]

In exchange for one-third of all profits, Turner agreed to provide the difference between the funds raised from advance subscriptions and the actual costs of producing an edition of three thousand of the Webster dictionaries—five hundred more than the first American edition. Barker signed an agreement with Webster's London attorney, retitled the work (*A Dictionary of the English Language,* by N. Webster, LL.D.), and eliminated Webster's religio-nationalistic references, including the preface.

Webster, in the meantime, wrote to his friends at Cambridge University to ensure an enthusiastic reception for the dictionary. The chancellor of the university responded by becoming one of the first subscribers, along with the Trinity College library, where Webster had done his final research for the dictionary. Not to be outdone by his rival at Cambridge, the chancellor of Oxford also subscribed, setting off a flow of subscriptions from all parts of England. In contrast to America's unenthusiastic response twenty years early, the eagerness of British sponsors put Americans to shame. Indeed, the British seemed determined to translate into reality Webster's vision four years earlier, when he was completing his dictionary at Cambridge, of unifying the English and American languages.

By September 30, the list of British subscribers had grown to 861, and early the following year, Barker was able to write to Turner:

> We have a highly respectable list of subscribers; among them many
> Colleges in Cambridge, two of its professors, three Heads of Houses,

DR. WEBSTER'S ENGLISH DICTIONARY.

PROPOSALS FOR REPRINTING

A DICTIONARY

OF

THE ENGLISH LANGUAGE:

INTENDED TO EXHIBIT

1. The Origin and the Affinities of every English Word, as far as they have been ascertained, with its Primary Signification, as now generally established.

2. The Orthography and the Pronunciation of Words, as sanctioned by reputable Usage, and where this Usage is divided, as determinable by a reference to the Principle of Analogy;

3. Accurate and Discriminating Definitions of Technical and Scientific Terms, with Numerous Authorities and Illustrations.

TO WHICH ARE PREFIXED

AN INTRODUCTORY DISSERTATION ON THE ORIGIN, HISTORY, AND CONNECTION OF THE LANGUAGES OF WESTERN ASIA AND OF EUROPE,

AND

A CONCISE GRAMMAR, PHILOSOPHICAL AND PRACTICAL, OF THE ENGLISH LANGUAGE.

BY N. WEBSTER, LL.D.

IN TWO VOLUMES QUARTO.

CONDITIONS OF PUBLICATION:

1. The Dictionary will be printed in 4to, with new types cast for the purpose, on a fine wove demy paper;—

2. The Work will appear in 12 Parts, each consisting of 20 sheets, at intervals of two months;—

3. Part I. will be published on *the 15th of February* next; Part II. on the first of April; and the continuation will be regularly put forth;—

4. The Dictionary will be published by subscription, price 7s. for each Part to Subscribers, who shall send their names for the whole Work, and 9s. to Non-Subscribers. The Subscription will continue open till the appearance of the Third Part.

5. The *total* price to Subscribers will be £4. 4s. and to Non-Subscribers, £5. 8s. ;—

6. The Work will be printed by Mr. Richard Taylor, of Red Lion Court, Fleet Street; and Subscribers are requested to send their names either direct, (*by Letters post-paid,*) or through their booksellers to the publishers,

MESSRS. BLACK, YOUNG, AND YOUNG,

Foreign Booksellers, 2, Tavistock Street, Covent Garden.

SUBSCRIBERS.

His Royal Highness the Duke of Sussex.
His Royal Highness the Duke of Gloucester, Chancellor of the University of Cambridge.
The Right Hon. Lord Aberdeen, Secretary of State for the Foreign Department.
The Right Hon. the Earl of Carlisle.
The Right Hon. Lord Grenville, Chancellor of the University of Oxford.
His Grace the Duke of Grafton.

The Right Rev. the Bishop of Lincoln, Master of Christ-College, Cambridge.
The Right Hon. Lord Viscount Milton, 2 *Copies.*
The Right Hon. Lord Palmerston, M.P. for the University of Cambridge.
The Right Hon. Robert Peel, M.P. Secretary of State for the Home Department.
The Right Hon. Lord Stafford.

The English edition of Webster's great *American Dictionary* was intended to unite the American and English orthographies of the English language. The circular shows elements of the title page, along with the names of the first subscribers. (Dawson Turner Papers, Wren Library, Trinity College, Cambridge University.)

both its MPs, the Dukes of Gloucester & Sussex & Grafton, Lords Aberdeen, Carlisle, Grenville, Stafford, Mr. [Robert] Peel, the Home Office, the Foreign Office, the London Institution, the Cathedral Library at York, & a number of eminent literary characters. Still we want the aid of the faithful. The book is the most learned book ever published in America . . . the most perfect Dictionary in existence. All English Lexicographers, compared to Webster, sink into nothing, *surly Sam* [Dr. Samuel Johnson] alone excepted.[10]

The English edition of Webster's dictionary was printed by Richard Taylor, of Red Lion Court, Fleet Street. The "Conditions of Publication" stated that the two-volume work

will appear in 12 Parts, each consisting of 20 sheets, at intervals of two months. . . . Part I, will be published on the *15th of February* next [1830]; Part II, on the first of April, and the continuation will be regularly put forth. . . . The Dictionary will be published by subscription, price 7s. for each part to Subscribers, who shall send their names for the whole Work, and 9s. to Non-Subscribers. The Subscription will continue open till the appearance of the Third Part. . . . The *total* price to Subscribers will be £4. 4s. and to Non-Subscribers, £5. 8s.[11]

After the first installment of the dictionary appeared, Barker wrote to Turner, "The cause of *Webster* flourishes. . . . I send you 4 copies of our *enlarged* List of Subscribers. . . . On examining this fresh list you will . . . find that the trade are taking us up: 4 booksellers (Baldwin, Deighton, Longman & Simpkins) take 70 copies between them: of the 4, Longman and Baldwin are principal proprietors of *Todd's Johnson*. The nobility & upper gentry are backward in subscribing: all the noblemen on our list were gained by my individual application."[12]

No less skilled a book peddler than Webster, Barker flooded the press with pseudonymously signed letters, which he wrote himself, praising the merits of the new dictionary. One letter signed "Bookseller"—probably Barker—said, "Nothing I have seen in the shape of a dictionary can be compared with it; it is admirable, unsurpassable. . . . It is a right noble monument of learning & talents, of judgment & discrimination, of industry, research & perseverance."[13]

In April 1830, when the second part of the dictionary appeared, Barker again wrote to Turner: "The cause of Webster continues to thrive, but the Nobility & upper gentry come forward slowly with their subscriptions, while the book sellers, speaking generally, behave handsomely. The grandees, will find themselves obliged to have the book in the end, & if they will not pay the subscription price by sending their names within the time allowed for subscription, faith! they will have to pay the *non*-subscription price, which will be so much the better for us."[14]

Barker sent each installment of "Dr. Webster's English Dictionary" to Webster as it appeared, and Webster, of course, never failed to respond, constantly adding new words and providing his English benefactor with unsolicited criticisms. In general, he told Barker, "I am well pleased with the execution. . . . I am glad to find my dictionary so well received in England; I hope your prospects of profit will be realized. I shall make efforts to add value to the work."[15]

Advances in science and industry forced Webster to amend the dictionary continually. In June, Webster sent Barker a letter noting that "*steam-carriage* is not in my book, for the invention is recent. But it may be well to add it, provided the thing has taken any definite form. I believe *rail-road & railway* are now used as synonymous—but it might be well to suggest under these words that a useful difference might be made—*rail-road* might be the name of the high way in which a *rail-way* is laid, but the *rail-way* to be limited to the rails & appendages which support the vehicles."[16] (In fact, the two words remained synonymous, with *railway* becoming the standard English word for what Americans now call a *railroad*.) In November, Webster asked Barker to add thirteen new words, including *dualism, dogmatic,* and *malaria.*

Webster was not pleased, however, with the changes Barker had made to the title page, nor with the preface that he had written and substituted for Webster's original. Barker had eliminated Webster's condescending references to "certain errors in the best English dictionaries" and the need for "the people of this country . . . [to] have an *American Dictionary of the English Language.*" Barker also eliminated references to Webster's theory of radical words.

"I must protest against the liberty you have taken," Webster wrote to Barker. "I beg you to reprint the page, according to my copy & send it to your subscribers." Webster believed Barker's changes would "expose the work to just criticism; & if so, you must take the responsibility on yourself, for I must disavow the article as it now stands."[17]

2

IN 1829, Webster's son-in-law William W. Ellsworth won election to Congress as a representative from Connecticut, and he and his wife, Emily, Webster's oldest daughter, moved to Washington, D.C., with their children. Ellsworth's first legislative initiative was the introduction of the new copyright law that his father-in-law had sought earlier from Daniel Webster.

With the Ellsworths in Washington and their other daughters scattered across the New England landscape, the sixty-nine-year-old Webster and his wife decided to spend the summer visiting as many of their children, grandchildren, and other relatives as possible, including his dysfunctional seventy-nine-year-old brother, Abram.

Sullivan June 1st 1830 Madison County

Dear Brother

I thought it well to let you know where I might be found in case you should come this way in the course of the summer. We live on the great road leading from Utica to Buffalo & about one & one half mile from the Canal. My Daughter who married Mr Adams is in Vernon 18 miles east of this place. We do hope you will come here this summer & bring sister with you. What pleasure it would give us to see you once more in this life. If we ever meet again on earth it must be soon[.] our days are almost numbered[.] you have lived beyond what is called the ordinary age of man & I fall but little short of fourscore. May God give us grace that we may "so number our days to apply our Hearts unto wisdom." . . . Do write to us soon & let us know whether your are coming or not. . . .

Your Affectionate Brother.[18]

Noah Webster went to see his older brother for the last time that October. Abram Webster died the following year, and his heartbroken younger brother determined to spend as much time as possible in his own remaining days visiting his children and grandchildren and luring them for frequent reciprocal visits to New Haven. Between visits, he wrote to them all, almost constantly—even sending an occasional note in Latin to his precocious four-year-old granddaughter Emily Ellsworth Fowler:

Novo Portu, Feb'y. die novo 1830

Carissima Nepte.

Epistola vestra, in Latina lingua scripta, a me recepta et perlecta est. Ago tibi gratias pro hoc testimonio amoris vestri. Hic amor est mihi gratissimus. Magna pars epistolae est recte composita. Gaudeo scire quo modo fratres vestri occupati sunt, sive ludendo, sive edendo, et noscere totam familiam patris vestri sanitate sui; praecipue matrem tuam convalescere. . . .

Perge, dilecta puella, in studio laudabile literorum, et opto te felicam esse.

vale sic vocit avus vester

New Haven, Feb. ninth day 1830

Dearest Grand Daughter,

Your letter, written in the Latin language has been received and read by me. I give you thanks for this testimony of your love. This affection is most gratifying to me. The greater part of the letter is correctly written. I rejoice to know, how your brothers are occupied, whether playing or eating, and to learn that the whole family of your father is well; especially that your mother is convalescent. . . .

Continue dear girl, the praiseworthy study of language and I wish you to be happy.

Farewell, your grandfather[19]

3

BY LATE 1830, Representative Ellsworth's efforts to obtain passage of his father-in-law's proposed amendment of the copyright law had met with nothing but rejection by the House Judiciary Committee. In mid-December, Webster decided to go to Washington to lobby personally for passage of the bill. It proved a brilliant decision.

The city of Washington greeted him as a national hero. "When I came here," he wrote to his daughter Harriet Fowler,

> I found members of both houses coming to me and saying, they had learned in my books, they were glad to see me, and ready to do me any kindness in their power. They all seemed to think, also, that my great labors deserve some uncommon reward. I know of nothing that has given me more pleasure in my journeys . . . than the respect and kindness manifested toward me in consequence of the use of my books. It convinces me that my fellow citizens consider me as their benefactor and the benefactor of my country.[20]

On December 28, President Jackson, the consummate Democrat, invited the old Federalist Webster "to dine with him, and I could not well avoid it."[21] To Webster, Jackson represented all the evils of popular rule by the uneducated and unpropertied. Webster had voted against Jackson in 1828, only to see Jackson win in a landslide over incumbent president John Quincy Adams. Jackson's victory crushed the last remnants of Federalism. Even Webster's old friend Oliver Wolcott had ceded his office as governor of Connecticut and returned to private business in New York.

Webster nevertheless refrained from engaging in political debate with Jackson. "The President," he wrote to Harriet,

> was very sociable and placed me, as a stranger, at his right hand. The party, mostly members of the two houses, consisted of about thirty. The table was garnished with artificial flowers placed in gilt urns, supported by female figures, on gilt waiters. We had a great variety of dishes, French and Italian cooking. I do not know the names. . . . I wonder at our great men who introduce foreign customs, to the great annoyance of American guests. To avoid annoyance as much as possible, the practice is to dine at home and go the President's to see and be seen, to talk and to nibble fruit, and to drink very good wines. As to *dining* at the President's table in the true sense of the word, there is no such thing.[22]

On the evening of January 3, 1831, the House of Representatives invited Webster to address "a respectable number of ladies and gentlemen." According to his daughter Emily Ellsworth, "It was an interesting lecture to all who heard it. Some complained it was too short. He spoke nearly an hour. The darkness and humidity of the weather prevented some from attending.

"I think, however, enough were present to get the bill through," she wrote to her mother. "I think all who heard him were convinced. He said nothing by way of self-praise—perfectly indirect. He urged no claims. He said, should the bill for extending the copyright law be carried successfully, he should rejoice for himself, for his family, for his country. I think it will succeed."[23]

On January 7, an elated Webster wrote to his wife:

Dear Becca

Emily & I have just returned from the Capitol, & we were in the gallery when the house of Repvs passed the Copyright bill, without a division. It is believed the bill will meet with no obstacles in the Senate. I have reason to think my presence here has been very useful in this affair; & I rejoice very much in the result. If the bill should pass in the Senate, it will add very much to the value of my property.

I begin to be invited to parties, but shall avoid them as much as possible, except those which are given by N. England people . . . it is all so disagreeable to me; & as I wish to avoid parties I have called on none of the heads of departments, & foreign ministers. Love to all.[24]

With Daniel Webster as sponsor in the Senate, Congress finished enacting Noah Webster's proposed copyright bill at the end of January, and the president signed it into law the next month. The new bill, which remained in effect in whole or in part until 1909, gave authors and proprietors the right to copyright their works for twenty-eight years and allowed their wives and children to renew the copyright for an additional fourteen years. Webster wrote to his son-in-law William Fowler, who had become professor of mineralogy and chemistry at Middlebury College: "This law will add much to the value of my property, and I cannot but hope I may now make dispositions of copyright which will make me comfortable during the remainder of my life, and secure to Mrs. Webster, if she should survive me, a decent independence."[25]

Before leaving Washington, Webster, ever the Yankee peddler, drew up a testimonial that he hoped Congress would transform into a formal resolution urging the nation's schools to adopt his "Series of books for systematic instruction in the English Language." The testimonial listed his *American Dictionary,* in both the abridged and unabridged editions, his dictionary for schools, and his *Elementary Spelling Book.* Failing enactment of a law, he felt an endorsement of some sort from Congress would be useful as a promotional device—even if it only amounted to the signatures of Congressmen on his testimonial.

"This paper," he wrote to Rebecca, "has been circulated in both houses of Congress, and is subscribed by more than a hundred of the Senators and Representatives . . . the signatures of such a respectable number of gentlemen from every state in the Union, will be of no inconsiderable use to me."[26]

Webster printed the paper in circular form. "The subscribers," it stated,

> highly appreciate Dr. Webster's purpose and attempt to improve the
> English language by rendering its orthography more simple, regular and
> uniform. The merits of Dr. Webster's *American Dictionary of the English
> Language,* are very extensively acknowledged. . . . We regard it as a great
> improvement on all the works which have preceded it. . . .
>
> The value and success of that work will no doubt contribute towards
> securing for the *Elementary Spelling Book,* by the same author, a currency
> with the public, corresponding to that which its predecessor, the *Ameri-
> can Spelling Book,* so long possessed . . . and render this book, in our
> opinion, highly valuable for the purposes of elementary instruction.
>
> It seems desirable that the children in this country should be in-
> structed, if possible, in one form of orthography and pronunciation; and
> it is still more important that they should not be taught an antiquated
> orthography rarely seen in books which they are afterwards to read.
>
> Dr. Webster's Dictionaries and Spelling book constitute a series of
> books for the purpose of instruction, which, we hope, will find their
> way into all our schools. We use them ourselves, and we most cheerfully
> recommend them to the general use of our fellow citizens.[27]

After obtaining the signatures of seventy-three representatives and thirty-one senators—including his cousin Daniel Webster—Noah Webster set off on a promotional tour, traveling as far north as Portland, Maine, to sell his new speller and his dictionaries. He stopped briefly in New Haven to see his family and to obtain additional endorsements from the president and faculty at Yale. He published the endorsements as a small pamphlet and mailed it to newspapers, schoolmasters, and ministers across the nation.

The pamphlet infuriated Lyman Cobb, who immediately tried to slow the Webster juggernaut with a barrage of articles—thirteen in all—denouncing Webster for inconsistencies and "errours."[28] Cobb did manage to sell several million copies of his own speller, but as publishers and printers adopted Webster's spellings in the readers they produced for schools, Webster's book became essential for acquiring the necessary reading skills, and it gradually forced competitive spellers such as Cobb's book off the market. In 1836, the publishing success of the *McGuffey Readers,* a series of books by the respected Cincinnati educator William Holmes McGuffey and his brother Alexander, indirectly secured a monopoly for Webster's speller in almost every classroom in the nation for the rest of the nineteenth century. In a triumph akin to that of Webster's original speller, the brilliantly written *McGuffey Readers* captured the entire school market almost overnight, displacing almost all older readers, including Webster's. But while destroying the fortunes of Webster's reader, the *McGuffey Readers* sent sales of Webster's speller soaring because of the McGuffeys' decision to use only Webster's orthography in their books. The choice of Webster's orthography forced every schoolmaster to teach students to read, write, and spell with

Series of books for systematic instruction in the English Language. By N. WEBSTER.

1. The AMERICAN DICTIONARY in quarto, containing ample etymologies of words, showing the affinity of the English language with many others, both in Asia and Europe; with copious, accurate and discriminating definitions, illustrated by examples.

2. An *Abridgment of the quarto, in an octavo form,* containing the chief etymologies, and brief definitions, with a key to the pronunciation. In this the words are divided into syllables; a synopsis of words differently pronounced by six different British orthoepists, is prefixed; and Walker's key to the pronunciation of classical and scripture proper names, is annexed.

3. A *Dictionary for schools, the counting house, and for families in moderate circumstances;* a manual containing more than forty thousand words, which are in common use, divided into syllables and accented, with a key to the pronunciation. To this are annexed tables of the moneys in use among commercial nations, reduced to their value in sterling and in dollars and cents.

4. An *Elementary Spelling Book,* in which words are classed according to their terminations; the lessons for spelling are divided into short sections, interspersed with familiar lessons for reading; rules and examples are given for forming derivative words; and the same key and the same orthography are used as in the school dictionary.

One very important object of this series of books, is, to reduce to *uniformity,* the orthography of a great number of words which are differently written by different authors. English books differ in the orthography of a multitude of words, and this diversity is extremely perplexing to all classes of people; but to none so much as to teachers. To increase the evil, the obsolete orthography of some classes of words is continued in English dictionaries, and copied into elementary books in this country, in which children are instructed in an orthography different from that which is found in books which they are afterwards to read. Books furnish no rules nor any settled usage on this subject. This unsettled state of orthography is deemed a reproach to the literature of England; it is embarrassing to our own citizens, as well as to foreigners who learn our language; and it appears to be an object as useful as it is honorable, to attempt, at this early period of the American republic, to impress a different character on our language.

The estimation in which this system is held, by gentlemen of erudition, appears from the following testimonials.

The merits of Dr. WEBSTER's *American Dictionary of the English Language,* are very extensively acknowledged by that part of the community for whose immediate use it was designed. We regard it as a great improvement on all the works which have preceded it. The *etymological* department throws new and striking light on the history of language; the *vocabulary* is enlarged by the addition of many thousand words, comprising the technical words of science and the arts, words not found in other dictionaries, and many of them the words for the precise meaning of which the general reader is most frequently at a loss; the *orthography* of several classes of words, instead of following cumbrous and obsolete modes of spelling, is conformed to the present usage of the best writers; and the *definitions* have a character of discrimination, copiousness, perspicuity, and accuracy, not found, we believe, in any other dictionary of the English language.

The value and success of that work will no doubt contribute towards securing for the *Elementary Spelling Book,* by the same author, a currency with the public, corresponding to that which its predecessor, the *American Spelling Book,* so long possessed. In this book, not only the orthography and pronunciation, with perhaps here and there a disputable exception, are conformed to the best modern usage; but, in addition to this improvement, the selection and classification of the spelling lessons—the adaptation of the reading lessons to the gradually expanding faculties of children—and the simplicity of the scheme for exhibiting the pronunciation of words, render this book, in our opinion, highly valuable for the purposes of elementary instruction.

It seems desirable that the children in this country should be instructed, if possible, in one form of orthography and pronunciation; and it is still more important that they should not be taught an antiquated orthography rarely seen in the books which they are afterwards to read.

Dr. Webster's Dictionaries and Spelling Book constitute a series of books for the purpose of instruction, which, we hope, will find their way into all our schools. We use them ourselves, and we most cheerfully recommend them to the general use of our fellow citizens.

The foregoing commendation is signed by
JEREMIAH DAY, *President of Yale College.*
SIMEON BALDWIN, *late Judge of the Superior Court.*
DAVID DAGGETT, *Judge of the Superior Court.*
Rev. SAMUEL MERWIN.
Rev. CLAUDIUS HERRICK.
BENJAMIN SILLIMAN, *Professor of Chemistry, &c. Yale College.*
Rev. HARRY CROSWELL.
WILLIAM BRISTOL, *Judge of the District Court.*
Rev. NATHANIEL W. TAYLOR, S. T. D.
JAMES L. KINGSLEY, *Professor of Hebrew, &c. Yale College.*
CHAUNCEY A. GOODRICH, *Professor of Rhetoric, &c. Yale College.*
Rev. LEONARD BACON.
DENISON OLMSTED, *Professor of Mathematics, &c. Yale College.*

A circular for Noah Webster's system of instruction, based on his books. Webster attempted to obtain a congressional resolution recommending them to elementary schools across America. (Webster Papers, New York Public Library.)

Webster's speller before they were able to progress to the *McGuffey Readers*. The McGuffeys thus helped entrench Webster's speller as the national standard of elementary schools throughout the nation.

Webster nevertheless recognized that nine new states had been added to the United States west of the Appalachian Mountains, where his name had less significance than in the original thirteen states. He appointed an agent to travel the West and sell his books on a commission basis. The agent also found a Western publisher for the speller, and it became as ubiquitous in Ohio, Indiana, Michigan, and Illinois classrooms as it was in those of the East and South.

Adding to the sales momentum of Webster's books was the addition of two more works—a *Biography, for the Use of Schools*,[29] which he wrote in 1830, and a *History of the United States*.[30] The former was a charming volume of thirty-seven concise biographies, of which twenty-one were of famous Americans such as George Washington and Benjamin Franklin. Seven figures from the scriptures, including Jesus, were among the remaining sixteen biographies, along with authors ranging from Homer to William Cowper. Webster's 350-page history traced the development of the United States from the origins of the human race to the discovery and settlement of America by western Europeans. An important work because of its widespread use, Webster's history tied every great development in the United States to Protestant Christianity and the guiding hand of God.

"Almost all the civil liberty now enjoyed in the world owes its origin to the principles of the Christian religion," he wrote.

> Men began to understand their natural rights, as soon as the reformation from popery began to dawn in the sixteenth century; and civil liberty has been gradually advancing and improving, as genuine Christianity has prevailed. By the principles of the Christian religion we are not to understand the decisions of ecclesiastical councils, for these are the opinions of mere men; nor are we to suppose that religion to be any particular church established by law, with numerous dignitaries, living in stately palaces, arrayed in gorgeous attire, and rioting in luxury and wealth, squeezed from the scanty earnings of the laboring poor.[31]

Webster said that his Puritan ancestors were

> the founders of the first genuine republic in the world, and affirmed that the principles of republican government have their origin in the Scriptures.
>
> For the progress and enjoyment of civil and religious liberty, in modern times, the world is more indebted to the Puritans in Great Britain and America, than to any other body of men, or to any other cause. . . . They rejected all ostentatious forms and rites; they were industrious in their callings, and plain in their apparel. They rejected all distinctions among men, which . . . exalt one class of men over another, in rights or property.

The Puritans who planted the first colonies in New England, established institutions on republican principles. They admitted no superiority in ecclesiastical orders, but formed churches on the plan of the independence of each church. They distributed the land among all persons, in free hold, by which every man, lord of his own soil, enjoyed independence of opinion and of rights. They founded governments on the principle that the people are the sources of power; the representatives being elected annually, and of course responsible to their constituents. And especially they made early provision for schools for diffusing knowledge among all their members of their communities, that the people might learn their rights and their duties. Their liberal and wise institutions, which were then novelties in the world, have been the foundation of our republican government.[32]

As his books found their way into classrooms, Webster was invited to preside at periodic teachers' conventions in Hartford and other New England cities. He also became an active member of the Society for the Improvement of Common Schools, which eventually brought compulsory universal public education to Connecticut and helped create a state system of public elementary schools, with uniform educational standards.

4

SALES OF WEBSTER'S DICTIONARY in England were outpacing those in America. E. H. Barker wrote to his financial patron Dawson Turner in the spring of 1830 that "the business thrives. . . . The subscription will close on Aug 1 to a certainty & we have good reason to expect that we shall have 1000 subscribers by that time. . . . We have been very favorably noticed in several newspapers. . . . The book gives great satisfaction to the subscribers. . . . It is a grand undertaking of mine, which will be eminently successful in the end."[33] By early July, Barker began planning a second edition of the dictionary and the publication of Webster's grammar—originally part II of Webster's *Institute*—as a separate book. "The Grammar," Barker wrote, "is very far superior to . . . any of our English grammars. We shall have to publish it in separate form."[34] Indeed, Barker was so enthusiastic about Webster's work that he made plans to publish Webster's *Elementary Spelling Book*. Webster's entire system of instruction would now make its way into English schools and eventually unify the English language throughout the world—with Webster's "American" orthography as the new standard.

In October, Barker wrote Turner:

The booksellers are a good deal surprised at the progress, which we have made, & the certainty of final success. Dr. Webster some years ago, when his work was not far advanced . . . wanted to make terms with the London publishers of Todd's Johnson for the reprint of his work in England, but these short-sighted gentlemen declined the offer, lest the sale of Todd's Johnson should be affected by such a reprint. They did not discover the value of the work: they did not see that it must ultimately rise on the ruins of Todd's Johnson, & that it was important for *them* to keep the market of English lexicography in their own hands. They will now have the merited satisfaction of seeing this work yield earlier & better profits than have been derived from Todd's *Johnson.*[35]

The last of the three thousand copies of the first edition of Webster's English dictionary were sold on January 30, 1832, and as in America, it was becoming the standard for English in Britain. Barker had freely confessed to Turner about his harvest of profits, but by the spring of 1832, Webster had yet to receive a penny—despite a flood of exasperatingly long, euphoric letters from Barker forecasting huge sales of the dictionary not only in England but in Canada, France, and Germany as well. Barker had an annoying habit of never saying in one or two words what he could say in ten or twenty—but he more than compensated for his extravagant use of words with a reticence to dispense money.

During the previous year, Barker had suggested that Webster accept payment in sheets, which later proved too costly to ship. In March 1832, Barker came up with an even more audacious scheme for not paying Webster: he sent a letter with a subscription sheet for another book that he planned to publish and suggested that "if any of your friends like to subscribe, let them pay you for the Nos., as they appear, & the amount, which you receive in this way, will be in the nature of a remittance made to you by me on account of your share in our English reprint of your *Dictionary*. But, while your friends will of course pay to you the *full* price of £3.3.0., we shall charge a copy to you *at the trade price* only £2.7.3. We shall *present* you with a copy for yourself, of course."

Then, almost parenthetically, Barker added, "I think that in less than 12 months we shall have covered all our expenses, & be in a condition to make a remittance to you as the first-fruits of your share [in the dictionary]. The advertising alone cost us £350 or nearer £400, because the duty on advertisements is heavy. . . . I continue to make collections for a *second* edition."[36]

Webster was furious—and exasperated by Barker's endless projections. He wanted some money, and instead of his usual warmth, he replied in the curt manner of a Connecticut Yankee schoolmaster:

Dear Sir,

You mention in your last letter that in less than a year, you suppose the sales of the American Dictionary will reimburse expenses & afford me some fruit of my labors. In a former letter you stated that you had printed 3000 copies. Now if 1200 copies will pay the outlay, then 1800 remain for profit. At £4-5-6 there would amount to between seven & eight thousand pounds—& at £5-10 to more than nine thousand pounds. If I am to receive anything from the work, I wish to receive it as conveniently it can be paid. I am advanced in life—I could apply the money to valuable purposes, & I wish not to leave any obligation on you to account with those who are to succeed me.

I would much rather choose to take a less sum than one *sixth* of the profits, provided it can be received at the present time. I wish you to make me an offer, as liberal as you can, of a sum in lieu of the sixth, & permit me to draw a bill for the amount at three months sight—or at farthest four months sight. If your offer should be reasonable, I would accept it, & give you an acquittance of all demand for the sixth of the whole impression.

PS I have not heard whether the 8avo [octavo] has been reprinted in England or Scotland. Nor have I seen any notice of the 4to [quarto] in the French or German journals.[37]

At the end of summer, more than two years after the English edition of Webster's dictionary had been published, E. H. Barker sent Webster an even wordier and more equivocal letter. He wrote of having received eight hundred subscriptions for a second edition of two thousand copies of the dictionary but said he needed £1,000 pounds of the profits from the first edition to "cover the expenses of *paper* & *print*" for the second. Sales of the first edition, he pleaded, had slowed, and "*profits* are not *yet* in sight. If I were in a condition to make you a *fair* offer for the value of your share in the work . . . I should willingly do so, but my outlay on these works precludes the possibility, as you will see when I inform you that I hold *four-sixths* of the property, & am therefore liable to pay *four-sixths* of the expenses."[38]

Barker promised to review the situation after Christmas, but added that Webster could help matters if he could sell copies of the English edition in America. Not only did the letter annoy Webster, he despaired of ever seeing a penny's profit from the English edition of his dictionary.

5

IN THE AUTUMN OF 1832, Webster refused to vote in the presidential election. He despised President Jackson as the embodiment of the evils of universal popular suffrage, which allowed the ignorant and unpropertied masses to vote. The Federalist party had disappeared, and Jefferson's Democratic-Republicans had split into two parties, the Democrats and the Republicans. Webster saw no difference between them. Both, he said, espoused the principle that "the *people* can govern themselves, and that a *democracy* is . . . a *free* government. . . . But in practice the word *people* denotes any collection of individuals either in meetings legally assembled, or in mobs, collected suddenly, no matter how, for any purpose good or bad."[39] He said the illiterate and unpropertied were too easily manipulated because they had no direct interests of their own to protect.

Webster's position isolated him, as never before, from America's political leadership and popular political thought. Even before the War of 1812, New Jersey and Maryland had abolished property ownership and tax paying as qualifications for voting, and after the war, Indiana, Alabama, Maine, New York, and Massachusetts had done the same. Even in his own state of Connecticut, Gov. Oliver Wolcott, of all people—Webster's close friend, Yale classmate, fellow Calvinist, and a former Federalist leader—had approved a new state constitution that granted universal male suffrage. And in state after state, the selection of presidential electors had been transferred from state legislatures to the people. Webster shook his head in disbelief.

After Jackson's reelection, in 1832, Rebecca Webster described her husband's feelings in a letter to one of her daughters: "Your Papa is sitting in his rocking chair with a paper in his hand. . . . Once in a while a deep groan escapes from him at the critical state of our country." Rebecca quoted her husband as saying, "What a dark cloud hangs over us and how will it end? In a dreadful hurricane I fear. We are now experiencing as a nation the curse of having 'a wicked man placed over us, with Satan standing at his right hand.' "[40]

Despite his political alienation, Webster remained the generous, hospitable man he had always been, and as in their earlier years, the Webster home was a center of social activity—for the Yale faculty, for visiting clergymen and old Federalists, and for noted figures in the arts such as Samuel Morse, the artist and inventor, and Jared Sparks, the historian and educator.

"Since I wrote you last," Rebecca wrote to her daughter, "I have had a large party . . . [with] as many of the faculty as we could *cram* in. The party went off well, for all seemed happy, especially Mrs. Leverett when she got alongside your father."[41]

In addition to his notable guests, a growing brood of Webster grandchildren came for frequent and extended visits. Their famous grandfather kept a plate filled with candies and raisins, luring them into his study and onto his lap for as long as he could keep them, to tell stories, teach them to read and write, and listen to tales of their adventures. He was somewhat intimidating, however, and they reserved another kind of love for their grandmother, who served as beloved confidante. When the oldest grandsons from the Ellsworth and Goodrich families attended Yale, Rebecca entertained them and their friends with musical parties, "old-time frolics," and at least one costume ball.[42]

6

IN 1832, Noah Webster began what he called "the most important enterprise of my life"—transcribing the Bible and all the marginal notes he had made in his own copy of the Bible into understandable American literary idiom.[43]

Throughout Webster's life, the Bible had been the nation's most widely read book—in and out of school. Although his speller and *Compendious Dictionary* had become the most important secular textbooks, the Bible remained the nation's most important text for divine truths, and he believed it was a key to his lifelong plan to create a single American language in the United States. "The language of the Bible," he said, "has no inconsiderable influence in preserving our national language."[44]

Few if any American households did not have at least one Bible to provide comfort, solace, family bonds, entertainment, instruction, and revelation. Before the dictionary, speller, or primer came the Bible: parents and teachers alike had used it to teach children to read, and Webster had always objected to that application because of its "uniform antique style."[45] A universally used text, he argued, should speak its message in a universally understood language. The 1611 text was written in the common language of that era, but nineteenth-century Americans could no longer understand it. The common man of 1833 deserved a text he could understand, and Webster set out to provide it—in a modern American English based on his orthography. By rewriting the Bible in the same language as his speller and dictionary, Webster would ensure that all Americans would read, write, and speak alike. The new Bible would complete his American system of education.

From the moment of his conversion, in the spring of 1808, Webster had kept his Bible—the King James Version of 1611—close to his person. Each time he sought solace from it, he made notes on the margins of its pages, correcting spellings, modernizing grammatical structures, and substituting modern Americanisms for archaic or difficult-to-understand terms. Such biblical emendations became part of his daily routine during the more than twenty years that he worked on his dictionary.

He was not the first American to try to modernize the language of the Bible, of course, but he was the first lexicographer and certainly the most skilled American linguist to attempt it.

"Some words have fallen into disuse," he explained, "and the signification of others in current popular use is not the same now as it was when they were introduced into the version. . . . Whenever words are understood in a sense differently from that which they had when introduced, and different from that of the original languages, they do not present to the readers the Word of God."[46]

Webster characterized his changes as falling into three categories:

1. The substitution of words and phrases now in good use for such as are wholly obsolete, or deemed below the dignity and solemnity of the subject.
2. The correction of errors in grammar.
3. The insertion of euphemisms, words and phrases which are not very offensive to delicacy, in the place of such as cannot, with propriety, be uttered before a promiscuous audience.[47]

Webster changed relative pronouns and articles to conform with modern usage. He substituted modern words for archaic ones, updated spellings, and systemized verb forms such as *should, would, shall,* and *will*. His changes were not radical or shocking; he did not, for example, eliminate the second-person-singular pronouns *thee, thy,* and *thou,* or the *-eth* verb endings—but he modernized and simplified the language just enough to allow ordinary eyes to move smoothly and without hesitation across the text. *Take no thought,* for example, became *be not anxious; Holy Ghost* became *Holy Spirit; tache* became *button; chapiter* became *capital;* and he replaced *which* with *who,* when it referred to a person, as in *Our Father who* instead of *Our Father which.*

Passages in the King James Version of 1611 with confusing pronouns—such as "And he shall be like a tree . . . that bringeth forth his fruit in his season, his leafe also shall not wither, and whatsoever he doeth shall prosper"—became clearer: "And he shall be like a tree . . . that bringeth forth its fruit in its season; its leaf also shall not wither; and whatsoever he doeth shall prosper."

Webster reduced the frequency with which the names *God* and *Christ* appeared. He had done the same with his speller a half century earlier, saying then, "Nothing has greater tendency to lessen the reverence which mankind ought to have for the Supreme Being than a careless repetition of God's name upon every trifling occasion." After studying earlier versions of the Bible, he found that the name of God had been inserted with far more frequency in the 1611 version than in earlier ones, on the theory that repetition of God's name would bring Him closer to the reader. Webster believed that excessive use of God's name in the 1611 Bible was directly responsible for the introduction into popular speech of such blasphemous exclamatory phrases as "Oh, God!"[48]

Webster's Bible substituted phrases such as *O that* (from earlier Bibles) for the 1611 Bible's *would God* or *would to God,* and *by no means* for *God forbid.* He also eliminated all sexually suggestive language, declaring that "many words and phrases are so offensive, especially to females, as to create a reluctance in young persons to attend bible classes and schools, in which they are required to read passages which cannot be repeated without a blush; and containing words which on other occasions a child could not utter without rebuke. The effect is to divert the mind from the *matter* to the *language* of the Scriptures, and thus, in a degree, frustrate the purpose of giving instruction."[49]

To accomplish his goal of desexualizing the Bible, he exorcised the word *whore* and all references to male genitalia; he all but eliminated the word *womb* and changed *fornication* to *lewdness* or *lewd deeds;* and he replaced *teats* with *breasts.*

Webster published his revised version of the Bible—*The Holy Bible . . . With Amendments of the Language*—in October 1833. He revised the first lines of Genesis to read:

In the beginning God created the heaven and the earth.

And the earth was without form, and void; and darkness *was* upon the face of the deep: and the Spirit of God moved upon the face of the waters.

And God said, Let there be light: and there was light.

And God saw the light, that *it was* good: and God divided the light from the darkness.

And God called the light Day, and the darkness he called Night: and the evening and the morning were the first day.

At the age of seventy-five, Noah Webster had completed his life's goal of creating a body of literature and a complete system of education in a single American language that would be studied by all Americans and unify them culturally as a single people. "In this edition" of the Bible, he explained, "I have further improved the language, & completed my design. . . . With this work my literary labors must close."[50]

Completion of his Bible took on particular meaning for him, coming as it did after the death, that same year, of Oliver Wolcott Jr., the last of his closest friends from Mother Yale. All the others were gone: Barlow, Trumbull, Dwight, Stiles, Meigs—and now Wolcott. Wolcott's death also left Webster as the only survivor among the original Federalists: Washington, Adams, Hamilton, Jay, Rush, King, Pickering, Watson, and the others were dead. Webster was the sole survivor—the last sentry at the gate that divided liberty from license.

To his consternation, his revised version of the Bible met with little interest from scholars, clerics, or churchgoers. "It wounds my feelings," he admitted, "to observe how indifferent the public are, and especially clergymen, to the correction of faults in the common version. . . . I wish a few clergymen would summon courage to commend my Bible to the public."[51] None did. In December 1835, as a courtesy to their distinguished alumnus, the Yale faculty issued a cryptic testimonial saying that "Dr. Webster's edition of the Bible . . . is approved and used by many clergymen and other gentlemen very competent to judge its merits."[52] Its rejection was so universal, however, that it became one of the rarest American Bibles ever produced. Webster had the few that he did not give to churches "handsomely bound," as gifts for each of his children and grandchildren.

7

JUST AS HE LAUNCHED HIS BIBLE into a sea of indifference, the fortunes of his great dictionary began to flounder—in England as well as America. His publishers in both countries went bankrupt: Sherman Converse in New York, and E. H. Barker, O.T.N., in Thetford, Norfolk—the latter after an unlikely scandal involving claims to his ancestral lands.

THE

HOLY BIBLE,

CONTAINING THE

OLD AND NEW TESTAMENTS,

IN THE

COMMON VERSION.

WITH

AMENDMENTS OF THE LANGUAGE,

BY NOAH WEBSTER, LL. D.

NEW HAVEN:

PUBLISHED BY DURRIE & PECK.

Sold by HEZEKIAH HOWE & Co., and A. H. MALTBY, *New Haven;*
and by N. & J. WHITE, *New York.*

1833.

The title page from Noah Webster's revision of the Bible into American English, from a facsimile edition. (Noah Webster Foundation.)

GENESIS.

CHAP. I.

1 *The creation of heaven and earth, 3 of the light, 6 of the firmament, 9 of the earth sepa-rated from the waters, 11 and made fruitful, 14 of the sun, moon, and stars, 20 of fish and fowl, 24 of beasts and cattle, 26 of man in the image of God. 29 Also the appointment of food.*

IN the *a* beginning God created the heaven and the earth.

2 And the earth was without form, and void; and darkness *was* upon the face of the deep: and the Spirit of God moved upon the face of the waters.

3 And God said, *b* Let there be light: and there was light.

4 And God saw the light, that *it was* good: and God divided 1 the light from the darkness.

5 And God called the light Day, and the darkness he called Night: 2 and the evening and the morning were the first day.

6 ¶ And God said, *c* Let there be 3 a firmament in the midst of the waters, and let it divide the waters from the waters.

7 And God made the firmament; and divided the waters which *were* under the firmament from the waters which *were* above the firmament: and it was so.

8 And God called the *d* firmament Heaven: and the evening and the morning were the second day.

9 ¶ And God said, *e* Let the waters under the heaven be gathered into one place, and let the dry *land* appear: and it was so.

10 And God called the dry *land* Earth, and the collection of waters he called Seas: and God saw that it *was* good.

11 And God said, Let the earth bring forth 4 grass, the herb yielding seed, *and* the fruit-tree yielding fruit after its kind, whose seed *is* in itself, upon the earth: and it was so.

12 And the earth brought forth grass, *and* herb yielding seed after its kind, and the tree yielding fruit, whose seed *was* in itself, after its kind: and God saw that it *was* good.

13 And the evening and the morning were the third day.

14 ¶ And God said, Let there be *f* lights in the firmament of the heaven, to divide 5 the day from the night: and let them be for signs, and for seasons, and for days, and years.

15 And let them be for lights in the firmament of the heaven, to give light upon the earth: and it was so.

16 And God made two great lights; the greater light *6* to rule the day, and

Before CHRIST, 4004.

a Psal. 33. 6.
& 136. 5.
Acts 14. 15.
& 17. 24.
Heb. 11. 3.

b 2 Cor. 4. 6.

1 Heb. *be-tween the light and between the darkness.*

2 Heb. *and the evening was, and the morning was, &c.*

c Ps. 136. 5.
Jer. 10. 12.
& 51. 15.

3 Heb. *ex-panse.*

d Jer. 51. 15.

e Job 38. 8.
Ps. 33. 7.
& 136. 6.

4 Heb. *ten-der grass.*

f Deut. 4. 19.
Ps. 136. 7.

5 Heb. *be-tween the day and be-tween the night.*

6 Heb. *for the rule of the day, &c.*

g Jer. 31. 35.

h 2 Esdr. 6. 47.

7 or, *creep-ing.*

8 Heb. *soul.*

9 Heb. *face of the firma-ment of heaven.*

i c. 8. 17.
& 9. 1.

k c. 5. 1.
& 9. 6.
1 Cor. 11. 7.
James 3. 9.
Ephes. 4. 24.
Col. 3. 10.

l Mat. 19. 4.

m c. 9. 1.

10 Heb. *seed-ing seed.*

n c. 9. 3.

the lesser light to rule the night: *he made* the stars also.

17 And God set them in the firmament of the heaven, to give light upon the earth.

18 And to *g* rule over the day, and over the night, and to divide the light from the darkness: and God saw that it *was* good.

19 And the evening and the morning were the fourth day.

20 And God said, *h* Let the waters bring forth abundantly the 7 moving creature that hath 8 life, and fowl *that* may fly above the earth in the 9 open firmament of heaven.

21 And God created great whales, and every living creature that moveth, which the waters brought forth abundantly af-ter their kind, and every winged fowl after his kind: and God saw that it *was* good.

22 And God blessed them, saying, *i* Be fruitful, and multiply, and fill the waters in the seas, and let fowl multiply in the earth.

23 And the evening and the morning were the fifth day.

24 ¶ And God said, Let the earth bring forth the living creature after his kind, cattle, and the creeping animal, and the beast of the earth after his kind: and it was so.

25 And God made the beast of the earth after his kind, and cattle after their kind, and every animal that creepeth upon the earth after his kind: and God saw that it *was* good.

26 ¶ And God said, *k* Let us make man in our image, after our likeness: and let them have dominion over the fish of the sea, and over the fowl of the air, and over the cattle, and over all the earth, and over every creeping animal that creepeth upon the earth.

27 So God created man in his *own* im-age, in the image of God created he him; *l* male and female created he them.

28 And God blessed them, and God said to them, *m* Be fruitful, and multiply, and replenish the earth, and subdue it: and have dominion over the fish of the sea, and over the fowl of the air, and over every living animal that moveth upon the earth.

29 ¶ And God said, Behold, I have given you every herb 10 bearing seed, which *is* upon the face of all the earth, and every tree, in which *is* the fruit of a tree yielding seed; *n* to you it shall be for food.

The first page of Genesis in Webster's American version of the Bible, from a facsimile edition. (Noah Webster Foundation.)

Barker was the son of a vicar whose legitimacy was suspect. Obsessed with the black mark on his family, Barker spent ten years accumulating evidence about his father's birth and sued the York jurisdiction. Ultimately, he won a verdict affirming his father's—and therefore his own—legitimacy.

Instead of folding up his birth certificate and returning to publishing, Barker let two charlatans lure him into a scheme involving a long-lost will of his great-uncle's that they said they had uncovered in a search of old records. The will gave Barker a claim to ancient Barker family estates, worth about £3,000 a year. In pursuit of the claim, Barker's associates ran up huge debts, bleeding the unsuspecting scholar of all his money, including the money he owed Webster. Investigators exposed the claim—along with his O.T.N. degree—as forgeries, and Barker was ruined. Although the charlatans had forged the will, Barker himself had invented the O.T.N., which meant nothing more than "Of *Thetford in Norfolk*," where he lived. He had tacked it onto his name to compensate for his lack of legitimate graduate degrees in the scholars' world in which he traveled. The court sentenced Barker to London's Fleet Prison, where he atoned, but he emerged a broken man after a year. He died a year later, in 1838, leaving "Dr. Webster's English Dictionary" without the aggressive promoter needed to publish a second edition and consummate its capture of the English market.

To make matters worse, just as Barker was about to emerge from prison, in 1837, a London schoolmaster, Charles Richardson, took advantage of Barker's absence by publishing his own *New Dictionary of the English Language*,[53] which restored most of the English spellings Webster had Americanized—with the exception of the *k*'s in *music, public,* and *traffic.* At seventy-two, Webster no longer had the energy to travel to England to find another publisher. Barker never published Webster's speller or grammar as he had promised to do, and Webster's dictionary quickly disappeared from English bookshops, along with his dream of unifying the English language.

Unfortunately, his *American Dictionary* was faring no better in America than in England. Five years after he first published it, Sherman Converse suffered irretrievable losses from various speculations and was as bankrupt as Barker. As in Britain, Webster was left with no publisher for a second edition to expand the dictionary's hold on the market. And as in Britain, it was neither Webster's fault nor that of his great dictionary that its publication came to an abrupt halt. It was just rotten luck.

In 1834, Joseph Worcester, the young man Webster had hired to abridge the *American Dictionary,* stepped into the void and published his own *Comprehensive Pronouncing and Explanatory Dictionary*,[54] which omitted all etymology and used an orthography midway between Dr. Johnson's and Webster's. Ironically, it was the *Palladium,* the Tory newspaper in Massachusetts that had assailed Webster so viciously for his political positions, that came to the old lexicographer's defense:

A gross plagiarism has been committed by Mr. J. E. Worcester on the literary property of Noah Webster, Esq. It is well known that Mr. Webster has spent a life, which is now somewhat advanced, in writing a dictionary of the English language, which he published in 1828. . . . Three abridgements have since been made . . . for families and primary schools. To aid in the drudgery of providing these abridgements, Mr. Webster employed Mr. Worcester, who after becoming acquainted with Mr. Webster's plan, immediately set about appropriating to his own benefit the valuable labors, acquisitions, and productions of Mr. Webster. He has since published a dictionary, which is a very close imitation of Webster's; and which, we regret to learn, has since been introduced into many of the primary schools of the country. We regret this, because the public, inadvertently, do an act of great injustice to a man who has rendered the country an invaluable service, and ought to receive the full benefit of his labors. If we had a statute which could fix its grasp on those who pilfer the products of the mind, as readily as our laws embrace the common thief, Mr. Worcester would hardly escape with a light mulct. At all events before people buy his ware, they would do well to inquire how he came by them.[55]

The editorial triggered a rapid-fire exchange of letters, with Worcester saying he had started work on his dictionary before working for Webster. Webster replied that Worcester had indeed stolen more than 120 definitions.

"My Quarto Dictionary [of 1828] cost me about *twenty years of labor and 20,000 dollars,*" Webster wrote. "For this labor and such expense I could never receive remuneration had the market been left open. . . . How unkind then was it, for *you,* who had been entrusted with the task of making an abridgement, and had been well rewarded for it, to sit down and introduce some of my improvements into a book of your own compilation."[56]

As he had done for his speller, Webster acted to protect the language against Anglicization by strengthening his dictionary's hold on the market. At the age of seventy-six, the old lexicographer began work on a second edition of his great *American Dictionary.* The *Hampshire Gazette* lamented, "It is sad to see that the veteran of letters, the venerable Dr. Webster, compelled, on the wintry verge of the autumn of life, to turn literary constable and endeavor almost singlehanded to drive the multifarious herd of poachers from his ancient and rightful province in literature."[57]

Even Webster recognized that at his age he would need help, and he hoped against all odds that his son, William, might at last have matured enough to help sustain the family's publishing enterprise. In 1831, William had married Rosalie Stuart, of Virginia, a distant relative of the Washingtons, and they had two sons. To help him support his family, his father had bought him a partnership in a small firm, where William proved himself as incompetent in business as he had been as a scholar. Within a year, William guided the firm into bankruptcy and saddled his father with debts on which the interest alone came to a staggering $1,500 a year. The proceeds from his dictionary could not even cover the interest, let alone the principal. His daughter Julia and son-in-law Yale professor Chauncey Goodrich came to his aid.

> Dear Parents.
>
> As the money lent to William is now lost, we are desirous to be considered as assuming the consequences of one half of this loss, by paying the interest of $1500 a year, until the proceeds of the Dictionary shall be an interest for your use; and as much longer as your convenience shall dictate.
>
> We are very affectionately and dutifully
> Your children
> Chauncey A Goodrich
> Julia W Goodrich[58]

Despite William's record of incompetence, Noah Webster was obsessed with ensuring his only son's success, and he decided to send William where even incompetents were amassing fortunes—to Cincinnati, the "Gateway to the West." Sales of Webster's speller were soaring out of sight everywhere in the United States, but nowhere higher than in Ohio and neighboring states, where the use of Webster's orthography in the popular *McGuffey Readers* forced every school to adopt the Webster speller to teach its children to read.

With sales of the speller flourishing in the West, Webster envisioned expanding sales of his other books, and he sent William to Cincinnati to form a publishing partnership devoted almost exclusively to producing Webster texts. William was to travel the West promoting and selling his father's texts, much as his father had done as a young man in the East. William left for Cincinnati in May 1835, and by August of the following year, he had managed to steer the firm to financial ruin by borrowing money at interest rates that were higher than the net profit from the books he produced. Noah Webster sold the firm's assets to pay its debts and found another printer to continue publishing the speller in the West; he shifted all other text production to Eastern printers.

In February 1837, still out of work in Cincinnati, William asked his father for funds to start a newspaper. The doting Noah was about to throw more money in his son's direction when the other Webster children rebelled. Writing on their behalf, Harriet Webster Fowler demanded that her father stop wasting precious family assets on the profligate young man.

She wrote the angriest letter her father ever received from any of his children: "William has already had quite too much of Fathers patrimony and in saying this I speak the opinion of each of my sisters, and when I look about and see how other young men labor to support themselves independently of their friends, I confess I feel ashamed of my brother, who is *willing* that continual sums be advanced for him by his father who has already advanced so much.—He ought to go and find employment."[59]

Clearly taken aback by his daughter's letter, Webster made his son find work on his own. After still another failure—on a dairy farm—William got a job as a clerk in an Indiana bank. After a promotion to teller, he wrote his parents that he planned to buy a house and settle permanently in Lafayette, Indiana.

8

IN THE SPRING OF 1837, a financial panic gripped the United States. Martin Van Buren, President Jackson's close ally and vice president, had been elected to succeed Jackson as president and was just assuming office when the panic struck. New York banks refused to pay out gold or silver coins; weaker banks failed everywhere; cotton and other commodity prices plunged 50 percent. The panic brought trade to a standstill. Webster called it God's retribution on Van Buren and Jackson for feigning a faith in popular democracy while slaughtering American Indians across the South.

"We are justly punished for our violations with the Indians," he wrote to his son, William, in Indiana. "*Ten millions* already expended in Florida, in driving a thousand Indians into the Swamps! And now military force is to be employed to drive the Cherokees from their native soil, in consequence of a treaty with a part of the tribe, who had no authority to make it. Was there ever a gov't so conducted. . . . I look on our public affairs with alarm."[60]

As the number of unemployed grew, the mobs Webster despised returned to the nation's streets, breaking into food warehouses in New York and other major cities. The old Federalist could not contain his anger and raised the shredded banner of Federalism for the last time. Using the pseudonym "Sidney," he sent an essay to the *New York Commercial Advertiser* and the *Spectator,* the newspapers he had once owned and edited.

"Why," he asked,

> do men wonder at outbreakings of popular violence? Many men and good citizens, too, appear to be *surprised* at the scenes which have taken place in Charleston, New York, Philadelphia, Baltimore, Vicksburg, Cincinnati, and St. Louis. Why, Gentlemen, these scenes do not surprise those who have studied history and mankind. . . .
>
> Now I appeal to history for the fact that there has never yet been a democratic government, that is, a government in which the whole populace have exercised the whole power of making laws and of choosing executive officers, which has been a free government. On the other hand, the annals of history show beyond contradiction, that such governments have ever been furious and implacable despotisms.

Our writers have uniformly charged the tyranny of civil government
to *Kings*, and true it is that Kings have often been tyrants. But it seems
never to have occurred to such writers that the people, so called, are just
as bad as Kings. By nature, all men have the same passions as Kings—
they are all selfish—*all* ambitious—*all*, from the king or President down
to the corporal of a militia company, aspiring to power, and striving for
superiority over their fellow men. Give the people the *power*, and they
are all tyrants as much as Kings. They are even more tyrannical; as they
are less restrained by sense of propriety or by principles of honor; more
under the control of violent passions, exasperated by envy and hatred
of the rich; stimulated to action by numbers; and subject to no responsibility. . . .

These outrages were foreseen and distinctly foretold by our ablest
statesmen forty and fifty years ago. The whole sin of the old Washington
federalists consisted in attempting to incorporate our government, or
establish by law, some power which should effectively control or prevent
such popular violence. It was perfectly well foreseen that, without some
provision of this kind, the *people* would, whenever they please, break over
the constitution and laws, and trample them under their feet. In what
has taken place, nothing strange or unexpected by sound statesmen has
taken place. Such scenes have characterized democratic governments
in every country where they have existed. They proceed from the universal depravity of man, and they will be repeated whenever occasions
of excitement occur.[61]

Webster's essay represented a dramatic reversal of his position five
decades earlier in *Sketches of American Policy*, in which he had insisted that
"all power is vested in the people. That this is their natural and unalienable
right, is a position that will not be disputed."

The essay provoked a storm of Jacksonian counterattacks. "It is the
essence of the Federal doctrines," said the *Daily Albany Argus*. "Here is the
same innate distrust and hatred of the people—the old habit of depreciat-
ing their intelligence and integrity—the same longing for a 'strong' federal
government, for an hereditary executive, and for elections and responsibility so remote as to be little else than power in perpetuity."[62]

After another article labeled Sidney antirepublican, Webster shot back
with another "Note from Sidney":

In the year 1777, when a British army was marching from the north
toward Albany, Sidney volunteered his services, shouldered the best
musket he could find, marched up the Hudson, in sight of the flames
and smoking ruins of Kingston, encountering the hardships of a soldier's
life, to which he had not been inured, to lend his feeble aid in checking
the enemy. This he did for the purpose of defending the country, in the
hope of establishing *Independence* and *a free republican government*. Had
he foreseen that a generation would have passed before this republican
government would be changed into the *tyranny of a party*; a tyranny
which has inflicted on the community, more losses, more distress, more

calamity than any monarch in Europe has inflicted on his subjects in half a century, and all this under the hypocritical pretext of republicanism; had Sidney foreseen all this, with the prostration, or imbecility of law, the popular outrages upon life, liberty and prosperity; the direct violations of constitution and law, and of the ordinances of God, in authorizing secular employments on the Sabbath, and all the baneful effects of party spirit and usurpation; he would not have moved a step to oppose the enemy. Sidney knows no difference in tyranny; the authors of it may be monarchs or republicans, but *tyranny* is the *same thing* and is to be resisted by every man who values his rights, and loves his family and his country. The men of the revolution did not fight for an *oligarchy;* they fought for a *commonwealth.*[63]

In the end, Webster's articles had little effect on national or even local political affairs. They were simply the last gasp of an angry old Federalist. Webster nevertheless obtained a measure of satisfaction a few months later, when his son-in-law Rep. William Wolcott Ellsworth won election as governor of Connecticut on the Whig party ticket, an anti-Jacksonian amalgam that captured twenty of twenty-one seats in the state Senate and two-thirds of the seats in the Assembly. Elated by Ellsworth's victory, Webster wrote to his son, William, "We shall have a great parade in May, when the Governor enters New Haven."[64]

The joy of his son-in-law's inauguration was followed by the equally joyous marriage of his "daughter"—his granddaughter Mary Southgate—on July 24. Shortly thereafter, Webster's daughter Harriet and her husband, William Fowler, moved to Amherst, Massachusetts, where Fowler assumed the chair of rhetoric and oratory at the college. For the first time in nearly fifty years, there were no children in the Webster home.

"We have parted with our last child," the forlorn scholar wrote Harriet. "Although Mary has good prospects, still when I think that a child leaves my house for life and forever, the painful thought affects me, and as I sit alone a tear is stealing down my cheek."[65]

In October 1838, Noah Webster celebrated his eightieth birthday. All his living children and grandchildren gathered around him—save his only son, William, and William's family. It was more than the old man could bear. Three years earlier, when William had left for Indiana, his father had written to his son that the separation was "as severe to me as any that I have ever experienced, except that of your leaving the church to which you belonged."[66] At eighty, the old man missed his son even more. William was his only surviving son—his only child bearing the family name—and he begged him to return home, promising to buy out the contract of his New York publisher and set William up as the new publisher of all the Webster books.

"The commission I now pay on his agency & yours," Webster wrote, "would support your family, & I have one or two other books that must be pushed into the market. I want your aid, & if my speller should continue in use, I can maintain your family, till you can find business. . . . I am becoming old & infirm & I want your aid. I hope you will not buy [a house], till you hear further from your affectionate father."[67]

In May 1839, William resigned from the bank in Lafayette, Indiana, and returned home to New Haven. His father foolishly terminated the contracts with his excellent and efficient New York publisher and, with William at his side, took personal control of publishing all his texts, at the age of eighty-one. He contracted with twenty different printers in more than a dozen states and Montreal, Canada, to produce his *Elementary Spelling Book*. These included G. & C. Merriam Co., a Springfield, Massachusetts, printer of textbooks, law books, and Bibles with a thriving bookshop.[68]

Webster signed up three agents to help William promote his books. He added several histories, primers, and grammars, and a wonderful *Manual of Useful Studies*—a small home library that parents in isolated areas without schools could use to teach their children reading, writing, arithmetic, history, and science. After William returned, Webster finished revising his *American Dictionary* and, to the horror of his family, mortgaged his home to get the funds to pay for its publication. Although he originally planned an edition of four thousand, they were able to convince him at least to limit production to three thousand copies.

It was a wise decision. Webster's personal approach to selling books—brilliantly successful before the turn of the century—was losing its effectiveness. The American population had exploded and scattered across twice the number of states. A new generation of printer-publishers had emerged, with an army of salesmen who traveled the nation to slake the unquenchable thirst of Americans for education and entertainment that was only available from books. They drew from a wellspring of books on history, biography, science, and literature. By 1840, publishers were selling 5.5 million books a year, of which 2.6 million were schoolbooks. Among the new giants was Webster's old printer from Worcester, Massachusetts—Isaiah Thomas—who had built his printing firm into a publishing empire. Elsewhere, the Harper Brothers built a publishing empire with so-called libraries that dwarfed Webster's *Manual of Useful Studies*. The Harper Family Library offered 187 titles; the Classical Library, 37 titles; the Library of Select Novels, 36; the Boy's and Girl's Library, 32; the Theological Library, 9; the Dramatic Library, 5. The Harper School District Library fed schools six different series with a total of 295 titles, which turned Webster's gallant little *Manual of Useful Studies* into a useless relic of the past. In effect, publishers had displaced authors as providers of educational books, and the market for books had grown too large for an eighty-one-year-old lexicographer, his son, and three agents to compete—even an eighty-one-year-old lexicographer named Webster.

Early in 1840, the *Hartford Times* accused Webster of interfering in state affairs by influencing his son-in-law Governor Ellsworth. Webster fired back an angry denial:

> I belonged to the school of Washington, but sometimes differed from the Federalists on particular points, as I did from their opposers. . . .
> I belong to no political party but to the class of citizens who love their country and strive to promote its interests, political, moral, literary, and religious. For many years past I have attended no political meetings, I have no communications with either party in public measures, and rarely give my vote at the polls. I speak and write my sentiments with freedom whenever occasion offers, and this I shall continue to do without fear or affection.[69]

On April 21, 1840, Noah Webster returned to Hartford, the city his great-great-grandfather had helped found in 1636, to deliver an address at the ceremonies commemorating the two-hundredth anniversary of the founding of the state of Connecticut.

After the ceremonies, Webster took his two youngest daughters, Eliza and Louisa, for their first look at the house in West Hartford where he was born. The grapevines had spread in wild profusion, and Webster told Eliza to cut some slips for her garden and "cherish them in memory of him." A year later, the young plant produced "only one grape in perfection," Eliza said, "so I wrapt it in cotton wool and put it in a tiny box and sent it to him."[70]

Webster's joy at the bicentennial and the return to his ancestral home was offset somewhat by his disgust with the presidential election campaign of 1840. Webster grew increasingly pessimistic about the nation's ability to remain one. The campaign was, he said, proof that ordinary people could not govern themselves. He was appalled by the conduct of both candidates—the Jacksonian puppet President Martin Van Buren and the Whig candidate, William Henry Harrison. Van Buren had no formal education, but Harrison had studied for three years at Hampden-Sydney College and then at the College of Physicians and Surgeons in Philadelphia, under the brilliant Benjamin Rush. Instead of exhibiting wisdom, both sought votes by parading as semiliterate frontiersmen, appealing to the lowest common denominator of voter.

"But the Log cabin," Webster lamented in a letter to his daughter Emily, the governor's wife, "oh how our country is degraded, when even men of respectability resort to such means to secure an election! I struggled, in the days of Washington, to sustain good principles—but since Jefferson's principles have prostrated the popular respect for sound principles, further efforts would be useless." Webster gave up "all expectation or hope" for wise self-government or national unity. "We deserve all our public evils. We are a degenerate and wicked people . . . and I quit the contest forever."[71]

Although the state bicentennial marked the last of Webster's public political statements, he continued writing texts. The second edition of Webster's dictionary came off the press in January 1841.[72] Ever hopeful of uniting the American and English languages, he sent a leather-bound presentation copy to England's Queen Victoria via American ambassador Andrew Stevenson. Ironically, Stevenson was a staunch Jacksonian who had served as Democratic speaker of the House during the previous administration. He nevertheless sent Webster's book to Lord Melbourne, the Queen's closest political adviser, and enclosed a letter that called Webster's work "one of high merit, and the result of forty years labor by its venerable author . . . with the hope that . . . it has been executed in a manner to manifest to the British Nation that the Americans have not forgotten the language of their Fathers."[73]

Lord Melbourne replied:

> Windsor Castle
> August 19, 1841

My dear Sir,

I beg leave to acknowledge your letter of the 12th inst.—I have delayed replying to it until I had an opportunity of presenting Mr. Noah Webster's Work to the Queen which I did yesterday, & I am now commanded by Her Majesty to request that you will convey to Mr. Webster her warm thanks for this mark of attention, & assure him that Her Majesty will highly value the Work, as well on account of its merits, as of the author & the kindred Country from which it comes.—Believe me—my dear Sir,

Yours faithfully

> Melbourne[74]

9

THE WEBSTERS' FIFTIETH WEDDING ANNIVERSARY was actually in May 1839, but they postponed their celebration until they could reunite their entire family. It took nearly three years to muster so large a group, but on May 4, 1842, the Webster clan gathered in New Haven at the home of his daughter Julia and her husband, Yale professor Chauncey Goodrich.

"All the children of the dear, dear old Patriarch and his wife Rebecca were invited to gather at brother Goodrich's," Eliza Webster Jones, Webster's fifth daughter, wrote in her touching "Account of the Festival of the Golden Wedding."[75] "Through the favor of a kind Providence, we came together in health and comfort at the appointed time, and sent a troup of happy little ones to escort the head of our house to the gathering table. Brother's parlor was filled. 35 of us were there."

After Julia and Eliza took their seats on either side of their father, Webster's six grandsons seated themselves on the carpet "like Turks before him, and a little wee thing of 3 years left her picture books and came and squatted down so innocently at the end of the row that all were greatly amused . . . all began in merry mood good 'Auld Lang Syne' and then 'Home Sweet Home' and tears of tenderness and joy followed."[76]

The family gathered about a table that ran along three sides of the room, with Noah and Rebecca Webster in the middle. The daughters sat along one leg of the table, the sons-in-law on the other, and the grandchildren were scattered among them appropriately. William, the only son, sat opposite Noah and Rebecca with his wife and children at the central table.

"Oh, it was a pleasant sight," said Eliza.

> When all were seated at the well filled board, brother G[oodrich] rose and fervently implored the blessing of heaven. We felt that God was with us and it was a cheerful meal. When we had finished brother Fowler [daughter Harriet's husband] made a few remarks expressive of our gratitude to God that we had been permitted to meet in such comfort, and that we were so united, loving and beloved, and returned solemn hearty thanks. Then we returned to the parlor to talk of old times and observe the happiness of the little folks whose eyes sparkled and whose smiles gladdened the hearts of us older folks who felt we were to part never to meet all together again, till we stand unsheltered before the Great Author of our being to learn where shall be our last eternal home. . . . At five we all went to Father's and took our tea in the home of our early days. In the evening before we parted, our beloved and revered parent called our attention, and kneeling, as we all did, fervently implored the blessing of heaven upon us, our children and our children's children to the latest generation. Oh shall not that prayer be heard? Then rising, he said, it was the happiest day of his life, to see us all together; so many walking in the truth and the others, children of promise. Oh . . . I cannot tell you half he said. Then he presented each of us with a Bible, his last gift, and with our names written by his own trembling hand; and we closed our meeting by singing "Blest be the tie that binds." Shall we ever forget it. Oh, no! the youngest there received some deep impression of the blessedness of nurturing a family in the fear of God.[77]

10

DURING THE SUMMER OF 1842, Webster made his annual visits to his daughters in Hartford and Amherst. On July 4 he made what would be his last Independence Day oration, to students at the college he had helped found in Amherst.

Early the following year, William was still floundering financially, and his father, obsessed with seeing his forty-two-year-old son succeed in life, again tried to help get him established in publishing. He bought his son a partnership in a printing firm in America's most lucrative market—New York. The firm reopened under the name Webster & Clark, on Fulton Street, but by mid-May, William was complaining. The walk from his home, in Brooklyn, to the shop in Manhattan was "hard on the feet." Publishing was an "uphill business." He found it difficult "to go on without credit & without cash."[78] Insurance was too costly. Ignoring admonitions from his oldest daughter, Emily, who actually adored William, and equally strong warnings from Emily's husband, Connecticut governor William Ellsworth, Webster gave William more money on May 18, along with a stack of books for William's shop. It was the last time he would be able to help his son.

Four days later, Webster returned from a long walk in the New Haven chill. He felt faint and had difficulty breathing. Over the next few days his respiratory problems grew worse. His children began gathering at his bedside to await the inevitable. As Eliza sat by his bed in his study, he asked after "the prospects of my trees and shrubbery, and especially of the grape vines, that were slips from the parent tree on his father's farm, the fruit of which was a favorite one when he was a very little boy." His son, William, whom he despaired of ever seeing again, arrived from New York in time to see his father. The old man was noticeably relieved. "The meeting between the dying man and his only son was deeply affecting. Father could then converse with ease and had a long conversation with him on business."[79]

When his eight-year-old grandson Henry Webster Jones, whom everyone called "Webster," entered the room, the old lexicographer reached out and gave the boy one of his legendary blue-backed spellers. "It was the last book he took in his hand and his last gift to his youngest grandchild."[80]

At ten minutes before eight on the evening of May 28, 1843, Noah Webster died peacefully, five months short of his eighty-fifth birthday. "I'm ready to go; my work is all done," he told his daughter Eliza.[81]

They buried the old Federalist in the Grove Street cemetery, next to Yale College, only two blocks from his home. He lies not far from Ezra Stiles, Timothy Dwight, Jedidiah Morse, and other friends from Yale. His infant son, Henry Bradford, who had died after a few weeks in 1806, is there as well. His funeral procession extended more than a mile, led by his wife, his children, and his grandchildren. The entire Yale student body and faculty followed, and in their turn, the schoolchildren of New Haven and nearby communities, who had learned to read and spell from Webster's little blue-backed spelling book.

As Webster's cortege moved quietly toward his grave, the anarchy he had fought so hard to defeat erupted in Philadelphia, of all places—where Webster's beloved Union had begun. Rioting erupted there between Protestants and Catholics, leaving twenty people dead and a hundred injured before the militia moved in to stop the bloodshed.

Webster's will left his wife his household effects and $750 a year for her and Louisa for the remainder of their lives. He gave $1,000 each to his daughters Emily, Harriet, and Eliza, and he gave Julia and Chauncey Goodrich his royalties of thirty-seven cents on the sale of each copy of his great dictionary for twenty-eight years. He distributed the rest of his property among all his daughters, and left his books and papers to William.

Webster's wife, Rebecca, joined her husband in the Grove Street cemetery four years later, in June 1847. William followed in 1869. William was never able to support his Southern wife in the style she demanded, and they separated. Their two sons, the only remaining men bearing Noah Webster's surname, fought and died on opposite sides in the Civil War.

Epilogue

NOAH WEBSTER LEFT HIS FAMILY fourteen hundred unsold copies of the self-published, second edition of the *American Dictionary,* of 1841, along with stocks of various editions of his other books. The Webster heirs sold exclusive rights to the dictionary to George and Charles Merriam, who had produced an edition of the speller in 1839. The Merriam brothers bought the remaining stock of 1828 and 1841 dictionaries, which they set aside as collector's items, and hired Webster's son-in-law Yale professor Chauncey Goodrich to edit an enlarged and improved edition. It appeared as one volume in 1847, and at $6 a copy was so successful that the Merriams were able to pay the Webster family $250,000 when they renewed the copyright.

In 1859, the Merriams hired a German scholar, C. A. F. Mahn, to rewrite and correct Webster's etymologies. At the time, German philologists were in the forefront of the new field of etymology, and Mahn converted Webster's work into the definitive 1859 edition of the *American Dictionary of the English Language.* With more than 140,000 words, it was the first dictionary ever to include illustrations. Mahn also eliminated Webster's many religio-nationalistic definitions and converted the dictionary into an objective work of scholarship that both established "Webster's" as a lasting standard of the English language in the United States and ended the use of English spellings. Mahn also reduced the scope of dictionaries to spellings, objective definitions, and scholarly etymology. With the 1859 edition of "Webster's," dictionaries ceased teaching morality and love of country; they withdrew from constitutional debates; they ceased telling parents how to raise their children—and make cranberry sauce.

In 1864, the Merriams hired American educator Noah Porter as editor in chief to produce a new "Webster's unabridged" edition. Porter became president of Yale College in 1871 but returned to Merriam after his retirement, in 1886, to produce the great *Webster's International Dictionary of the English Language,* of 1890. Since 1900, Merriam has produced two more editions of *Webster's New International Dictionary,* along with smaller versions, including the popular *Merriam-Webster's Collegiate Dictionary.*

A portrait of Noah Webster superimposed on a page of the original, handwritten manuscript for his seventy-thousand-word *American Dictionary of the English Language,* first published in 1828. To the right is a copy of his *Elementary Spelling Book,* which he published in 1829 as a replacement for his original *American Spelling Book* of 1789; it stands on a copy of Webster's *Compendious Dictionary* of 1806 and leans against G. & C. Merriam's colossal one-volume *Webster's International Dictionary,* published in 1890 under the editorship of former Yale president Noah Porter. (Library of Congress.)

Ironically, the name of Webster, the father of American copyright laws, eventually passed into the public domain, and anyone may produce a dictionary bearing the name "Webster's." A 1917 court ruling, however, forces all but Merriam-Webster Inc., the successor firm of the Merriam brothers, to publish a disclaimer: "This dictionary is not published by the original publishers of Webster's dictionary or their successors."

After Noah Webster's death, his family sold the rights to his *Elementary Spelling Book* to George F. Coolidge & Brother, a New York printer that built and installed "the fastest steam press in the United States" to print nothing but Webster spellers. Coolidge produced 525 books an hour—5,250 a day and about 1.5 million a year—until 1857, when Coolidge sold the rights to Merriam.[1] By that time, *The Elementary Spelling Book* was indeed the national standard, with virtually all children in American schools fulfilling Webster's dream by learning to "speak alike."

"Above all other people," declared Mississippi senator Jefferson Davis— ironically, on the eve of the Civil War, in 1859—"we are one, and above all books which have united us in the bond of common language, I place the good old Spelling-Book of Noah Webster. We have a unity of language no other people possesses, and we owe this unity, above all else, to Noah Webster's Yankee Spelling-Book."[2]

Although the Civil War interrupted sales and shipments to the South, the war's end saw sales of Webster's speller leap to nearly 1.6 million copies a year—largely because of demand by former slaves, who equated literacy to liberty and no longer faced state laws making it a crime to teach blacks how to read or write.

In 1880, Webster's speller continued to command "the largest sale of any book in the world except the Bible," according to William H. Appleton, whose firm printed the book for the Merriams. "We sell a million copies a year. . . . We sell them in cases of seventy-two dozen, and they are bought by all the large dry-goods houses and supply stores, and furnished by them to every cross-roads store in the country."[3] By the end of the century, estimated total sales of the speller reached between 70 and 100 million, with pirated editions making an accurate count impossible.

The speller not only was the foundation of classroom instruction, it made the spelling bee the most popular form of home entertainment well into the twentieth century, when radio displaced it as entertainment in American living rooms. At the same time, new teaching methods began driving Webster's speller from American classrooms. Teachers found that phonics, the whole-word method, and other approaches to reading instruction were more effective than the alphabet method and the syllabarium, on which Webster had based his speller.

Schools in the rural South, however, continued to use the speller into the late 1930s, and it remained in print in limited quantities—primarily as a collector's item—as late as 1987. Facsimile editions continue to be printed for sale by the Noah Webster Foundation and Historical Society of West Hartford, Connecticut.

Tragically, as Webster's speller disappeared from American classrooms, the philosophy that sired it also began to vanish. Unlike the books that replaced it, Webster's speller did not teach children only to spell and read. It taught them to embrace their nation and their nation's political system. For more than a century, Webster's speller unified millions of children of different nationalities, races, religions, language groups, and political systems by teaching them the common language of America. For a brief moment each day in every American school, the speller bonded them in a common family, with one moral code and one political philosophy, based on love of country and the common good. Webster's "national language" was their "band of national union."

Ironically, two centuries after he first published the speller, bilingual education and multicultural education have replaced Webster's system of education in many American schools. English as a second language often takes precedence over English as a first language. Instead of national unity, many schools promote cultural differences and rank ancestral tongues alongside the language of the United States. The net result has been the creation of a huge new nation within the United States—a nation whose children are growing up semiliterate in both English and their native tongues[4] and who are developing little or no love or allegiance to their new land. As the dissimulative purveyors of multilingualism divide the nation culturally under the banner of individual liberty, they will all but surely divide the nation politically and provoke anarchy, as their predecessors have done throughout history.

Webster traced the social and political upheaval, from ancient Babel to his own America, to linguistic and cultural disunity. The nation's freedom and independence, he predicted, would depend on every immigrant child absorbing the language and culture of the United States as his or her own and abandoning the language and customs of his or her foreign origins. Webster's life was not about a dictionary. It was about creating a new nation—the *United* States of America—and making everyone in America an American.

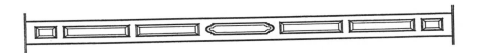

Notes

Abbreviations

BL   Beinecke Rare Book and Manuscript Library, Yale University, New Haven, Connecticut
LC   Library of Congress, Washington, D.C.
NW   Noah Webster
NYPL   New York Public Library
NWH   Noah Webster House
Wren   Wren Library, Trinity College, Cambridge University
YL   Sterling Memorial Library, Yale University, New Haven, Connecticut

Chapter 1. Patriot

1. Harold Underwood Faulkner and Tyler Kepner, *America: Its History and People* (New York: Harper & Brothers, 1942), 19.

2. NW, *Family of John Webster* (1836, unpublished), YL.

3. After leaving Massachusetts, Williams and a group of his followers founded the town of Providence and the colony of Rhode Island, a settlement in which government ruled "only in civil things." For the first time in any Christian country, church and state were separated and religious toleration was established by law.

4. W. S. Porter, *Historical Notices of Hartford* (unpublished), 3, Hartford Public Library.

5. Daniel Steele Durrie, *Steele Family: A Genealogical History of John and George Steele, (Settlers of Hartford, Conn.) 1635–1636, and Their Descendants* (Albany, N.Y.: J. Munsell, 1862).

6. The Fundamental Orders of 1639 created a self-governing state under the authority of two general courts, one legislative, the other administrative. The governor and magistrates were to be elected by "vote of the country"—that is, by all male freemen, or landowners, without regard to religion.

7. Sylvester Judd, *History of Hadley* (unpublished), 237, Hadley Public Library.

8. Emily Ellsworth Fowler Ford, *Notes on the Life of Noah Webster* (New York: privately printed, 1912), I:9.

9. Isaac Watts (1674–1748), an English theologian, educator, hymn writer, and author, whose popular works helped shape American education at home and in church. A Puritan, Watts composed hymns and works for children that presented a benevolent Deity. His texts urged a gentle approach to pedagogy. They did not proscribe the rod but counseled reason in imparting knowledge and emphasized the difference between teaching and preaching.

10. NW, introduction to *A Grammatical Institute of the English Language,* part I (Hartford: Hudson & Goodwin, 1783), 6.

11. NW to Henry Barnard, March 10, 1840, Barnard Papers, New-York Historical Society.

12. Ibid.

13. Ford, *Notes*, I:14.

14. NW to Oliver Wolcott Jr., May 25, 1793, Connecticut Historical Society.

15. Ford, *Notes*, I:15.

16. Ibid., I:16.

17. Led by Connecticut's Jonathan Edwards, a fiery orator who had graduated with Yale's Old Light class of 1720, the New Light ministers opened their congregations to all. They promised that God would save all people from the fires of hell if they would convert and lead saintly lives on earth. Disenfranchised colonists who had despaired of ever reaching heaven flocked to hear the soaring New Light oratory and its messages of hope for salvation. They sang and cried and stretched their arms to heaven in anguished pleas to God. The Great Awakening created a new church that lured converts in numbers never seen before in the colonies.

18. Thomas Clap, *The Religious Constitution of Colleges, Especially of Yale-College in New Haven in the Colony of Connecticut* (New-London: T. Green, 1754).

19. Brooks Mather Kelley, *Yale: A History* (New Haven: Yale University Press, 1974), 66.

20. Under traditional gradation, the son of a Connecticut governor or Yale president stood, marched, or sat at the head of his class in processions, in church, in recitation rooms, and in the dining hall. Next in rank came grandsons of governors and sons of trustees (ranked by length of service on the corporation), the sons of large landowners, and so on. Farm boys and merchants' sons came last. The end of gradation pleased high-ranked students as well as the low-ranked, for they were spared the humiliating punishment of public *de*gradation to lower ranks when they committed misdemeanors (Kelley, *Yale*, 75–76).

21. When Webster arrived at Yale, freshmen concentrated on Latin (Virgil and Cicero's orations), the Greek New Testament, and arithmetic. Sophomores studied Horace in Latin, more of the Greek Testament, and Thomas Vincent's *Explicatory Catechism*. Sophomores also studied logic, geography, algebra, geometry, rhetoric, and English grammar. Juniors studied more of the Greek Testament, of Cicero's orations, and of the *Explicatory Catechism*, in the divinity sector. In addition, they studied trigonometry, natural philosophy (sciences), surveying, the calculation of eclipses, conic sections, and fluxions (calculus). Juniors had but two classes a day—one at eleven, the other in the late afternoon—but they were expected to spend their free time in their rooms studying. Seniors met only once a day, at eleven, but were also expected to spend their free time studying in their rooms. The core of the senior curriculum was ethics, metaphysics, philosophy, two difficult theology courses, and some mathematics and science. Juniors and seniors also had to dispute, or debate, twice a week: once in Latin, according to syllogistic rules, and once, forensically, in English (Kelley, *Yale*, 80–81).

22. Ibid., 42.

23. On Mondays, Wednesdays, and Thursdays, Buckminster and his class worked on Cicero's orations, the Greek Testament, logic, and arithmetic; on Tuesdays and Fridays, students prepared and declaimed their own original florid orations in English, Latin, and Greek. Saturday mornings were devoted to divinity studies—largely lectures by President Daggett. Saturday afternoons and evenings provided them with their only free time, which they usually spent splitting wood and doing other chores.

24. Kelley, *Yale*, 42.

25. When it was built, in 1753, Connecticut Hall represented the perfection of colonial architecture—it was a simple two-story brick-faced rectangle with a peaked roof and two evenly placed entrances along its long eastern wall. Yale students had previously boarded with local families, and completion of Connecticut Hall assured parents that their boys would be under constant supervision of the faculty.

26. Ford, *Notes*, I:22.

27. Kelley, *Yale*, 57.

28. Harry R. Warfel, *Noah Webster, Schoolmaster to America* (New York: Macmillan Company, 1936; reprint, Octagon Books, New York, 1966), 84.

29. Ibid., 6.

30. NW, *Sketches of American Policy* (Hartford: Hudson & Goodwin, 1785), 31.

31. Ibid., 28.

32. NW, *American Magazine*, May 1788, 367–68.

33. NW, "An Address to Young Ladies," in *A Collection of Essays and Fugitiv Writings on Moral, Historical, Political and Literary Subjects* (Boston: I. Thomas and E. T. Andrews, 1790), 410–14.

34. Kelley, *Yale*, 84.

35. Ibid., 89.

36. Ibid.

37. Ford, *Notes*, I:18 n–19 n; 35. Yale students accounted for more than half the officers in the Connecticut militia during the Revolutionary War. Ironically, Yale College now bans all American government military activities on campus, including the Reserve Officers Training Corps.

38. Kelley, *Yale*, 85.

39. Ibid., 89.

40. James Woodress, *A Yankee's Odyssey: The Life of Joel Barlow* (Philadelphia and New York: J. B. Lippincott Company, 1958), 39.

41. Ford, *Notes*, I:19.

42. Ibid., I:20.

43. Zephaniah Swift to NW, December 13, 1776, in Ford, *Notes*, I:23.

44. Latin manuscript, May 4, 1776, in Webster's hand, Webster Papers, BL; English translation by Douglas Kneeland, the Hotchkiss School and Swarthmore College.

45. Woodress, *Yankee's Odyssey*, 41.

46. Kelley, *Yale*, 83.

47. Warfel, *Noah Webster*, 29.

48. NW, Diary, in Ford, *Notes*, I:20.

49. Ibid., I:21.

50. Woodress, *Yankee's Odyssey*, 44.

51. Fragment, Webster Papers, BL.

52. Kelley, *Yale*, 88.

53. North Callahan, *Royal Raiders: The Tories of the American Revolution* (Indianapolis and New York: Bobbs-Merrill Company, 1963), 155; Richard B. Morris, *Encyclopedia of American History* (New York: Harper & Brothers, 1953), 96.

54. Callahan, *Royal Raiders*, 155.

55. Ford, *Notes*, I:28.

56. NW to the Editor of the *Palladium*, February 17, 1835, Webster Papers, NYPL.

57. Franklin B. Dexter, ed., *The Literary Diary of Ezra Stiles* (New York, 1901), II:284.

58. Kelley, *Yale*, 88.

59. Ford, *Notes*, I:31.

60. The Reverend Joseph Buckminster to NW, October 30, 1779, NYPL.

61. Ford, *Notes*, I:35.

62. Kelley, *Yale*, 95. The commander of the British fleet was furious when he saw the troops onshore withdraw without burning New Haven. "That place," he said, "has the largest university in America, and might with propriety be styled the parent and nurse of rebellion." The troops compensated for their charity at New Haven by burning nearby Fairfield and Norwalk a few days later (ibid.).

63. Naphthali Daggett to Henry Daggett, New Haven, April 10, 1778, YL.

Chapter 2. Schoolmaster

1. NW, *Memoir of Noah Webster, LL.D.* (unpublished), no. 5, YL.; Ford, *Notes*, I:38.

2. NW, *Memoir of Noah Webster, LL.D.* (unpublished), no. 5; YL.

3. Reeve attracted so many apprentices he could no longer accommodate them in his offices. He moved them into a freestanding structure in his backyard, where he housed his law library and delivered a series of 139 lectures on all aspects of the law. Called the Litchfield Law School, it was the nation's first formal institution of its kind and remained the preeminent law school in America until 1833, by which time competition from university law schools

forced it to close. See Harlow G. Unger, *Encyclopedia of American Education* (New York: Facts On File, 1996), 1:806.

4. NW, *Memoir*, xv.

5. Born in New London, Connecticut, John Butler (1728–96) recruited a combined force of loyalists and Indians that defeated the Continentals in the Wyoming Valley of northeastern Pennsylvania. The Indians committed a series of atrocities—the Wyoming Massacre—before moving with the rangers to Elmira, New York. Gen. John Sullivan's forces defeated them in 1779. Butler's son Walter N. Butler, who died in 1781, marched in his father's footsteps. He led Butler's Rangers in an assault on Cherry Valley, New York, in 1778, with Joseph Brant's Indians, who perpetrated the Cherry Valley Massacre on November 11. John Butler was named British commissioner of Indian affairs in Niagara, Canada, after the Revolutionary War and was knighted.

6. Woodress, *Yankee's Odyssey.*

7. Ford, *Notes*, I:40.

8. NW, "On Education," *American Magazine*, December 1787, 21.

9. Samuel Butler (1612–80), *Hudibras*, part II, canto I, l. 843. The universally misunderstood and misapplied Puritan belief in the principle of sparing the rod and spoiling the child was actually part of a couplet in a poem that viciously satirized Puritan life and that most Puritans never read. Rather than applying to children generally, as Puritans liked to believe, the line was the second in a couplet advocating release of erotic passions: "Love is a boy by poets styl'd;/ Then spare the rod and spoil the child."

10. NW, *A Collection of Essays and Fugitiv Writings.*

11. Ford, *Notes*, I:49.

12. *Connecticut Courant and Weekly Intelligencer* (Hartford), June 5, 1781.

13. Ford, *Notes*, I:46.

14. NW, "An Address to Young Ladies," in *A Collection of Essays and Fugitiv Writings*, 410–11.

15. NW, "Laws Respecting Females," in *A Manual of Useful Studies; for the Instruction of Young Persons of Both Sexes, in Families and Schools* (New Haven, 1839), vi, 79.

16. NW, *Dissertation in English on the Universal Diffusion of Literature as Introductory to the Universal Diffusion of Christianity* (September 1781, unpublished), NYPL.

17. Woodress, *Yankee's Odyssey*, 75.

18. NW, "On Education," *American Magazine*, December 1787, 21.

19. Sir Henry Clinton, "Declaration to the Inhabitants," *New-York Packet* (Fishkill), December 29, 1780.

20. NW, "Observations on the Revolution," *New-York Packet*, January 17, 1782.

21. NW, ibid., January 31, 1782.

22. NW, ibid., February 7, 1782.

23. NW, *Memoir*, no. 7.

24. Ibid., no. 6.

25. Ibid.

26. NW, introduction to *Grammatical Institute*, I:6.

27. Thomas Dilworth, *A New Guide to the English Tongue* (London, 1740). Benjamin Franklin published the first American edition—a reprint of the eighth English edition—in Philadelphia in 1747. A New York printer issued a second American edition in 1754. Dilworth's remained the standard spelling book in England until just after 1800.

28. Thomas H. Palmer, "The Teacher's Manual" (Prize Essay), *Common School Journal* 2 (1840):301.

29. NW, introduction to *Grammatical Institute*, I:5.

30. NW to John Canfield, January 6, 1783, NYPL.

31. Horace E. Scudder, *Noah Webster* (Boston: Houghton, Mifflin and Company, 1882), 36.

32. A Canaanite military center during the second millennium B.C.E., it stood about seven miles northwest of Dan, in what is now northern Israel (1 Kings 15:20; 2 Kings 15:29; 2 Samuel 20:14–18).

33. Son of Baladan, one of the kings of Babylon (Isaiah 39:1; 2 Kings 20:12).

34. NW, *Introduction to Grammatical Institute,* I:10.
35. Ibid., I:24.
36. Chauncey A. Goodrich, "Life and Writings of Noah Webster, LL.D.," *American Magazine* 2 (1849): 9.
37. NW, To the General Assembly of Connecticut, October 24, 1782, Webster Papers, NYPL.
38. NW, *Grammatical Institute,* I:102–3.
39. Ibid.
40. Ibid., I:106–11.
41. Editorial, *New Haven Daily Herald,* January 4, 1842.
42. The Reverend Increase N. Tarbox, "Noah Webster," *Congregational Quarterly* 7, no. 1 (January 1865): 4.
43. NW, "On Education," *American Magazine,* December 1787, 22.
44. John Tebbel, *A History of Book Publishing in the United States* (New York: R. R. Bowker Company, 1972), 1:46, 139–40.
45. It was Webster's maternal great-great-great-grandfather William Bradford, governor of the Plymouth Colony, who first proclaimed a day of thanksgiving and prayer, after the first harvest by the Plymouth colonists, in 1621. In 1623, during a long drought, days of fasting and prayer climaxed with a day of thanksgiving after the clouds erupted with torrents of rain during a sequence of prayers. Gradually, New Englanders began a custom of celebrating a day of thanksgiving after the harvest. During the American Revolution, the Continental Congress suggested an annual national Day of Thanksgiving.
46. Ford, *Notes,* I:56.

Chapter 3. Author

1. NW to John Canfield, January 6, 1783, NYPL.
2. "Memorial to the Legislature of New York," January 18, 1783, NYPL.
3. NW, "To the General Assembly of Connecticut"; "Memorial to the Legislature of New York"; NYPL.
4. NW *Memoir,* no. 9.
5. John Trumbull, *M'Fingal* (New Haven, 1775; rev. ed., Hartford, 1782). Modeled on Samuel Butler's *Hudibras* (1663–78), *M'Fingal* mocks extremists on both sides of the Revolution, especially the pompous Tory M'Fingal, a Scottish American who, after being tarred and feathered, repents and embraces the colonist cause.
6. NW, *Memoir,* no. 9.
7. Ibid.
8. Ibid.
9. Faulkner and Kepner, *America,* 106.
10. Merrill Jensen, *The New Nation: A History of the United States During the Confederation, 1781–1789* (New York: Alfred A. Knopf, 1967), 39.
11. NW, *Memoir,* no. 10.
12. NW's article appeared in two parts in the *Connecticut Courant* (Hartford), on August 23 and September 2, 1783, under the pseudonym "Honorius." Pseudonyms were common then and are still common in Britain.
13. Ibid., September 2, 1783.
14. Ibid.
15. Ibid.
16. Ford, *Notes,* I:66.
17. Like many books of the era, Webster's speller and his other children's texts were only about three and a half inches wide and about six and a quarter inches tall.
18. NW, *Memoir,* no. 9.

19. NW, introduction to *Grammatical Institute,* I:8.

20. Ibid., I:10.

21. In the preface to his *Schoolmaster's Assistant,* Dilworth wrote:

> While I am speaking of the Education of Children, I hope I shall be forgiven, if I drop a Word or two relating to the fair Sex. — It is a general Remark, that they are so unhappy as seldom to be found either to Spell, Write or Cypher well: And the Reason is very obvious, because they do not stay at their Writing Schools long enough. A Year's Education in Writing, is, by many, thought enough for Girls; and by others it is thought Time enough to put them to it, when they are Eighteen or Twenty Years of Age; whereas by sad Experience, both these are found to be, the one too short a Time, and the other too late. I am
>
> You and your Children's Well-wisher,
Thomas Dilworth.

22. Every speller in use in America before Webster's originated in England, including the widely used *New-England Primer.* Though printed in Boston after 1690, it was originally published in London in 1680 for use in the colonies, and its contents did not change with the shift in printing site.

23. NW, introduction to *Grammatical Institute,* I:14–15.

24. Ford, *Notes,* I:62–64.

25. John Pickering (1777–1846) became a prominent lawyer and scholar, eventually compiling a lexicon of the Greek language.

26. Timothy Pickering to his wife, October 31, 1783, in Octavius Pickering, *The Life of Timothy Pickering* (Boston, 1867).

27. NW, "Memorial to the Legislature of New York," for copyright protection of the *Grammatical Institute,* January 18, 1783, NYPL.

28. NW, introduction to *Grammatical Institute,* I:12.

29. Ford, *Notes,* I:63.

30. Ibid., I:74.

31. NW, *Memoir,* no. 10.

32. Ibid.

33. Ibid., no. 11.

34. Samuel Adams to NW, Boston, April 30, 1784, in Ford, *Notes,* II:451–53, citing William V. Wells, *The Life and Public Services of Samuel Adams,* III:207.

35. NW, "Policy of Connecticut" (signed "Honorius"), *Connecticut Courant,* May 18 and May 25, 1784.

36. NW, *Freeman's Chronicle* (Hartford), July 5, 1784.

37. NW to James Madison, July 5, 1784, LC.

38. Ford, *Notes,* I:79–80.

39. "Thomas Dilworth" letter, *Connecticut Journal* (New Haven), July 14, 1784; cited in Emily Ellsworth Ford Skeel, *A Bibliography of the Writings of Noah Webster,* ed. Edwin H. Carpenter Jr. (New York: New York Public Library, 1958; reprint, New York: New York Public Library and Arno Press, 1971), appendix 3, 484.

40. NW, "To Dilworth's Ghost . . . " (dated January 19, 1785), *Weekly Monitor and American Advertiser* (Litchfield), February 1, 1785; cited in Harry R. Warfel, ed., *Letters of Noah Webster* (New York: Library Publishers, 1953), 19.

41. Ibid.

42. Ibid.

43. NW, "To the Printer" (dated July 5, 1784), *Freeman's Chronicle,* cited in Warfel, *Letters,* 9–11.

44. NW to "Dilworth's Ghost," *Weekly Monitor,* February 15, 1785, cited in Warfel, *Letters,* 25–31.

45. Ibid.

46. Ford, *Notes,* I:81.

47. Ibid., I:85.

48. Ibid., I:80–82.

49. Ibid., I:85.

50. Ibid., I:84.

51. Webster's articles were published concurrently, beginning January 3, 1785, in two Hartford periodicals, the *Connecticut Courant* and *American Mercury,* a new publication started by Webster's friend the poet Joel Barlow.

52. Only twenty-five at the time and three years older than Webster, Hamilton moved to Albany, New York, in 1781 to get his law degree, after five years of gallant service in the Revolution. At twenty-one, he had organized a company, and he served with distinction in the New York and New Jersey campaigns. After serving as Washington's aide-de-camp and personal secretary in 1777, he took command of a battalion that helped engineer the British defeat at Yorktown. In 1783, the year before Webster entered the Federalist camp, Hamilton moved to the Federalist capital, New York City.

53. A linear descendant of America's original Webster, Pelatiah Webster graduated from Yale in 1746, thirty-two years before Noah. Although he started his adult years as a minister and a teacher, he became a merchant in 1777. After they seized a shipload of his flour and iron bound for patriots in Boston, the British captured Webster, confiscated the rest of his property, and jailed him for almost a year.

54. Timothy Dwight, *Conquest of Canaan* (New Haven, 1787).

55. NW, *Grammatical Institute,* III:3–4.

56. NW, *An American Selection of Lessons in Reading and Speaking, Calculated to Improve the Minds and Refine the Taste of Youth and Also to Instruct Them in Geography, History, and Politics of the United States, to Which Is Prefixed, Rules in Elocution, and Directions for Expressing the Principle Passions of the Mind. Being the Third Part of a Grammatical Institute, Greatly Enlarged,* v–vi. Webster's first reader first appeared in 1785 but was enlarged and given the title noted here in 1787.

57. Scudder, *Noah Webster,* 47.

58. Ibid., 183.

59. Dwight, *Conquest.*

60. Ford, *Notes,* I:87.

61. Ibid.

62. Ibid., I:89.

63. Joel Barlow, *Vision of Columbus* (New Haven, 1787).

64. Ford, *Notes,* I:87.

65. Ibid., I:89.

66. NW to Jedidiah Morse, May 15, 1797, NYPL; NW, *Memoir of the Author* (August 1847), xvi, NYPL. (*Note:* This memoir is an otherwise unidentified printed document separate from the handwritten manuscript entitled *Memoir of Noah Webster, LLD.*)

67. NW, *Sketches of American Policy* (Hartford: Hudson & Goodwin, 1785).

68. *The Federalist* (New York, 1788) collected into two volumes a series of eighty-five essays, edited by Alexander Hamilton. Appearing in 1787 and 1788, about fifty essays were written by Hamilton, the others by James Madison and John Jay. The essays explained the republican principles underlying the national government, as outlined in the proposed Constitution, and urged New Yorkers to vote for ratification. Seventy-seven of the essays first appeared in the New York City newspaper the *Independent Journal* between October 17, 1787, and April 12, 1788, and refuted the arguments opposing ratification. Published next in pamphlet form, the earliest essays bore the signature "A Citizen of New York" and the later ones the pseudonym "Publius."

69. John Dos Passos, *The Men Who Made the Nation* (New York: Doubleday & Company, 1957), 72.

70. Alexander Hamilton to James Duane, September 3, 1780, in John C. Hamilton, ed., *The Works of Alexander Hamilton* (New York, 1850–51), I:150–68; Jensen, *The New Nation,* 51.

71. Jensen, *The New Nation,* 79.

72. Pelatiah Webster, "The Political Union and Constitution of the Thirteen United States of North-America," *Pennsylvania Packet* (Philadelphia), February 1783, from his more detailed work *A Dissertation on the Political Union and Constitution of the Thirteen States, of North-America:*

Which Is Necessary to Their Preservation and Happiness; Dos Passos, *The Men Who Made the Nation,* 73.

73. NW to Jedidiah Morse, May 15, 1797, NYPL.

74. Ford, *Notes,* I:68.

75. NW to James Madison, August 20, 1804, in *A Collection of Papers on Political, Literary and Moral Subjects* (1843); Warfel, *Letters,* 255–57.

76. See note 68.

77. *Preface to Debates in the Convention: A Sketch Never Finished nor Applied,* in Gaillard Hunt and James Brown Scott, eds., *Notes of Debates in the Federal Convention of 1787 Which Framed the Constitution of the United States of America* (New York: Oxford University Press, 1920; reprint, New York: W. W. Norton & Company, 1987); first published in Henry Gilpin, ed., *The Papers of James Madison* (Washington, 1840), II:709.

78. NW to Jedidiah Morse, May 15, 1797, NYPL.

79. James Madison to NW, Madison Papers, LC, cited in Scudder, *Noah Webster,* 114.

80. NW, *Memoir,* no. 12.

81. NW, *Sketches,* 3–4.

82. Ibid., 5.

83. Ibid., 6.

84. Ibid., 6–7.

85. Ibid., 27–28.

86. Ibid., 30–31.

87. Ibid.

88. Ibid. Webster includes a footnote comparing such a governmental form to "the harmony of nature in the planetary system. The moon is an inferior planet subject to the earth. The earth and other planets govern their secondary planets and at the same time, are governed by the sun, the common center of our system."

89. Ibid., 34–37.

90. Ibid.

91. Ibid., 30–31.

92. Ibid.

93. Ibid.

94. Ibid., 44–48.

95. Ibid.

96. Ibid.

97. Ibid.

98. Ibid.

Chapter 4.　Yankee Peddler

1. Ford, *Notes,* I:129.

2. Ibid., I:130.

3. Ibid., I:131.

4. Warfel, *Noah Webster,* 121.

5. Ibid., 132.

6. Ibid., 72.

7. Ford, *Notes,* I:106.

8. *Maryland Journal,* May 25, 1785, cited in Warfel, *Noah Webster,* 124.

9. Ford, *Notes,* I:133.

10. Ibid., I:135–36.

11. William Waller Henning, ed., *The Statutes at Large; Being a Collection of All the Laws of Virginia, from the First Session of the Legislature, in the Year 1619* (1819–23), II:517. Berkeley made his oft-quoted comment in a 1671 reply to an inquiry from the Commissioners of Trade and Plantations.

12. The second-oldest institution of higher education in the United States, William and Mary was founded in 1693 by the Scottish churchman James Blair to help alleviate the shortage of ministers in the colonies.

13. Ford, *Notes*, I:146.

14. Warfel, *Noah Webster*, 123.

15. Ford, *Notes*, I:136–37.

16. Ibid., I:139.

17. Ibid.

18. Warfel, *Noah Webster*, 126.

19. Scudder, *Noah Webster*, 192–208.

20. Ibid.

21. Ibid.

22. Ford, *Notes*, I:141.

23. Ibid.

24. Timothy Pickering to NW, October 19, 1785, NYPL.

25. NW to Timothy Pickering, October 28 (1785), in *Massachusetts Historical Society Proceedings*, November 1909, xliii.

26. Warfel, *Noah Webster*, 130.

27. Martha Washington had three grandchildren by her previous marriage, to Daniel Parke Custis.

28. NW, *Memoir*, no. 14.

29. NW, Diary, in Ford, *Notes*, I:143.

30. NW to George Washington, December 16, 1785, in Warfel, *Letters*, 39–41.

31. Ibid.

32. Ford, *Notes*, I:145.

33. *Maryland Gazette* (Annapolis), January 10, 1786.

34. Ford, *Notes*, I:147.

35. NW to Daniel Webster, September 30, 1826, NYPL.

36. Ford, *Notes*, I:149.

37. Ibid.

38. Thomas Dilworth, *A New Guide to the English Tongue* (London, 1740).

39. Leonard W. Labaree, Ralph L. Ketcham, Helen B. Boatfield, and Helene H. Fineman, eds., *The Autobiography of Benjamin Franklin* (New Haven: Yale University Press, 1959).

40. Initially stocked with classics such as Homer's *Iliad* and Plutarch's *Lives*, Franklin's library became a largely practical collection of atlases, histories, and handbooks on everything from husbandry to mechanics. It contained not a single book on theology.

41. Franklin's *Proposals* called for all young men to study handwriting, drawing, arithmetic, accounts, geometry, astronomy, English grammar, composition, rhetoric, history, geography, ethics, natural history, gardening, commerce, principles of mechanics, science, and agriculture. In 1751, he added more details to his *Proposals* with a new work, *Idea of the English School*, which called for a curriculum lasting six years, designed not to produce scholars, poets, or scientists but "youth . . . fitted for learning any business, calling or profession, except such wherein languages are required." Students, he said, would learn the skills "to pass through life and execute the several offices of civil life, with advantage and reputation to themselves and country" (Unger, *Encyclopedia of American Education*, II:384).

42. NW, *Old South Leaflets*, VIII:396, cited in Ervin C. Shoemaker, *Noah Webster, Pioneer of Learning* (New York: Columbia University Press, 1936).

43. H. L. Mencken, *The American Language*, 4th ed. (New York: Alfred A. Knopf, 1936).

44. NW, *Memoir*, no. 17.

45. Even Dr. Samuel Johnson, the great scholar and lexicographer, who was a great friend of Elphinston and dined with him quite often, said of him, after looking at the grammar, "He has a great deal of good about him, but he is also very defective in some respects; his inner part is good, but his outward part is awkward." *Principles* was first published in 1765, and a second edition was issued the following year, when Elphinston was a schoolmaster at

Brompton. After giving up teaching, Elphinston devoted himself full-time to writing—first a series of absurd translations of French works that earned him universal derision, and then a monumental work that set forth his fantastic system of quasiphonic spelling. Published in 1790, the two-volume work bore the unlikely title *Propriety Ascertained in Her Picture, or Inglish Speech and Spelling under Mutual Guides*. In 1791, he published *Forty Years of Correspondence Between Geniusses ov Boath Sexes and James Elphinston* "in 6 pocket volumes, foar ov oridginal letters, two ov poetry."

46. NW to Benjamin Franklin, "Thursday Evening" (probably June 22, 1786), American Philosophical Society, Philadelphia.

47. Scudder, *Noah Webster*, 254–55.

48. Rittenhouse would later help organize the First Bank of the United States and become first director of the U.S. Mint.

49. George W. Corner, ed., *The Autobiography of Benjamin Rush* (Princeton: Princeton University Press, 1948).

50. Rush proposed development of a three-tier system of education in Pennsylvania. A free school in each district or township would teach reading, writing, arithmetic, and the English and German languages. At the next tier, four regional colleges would teach mathematics and the higher branches of science. At the highest tier, a university in the state capital, Philadelphia, would teach law, medicine, divinity, politics, economics, and natural philosophy (advanced science).

"The state," he explained, would thus be "tied together by one system of education. The university will in time furnish masters for the colleges and colleges will furnish masters for the free schools, while the free schools, in their turn, will supply the colleges and the university with scholars, students and pupils. The same systems of grammar, oratory and philosophy, will be taught in every part of the state, and the literary features of Pennsylvania will thus designate one great, and equally enlightened family" (*Essays, Literary, Moral and Philosophical* [Philadelphia, 1806]).

51. Ford, *Notes*, I:150.

52. Ibid., I:151.

53. Ibid.

54. Ibid.

55. NW, "Origin of the Copyright Laws of the United States," in *A Collection of Papers on Political, Literary and Moral Subjects* (New York: Webster & Clark, 1843).

56. A leader in the South Carolina legislature from 1776 to 1783, Ramsay was taken hostage by the British after they captured Charleston and was imprisoned for eleven months. He was a powerful member of the Continental Congress in 1782–84 and 1785–86.

57. Cited (n.d.) in Warfel, *Noah Webster*, 139.

58. Ford, *Notes*, I:155.

59. Ibid., I:156.

60. NW to Hudson & Goodwin, May 5, 1784, NYPL.

61. Ibid.

62. John Wheelock (1754–1817) succeeded his father, founder Eleazer Wheelock, to the Dartmouth College presidency in 1779. Although he began his college education at Yale, he transferred to Dartmouth and became a member of that school's first graduating class in 1771. His students would include Noah Webster's younger cousin Daniel Webster, who would graduate in the class of 1801.

63. NW to Benjamin Franklin, May 24, 1786, American Philosophical Society, Philadelphia.

64. NW to Timothy Pickering, May 25, 1786; cited in Warfel, *Letters*, 51–52.

65. Warfel, *Noah Webster*, 138.

66. Ford, *Notes*, I:157.

67. Ibid., I:159.

68. *New Haven Gazette*, June 21, 1786.

69. Stiles, *Literary Diary*, 230, cited in Ford, *Notes*, I:116.

70. The *Massachusetts Sentinel* (Boston), July 12, 1786, carried this announcement:

To-morrow evening, at half after seven o'clock, in Mr. Hunt's School-House, Mr. Webster will begin a short Course of LECTURES on the *English Language* and on *Education*. The course will consist of Six Lectures; the heads of which are the following.

    I. Introduction. Origin of the English Language. Derivation of the European Languages from the ancient Celtic. General History of the English Language. Its Copiousness. Effect of this. Irregularity of its Orthography. Causes of this.

    II. Elements of the English Language investigated. Rules of Pronunciation. Different Dialects of the Eastern, the Middle, and the Southern States.

    III. Some Differences between the English and Americans considered. Corruption of Language in England. Reasons why the English should not be our Standard, either in Language or Manners.

    IV. Prevailing Errors in the use of Words. Errors of Grammarians in the Arrangements of the Verbs. Consequences of these in the most correct Writings.

    V. Poetry. Principles of English Verse explained. Use and effect of the several Pauses. Effects of different poetic Measures illustrated by Examples.

    VI. General Remarks on Education. Defects in our mode of Education. Influence of Education on Morals, and of Morals on Government. Female Education. Connection between the Mode of Education and the Form of Government. Effects of an European Education in America. Tour of America a useful Branch of Education. Conclusion.

    Tickets to be sold at the Post-Office, and at Mr. Batelle's Book-Store in Marlborough-Street, at 12s. the course, for Gentlemen, 6s. the course for Ladies, and 3s. a Ticket for an evening.

    After the course shall be finished, a lecture will, if desired, be delivered for the benefit of the poor; consisting of remarks on the population, agriculture, literature, climate and commerce of the United States, taken mostly from actual observation. After the first lecture the evenings proposed are Monday, Wednesday and Friday, the evening after Commencement excepted.

    Those who purchase a Ticket for the first evening may afterwards take a Ticket for the course at 9s. *Boston July* 12, 1786.

71. Benjamin Franklin to NW, June 18, 1786, NYPL.
72. NW to Benjamin Franklin, June 23, 1786, American Philosophical Society, Philadelphia.
73. Benjamin Franklin to NW, July 9, 1786, NYPL.
74. NW to Hudson & Goodwin, July 24, 1786, NYPL.
75. NW to Hudson & Goodwin, August 29, 1786, NYPL.
76. NW to Timothy Pickering, August 10, 1786, NYPL.
77. Ibid.
78. [NW], anonymous letter "On Redress of Grievances," *Essex Journal* (Newburyport, Massachusetts), September 13, 1786, cited in Warfel, *Noah Webster*, 145.
79. NW, *A Collection of Essays and Fugitiv Writings* (Boston, 1790), 130.
80. NW, "The Devil Is in You" (signed "Tom Thoughtful"), *United States Chronicle* (Providence, Rhode Island), October 6, 1786, cited in Warfel, *Noah Webster*, 146–47.
81. *Connecticut Courant*, October 18, 1786.
82. Warfel, *Noah Webster*, 147–48.
83. NW to Hudson & Goodwin, August 29, 1786, NYPL; Ford, *Notes*, I:168.
84. Ford, *Notes*, I:163.
85. Morris, *Encyclopedia of American History*, 115.
86. NW to Benjamin Franklin, October 28, 1786, American Philosophical Society, Philadelphia.
87. *Connecticut Courant* (Hartford), November 20, 1786.
88. Ford, *Notes*, I:169.

Chapter 5. Essayist

1. Jensen, *The New Nation,* 310.
2. Warfel, *Noah Webster,* 159.
3. NW, introduction to *An American Dictionary of the English Language* (New York: S. Converse, 1828), n.p. [xl].
4. NW, Diary, in Ford, *Notes,* I:215.
5. NW to Gov. James Bowdoin, March 21, 1787, in Warfel, *Noah Webster,* 160–61.
6. Warfel, *Noah Webster,* 161.
7. *Freeman's Journal* (Philadelphia), April 20, 1787.
8. Ibid., April 27, 1787.
9. NW, "To the Public" (signed "Adam"), *Independent Gazeteer, or The Chronicle of Freedom* (Philadelphia), May 10, 1787; see also Warfel, *Letters,* 62–68.
10. Ford, *Notes,* I:173–75.
11. Ibid., chapter VI, "Rebecca Webster's Forbears," I:249–67.
12. Ibid., I:263.
13. NW, Diary, in Ford, *Notes,* I:211–16.
14. NW to Rebecca Greenleaf, June 20, 1787, YL.
15. NW, Diary, in Ford, *Notes,* I:215.
16. *Freeman's Journal,* June 21, 1787.
17. The full title of the revised reader was actually *An American Selection of Lessons in Reading and Speaking. Calculated to Improve the Minds and Refine the Taste of Youth. And Also to Instruct Them in the Geography, History, and Politics of the United States. To Which Is Prefixed, Rules in Elocution, and Directions for Expressing the Principal Passions of the Mind. Being the Third Part of a Grammatical Institute of the English Language. The Third Edition, Greatly Enlarged* (Philadelphia: Young and McCullough, 1787).
18. Jedidiah Morse (1761–1826), *Geography Made Easy* (New Haven, 1784). Morse's book was the first American geography book. It went through twenty-five editions during his lifetime.
19. Morse's expanded geography text with Webster's history was published in 1789 as *The American Geography.* He reissued it as *The American Universal Geography, Elements of Geography* (for children) in 1795 and as *American Gazeteer* (for adults) in 1797.
20. NW to Rebecca Greenleaf, August 28, 1787, YL.
21. NW, Diary, in Ford, *Notes,* I:219.
22. "Saturday August 18. In Convention Mr. Madison submitted . . . the following powers as proper to be added to those of the General Legislature . . . To secure to literary authors their copy rights for a limited time" (Hunt and Scott, eds., *Notes of Debates in the Federal Convention of 1787,* 477).
23. Text from *Funk & Wagnalls New Encyclopedia* (1993), 7:158.
24. NW, Diary, in Ford, *Notes,* I:219–20.
25. NW, *Memoir,* no. 18.
26. NW to Rebecca Greenleaf, September 15, 1787, YL.
27. NW, Diary, in Ford, *Notes,* I:220.
28. NW, *Memoir,* no. 19.
29. NW, *An Examination into the Leading Principles of the Federal Constitution Proposed by the Late Convention Held at Philadelphia. With Answers to the Principal Objections That Have Been Raised Against the System,* "by a Citizen of America" (Philadelphia: Prichard & Hall, 1787).
30. Ibid.
31. Warfel, *Noah Webster,* 167.
32. NW to Rebecca Greenleaf, October 11, 1787, YL.
33. NW, Diary, in Ford, *Notes,* I:221.
34. NW, Diary, ibid., I:224.
35. The complete title was *The American Magazine, Containing a Miscellaneous Collection of Original and Other Valuable Essays, in Prose and Verse, and Calculated Both for Instruction and Amusement.*
36. *American Magazine,* December 1787, 3.

37. Hunt and Scott, eds., *Notes of Debates in the Federal Convention of 1787,* 477.

38. *American Magazine,* December 1787, 22–23.

39. J.-P. Brissot de Warville, *New Travels in the United States of America, Performed in 1788* (London, 1792), I:133–35.

40. Ford, *Notes,* I:225–26.

41. Noah Webster Sr. to NW, February 16, 1788, in Ford, *Notes,* I:175–76.

42. Timothy Dwight, *Triumph of Infidelity* (New Haven, 1788).

43. *American Magazine,* December 1787, 15.

44. NW to Rebecca Greenleaf, January 27, 1788, YL.

45. Ebenezer Hazard to Jeremy Belknap, August 26, 1788, Belknap Papers, Massachusetts Historical Society.

46. Scudder, *Noah Webster,* 114.

47. *American Magazine,* December 1787, 15–16.

48. NW to Rebecca Greenleaf, February 10, 1788, YL.

49. Joel Barlow, *Vision of Columbus* (Hartford: Hudson & Goodwin, 1787).

50. Woodress, *Yankee's Odyssey,* 85.

51. Ibid.

52. NW, Diary, in Ford, *Notes,* I:232.

53. NW to George Washington, July 14, 1788, NYPL.

54. George Washington to NW, July 31, 1788, NYPL.

55. Ford, *Notes,* I:230.

56. Ibid., I:232.

57. Ibid.

58. *Daily Advertiser* (New York), July 22, 1788.

59. Ibid., August 2, 1788.

60. Ford, *Notes,* II:461–65.

61. NW, Diary, in Ford, *Notes,* I:234.

62. NW to Hudson & Goodwin, September 4, 1788, New-York Historical Society.

63. NW, Diary, in Ford, *Notes,* I:235.

64. Ibid., I:236.

65. James Greenleaf to NW, November 24, 1788, NYPL.

66. Nathaniel W. Appleton to NW, November 30, 1788, NYPL.

67. NW, Diary, in Ford, *Notes,* I:238.

Chapter 6. Public Servant

1. NW, *Dissertations on the English Language: With Notes Historical and Critical. To Which Is Added . . . an Essay on a Reformed Mode of Spelling, with Dr. Franklin's Arguments on the Subject* (Boston: Isaiah Thomas & Co., 1789).

2. Scudder, *Noah Webster,* 192–208.

3. Ibid.

4. Warfel, *Noah Webster,* 190.

5. Ford, *Notes,* I:202.

6. Ibid., I:203.

7. NW to James Greenleaf, September 20, 1789, in Ford, *Notes,* I:206–7.

8. Warfel, *Noah Webster,* 194.

9. NW, Diary, in Ford, *Notes,* I:246.

10. In a letter to her daughter Harriet Fowler dated October 20, 1832, Mrs. Webster wrote: "My portrait by Flagg is considered by most of my acquaintance as a better likeness than common. The face, & form, are too large, but the expression is acknowledged to be correct & I doubt whether, if I should sit for Mr. Flag [*sic*] again, he would paint a more perfect likeness. I think too that it would hardly be doing justice to the artist to tax him so far; when the Portrait is pronounced by most people good."

On December 1, she wrote, "I am much pleased that you think my likeness striking. The artist gained at least twenty customers in this naighborhood [*sic*] in consequence of succeeding so well with me. I believe he is satisfied with the patronage of New Haven and now returned to New York."

11. NW, Diary, in Ford, *Notes*, I:246.

12. James Greenleaf to Noah Webster, December 24, 1789, in Ford, *Notes*, I:273.

13. Rebecca Webster to John Greenleaf, December 4, 1789, in Ford, *Notes*, I:270–71.

14. Ibid.

15. Ford, *Notes*, I:272.

16. Researchers at Noah Webster House have been unable to document the puzzling custom that so disgusted Rebecca Webster.

17. Ford, *Notes*, I:272.

18. Rebecca Webster to John Greenleaf, December 4, 1789, in Ford, *Notes*, I:271.

19. John Trumbull to Oliver Wolcott, December 9, 1789, in Ford, *Notes*, I:269.

20. Rebecca Webster to John Greenleaf, December 4, 1789, in Ford, *Notes*, I:270.

21. NW, *Attention! or, New Thoughts on a Serious Subject: Being an Enquiry into the Excise Laws of Connecticut; Addressed to the Freemen of the State*, "by a Private Citizen" (Hartford: Hudson & Goodwin, 1789).

22. Warfel, *Noah Webster*, 198–99.

23. Benjamin Rush to NW, December 29, 1789, in Ford, *Notes*, I:274–75.

24. NW to George Washington, December 16, 1785, Historical Society of Pennsylvania, reprinted in Warfel, *Letters*, 39–41.

25. *An Introduction to English Grammar. Being an Abridgement of the Second Part of the Grammatical Institute* (Philadelphia: W. Young, 1788).

26. NW, *The Little Reader's Assistant; Containing I. A number of Stories, Mostly Taken from the History of America, and Adorned with Cuts. II. Rudiments of English Grammar. III. A Federal Catechism, Being a Short and Easy Explanation of the Constitution of the United States. IV. General Principles of Government and Commerce. All adapted to the Capacities of Children.* (Hartford: Elisha Babcock, 1790).

27. NW, Diary, in Ford, *Notes*, I:329.

28. NW, *An American Selection of Lessons in Reading and Speaking. Calculated to Improve the Minds and Refine the Taste of Youth. And Also to Instruct Them in the Geography, History, and Politics of the United States. To Which Is Prefixed, Rules in Elocution, and Directions for Expressing the Principal Passions of the Mind. Being the Third Part of a Grammatical Institute of the English Language. The Third Edition, Greatly Enlarged* (Philadelphia: Young and McCulloch, 1787).

29. NW, *A Collection of Essays and Fugitiv Writings, on Moral, Historical, Political and Literary Subjects* (Boston: I. Thomas and E. T. Andrews, 1790).

30. NW, preface in Ibid.

31. Ezra Stiles to NW, August 27, 1790, NYPL.

32. Jeremy Belknap to Ebenezer Hazard, September 14, 1790, Massachusetts Historical Society.

33. Daniel George to NW, September 27 and November 23, 1790, in Ford, *Notes*, I:290–91.

34. NW to Daniel George, October 18, 1790, in Ford, *Notes*, I:291.

35. Nathaniel W. Appleton to NW, July 11, 1790, in Ford, *Notes*, I:284.

36. Charles Van Doren and Robert McHenry, eds., *Webster's American Biographies* (Springfield, Mass.: Merriam-Webster, 1984).

37. Jeremy Belknap to NW, "Saturday noon" (1789), in Ford, *Notes*, I:302.

38. *See* note 26 above.

39. Benjamin Franklin (pseudonym: "Richard Saunders"), *Poor Richard's Almanack* (Philadelphia), 1730–57.

40. NW, *The Prompter, or a Commentary on Common Sayings and Subjects, Which Are Full of Common Sense, the Best Sense in the World* (Hartford: Hudson & Goodwin, 1791).

41. NW to Timothy Pickering, March 10, 1792, in Ford, *Notes*, I:309–10.

42. *See* note 39.

43. NW, preface to *The Prompter*, n.p. [iii].

44. Ibid., contents page [ii].

45. Ibid., 64–66.

46. Ibid., 33.

47. NW, Diary, in Ford, *Notes*, I:329–43.

48. Ibid., I:345.

49. Ibid., I:243.

50. Ibid., I:334.

51. NW, *The Farmer's Catechizm; Containing Plain Rules of Husbandry—and Calculated for the Use of Schools* (No title page; 1790, according to Ford, *Notes*, II:528).

52. George Washington to NW, August 28, 1790, NYPL.

53. NW, Diary, in Ford, *Notes*, I:337.

54. Jensen, *The New Nation*, 117.

55. NW, Diary, in Ford, *Notes*, I:332.

56. It would not be until 1796 that Britain's Edward Jenner would develop a safe vaccine from cowpox, an extremely mild form of smallpox found in cows.

57. Warfel, *Noah Webster*, 211.

58. Ibid., 210.

59. Ibid., 211.

60. Ibid., 209.

61. NW, "Oration before the Connecticut Society for the Promotion of Freedom," May 9, 1793, cited in Scudder, *Noah Webster*, 139–40; Warfel, *Noah Webster*, 214–15.

62. NW, *Effects of Slavery, on Morals and Industry* (Hartford: Hudson & Goodwin, 1793).

63. *See* note 61.

64. NW, "To the Public," *Herald* (New York), June 9, 1794, in Scudder, *Noah Webster*, 140–42.

65. NW, "To the Inhabitants of Hartford," *Connecticut Courant* (Hartford), September 10, 1792.

66. NW, Diary, in Ford, *Notes*, I:361.

67. Ibid., I:362.

68. Ibid., I:436.

69. John C. Miller, *The Federalist Era, 1789–1801* (New York: Harper & Brothers, 1960), 127.

70. NW, "To the Public," *Herald* (New York), March 4, 1794.

71. Miller, *Federalist Era*, 127.

72. Warfel, *Noah Webster*, 226.

73. Woodress, *Yankee's Odyssey*, 119–23.

74. Ibid., 128–30.

75. Ibid., 238.

76. Ibid.

77. NW to Joel Barlow, October 13, 1808, in Warfel, *Letters of Noah Webster*, 308–9.

78. John Ferling, *A Life of John Adams* (New York: Henry Holt and Company, 1996).

79. NW, "To the Public," *Herald* (New York), March 4, 1794.

80. Ibid.

81. Ibid.

82. Meade Minnigerode, *Jefferson—Friend of France* (New York: G. P. Putnam & Sons, 1928), 142.

83. Ibid., 144.

84. NW, *American Minerva* (New York) December 9, 1793.

85. Minnegerode, *Jefferson*, 207.

86. NW to Joel Barlow, *Spectator* (New York), November 16, 1798; cited in Warfel, *Letters*, 187–94.

87. Ibid.

88. Miller, *Federalist Era*, 133.

89. Minnigerode, *Jefferson*, 191.

90. Miller, *Federalist Era*, 130.

91. Ibid.

92. Minnigerode, *Jefferson*, 191.

93. Ibid.

94. Ibid., 184.

95. Ibid., 202–3.

96. NW, *American Minerva*, December 26, 1793.

97. Miller, *Federalist Era*, 135.

98. Minnigerode, *Jefferson*, 236.

98. Warfel, *Noah Webster*, 216.

100. Minnigerode, *Jefferson*, 236.

101. Miller, *Federalist Era*, 137.

102. *Greenleaf's New-York Journal*, August 28, 1793.

103. Minnigerode, *Jefferson*, 282.

104. Paul Leicester Ford, ed., *The Writings of Thomas Jefferson* (New York: G. P. Putnam & Sons, 1892–99), Vol. I.

105. NW, *Memoir*, no. 28.

106. Miller, *Federalist Era*, 137; Minnigerode, *Jefferson*, 265.

107. Minnigerode, *Jefferson*, 323–24.

108. NW, *Herald* (New York), March 4, 1797.

109. Warfel, *Noah Webster*, 221.

110. NW to Oliver Wolcott, September 16, 1793, Connecticut Historical Society.

111. NW, Diary, in Ford, *Notes*, I:443.

112. The original affidavit is in the Sterling Memorial Library, Manuscripts and Archives, Yale University.

113. Webster's diary lists the dinner on August 12. The most likely explanation for the discrepancy is that by the time he traveled to Hartford in September to swear out the affidavit, he confused the date of his initial letter to Wolcott about the dinner with the date of the dinner itself.

114. NW to Oliver Wolcott, September 26, 1793, Connecticut Historical Society.

115. Minnigerode, *Jefferson*, 319.

116. Oliver Wolcott to NW, September 19, 1793, in Ford, *Notes*, I:369.

117. NW to Oliver Wolcott, September 26, 1793, Connecticut Historical Society.

118. NW to Oliver Wolcott, October 10, 1793, Connecticut Historical Society.

Chapter 7. Editor

1. NW, *Memoir of Noah Webster, LL.D.* (unpublished; handwritten manuscript), Sterling Memorial Library, Manuscripts and Archives, Yale University.

2. NW to Oliver Wolcott, October 10, 1793, Connecticut Historical Society.

3. NW, *Memoir*, no. 26.

4. NW, Diary, in Ford, *Notes*, I:443.

5. Ford, *Notes*, I:366–67.

6. Minnigerode, *Jefferson*, 338.

7. Ibid.

8. Ford, *Notes*, I:376–77.

9. Minnigerode, *Jefferson*, 350.

10. Ibid.

11. Minerva is the name of the Roman goddess of wisdom.

12. *American Minerva*, December 9, 1793.

13. *Herald: A Gazette for the Country*, June 4, 1794.

14. Ford, *Notes*, I:377.

15. *American Minerva*, December 26, 1793.

16. Paine spent eleven months in prison until James Madison intervened, following Robespierre's downfall.

17. The Saint Bartholomew's Day Massacre, August 24, 1572, when the River Seine flowed red with the blood of Protestants, following a purge of Huguenot leaders by King Charles IX. Estimates of the number of victims vary from two thousand to one hundred thousand.

18. Scudder, *Noah Webster*, 135–36; NW, *Revolution in France* (New York: George Bunce & Co., 1794).

19. NW, "To the Public," *American Minerva* (New York), March 4, 1797.

20. NW, *Spectator*, November 16, 1798.

21. NW, *Memoir*, no. 29.

22. NW to George Washington, April 20, 1794, National Archives, Washington, D.C.

23. Ford, *Notes*, I:382–84.

24. Warfel, *Noah Webster*, 229–30.

25. Minnigerode, *Jefferson*, 357.

26. Ibid., 346.

27. NW, *Memoir*, no. 29.

28. Ford, *Notes*, I:386.

29. Minnigerode, *Jefferson*, 353–54.

30. Ibid., 365.

31. Ibid., 358.

32. Ibid., 360.

33. Ibid., 361.

34. Ibid.

35. Ibid., 362.

36. Ibid.

37. Ibid., 378. Genet (1763–1834) became a U.S. citizen and the father of six children by Cornelia Clinton. One of his great-great-grandsons, Edmond Charles Clinton Genet, was the first American aviator killed in World War I, in the skies over France with the Lafayette Escadrille, a group of American fliers who volunteered to fight with the Allies before the United States entered the war.

38. Warfel, *Noah Webster*, 275–76.

39. NW, "To the Public," *Herald*, June 9, 1974.

40. NW, "To the Friends of the Minerva," *American Minerva*, June 28, 1794.

41. Nathaniel W. Appleton to NW, July 26, 1794, NYPL.

42. NW to Oliver Wolcott, July 30, 1795, Connecticut Historical Society.

43. Oliver Wolcott to NW, August 1, 1795, NYPL.

44. Paul Leicester Ford, ed., *The Writings of Thomas Jefferson*, VII:31.

45. Warfel, *Noah Webster*, 234.

46. NW, "To the Public," *Herald*, May 1, 1796.

47. NW to Daniel Webster, New Haven, September 6, 1834.

48. Thomas Dawes Jr. to NW, February 9, 1795, in Ford, *Notes*, I:396–98.

49. NW to Oliver Wolcott, July 30, 1795, Connecticut Historical Society.

50. NW to Theodore Sedgwick, January 2, 1795, Massachusetts Historical Society.

51. NW to Oliver Wolcott, March 8, 1795, Connecticut Historical Society.

52. Ibid.

53. NW to Oliver Wolcott, July 30, 1795, Connecticut Historical Society.

54. Timothy Pickering to NW, February 18, 1796, NYPL.

55. Richard Bayley (1745–1801), *An Account of the Epidemic Fever Which Prevailed in the City of New York, During Part of the Summer and Fall of 1795* (New York: T. and J. Swords, 1796), 7–8.

56. Warfel, *Noah Webster*, 243–44.

57. NW, *American Minerva*, April 11, 1794.

58. NW to the Physicians of Philadelphia, New York, Baltimore, Norfolk, and New Haven, October 31, 1795, in Warfel, *Letters*, 130–33.

59. Warfel, *Noah Webster*, 243.

60. NW to Thomas Greenleaf, November 10, 1795, in Warfel, *Letters*, 133. Greenleaf was editor of the *Argus* and unrelated to Rebecca Greenleaf Webster's family.

61. James Hardie (1758–1826), *An Account of the Malignant Fever, Lately Prevalent in the City of New-York* (New York: Hurtin and M'Farlane, 1799).

62. Benjamin Rush, *An Account of the Bilious Remitting Yellow Fever As It Appeared in the City of Philadelphia in the Year 1793* (Philadelphia, 1794).

63. Warfel, *Noah Webster,* 247–48.
64. NW, *American Minerva,* October 24, 1797.
65. NW, *A Brief History of Epidemic and Pestilential Diseases; with the Principal Phenomena of the Physical World, Which Precede and Accompany Them, and Observations Deduced from the Facts Stated,* 2 vols. (Hartford: Hudson & Goodwin, 1799).
66. NW, *American Minerva,* October 14, 1797.
67. Ford, *Notes,* I:412. A century later, a wave of immigration would transform the area around Webster's "pretty cottage and garden" into the teeming slums of the Lower East Side of Manhattan, in the shadow of the Brooklyn Bridge.
68. Ford, *Notes,* I:413–14.
69. Abram Webster to NW, July 27, 1796, in Ford, *Notes,* I:407–8.
70. Miller, *Federalist Era,* 196–97.
71. NW to Timothy Pickering, November 24, 1796, Massachusetts Historical Society.
72. Abram Webster to NW, January 3, 1797, in Ford, *Notes,* I:410–11.
73. Ferling, *John Adams,* 310.
74. Miller, *Federalist Era,* 198.
75. NW, *American Minerva* and *Herald,* April 29, 1787.
76. Ibid. Philip Mazzei (1730–1816) was a Florentine physician who became a wine merchant in London. From 1773 to 1778, he tried to introduce viniculture in Virginia and developed a friendship with Jefferson. After returning to Europe, he sent Jefferson regular intelligence reports on European political affairs. He wrote several works of "historical and political researches" on the United States.
77. Webster notes: "This letter I first translated in the Minerva & Herald papers of my own, April 29 & May 3, 1797. I found it in the Paris *Moniteur* of January 29 of that year, a file of which I received from my friend Mr. Epaphras Jones, who had just returned from France." Both the French version and the English translation, in Webster's handwriting, are in the Webster manuscript collection at the New York Public Library.
78. Abram Webster to NW, April 21, 1797, in Ford, *Notes,* I:411–12.
79. NW, "To the Public," *Herald,* March 4, 1797.
80. NW to Rufus King, May 30, 1797, in Warfel, *Letters,* 149–50.
81. NW to Rufus King, June 1, 1797, in Warfel, *Letters,* 150–59.
82. Miller, *Federalist Era,* 208–9.
83. Warfel, *Noah Webster,* 234.
84. Ibid.

Chapter 8.   Philosopher

1. Warfel, *Noah Webster,* 241.
2. NW, *American Minerva,* April 11, 1794.
3. NW to Timothy Pickering, April 13, 1798, in Ford, *Notes,* I:433–34.
4. Rufus King to NW, January 16, 1798, NYPL.
5. NW to E. Waddington, July 6, 1798, in Warfel, *Letters,* 181–82.
6. Ibid.
7. *Spectator,* March 17, 1794.
8. Ford, *Notes,* I:450–53.
9. Ibid.
10. Ibid.
11. NW, Diary, in Ford, *Notes,* I:485.
12. Ezra Stiles (1727–1795), Webster's longtime friend and former teacher, had died of hepatitis after seventeen years as Yale's president.
13. Ford, *Notes,* I:453.
14. Ibid., II:108.
15. Ibid., II:113.
16. Ibid., I:450.

17. NW, *A Brief History of Epidemic and Pestilential Diseases; with the Principal Phenomena of the Physical World, Which Precede and Accompany Them, and Observations Deduced from the Facts Stated.* 2 vols. (Hartford: Hudson & Goodwin, 1799).

18. Jeremy Belknap to NW, January 13, 1798, in Ford, *Notes*, I:437–38.

19. Benjamin Rush to NW, April 27, 1798, NYPL.

20. Samuel Latham Mitchill to NW, September 17, 1798, NYPL.

21. Warfel, *Noah Webster*, 255.

22. NW to Benjamin Rush, April 6, 1798, in Ford, *Notes*, I:458–59.

23. Warfel, *Noah Webster*, 252.

24. Ibid., 253.

25. Ibid.

26. Ibid.

27. NW to Benjamin Rush, February 15, 1799, in Warfel, *Letters*, 196–98.

28. NW to Benjamin Rush, September 11, 1801, in Warfel, *Letters*, 235–37.

29. Warfel, *Noah Webster*, 264.

30. Richard B. Morris, *Encyclopedia of American History* (New York: Harper & Brothers, 1953), 129.

31. Ibid.

32. NW, "To the Public," *Herald*, May 1, 1796.

33. NW to Timothy Pickering, July 17, 1798, Massachusetts Historical Society.

34. Ibid.

35. Miller, *Federalist Era*, 236; Woodress, *Yankee's Odyssey*, 194–96.

36. NW, "To Joel Barlow," *Spectator*, November 16, 1798.

37. Woodress, *Yankee's Odyssey*, 198.

38. Ibid., 199.

39. Ford, *Notes*, II:166.

40. Henry (Light-Horse Harry) Lee (1756–1818), *Resolutions Presented to the House of Representatives on the Death of Washington*, December 1799.

41. NW to Alexander Hamilton, undated (September 1800), in Warfel, *Letters*, 222–26.

42. Ibid.

43. NW, *Spectator*, January 17, 1801.

44. Thomas Jefferson, Inaugural Address, March 4, 1801, LC.

45. William Coleman to Harry Croswell, January 20, 1803, in Ford, *Notes*, I:503 n.

46. Samuel Bayard to NW, September 21, 1801, NYPL.

47. NW to Samuel Bayard, March 2, 1802, LC.

48. NW to Oliver Wolcott, October 13, 1801, Connecticut Historical Society.

49. NW to Rufus King, June 12, 1801, in Warfel, *Letters*, 231.

50. NW to James Madison, July 18, 1801, LC.

51. NW, "An Address to the President of the United States on the Subject of His Administration," in *Miscellaneous Papers: on Political and Commercial Subjects* (New York: E. Beldon & Co., 1802), 1–76.

52. Warfel, *Noah Webster*, 272.

53. Ford, *Notes*, I:533–34.

54. Ibid., I:534–35.

55. Ibid., I:535.

56. Ibid., I:535–36.

57. NW to Benjamin Rush, December 15, 1800, in Ford, *Notes*, I:478–79.

58. Warfel, *Noah Webster*, 278–79.

59. Ibid., 280.

60. E. Jennifer Monaghan, *A Common Heritage: Noah Webster's Blue-Back Speller* (Hamden, Conn.: Archon Books, 1983), 83.

61. Ibid., 88.

62. Warfel, *Noah Webster*, 304.

63. Rebecca Greenleaf Webster to NW, December 11, 1803, in Ford, *Notes*, I:537–38.

64. Ibid.

65. Emily Webster to NW, December 17, 1803, in Ford, *Notes,* I:536.

66. Ibid., I:536–37.

67. Timothy Dwight to NW, May 6, 1784, cited in Monaghan, *Common Heritage,* 91.

68. NW to Joseph Priestly, Letter IX, January 1800, in Warfel, *Letters,* 211.

69. NW, *Elements of Useful Knowledge. Containing a Historical and Geographical Account of the United States: For the Use of Schools* (vol I., Hartford: Hudson & Goodwin, 1802; vol. II, New Haven: Sidney's Press, 1804).

70. Ibid., vol. III, *Containing a Historical and Geographical Account of the Empires and States in Europe, Asia and Africa, with Their Colonies. To Which Is Added, a Brief Description of New Holland, and the Principal Islands in the Pacific and Indian Oceans. For the Use of Schools* (New Haven: Bronson, Walter & Co. O. Steele & Co. Printers, 1806); *History of Animals; Being the Fourth Volume of Elements of Useful Knowledge. For the Use of Schools and Young Persons of Both Sexes* (New Haven: Howe & Deforest. Walter & Steele, Printers, 1812).

71. John Walker (1732–1807), *Principles of English Pronunciation* (London, 1791), "for schools and polite readers."

72. Warfel, *Noah Webster,* 189.

73. John Entick (1703?–1773), *New Spelling Dictionary of the English Language* (London, 1764).

74. Samuel Johnson (1709–1784), *Dictionary of the English Language,* 2 vols. (London, 1755).

75. Samuel Johnson Jr. (1757–1836), *A School Dictionary* (New Haven, 1798).

76. Jonathan Green, *Chasing the Sun: Dictionary Makers and the Dictionaries They Made* (New York: Henry Holt and Co., 1996); Shoemaker, *Noah Webster,* 218–19.

77. Green, *Chasing the Sun,* 292; Shoemaker, *Noah Webster,* 219.

78. Caleb Alexander (1775–1828), *The Columbian Dictionary of the English Language* (Boston, 1800).

79. Warfel, *Noah Webster,* 289.

80. Ibid., 290–91.

81. *Gazette of the United States* (Philadelphia), June 12, 1800.

82. Warren Dutton, *Palladium* (Boston), October 2 and November 6, 1801.

83. NW, "To the New England Palladium," November 10, 1801, in Warfel, *Letters,* 245–47.

84. Warfel, *Noah Webster,* 297–98.

85. NW, *A Compendious Dictionary of the English Language. In Which Five Thousand Words Are Added to the Number Found in the Best English Compends; the Orthography Is, in Some Instances Corrected; the Pronunciation Marked by an Accent or Other Suitable Directions; and the Definitions of Many Words Amended and Improved. . . .* (New Haven: S. Babcock, 1806).

86. *Tho* is still listed in dictionaries today as a variation of *though* or as a poetic abbreviation of it.

87. *The Merchant of Venice* IV.i.184.

88. *King Richard II* II.i.40.

89. NW, *Compendious,* S.V. "Tung, n."

90. Ibid., preface, n.p.

91. NW to David Ramsay, October, 1807, in Warfel, *Letters,* 287.

92. Ibid.

93. NW, *Compendious,* title page.

94. NW, *A Dictionary of the English Language; Compiled for the Use of Common Schools in the United States* (New Haven: S. Babcock, 1807).

95. Samuel Latham Mitchill to NW, June 19, 1807, in Ford, *Notes,* II:20–22.

96. Lindley Murray to NW, "Holdgate, near York, 1803," in *An American Dictionary of the English Language* (New York: S. Converse, 1828), vol. I, n.p., in advertisement for "A Philosophical and Practical Grammar of the English Language," following introduction.

97. Warfel, *Noah Webster,* 318.

98. John Quincy Adams to NW, November 5, 1806, NYPL.

99. Thomas Dawes Jr. to NW, August 14, 1806, in Ford, *Notes,* II:8–9.

100. NW to Thomas Dawes, August 5, 1809, *Monthly Anthology and Boston Review* VI (September 1809): 205–11.

101. NW, *An American Dictionary of the English Language*. . . . 2 vols. (New York: S. Converse, 1828).
102. NW, *Dissertations*, appendix.
103. NW to John West, August 18, 1807, YL.
104. NW, "To the Friends of Literature in the United States," February 27, 1807, NYPL.
105. Ibid.
106. Oliver Wolcott to NW, September 19, 1807, in Ford, *Notes*, II:26–27.
107. Rufus King to NW, May 25, 1807, in Ford, *Notes*, II:18–21.
108. NW, "To the Friends of Literature in the United States," August 1807, in Warfel, *Letters*, 279–81.
109. James M. Banner Jr., *To the Hartford Convention: The Federalists and the Origins of Party Politics in Massachusetts, 1789–1815* (New York: Alfred A. Knopf, 1970), 114–15; *see also* Timothy Pickering to Caleb Strong, November 22, 1803, to George Cabot, January 29, 1804; and to Rufus King, March 4, 1804, Pickering Manuscripts, Massachusetts Historical Society.
110. NW to Stephen Jacob, October 3, 1803; Boston Public Library.
111. Woodress, *Yankee's Odyssey*, 241.
112. NW to Joel Barlow, October 19, 1807, in Warfel, *Letters*, 292–94.
113. It would be seventy years, however, before such a university would begin to take shape in America—appropriately enough at America's first college, Harvard.
114. Woodress, *Yankee's Odyssey*, 242.
115. NW to Joel Barlow, November 12, 1807, in Warfel, *Letters*, 294–300.

Chapter 9. Lexicographer

1. The plan for a national university did not die completely. In 1821, a group of private benefactors founded the Columbian Institution for the Promotion of Arts and Sciences and Columbian College, with Barlow and Webster's Yale classmate Josiah Meigs as the first president. He died the following year. In 1832, Congress granted the college $25,000, and it ultimately became George Washington University—not the "national university" its namesake had envisioned, but nonetheless an outstanding private institution.
2. Noah Webster Sr. to NW, June 9, 1807, in Ford, *Notes*, II:20.
3. NW to Oliver Wolcott, May 13, 1808, Connecticut Historical Society.
4. NW (pseudonym: "Public Spirit"), "To All American Patriots," *Connecticut Herald*, May, 1808.
5. NW to Joel Barlow, October 13, 1808, in Woodress, *Yankee's Odyssey*, 269.
6. NW to David Ramsay, October 1807, in Warfel, *Letters*, 291.
7. NW to Thomas Dawes, July 25, 1809, in Warfel, *Letters*, 318–24.
8. *Monthly Anthology and Boston Review* II (April 1805): 200 (This was the publication of the Anthology Society of Boston).
9. Green, *Chasing the Sun*, 316.
10. NW to David Ramsay, October, 1807, in Warfel, *Letters*, 290–92.
11. Morris, *Encyclopedia of American History*, 143.
12. Ibid., 143–44.
13. NW to Josiah Quincy, February 12, 1811, in Ford, *Notes*, II:101–2.
14. Ford, *Notes*, II:106–8.
15. Ibid., II:170 n.
16. Ibid., II:106–8.
17. The house burned down in 1838.
18. Hannah More (1745–1833), English writer, reformer, and philanthropist, whose forgettable plays included two tragedies, *Percy* (1777) and *The Fatal Falsehood* (1779).
19. Ford, *Notes*, II:108–9.
20. Ibid., II:168.
21. Ibid., II:110.
22. Ibid., II:116.

23. NW, *Hampshire Gazette* (Northampton, Mass.), December 3, 1817; *An Address Delivered Before the Hampshire, Franklin and Hampden Agricultural Society, at Their Annual Meeting in Northampton* (Northampton: Thomas W. Shepard & Co., 1818).

24. Ford, *Notes*, II:169.

25. Ibid., II:166 n–167 n.

26. Ibid., II:116.

27. Ibid., II:115.

28. NW, *Family Prayers* (unpublished), 3–5, NYPL.

29. Ford, *Notes*, II:169.

30. William Wolcott Ellsworth to NW, November 9, 1813, YL.

31. NW to Thomas Dawes, July 25, 1809, in Warfel, *Letters*, 318–24.

32. NW to John Jay, May 19, 1813, NYPL.

33. Ford, *Notes*, II:145–46.

34. Joseph Lyman to NW and others, January 5, 1814, in Ford, *Notes*, II:124.

35. NW, Circular for the Conference, signed by Joseph Lyman, chairman, January 5, 1814.

36. Ibid.

37. Ibid.

38. Thomas Dawes to NW, February 17, 1814, in Ford, *Notes*, II:129–30.

39. James Kent to NW, October 8, 1814, in Ford, *Notes*, II:133–34.

40. Abram Webster to NW, December 3, 1814, in Ford, *Notes*, II:134–36.

41. Morris, *Encyclopedia of American History*, 153.

42. Ibid.

43. Ibid.

44. Zephaniah Swift (1759–1823), *Digest of the Laws of the State of Connecticut*, 2 vols. (Hartford, 1822–23). (Volume II was published posthumously.) The work was used throughout the country as a basis for legal instruction for many years after Swift's death, and he was remembered more as Connecticut's leading scholar than for his role at the Hartford Convention.

45. Warfel, *Noah Webster*, 328.

46. Ford, *Notes*, II:167 n.

47. NW to Solomon Smead, March 30, 1820, NYPL.

48. NW, *Address Delivered at the Laying of the Corner Stone of the Building Now Erecting for the Charity Institution in Amherst, August 9, 1820* (Boston: Ezra Lincoln, 1820).

49. NW, "To the Board of Trustees of Amherst Academy," in Warfel, *Letters*, 404–5.

50. John Jay to NW, October 29, 1821, NYPL.

51. NW to John Jay, November 8, 1821, NYPL.

52. *The Synopsis of Radical Words* was never published. The manuscript is in the New York Public Library.

53. NW, introduction to *American Dictionary of the English Language*, n.p. [i].

54. Richard M. Rollins, *The Long Journey of Noah Webster* (Philadelphia: University of Pennsylvania Press, 1980), 129.

55. NW to John Jay, November, 1821, in Ford, *Notes*, II:160–63.

56. John Jay to NW, December 3, 1821, NYPL.

57. NW to Harriet Webster Cobb, March 19, 1822, in Warfel, *Letters*, 408–09.

58. Webster's house stood at the corner of Temple and Grove Streets, a site that Yale University acquired for Silliman College in 1938. The Webster home was dismantled and moved to Henry Ford's Greenfield Village, in Dearborn, Michigan, where it stands today.

59. Jedidiah Morse, *The American Geography* (New Haven: S. Babcock, 1789).

60. Ford, *Notes*, II:197–98.

61. John S. Morgan, *Noah Webster* (New York: Mason/Charter, 1975), 179.

62. Ford, *Notes*, II:198.

63. NW to Rebecca Webster, "At Sea," n.d. (written over several days, beginning June 15, 1824), in Ford, *Notes*, II:199–202.

64. Ibid.

65. NW to Rebecca Webster, July 10, 1824, in Ford, *Notes*, II:205–6.

66. G. de Bertier de Sauvigny, *La France et les Français vus par les voyageurs americains, 1814–1848* (Paris: Flammarion, 1982), 62–66.
67. NW to "My Dear Becca & All My Dear Family," July 21, 23, 25, in Ford, *Notes*, II:210–16.
68. Warfel, *Noah Webster*, 354.
69. NW to "My Dear Becca & All My Dear Family," in Ford, *Notes*, II:210–16.
70. Ibid.
71. NW to Rebecca Greenleaf Webster, August 1, 1824, in Ford, *Notes*, II:220–23.
72. Ibid.
73. NW to "My Dear Becca & All My Dear Family," in Ford, *Notes*, II:210–16.
74. Ibid.
75. Ibid.
76. Harriet Webster Cobb to NW, July 24, 1824, in Ford, *Notes*, II:217–18.
77. NW to Rebecca Greenleaf Webster, August 1, 8, 9, 1824, in Ford, *Notes*, II:220–23.
78. Samuel Lee to NW, August 11, 1824, NYPL.
79. NW to Rebecca Greenleaf Webster, August 20, 1824, in Ford, *Notes*, II:227–28.
80. Ibid., II:228–30.
81. NW to Eliza Steele Webster, August 19, 1824, in Ford, *Notes*, II:224–27.
82. Rebecca Greenleaf Webster to NW, August 27, 1824, in Ford, *Notes*, II:235–39.
83. Harriet Webster Cobb to William Greenleaf Webster, August 1824, in Ford, *Notes*, II: 230–31.
84. NW to Rebecca Greenleaf Webster, September 8, 1824, in Ford, *Notes*, II:239–40.
85. NW to Rebecca Greenleaf Webster, September 19, 1824, in Ford, *Notes*, II:244–45.
86. NW to Rebecca Greenleaf Webster, September 24, 1824, in Ford, *Notes*, II:246–47.
87. NW to Rebecca Greenleaf Webster, October 16, 1824, in Ford, *Notes*, II:248–51.
88. Samuel J. Hitchcock to NW, November 11, 1824, NYPL.
89. NW to Samuel Lee, December 20, 1824, in Ford, *Notes*, II:271–73.
90. NW to Rebecca Greenleaf Webster, February 15, 1825, in Ford, *Notes*, II:283–84.
91. Ford, *Notes*, II:293.
92. Henry Todd (1763–1845) was an English clergyman who edited various works of Milton and Spenser. He improved the etymologies in Dr. Johnson' original dictionary and added more than fifteen thousand new entries, to give the 1818 edition of "Todd's Johnson" about fifty-eight thousand words.
93. Daniel Webster to NW, October 14, 1826, in Ford, *Notes*, II:300–301.

Chapter 10. Elder Statesman

1. Green, *Chasing the Sun*, 326.
2. Ibid., 325.
3. Ibid., 326.
4. Rebecca Webster to Harriet Webster Fowler, February 16, 1829, NYPL.
5. NW, preface to *American Dictionary of the English Language* (New York: S. Converse, 1828), n.p. [ii].
6. Ibid., [iii].
7. NW, *American Dictionary of the English Language* (New York: S. Converse, 1828).
8. Scudder, *Noah Webster*, 261–62.
9. Edmund Henry Barker to Dawson Turner, August 2, 1829, Wren.
10. Edmund Henry Barker to Dawson Turner, February 2, 1830, Wren.
11. The advertisement for the dictionary began:

    Dr. Webster's English Dictionary. Proposals for Reprinting *A Dictionary of the English Language*: Intended to Exhibit
    1. The Origin and the Affinities of every English Word, as far as they have been ascertained, with its Primary Signification, as now generally established.

2. The Orthography and the Pronunciation of Words, as sanctioned by reputable Usage, and where this Usage is divided, as determinable by a reference to the Principle of Analogy;

3. Accurate and Discriminating Definitions of Technical and Scientific Terms, with Numerous Authorities and Illustrations.

To which are prefixed an Introductory Dissertation on the Origin, History, and Connection of the Languages of Western Asia and of Europe, and a Concise Grammar, Philosophical and Practical, of the English Language.

By N. Webster, LL.D.

In Two Volumes Quarto

Turner Papers, Wren Library.

12. Edmund Henry Barker to Dawson Turner, March 13, 1830, Wren.

13. Edmund Henry Barker to Dawson Turner, April 11, 1830, Wren.

14. Ibid.

15. NW to Edmund Henry Barker, April 15, 1831, Bodleian Library, Oxford University.

16. NW to Edmund Henry Barker, June 21, 1830, Bodleian Library, Oxford University.

17. NW to Edmund Henry Barker, April 25, 1831, Bodleian Library, Oxford University.

18. Abram Webster to NW, June 1, 1830, in Ford, *Notes*, II:316–17.

19. NW to Emily Ellsworth Fowler, in Ford, *Notes*, II:315–16.

20. NW to Harriet Webster Fowler, December, 1830, in Warfel, *Noah Webster*, 391–92.

21. NW to Harriet Webster Fowler, December 29, 1830, in Warfel, *Letters*, 423–24.

22. Ibid.

23. Emily Webster Ellsworth to Rebecca Greenleaf Webster, ibid., 392–93.

24. NW to Rebecca Greenleaf Webster, January 7, 1831, NYPL.

25. NW to William Chauncey Fowler, January 29, 1831, in Warfel, *Letters*, 424–25.

26. NW to Rebecca Greenleaf Webster, February 16, 1831, NYPL.

27. NW, "To the Friends of Literature," February 16, 1831, YL.

28. Warfel, *Noah Webster*, 393–94.

29. NW, *Biography, for the Use of Schools* (New Haven: Hezekiah Howe, 1830).

30. NW, *History of the United States to Which Is Prefixed a Brief Historical Account of Our* [English] *Ancestors from the Dispersion at Babel, to Their Migration to America and of the Conquest of South America by the Spaniards* (New Haven: Durrie & Peck, 1832).

31. Ibid.

32. Ibid.

33. Edmund Henry Barker to Dawson Turner, May 19, 1830, Wren.

34. Edmund Henry Barker to Dawson Turner, July 7, 1830, Wren.

35. Edmund Henry Barker to Dawson Turner, October 14, 1830, Wren.

36. Edmund Henry Barker to NW, March 29, 1832, NYPL.

37. NW to Edmund Henry Barker, May 5, 1832, Bodleian Library, Oxford University.

38. Edmund Henry Barker to NW, September 27, 1832, NYPL.

39. NW, "A Voice of Wisdom" (signed "Sidney"), *New York Commercial Advertiser* and the *Spectator*, November 20, 1837.

40. Rebecca Greenleaf Webster to Harriet Webster Fowler, New Haven, 1833, in Warfel, *Noah Webster*, 432–33.

41. Warfel, *Noah Webster*, 420.

42. Ibid.

43. NW to Messrs. Morse, February 24, 1834, NYPL.

44. Warfel, *Noah Webster*, 407.

45. Ibid., 402.

46. NW, preface to *The Holy Bible, Containing the Old and New Testaments, in the Common Version. With Amendments of the Language* (New Haven: Durrie & Peck, 1833), iii.

47. Ibid., iv.

48. Scudder, *Noah Webster*, 172–78.

49. Warfel, *Noah Webster*, 411.

50. Ibid., 413.

51. Ibid., 412.

52. Testimonial, Webster Papers, NYPL.

53. Charles Richardson (1775–1865), *A New Dictionary of the English Language* (London, 1835–37). Richardson's *New Dictionary* was actually an expanded version of the lexicon he had published in *The Encyclopaedia Metropolitana*, in 1818. The *New Dictionary* borrowed from Webster and Dr. Johnson, using Webster's (incorrect, as it turned out) etymologies based on "radical" forms of each word and Dr. Johnson's charming illustrative passages to show how derived meanings developed.

54. Joseph Emerson Worcester (1784–1865), *Comprehensive Pronouncing and Explanatory Dictionary of the English Language* (1830).

55. *Palladium* (Worcester, Mass.), November 26, 1834, quoted in Green, *Chasing the Sun*, 328–29.

56. NW, *Palladium* (Worcester, Mass.), February 18, 1835, quoted in ibid., 329.

57. Warfel, *Noah Webster*, 396.

58. Chauncey A. Goodrich and Julia W. Goodrich to NW and Rebecca Greenleaf Webster, n.d., in Ford, *Notes*, II:327–28.

59. W. C. Fowler and Harriet Fowler to NW, February 13, 1837, NYPL.

60. NW to William Greenleaf Webster, April 8, 1838, NYPL. In 1830, the Jackson-controlled Congress had passed the Removal Act that ordered forcible expulsion of the Cherokees from their hereditary lands in Georgia and the western Carolinas. The act violated a treaty signed by George Washington and the Cherokees in 1891.

61. NW, "A Voice of Wisdom" (signed "Sidney"), *New York Commercial Advertiser* and the *Spectator*, August 29, 1837.

62. "The Federal Tone and Spirit," *Daily Albany Argus*, November 30, 1837.

63. NW, "Note from Sidney," *New York Commercial Advertiser* and the *Spectator*, December 21, 1837.

64. NW to William Greenleaf Webster, April 8, 1838, NYPL.

65. NW to Harriet Webster Fowler, in Warfel, *Noah Webster*, 417.

66. NW to William Greenleaf Webster, June 27, 1835, YL.

67. NW to William Greenleaf Webster, May 1, 1839, YL.

68. Its founders, George and Charles Merriam, were Hartford boys from a newspaper and book publishing family; they had originally moved to Springfield, just twenty-five miles to the north, to found a newspaper, but abandoned the idea in favor of book publishing.

69. Warfel, *Noah Webster*, 429–30.

70. Ford, *Notes*, II:364.

71. NW to Emily Webster Ellsworth, July 3, 1840, quoted in Rollins, *The Long Journey*, 141.

72. NW, *An American Dictionary of the English Language* (New Haven: Published by the Author, 1841).

73. Copy, Webster Papers, NYPL.

74. Ibid.

75. Eliza Webster Jones, "An Account of the Festival of the Golden Wedding," May 1842, in Ford, *Notes*, II:359–61.

76. Ibid.

77. Ibid.

78. Monaghan, *A Common Heritage*, 189–90.

79. Eliza Webster Jones, "Account by Eliza Webster Jones 'For My Little Boy,'" in Ford, *Notes*, II:362–71.

80. Ibid., II:365.

81. Ibid., II:367.

Epilogue

1. H. L. Mencken, *The American Language*, 385.

2. Warfel, *Noah Webster*, 396. Mississippi senator Jefferson Davis (1808–1889) was elected president of the Confederate States of America in 1862.

3. Monaghan, *A Common Heritage*, 193.

4. A 1994 study by the New York City Board of Education found that more than 90 percent of the students who started bilingual education in the sixth grade were unable to pass an English language test after three years of bilingual instruction.

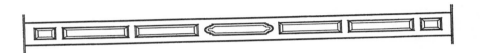

Selected Bibliography
of Principal Sources

Babbidge, Homer D. Jr. *Noah Webster: On Being American, Selected Writings, 1783–1828*. New York: Frederick A. Praeger, 1967.

Banner, James M. Jr. *To the Hartford Convention: The Federalists and the Origins of Party Politics in Massachusetts, 1789–1815*. New York: Alfred A. Knopf, 1970.

Callahan, North. *Royal Raiders: The Tories of the American Revolution*. Indianapolis and New York: Bobbs-Merrill Company, 1963.

Cremin, Laurence A. *American Education: The Colonial Experience, 1607–1783*. New York: Harper & Row, 1970.

———. *American Education: The National Experience, 1783–1876*. New York: Harper & Row, 1979.

Curti, Merle. *The Social Ideas of American Educators*. New York: Charles Scribner's Sons, 1935.

Dos Passos, John. *The Men Who Made the Nation*. Garden City, N.Y.: Doubleday & Company, 1957.

Faulkner, Harold Underwood, and Tyler Kepner. *America: Its History and People*. New York: Harper & Brothers, 1942.

Ferling, John. *A Life of John Adams*. New York: Henry Holt and Company, 1996.

Ford, Emily Ellsworth Fowler. *Notes on the Life of Noah Webster*. 2 vols. New York: privately printed, 1912.

Green, Jonathan. *Chasing the Sun: Dictionary Makers and the Dictionaries They Made*. New York: Henry Holt and Company, 1996.

Hicks, John D. *A Short History of American Democracy*. Boston: Houghton, Mifflin Company, 1946.

Jensen, Merrill. *The New Nation: A History of the United States During the Confederation, 1781–1789*. New York: Alfred A. Knopf, 1967.

Kelley, Brooks Mather. *Yale: A History*. New Haven: Yale University Press, 1974.

Mencken, H. L. *The American Language*. 4th ed. New York: Alfred A. Knopf, 1936.

Miller, John C. *The Federalist Era, 1789–1801*. New York: Harper & Brothers, 1960.

Minnigerode, Meade. *Jefferson—Friend of France*. New York: G. P. Putnam's Sons, 1928.

Monaghan, E. Jennifer. *A Common Heritage: Noah Webster's Blue-Back Speller*. Hamden, Conn.: Archon Books, 1983.

Morgan, John S. *Noah Webster*. New York: Mason/Charter, 1975.

Morris, Richard B. *Encyclopedia of American History*. New York: Harper & Brothers, 1953.

Rollins, Richard M. *The Long Journey of Noah Webster*. Philadelphia: University of Pennsylvania Press, 1980.

Sauvigny, G. de Bertier de. *La France et les Français vus par les voyageurs américains, 1814–1848*. Paris: Flammarion, 1982.

Savy, Nicole, and Georges Vigne. *Le siècle des dictionnaires*. Paris: Ministère de la Culture et de la Communication, Editions de la Réunion des Musées Nationaux, 1987.

Schaer, Roland, dir. *Tous les savoirs du monde*. Paris: Flammarion, 1996.

Scudder, Horace E. *Noah Webster.* Boston: Houghton, Mifflin and Company, 1882.

Shoemaker, Ervin C. *Noah Webster, Pioneer of Learning.* New York: Columbia University Press, 1966.

Skeel, Emily Ellsworth Ford. *A Bibliography of the Writings of Noah Webster.* Edited by Edwin H. Carpenter Jr. New York: New York Public Library, 1958; reprint, New York: New York Public Library and Arno Press, 1971.

Unger, Harlow G. *Encyclopedia of American Education.* 3 vols. New York: Facts On File, 1996.

Warfel, Harry R., ed. *Letters of Noah Webster.* New York: Library Publishers, 1953.

———. *Noah Webster, Schoolmaster to America.* New York: Macmillan Company, 1936; reprint, New York: Octagon Books, 1966.

Woodress, James. *A Yankee's Odyssey: The Life of Joel Barlow.* Philadelphia and New York: J. B. Lippincott Company, 1958.

Works by Noah Webster

An American Dictionary of the English Language. New York: S. Converse, 1828.

An American Selection of Lessons in Reading and Speaking. . . . Philadelphia: Young and McCulloch, 1787–88.

The American Spelling Book. . . . Boston: Isaiah Thomas and Ebenezer T. Andrews, 1789.

A Brief History of Epidemic and Pestilential Diseases. . . . 2 vols. Hartford: Hudson & Goodwin, 1799.

A Collection of Essays and Fugitiv Writings on Moral, Historical, Political and Literary Subjects. New York: Webster & Clark, 1843.

A Collection of Papers on Political, Literary and Moral Subjects. New York: Webster & Clark, 1843.

A Compendious Dictionary of the English Language. New Haven: S. Babcock, 1806.

Dissertations on the English Language. Boston: Isaiah Thomas & Co., 1789.

Effects of Slavery, on Morals and Industry. Hartford: Hudson & Goodwin, 1793.

The Elementary Spelling Book; Being an Improvement on the American Spelling Book. Philadelphia: Kimber & Sharpless, 1829.

An Examination into the Leading Principles of the Federal Constitution Proposed by the Late Convention Held at Philadelphia. With Answers to the Principal Objections That Have Been Raised Against the System. By a Citizen of America. Philadelphia: Prichard & Hall, 1787.

A Grammatical Institute of the English Language. . . . Part I, Hartford: Hudson & Goodwin, 1783. Part II, Hartford: Hudson & Goodwin, 1784. Part III, Hartford: Barlow & Babcock, 1785.

History of the United States. . . . New Haven: Durrie & Peck, 1832.

The Holy Bible, Containing the Old and New Testaments, in the Common Version. With Amendments of the Language. New Haven: Durrie & Peck, 1833.

A Manual of Useful Studies; for the Instruction of Young Persons of Both Sexes, in Families and Schools. New York: S. Babcock, 1839.

Memoir of Noah Webster, LL.D. Unpublished manuscript handwritten by NW. 69 pages. Sterling Memorial Library, Manuscripts and Archives.

The New American Spelling Book, for the Use of Primary Schools in the United States. New Haven: Durrie & Peck and S. Babcock, 1833.

The Prompter, or a Commentary on Common Sayings and Subjects, Which are Full of Common Sense, the Best Sense in the World. Hartford: Hudson & Goodwin, 1791.

Revolution in France. . . . By an American. . . . New York: George Bunce & Co., 1794.

Sketches of American Policy. Hartford: Hudson & Goodwin, 1785.

Manuscript Collections

Bibliothèque de l'Institut de France (Paris, France).

Bibliothèque Historique de la Ville de Paris (Paris, France).

Bibliothèque Nationale de France (Paris, France).

Bienecke Rare Book and Manuscript Library, Yale University (New Haven, Conn.). Webster Collection.

The Bodleian Library, Oxford University (England). Duke Humfrey's Library. Miscellaneous Manuscripts: Webster Letters.

Library of Congress, Washington, D.C. Manuscripts and Archives. Miscellaneous Manuscripts.

New York Public Library (New York). Manuscripts and Archives. Webster Collection.

Noah Webster House (West Hartford, Conn.).

Sterling Memorial Library, Yale University (New Haven, Conn.). Archives and Manuscripts. Webster Family Papers.

Wren Library, Trinity College, Cambridge University (England). Dawson Turner Papers.

General References

Biographical Dictionary of American Educators.
Dictionary of American Biographies.
Dictionary of National Biographies.
Le Dictionnaire de l'Académie Française, 1694–1994: Sa naissance et son actualité.
Encyclopedia of American Education.
Encyclopaedia Britannica.
Funk & Wagnall's New Encyclopedia.
Webster's American Biographies.
Webster's New Biographical Dictionary.

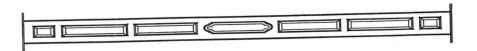

Index